Ethical Obligations and Decision Making in Accounting

Text and Cases

Ethical Obligations and Decision Making in Accounting

Text and Cases

Steven M. Mintz, DBA, CPA

Professor of Accounting
California Polytechnic State University,
San Luis Obispo

Roselyn E. Morris, PhD, CPA

Chair and Professor of Accounting
Texas State University-San Marcos

McGraw-Hill Irwin

Boston   Burr Ridge, IL   Dubuque, IA   New York   San Francisco   St. Louis
Bangkok   Bogotá   Caracas   Kuala Lumpur   Lisbon   London   Madrid   Mexico City
Milan   Montreal   New Delhi   Santiago   Seoul   Singapore   Sydney   Taipei   Toronto

McGraw-Hill
Irwin

EHTICAL OBLIGATIONS AND DECISION MAKING IN ACCOUNTING: TEXT AND CASES

Published by McGraw-Hill/Irwin, a business unit of The McGraw-Hill Companies, Inc., 1221 Avenue of the Amcricas, New York, NY, 10020. Copyright © 2008 by The McGraw-Hill Companies, Inc. All rights reserved. No part of this publication may be reproduced or distributed in any form or by any means, or stored in a database or retrieval system, without the prior written consent of The McGraw-Hill Companies, Inc., including, but not limited to, in any network or other electronic storage or transmission, or broadcast for distance learning.

Some ancillaries, including electronic and print components, may not be available to customers outside the United States.

This book is printed on acid-free paper.

2 3 4 5 6 7 8 9 0 QPD/QPD 0 9 8 7

ISBN 978-0-07-340399-1

MHID 0-07-340399-7

Editorial director: *Stewart Mattson*
Editorial assistant: *Colleen Honan*
Associate marketing manager: *Daniel Wiencek*
Senior project manager: *Susanne Riedell*
Lead production supervisor: *Michael R. McCormick*
Lead designer: *Matthew Baldwin*
Senior media project manager: *Rose M. Range*
Cover design: *Matthew Baldwin*
Cover image: *© Creatas/PunchStock*
Typeface: *10/12 Times New Roman*
Compositor: *Laserwords Private Limited, Chennai, India*
Printer: *Quebecor World Dubuque Inc.*

Library of Congress Cataloging-in-Publication Data

Mintz, Steven M.
    Ethical obligations and decision making in accounting : text and cases / Steven M. Mintz,
Roselyn E. Morris.—1st ed.
        p. cm.
    Includes index.
    ISBN-13: 978-0-07-340399-1 (alk. paper)
    ISBN-10: 0-07-340399-7 (alk. paper)
    1. Accountants—Professional ethics—United States—Case studies. I. Morris, Roselyn E.
II. Title.
HF5616.U5M535 2008
174'.4—dc22

2007000135

www.mhhe.com

To my parents for being ethical role models for me growing up and to Rosanne Feild whose love, dedication, support and commitment made it possible for me to write the text.

—**Steve Mintz**

To my mother, who taught me love and values, and to my daughters, Rachel and Ruth, who give me inspiration.

—**Rosie Morris**

"The choices we make dictate the life we lead." We hope this book serves to inspire students to strive for excellence in whatever they do and to always be sensitive to ethical issues.

—**Steve and Rosie**

About the Authors

STEVEN M. MINTZ, D.B.A., CPA, is Professor of Accounting in the Orfalea College of Business at the California Polytechnic State University, San Luis Obispo. Dr. Mintz received his Doctor of Business Administration degree in 1978 from George Washington University.

Dr. Mintz has researched, published, and taught ethics for more than twenty years. He previously served on the Professional Ethics Committees of the California and Texas Societies of CPAs. He has developed continuing education courses for CPAs on Independence and on the state board of accountancy rules of professional conduct in California, Michigan, New York, and Texas. Dr. Mintz has researched and spoken extensively on the need to teach accounting students about their ethical obligations as future members of the accounting profession. He has had more than 20 research papers published on a variety of issues including reflective learning and ethics education and virtue ethics in accounting. He has also written several cases on accounting ethics that have been published in academic journals. Dr. Mintz's first book on accounting ethics, *Cases in Accounting Ethics & Professionalism,* was published by McGraw-Hill/Irwin.

The California Society of CPAs honored Dr. Mintz for his contributions to the development of the accounting profession and his influence on its future members by selecting him as the recipient of the 1988 Faculty Excellence Award. In 1998 the Inland Empire Hispanic Chamber of Commerce recognized his contributions to the community by honoring his service to education.

ROSELYN E. MORRIS, PhD, CPA, is the chair of the Accounting Department at the McCoy College of Business, Texas State University-San Marcos. Dr. Morris received her Ph.D. in business administration in 1993 from the University of Houston. Since joining the McCoy College of Business Administration in 1993, Dr. Morris has served as Interim Chair for the Department of Accounting and as Associate Dean for Undergraduate Programs for the McCoy College of Business.

Dr. Morris's awards include the Texas Society of CPAs (TSCPA) Outstanding Educator, the McCoy College Teaching Excellence Award, and the Technology Innovation Award from the *Accounting Instructors' Report.*

Her teaching and research areas include auditing independence and ethics, and she has been active in the Texas accounting profession since 1976. She is actively involved in both the local and state levels of TSCPA where she served as chair of the Relations with Educational Institutions Committee. She currently serves on the Editorial Board and Professional Ethics Committees and is a foundation member on the Accounting Education Foundation. She is also a member of the Qualifications Committee of the Texas Board of Public Accountancy. Dr. Morris is the faculty sponsor for Beta Gamma Sigma, past faculty sponsor of Tau Alpha Chi, and co-sponsor for the Accounting Club and Beta Alpha Psi at Texas State. Additionally, she is very active in a variety of civic organizations and was inducted into the San Marcos Women's Hall of Fame.

Preface

Why Did We Write This Book?

The recent accounting scandals at companies such as Enron and WorldCom make it clear that ethics is of primary importance in the training of new accountants. Texas now requires accountants sitting for the CPA exam to have passed a course in ethics; other states are soon to follow suit. Accounting instructors should be at the forefront of the ethics education movement; in particular, those of us who have worked in the profession or who hold professional certifications understand the importance of following the profession's codes of ethics. All accounting instructors, regardless of background or teaching approach, know the importance of ethical behavior to the smooth functioning of the financial markets.

Ethical Obligations and Decision Making in Accounting was written to guide accountants through the post-Enron age. Our book is entirely devoted to helping students cultivate the ethical commitment needed to ensure that their work meets the highest standards of integrity, independence, and objectivity.

We wrote this book with these aims in mind:

- To help accounting students fully understand how a commitment to ethics can enable accounting professionals to meet their ethical obligations to investors and creditors.
- To define an integrated ethical framework built on ethical reasoning and detailed explanations of the principles of ethical behavior in the AICPA Code of Professional Conduct. This framework highlights the importance of adhering to generally accepted accounting principles (GAAP) and generally accepted auditing standards (GAAS).
- To provide the ethical grounding that accounting students need to reconcile conflicts between stakeholder interests that can occur in the performance of audit, tax, and consulting services.
- To examine the broad elements of the financial reporting system that dictate whether ethical decisions will be made in business and accounting, including the ethics of the internal control environment, the effectiveness of accounting and auditing within an ethical framework, and board of director and audit committee responsibilities under the Sarbanes-Oxley Act.
- To aid the student in understanding the failures of corporate governance that led to the scandals at Enron and WorldCom.

The philosophy of this text is that accounting ethics is best discussed in the context of professional obligations. CPAs serve as internal accountants and auditors, external auditors, tax preparers and advisors, and consultants to their clients. The ethical standards laid down in the AICPA Code pertain to the performance of professional services. Just knowing the ethics is only part of the story: The challenges for CPAs arise in the context of their roles as members of management and external auditors, and the pressures exerted by superiors and clients test the CPA's commitment to ethical behavior.

About this Textbook

Ethical Obligations and Decision Making in Accounting is designed to provide the instructor with the best flexibility and pedagogical effectiveness of any book on the market.

To that end, it includes numerous features designed to make both learning and teaching easier, such as:

- Twelve cases covering the scandals that led to Sarbanes-Oxley are incorporated into the text. Another 65 cases are available to assign as homework; 11 of these cover accounting scandals, and the remaining 54 are original. The cases explore these events from a strictly ethical point of view rather than simply rehashing common information.
- Three of the cases—Bhopal, India, in Chapter 3, The Hollinger Chronicles in Chapter 5, and Imperial Valley Thrift & Loan in Chapter 5—are longer, more complex cases that can be assigned to students as a separate course project or serve as a final examination.
- The book is comprehensive enough to serve as a stand-alone text yet flexible enough to act as a supplementary text within an auditing or financial accounting course.
- There is sufficient case and problem material to allow the instructor to vary the course over at least two to three terms.
- The writing style is pitched specifically to students, making the material easy to follow and absorb.
- Chapter 7 covers the critical issues facing the accounting profession including how to control earnings management and how to improve the quality of financial reports.
- Nearly 120 end-of-chapter questions throughout the book provide the opportunity for helpful and stimulating in-class review of text concepts.

The **Instructor's Resource CD-ROM** included with the book offers the finest teaching support of any accounting ethics text. A comprehensive **Instructor's Manual** provides teaching notes, grading suggestions and rubrics, sample syllabi, extra cases and projects, and guidelines for incorporating writing into the accounting ethics course; the **Test Bank** provides a variety of multiple choice, short answer, and essay questions for building quizzes and tests; and **PowerPoint** presentations for every chapter make a convenient and powerful lecture tool.

Acknowledgements

We greatly appreciate the insight and suggestions provided by the following reviewers of this text:

Dennis Elam
University of North Texas

Richard Mark
University of Texas at Arlington

Aundrea Kay Guess
St. Edward's University

L. Kevin McNelis
New Mexico State University

Cynthia Jeffrey
Iowa State University

Kevin M. Misiewicz
University of Notre Dame

Lawrence Kalbers
Loyola Marymount University

Aileen Smith
Stephen F. Austin University

Carol Lawrence
University of Richmond

Charles Stanley
Baylor University

We also appreciate the assistance and guidance given us on this project by the staff of McGraw-Hill/Irwin, including Stewart Mattson, editorial director; Dan Wiencek, marketing manager; Robin Reed, developmental editor (Carlisle Publishing Services); Colleen Honan, editorial assistant; Susanne Riedell, senior project manager; Michael McCormick, lead production supervisor; Matthew Baldwin, lead designer; and Rose Range, media project manager.

Finally, we would like to acknowledge the contributions of our students, who have provided invaluable comments and suggestions on the content and use of these cases.

If you have any questions, comments, or suggestions concerning *Ethical Obligations and Decision Making in Accounting,* please send them to us through our publisher.

Steve Mintz

Rosie Morris

Brief Contents

Table of Contents

Chapter 4
Ethics in Accounting: Ethical Obligations and Decision Making 101

Chapter 5
Professional Responsibilities and Ethical Obligations in Auditing 139

Ethical Obligations and Decision Making in Accounting

Text and Cases

1

Integrity: The Basis for Ethics in Accounting

Have the courage to say no. Have the courage to face the truth. Do the right thing because it is right. These are the magic keys to living your life with integrity . . . .

W. Clement Stone (1902–2002)

What Is Ethics?

There are various ways to define *ethics*. The simplest may be to say that ethics deals with "right" and "wrong." However, it is difficult to judge what may be right or wrong in a particular situation without some frame of reference.

Ethics must be based on accepted standards of behavior. For example, in virtually all societies and cultures, it is wrong to kill someone or steal property from someone else. These standards have developed over time and come from a variety of sources including:

- The influence of religious writing and interpretations.
- The influence of philosophical thought.
- The influence of community (societal) values.

In addition, the ethical standards for a profession, such as the accounting profession, are heavily influenced by the practices of those in the profession, state laws and regulations, and the expectations of society.

Definition

Ethics deals with well-based standards of how people ought to act. Ethics does not describe the way people do act. It deals with the way people should act, and it is prescriptive (normative), not descriptive. Ethical people always strive to make the right decision in all circumstances. They do not rationalize their actions based on their own perceived self-interests. Ethical decision making entails following certain well-established norms of behavior.

Laws versus Ethics

Being ethical is not the same as following the law. While ethical people always try to be law abiding, there may be instances when your sense of ethics tells you it is best not to follow the law in a particular instance. These situations are rare and should be based on sound ethical reasons.

Assume that you are driving 45 miles per hour on a two-lane divided roadway (double yellow line) going east. All of a sudden, you see a young boy jump out to retrieve a ball. The boy is close enough to your vehicle that you know you cannot continue straight down the roadway and stop in time to avoid hitting him. You quickly look to your right and notice about 10 other children off the road. You cannot avoid hitting one or more of them if you swerve to the right to avoid hitting the boy in the middle of the road. You glance to the left on the opposite side of the road and notice no traffic going west or any children off the road. What should you do?

Ethical Perspective

If you cross the double yellow line that divides the roadway, you have violated the motor vehicle laws. We are told never to cross a double yellow line and travel into oncoming traffic. The ethical action would be to do just that because you have determined that it appears to be safe. It is better to risk a ticket than hit the boy in the middle of your side of the road or those children off to the side of the road.

Laws and Ethical Obligations

Laws create a minimum set of standards. Ethical people often go beyond what the law requires because the law cannot cover every situation a person might encounter. When the facts are unclear and the legal issues uncertain, an ethical person should decide what to do on the basis of well-established standards of ethical behavior.

Ethical people often do less than is permitted by the law and more than is required. A useful perspective is to ask:

What does the law require of me?

What do ethical standards of behavior demand of me?

How should I act to conform to both?

The Gray Area

When the rules are unclear, an ethical person looks beyond his own self-interest and evaluates the interests of all the parties potentially affected by the action or decision. These parties are known as the *stakeholders*. Ethical decision making requires that a decision maker should, at least sometimes, be willing to take an action that might not be in his best interest.

Distinguishing between Ethics and Morality

The term *ethics* is derived from the Greek word *ethikos,* which itself is derived from the Greek word *ethos,* meaning custom or **character.** Morals are from the Latin word *moralis,* meaning customs, with the Latin word *mores* being defined as "manners, morals, **character.**" Therefore, ethics and morals are essentially the same.

In philosophy, ethical behavior is that which is "good." The Western tradition of ethics is sometimes called *moral philosophy.* The field of ethics or moral philosophy involves developing, defending, and recommending concepts of right and wrong behavior. These concepts do not change as one's desires and motivations change. They are not relative to the situation. They are immutable. Moral philosophies will be discussed in the next chapter. The primary objective of this chapter is to describe the character traits that enable a person to act with integrity.

Values and Ethics

Values are basic and fundamental beliefs that guide or motivate attitudes or actions. Values are concerned with how a person will behave in certain situations whereas ethics is concerned with how a moral person should behave. A person who values prestige, power, and wealth is likely to act out of self-interest whereas a person who values honesty, integrity, and trust typically acts in the best interests of others. It does not follow that acting in the best interests of others precludes acting in one's own self-interest. Indeed, the Golden Rule prescribes that we should treat others the way we want to be treated.

The Golden Rule requires that we try to understand how our actions affect others and that we need to put ourselves in the place of the other person on the receiving end of the action. The Golden Rule is best seen as a consistency principle in that we should not act one way toward others but have a desire to be treated differently in a similar situation. In other words, it would be wrong to think that separate standards of behavior exist to guide our personal lives but a different standard (a lower one) exists in business.

Religious and Philosophical Foundations of Ethics

Virtually all of the world's great religions contain in their religious texts some version of the Golden Rule: "Do unto others as you would wish them do unto you." In other words, we should treat others the way we would want to be treated. This is the basic ethic that guides all religions. If we believe that honesty is important, we should be honest with others and expect the same in return. One result of this ethic is the concept that every person shares certain inherent human rights that will be discussed later in this chapter and the next. Exhibit 1.1 provides some examples of the universality of the Golden Rule in world religions provided by the character education organization "Teaching Values."[1]

Integrity is the key to carrying out the Golden Rule. A person of integrity acts with truthfulness, courage, sincerity, and honesty. *Integrity* means to have the courage to stand by your principles even in the face of pressure to bow to the demands of others. Integrity

EXHIBIT 1.1
The Universality of the Golden Rule in the World Religions

Religion	Expression of the Golden Rule	Citation
Buddhism	Hurt not others in ways that you yourself would find hurtful.	Udana-Varga 5,1
Christianity	All things whatsoever ye would that men should do to you, Do ye so to them; for this is the law and the prophets.	Matthew 7:1
Confucianism	Do not do to others what you would not like yourself. Then there will be no resentment against you, either in the family or in the state.	Analects 12:2
Hinduism	This is the sum of duty, do naught onto others what you would not have them do unto you.	Mahabharata 5, 1517
Islam	No one of you is a believer until he desires for his brother that which he desires for himself.	Sunnah
Judaism	What is hateful to you, do not do to your fellowman. This is the entire Law; all the rest is commentary.	Talmud, Shabbat 3id
Taoism	Regard your neighbor's gain as your gain, and your neighbor's loss as your own loss.	Tai Shang Kan Yin P'ien
Zoroastrianism	That nature alone is good which refrains from doing another whatsoever is not good for itself.	Dadisten-I-dinik, 94, 5

has particular importance for certified public accountants (CPAs) who often are pressured by their employers and clients to give in to their demands. The ethical responsibility of a CPA in these instances is to adhere to the ethics of the accounting profession and not to subordinate professional judgment to others. Integrity encompasses the whole of the person and is the foundation of the ancient Greek philosophy of virtue.

The origins of Western philosophy trace back to the ancient Greeks including Socrates, Plato, and Aristotle. The ancient Greek philosophy of virtue deals with questions such as this: "What is the best sort of life for human beings to live?" Greek thinkers saw the attainment of a good life as the *telos,* the end or goal of human existence. For most Greek philosophers, the end is *eudaimonia*, which is usually translated as "happiness." However, to the Greeks, the end goal of happiness meant much more than to experience pleasure or satisfaction. The ultimate goal of happiness was to attain some objectively good status, the life of excellence. The Greek word for excellence is *arete*, the customary translation of which is "virtue." Thus for the Greeks, the "excellences" or "virtues" were the qualities that made a life admirable or excellent. They did not restrict their thinking to characteristics we regard as moral virtues, such as courage, justice, and temperance but included others we think of as nonmoral such as wisdom.[2]

Modern philosophies have been posited as ways of living an ethical life. Unlike virtue theory, these philosophies rely more on methods of ethical reasoning, and they can be used to facilitate ethical decision making. We provide a brief overview of these philosophies in this chapter with more extensive coverage in Chapter 2.

Teleology

Recall that *telos* is the Greek word for "end" or "purpose." In teleology, an act is considered morally right or acceptable if it produces some desired result, such as pleasure, the realization of self-interest, utility, wealth, and so on. Teleologists assess the moral worth of behavior by looking at its consequences, and thus moral philosophers often refer to these theories as consequentialism. Two important teleological philosophies that typically guide decision making in individual business decisions are egoism and utilitarianism.[3]

Egoism

Egoism defines right or acceptable behavior in terms of its consequences for the individual. *Egoists* believe that the individual should "Do the act that promotes the greatest good for oneself."[4]

One form of egoism emphasizes a more direct action to bring about the best interests of society and therefore is more consistent with Adam Smith's belief that society's interest is better served when an individual pursues long-run self-interest.[5] *Enlightened egoists* allow for the well-being of others because they help achieve some ultimate goal for the decision maker, although their own self-interest remains paramount.[6]

Let's examine the following example from the perspective of egoism. The date is Friday, January 15, 2008, and the time is 5 p.m. It is the last day of fieldwork on the audit of What's It To U, Inc. You are the staff auditor in charge of receivables. You are wrapping up the test of subsequent collections of accounts receivable to determine whether certain receivables that were outstanding on December 31, 2007, and that were not confirmed by the customer as being outstanding, have now been collected. If these receivables have been collected and in amounts equal to the year-end outstanding balances, you will be confident that the December 31 balance is correct and this aspect of the audit of receivables can be relied on. One account receivable for $1 million has not been collected even though it is 90 days past due. You go to your supervisor and discuss whether to establish an allowance for uncollectibles for part or the entire amount. Your supervisor contacts the manager in charge of the audit who goes to the chief financial officer (CFO) of the client to discuss the matter. The CFO says in no uncertain terms that you should not record an allowance of any amount. The CFO does not want to reduce earnings below the current level because that will cause the company not to meet financial analysts' estimates of earnings for the year. Your supervisor informs you that the firm will go along with the client on this matter even though the $1 million amount is material. In fact, it is 10 percent of the overall accounts receivable balance at December 31.

The junior auditor faces a challenge to integrity in this instance. The client is attempting to circumvent generally accepted accounting principles (GAAP). The ethical obligation of the staff auditor under generally accepted auditing standards (GAAS) is to maintain independence and not to subordinate judgment to the client.

If you are an egoist, you might conclude that it is in your best interests to go along with the client. After all, you do not want to lose the client. An enlightened egoist might reason that it is in her long-run interests to go along with the firms' position to support the client because she may not advance within the firm unless she is perceived to be a "team" player.

Utilitarianism

The utilitarian theory was first formulated in the eighteenth century by Jeremy Bentham (1748–1832) and later refined by John Stuart Mill (1806–1873). *Utilitarians* look beyond self-interest to consider impartially the interests of all persons affected by an action. According to the utilitarian principle, a decision is ethical if it provides greater net utility to the stakeholders than any other alternative decision.[7]

Utilitarianism emphasizes the consequences of an action on the individuals affected by the action. Utilitarians recognize that trade-offs exist in decision making. The utilitarian is concerned with balancing social harms and benefits to reach a decision that maximizes net benefits and minimizes overall harm for all stakeholders.

Utilitarian decision making relies on a systematic comparison of the costs and benefits of alternatives. Using such a cost-benefit analysis, a utilitarian decision maker calculates the utility of the consequences of all possible actions and then selects the one that results in the greatest benefit.[8]

Utilitarianism is a common approach in certain types of business decisions, such as performance measurements and evaluations. As a tool of ethical analysis, however, it suffers from two difficulties. First, it is often very difficult if not impossible to foresee all consequences of a decision. Accurate forecasts of outcomes are required in business situations in which very little data or experience is available. Second, many decisions have consequences that are difficult to measure.[9]

Let's go back to our audit example. It would be difficult to quantify the possible effects of going along with the client. How can a utilitarian measure the costs to the company of having to write off a potential bad debt after the fact including possible higher interest rates to borrow money in the future because of a decline in liquidity? The results could lead to pressures in financing business operations that threaten the viability of the company.

Utilitarian philosophers are conventionally divided into two types, act-utilitarians and rule-utilitarians. An *act-utilitarian* examines the specific action itself rather than the general rules governing the action to assess whether it will result in the greatest utility.[10] For example, a rule such as "don't subordinate judgment*"* would serve only as a general guide for an act-utilitarian. If the overall effect of giving in to the client's demands brings net utility to all of the stakeholders, then the rule is set aside.

A *rule-utilitarian* determines behavior based on principles, or rules, designed to promote the greatest utility. For the rule-utilitarian, actions are justified by appeal to rules such as "Don't subordinate judgment," or "Don't deceive." According to the rule-utilitarian, an action is selected because it is required by the correct moral rule that everyone should follow. The correct moral rule is that which maximizes intrinsic value and minimizes intrinsic disvalue. For example, a rule such as "Don't deceive" might be interpreted as requiring the full disclosure of the possibility that the client will not collect on a material, $1 million receivable. A rule-utilitarian might reason that the long-term effect of deceiving the users of financial statement information is a breakdown of the trust that exists between the users and preparers and auditors of financial information.

Deontology

Deontology is derived from the Greek word *deon* meaning "duty." Deontologists believe that moral norms establish the basis for action. Unlike utilitarianism, the norms are based on the rights of individuals and on the motivations associated with a particular behavior rather than on its consequences. Deontology differs from rule utilitarianism in that the moral norms (or rules) are based on reason, not outcomes.

Rights Principles

The Golden Rule that we should treat others the way we would wish to be treated creates certain rights for others and obligations for decision makers. Rights principles grant you certain moral or human rights because you are a human being. These rights relate to the duties of others not to violate your rights and, in turn, you have duties not to violate their rights. If you have a right to free speech, I have a duty not to violate your right as long as your speech does not violate my rights.[11]

Formulations of *rights theories* first appeared in the seventeenth century in writings of Thomas Hobbes and John Locke. Modern rights theory is associated with the eighteenth century philosopher Immanuel Kant (1724–1804). He created several formulations of his *categorical imperative*. This principle requires that everyone should be treated as a free and equal person and proposes that everyone has a correlative duty to treat others in this way. According to the theory, an action is morally correct if it is motivated by a sense of obligation, not because an action may be taken merely to advance one's personal interests. One version of Kant's categorical imperative emphasizes the universality of moral actions. The principle is stated as follows: "Act only according to that maxim [reason for acting] by which you can at the same time will that it should become universal law."[12]

Kant argues that an action is morally right only if you would be willing to have everyone act the same way in a similar situation. Thus, the principle provides both universal (have everyone act) and reversible (you would be the recipient of the acts of others) criteria for determining moral right and wrong.[13]

A second formulation of the categorical imperative states, "Act so that you treat humanity, whether in your own person or that of another, always as an end and never as a means only."[14] Kant argues that people should never be treated only as a means to an end but as ends themselves or as a means and ends. Thus, when using people to accomplish your purposes, you have a duty to respect them as human beings and to promote their ability to realize their desired ends or goals. In this way, deontologists consider one's moral motivation in acting.

One problem with deontological theory is that it relies on moral absolutes: absolute principles and absolute conclusions. The notions of rights and duties are completely separated from the consequences of one's actions. This could lead to making decisions that might adhere to one's moral rights and another's attendant duties to those rights but that also produces disastrous consequences for some.

Another problem with deontological moral systems is that there is no clear way to resolve conflicts between moral duties. One of the most widely discussed cases of this kind is taken from William Styron's *Sophie's Choice*. Sophie and her two children are at a Nazi concentration camp. A guard confronts Sophie and tells her that one of her children will be allowed to live and one will be killed. Sophie must decide which child will be killed.

She can prevent the death of either of her children but only by condemning the other to be killed. The guard makes the situation even more painful for Sophie by telling her that if she chooses neither, both will be killed. With this added factor, Sophie has a morally compelling reason to choose one of her children. But for each child, Sophie has an apparently equally strong reason to save him or her. Thus, the same moral precept gives rise to conflicting obligations.[15]

Thank goodness we do not face such morally excruciating decisions in accounting. The ultimate obligation of an accountant and an auditor is to honor the public trust. The public interest obligation that is embedded in the profession's codes of ethics requires that if a conflict exists between the obligations of a decision maker to others, the decision maker should always decide based on protecting the right of the public (i.e., investors and creditors) to receive accurate and reliable financial information. However, when this right conflicts with auditors' ethical obligations, such as confidentiality, the auditor has an ethical dilemma.

Acting with Integrity

According to Mintz, "Integrity is a fundamental trait of character that enables a CPA to withstand client and competitive pressures that might otherwise lead to the subordination of judgment."[16] A person of integrity will act out of moral principle, not expediency. That person will do what is right even if it means the loss of a client.

For example, assume that your tax client fails to inform you about an amount of earned income for the year and you confront the client on this issue. He tells you not to record it and reminds you there is no W-2 form or 1099 form to evidence the earnings. The client adds that you will not get to audit the company's books anymore if you do not adhere to his wishes.

If you are a person of integrity, you will not allow the client to dictate how the tax rules should be applied in the client's situation. You are the professional, know the tax law best, and have an ethical obligation to report taxes in accordance with the law. If you go along with the client and the Internal Revenue Service (IRS) investigates and sanctions you for failing to follow the IRS Tax Code, you could suffer irreparable harm to your reputation. The point is that a professional must never let loyalty cloud good judgment and ethical decision making.

The Moral Point of View

Traits of character such as honesty, integrity, and trustworthiness enable a person to act with virtue and apply the moral point of view. Kurt Baier, a well-known moral philosopher, discusses the moral point of view as being one that emphasizes practical reason and rational choice.[17] To act ethically means to incorporate ethical values into decision making and to reflect on the rightness or wrongness of alternative courses of action.

Aristotle believed that deliberation (reason and thought) precedes the choice of action and that we deliberate about things that are in our power (voluntary) and can be realized in action. The deliberation that leads to the action always concerns the choices, not the ends. We take the end for granted—a life of excellence or virtue—and then consider in what manner and by what means it can be realized.[18]

We conclude this section by emphasizing that the ends do *not* justify the means. The process you follow to decide on a course of action is more important than achieving the end goal. If this were not true from a moral point of view, we could rationalize all types of actions in the name of achieving a desired goal even if that goal does harm to others while satisfying our personal needs and desires.

What makes a person of goodwill? What enables a person to treat others with respect, caring, and fairness? It is someone who internalizes the ethical values discussed in the following sections and lives life consistently, both at home and at work, in accordance with those same values.

Personal Integrity

Given that integrity is an essential characteristic for a CPA in the performance of professional services, it is important that the CPA also have personal integrity. Integrity, indeed all of ethics, is not a spigot that can be turned on or off from one's personal to professional life. As the ancient Greeks pointed out, we learn how to be ethical by practice and exercising those virtues that enable us to lead a life of excellence.

The Six Pillars of Character_SM

The Josephson Institute of Ethics identifies Six Pillars of Character that provide a foundation to guide ethical decision making. These ethical values include trustworthiness, respect, responsibility, fairness, caring, and citizenship. Josephson believes that the Six Pillars act as a multilevel filter through which to process decisions. So being trustworthy is not enough; we must also be caring. Adhering to the letter of the law is not enough; we must accept responsibility for our actions or inactions.[19]

Trustworthiness

The dimensions of trustworthiness include being honest, acting with integrity, being reliable, and exercising loyalty in dealing with others.

Honesty

Honesty is the most basic ethical value and means that we should express the truth as we know it and without deception. In accounting, the full disclosure principle requires that the accounting professional should disclose all of the information that owners, investors, governments, and creditors need to make informed decisions. To withhold relevant information is dishonest.

Let's assume that you are a member of a case discussion group in your Intermediate Accounting II class. In the initial meeting with all members, the leader asks whether anyone there has not completed Intermediate I. You failed the course last term and are retaking it concurrently with Intermediate II. However, you feel embarrassed and say nothing. Perhaps the leader believes it is important because the case assigned to your group uses knowledge gained from Intermediate I. You internally justify the silence by thinking: "Well, I did complete the course, albeit with a grade of F." This is an unethical position. You are rationalizing silence by interpreting the question in your own self-interest rather than in the interests of the entire group. The other members need to know whether you have completed Intermediate I because the leader may choose not to assign a specific project to you that requires the Intermediate I prerequisite knowledge.

Integrity

The integrity of a person is an essential element in trusting that person.

MacIntyre in his account of Aristotelian virtue states, "There is at least one virtue recognized by tradition which cannot be specified except with reference to the wholeness of a human life—the virtue of integrity or constancy."[20] A person of integrity takes time for self-reflection so that the events, crises, and challenges of everyday living do not determine the course of that person's moral life. Such a person is trusted by others because that person is true to her word.

Going back to the previous example, if you encounter a conflict with another group member who pressures you to plagiarize a report that the two of you are working on from one available on the Internet, you'll be acting with integrity if you refuse to go along. Integrity requires that you have the courage of your convictions. You know it's wrong to plagiarize other material. Someone worked hard to get the report published. You wouldn't want another person to take material you had published without permission and proper citation. Why do it to that person? If you do it simply because it might benefit you, you are acting out of self-interest, or egoism, and that is wrong!

Reliability

Others rely on the promises that we make to them, and we have a moral duty to follow through with action. Our ethical obligation for promise keeping includes avoiding bad faith excuses and unwise commitments. Imagine that you are asked to attend a group meeting on Saturday and you agree to do so. That night your best friend calls and says he has two tickets to the basketball game between the Dallas Mavericks and San Antonio Spurs. You decide to go to the game instead of the meeting. You've broken your promise. You did it out of self-interest. You figured, who wouldn't want to see the Spurs play? What's worse is that you call the group leader and say you can't attend the meeting because you're sick. Now you've also lied. You've started the slide down the proverbial ethical slippery slope, and it will be difficult to climb back up to the top.

Loyalty

We all should value loyalty in friendship. After all, you wouldn't want the friend who called you to go to the basketball game to telephone the group leader later in the day and say you went to the game instead of the group meeting.

Loyalty requires that our friend should not violate the confidence we place in him. In accounting, loyalty requires that we keep financial and other information confidential when it deals with our employer and client. For example, if you are the in-charge accountant on an audit of a client for your CPA firm-employer and you discover that the client is "cooking the books," you shouldn't telephone the local newspaper and tell the story to a reporter. Instead, you should go to the partner in charge of the engagement and tell her. Your ethical obligation is to report what you have observed to your supervisor and let her take the appropriate action.

There are limits to the confidentiality obligation. For example, let's assume that you are the accounting manager at a publicly owned company and your supervisor pressures you to keep silent about the manipulation of financial information. The chief executive officer (CEO) and board of directors support your supervisor. Out of a misplaced duty of loyalty in this situation, you might rationalize your silence. However, loyalty is the ethical value that should never take precedence over other values such as honesty and integrity. Otherwise, we can imagine all kinds of cover-ups of information in the interest of loyalty or friendship.

The prior examples could represent situations in which you consider taking a matter outside your employer or circumvent the firm-employer relationship to air your concerns. Be careful if you choose to do this and get legal advice before acting. While acting out of conscience and a sense of what the right thing to do is the highest ethical choice you can make, it is important to be aware of the consequences of your actions before taking the ultimate step of whistle-blowing.

While attending a Josephson Institute of Ethics training program for educators in 1992, one of your authors heard Michael Josephson make an analogy about loyal behavior that sticks with him to this day. Josephson said, "Dogs are loyal to their master while cats are loyal to the house." How true it is that dogs see their ultimate allegiance to their owner while cats get attached to the place they call home—their own personal space. In a business context, this means that a manager should try to encourage "cat" behavior in the organization (sorry, dog lovers). In that way, if a cover-up of a financial wrongdoing exists, the cat loyalty mentality incorporated into the business environment dictates that the information should be disclosed because it is not in the best interests of the organization to hide or ignore it. If we act with dog loyalty, we will cover up for our supervisor who has a say about what happens to us in the organization. It may be an understandable position, perhaps, but it is unethical all the same. Moreover, once we go along with the cover-up, we have started the slide down the ethical slippery slope. There may be no turning back. In fact, our supervisor may come to us next period and expect the same cover-up in a similar situation. If we refuse, the first instance could be brought up and used as a threat against us because we've already violated ethical standards once and don't want to get caught.

Often when we cover up information, it becomes public knowledge later. The results at that time could be much worse. This could be a practical consideration in deciding on a course of action, but it is not an ethical one. What's most important is to emphasize that we should act ethically not out of a fear for the consequences of hiding information. We should act ethically out of a positive sense that it is the right way to behave.

Respect

All people should be treated with dignity. We don't have an ethical duty to hold all people in high esteem, but we should treat everyone with respect regardless of their circumstances in life. The Golden Rule encompasses respect for others through notions such as civility, courtesy, decency, dignity, autonomy, tolerance, and acceptance.[21]

By age 16, George Washington had copied out by hand 110 *Rules of Civility & Decent Behavior In Company and Conversation.* They are based on a set of rules composed by French Jesuits in 1595. While many of the rules seem out of place in today's society, it is worthwhile noting the first rule: "Every Action done in Company, ought to be with Some Sign of Respect, to those that are Present."[22]

Washington's vernacular was consistent with the times as indicated by the last of his rules: "Labour to keep alive in your Breast that Little Spark of Celestial fire Called Conscience."[23] There are many definitions of conscience, but the one your authors find most relevant comes from the lexical database for the English language by the Cognitive Science Laboratory at Princeton University. The definition is "Motivation deriving logically from ethical or moral principles that govern a person's thoughts and actions."[24]

As a member of the case discussion group, it would be wrong for you to treat another member with discourtesy or prejudice because you have prejudged that person on the basis of national origin or some other factor rather than her abilities and conduct. You would not want to be treated unfairly because of how you dress or walk or talk, so others should not be judged based on similar considerations. We should judge people based on their character.

The Nobel Prize peace activist Dr. Martin Luther King said it best in his "I Have a Dream" speech delivered on the steps at the Lincoln Memorial in Washington, D.C., on August 28, 1963. Dr. King said the following in reference to the true meaning of the nation's creed, "We hold these truths to be self-evident; that all men are created equal":

"I have a dream that my four children will one day live in a nation where they will not be judged by the color of their skin but by the content of their character."[25]

Responsibility

Josephson points out that our capacity to reason and our freedom to choose make us morally autonomous for our actions and decisions. We are accountable for what we do and who we are.[26]

A responsible person carefully reflects on alternative courses of action using ethical principles. A responsible person acts diligently and perseveres in carrying out moral action. Imagine that you were given the task by your group to interview five CPAs in public practice about their most difficult ethical dilemma. You decided to ask one person who is a friend of the family about five dilemmas that person faced in the practice of public accounting. Now, even if you made an "honest" mistake in interpreting the requirement, it is clear that you did not exercise the level of care (due care) that might be expected in this instance in carrying out the task to interview five different CPAs. The due care test is whether a "reasonable person" would conclude that you had acted with the level of care, or diligence, expected in the circumstance. The courts have used this test for many years to evaluate the actions of professionals.

Fairness

A person of fairness treats others equally, impartially, and openly. In business, we might say that the fair allocation of scarce resources requires that those who have earned the right to a greater share of corporate resources as judged objectively by performance measures should receive a larger share than those whose performance has not met the standard.

Let's assume that your instructor told the case study groups at the beginning of the course that the group with the highest overall numerical average would receive an A grade, the group with second highest a B, and so on. At the end of the term, the teacher gave the group with the second highest average—90.5—an A and the group with the highest average—91.2—a B. Perhaps the instructor took subjective factors into account in deciding on the final grading. You might view the instructor's action as unfair to the first group. As Michael Josephson points out, "Fairness implies adherence to a balanced standard of justice without relevance to one's own feelings or inclinations."[27]

Caring

Edmund L. Pincoffs, a philosopher who formerly taught at The University of Texas at Austin, believes that virtues such as caring, kindness, sensitivity, altruism, and benevolence enable a person who possesses these qualities to consider the interests of others.[28] Josephson believes that caring is the "heart of ethics, and ethical decision-making."[29]

The essence of caring is empathy. Empathy is the ability to understand, be sensitive to, and care about the feelings of others. Caring and empathy support each other and enable a person to put himself in the position of another. This is essential to ethical decision making.

Let's assume that the morning of an important group meeting, your child comes down with temperature of 103 degrees. You call the group leader and say that you can't make it to the meeting. Instead, you suggest taping the meeting so that you can listen to the discussions later that day and telephone the leader with any questions. The leader reacts angrily, stating that you aren't living up to your responsibilities. Assuming that your behavior is not part of a pattern, you would have a right to be upset with the leader who seems uncaring. In the real world, emergencies do occur, and placing your child's health and welfare above all else should make sense in this situation to a person of rational thought. You also acted diligently by offering to listen to the discussions and, if necessary, follow up with the leader.

Putting yourself in the place of another is sometimes difficult to do because the circumstances are unique to that person's situation. For example, what would you do if a member of your team walks into a meeting bleary eyed? You might ignore it, or you might ask that person if everything is all right. If you do and are informed that the person was up all night with a crying baby, you might say something like: "If there's anything I can do to lighten the load for you today, just say the word."

A person who can empathize seems to know just what to say to make the other person feel better about circumstances. On the other hand, if you have never been married and have not had children, you might not be able to understand the feelings of a mother who has just spent the night trying to comfort a screaming child.

Citizenship

Josephson points out that "citizenship includes civic virtues and duties that prescribe how we ought to behave as part of a community."[30] An important part of good citizenship is to obey the laws, be informed of the issues, volunteer in your community, and vote in elections.

The accounting profession is a community with values and standards of behavior. These are embodied in the various codes of conduct in the profession. CPAs should strive to live up to basic principles including honoring the public trust, acting with integrity in the performance of professional services, being independent of clients, making decisions objectively, and exercising due care in the performance of services.[31] The American Institute of Certified Public Accountants (AICPA) Code of Professional Ethics guides the ethical behavior of CPAs and is the basis for discussing the professional obligations of CPAs to the public, clients, and employers. More will be said about the Code in Chapter 4.

Virtue, Character, and CPA Obligations

Aristotle's conception of virtues can be used as positive traits of character to identify ethical standards in the accounting profession. These virtues enable CPAs to have integrity—the inner strength of character to withstand pressures that might otherwise overwhelm and negatively influence their professional judgment. A summary of the virtues is listed in Exhibit 1.2.[32]

Scope and Organization of the Text

The ethics standards in accounting are more stringent than those in business or any other field because CPAs render opinions on a company's financial statements. CPAs must be objective and maintain their integrity for that opinion to be useful. Furthermore, investors and creditors rely on that opinion for their decision making. They might buy or sell stock and loan money or not loan money based on the opinion. Indeed, the public interest demands that CPAs should be beyond reproach in forming and rendering an audit opinion. The audit opinion contributes to a well-functioning financial market place. A brief overview of audit opinions and the audit process will be provided in Chapter 5 so that students can better appreciate why accounting scandals at companies such as Enron and WorldCom occurred.

EXHIBIT 1.2
Virtue and Ethical Obligations of CPAs

Aristotle's Virtues	Ethical Standards for CPAs
Trustworthiness, benevolence, altruism	*Integrity*
Honesty, **integrity**	Truthfulness, nondeception
Impartiality, open-mindedness	Objectivity, independence
Reliability, dependability, faithfulness	Loyalty (confidentiality)
Trustworthiness	Due care (competence and prudence)

The philosophy of this text is that accounting ethics is best discussed in the context of professional obligations. CPAs serve as internal accountants and auditors, external auditors, tax preparers and advisors, and consultants to their clients. The ethical standards that are described in the AICPA Code pertain to the performance of professional services. Just knowing the ethics is only part of the story. The challenges that exist for CPAs take place in the context of their roles as members of management and external auditors. Pressures that test their commitment to ethical behavior are exerted on CPAs by superiors and clients.

By necessity, the text covers financial reporting and auditing. These are two subject areas with stand-alone courses. However, the coverage in this text is designed to be complementary and supportive of those courses. Most students will have taken the intermediate accounting sequence before using this book, so the financial reporting areas relevant to accounting ethics such as financial statement reporting and disclosure already will have been covered. As for auditing, the ethical responsibilities of CPAs who audit public companies cannot be separated from the audit standards that guide the investigation of a company's financial statements. Coverage in the book is basic, and it allows students who have not had the auditing course to get up to speed with those who might have already completed the course.

Chapter 2 describes the ethical reasoning methods in accounting that were introduced in this chapter. The ethical reasoning methods have application to CPAs in the performance of professional responsibilities because the Principles of the AICPA Code are based on virtue, utilitarianism, and rights principles.

Chapter 3 discusses ethics in business. Because CPAs are part of an organization, it is important to understand how their responsibilities relate to those of the CEO and CFO, the latter of whom has supervisory authority over accountants and auditors. The environment that creates the pressure on CPAs to deviate from financial reporting, auditing, and ethics standards is critical to understand before encountering the ethical obligations of CPAs to their employers and clients.

Chapter 4 describes the ethics standards in accounting as embodied in the AICPA Code. The ethical obligations of CPAs are discussed in the performance of accounting, auditing, tax, and consulting services. This chapter also presents the Sarbanes-Oxley Act (SOX) of 2002 that changed the landscape in accounting forever. SOX establishes the Public Company Accounting Oversight Board (PCAOB) to regulate public company audits, taking away that responsibility from the AICPA. The PCAOB was formed after the accounting scandals of the late 1990s and early 2000s. The accounting scandals are discussed primarily in Chapters 5 and 7.

Chapter 5 emphasizes ethics and audit responsibilities. CPAs render opinions on their clients' financial statements. These opinions carry a great deal of weight in the financial marketplace. After the Enron and WorldCom scandals, the financial markets went down precipitously. The effect of false financial statements and the impact of improper audit opinions can be seen by studying these and other failures.

Chapter 6 describes the legal obligations of CPAs within the framework of ethical standards. The consequences for violating ethical standards often lead to a lawsuit against accountants and auditors filed by investors and creditors who rely on financial statement information for decision making. Future accounting professionals need to understand their legal liabilities as CPAs and what is expected of them to satisfy the public interest.

Finally, Chapter 7 deals with issues related to earnings management, the quality of financial reporting, and corporate governance. These issues arose in the accounting scandals, and they provide serious challenges to the ethics of CPAs in carrying out their professional obligations. Companies should rely on systems of corporate governance including the audit committee of the board of directors, internal controls, the external audit, and other provisions of SOX to ensure that the financial statements are free of material misstatement.

Earnings management issues exist in the context of financial reporting and link directly to intermediate accounting courses. Earnings management occurs when net income is determined not in accordance with GAAP but in a way that meets the needs and wants of management. Often, the incentive to meet or exceed financial analysts' earnings estimates leads to earnings management. It is within this framework that the ethics of CPAs are directly challenged.

When financial statements are not accurate and reliable because of earnings management or other techniques used to "cook the books," the quality of financial reporting seriously declines. The result can lead to an accounting scandal.

This is a comprehensive book of text and cases in accounting ethics. The discussion links to areas of accounting practice such as accounting, auditing, tax, and consulting services because these are the areas of practice students will enter after graduating from college.

Conclusion

When was the last time you picked up a newspaper and read a story about someone doing the right thing because it was the right thing to do? Such stories are rare these days. We seem to read and hear more about pursuing one's own selfish interests as the motivation for action. It might be called the "What's-in-it-for-me?" approach to life. Nothing could be more contrary to leading a life of virtue. Ralph Waldo Emerson in his classic essay on friendship said, "The only reward of virtue is virtue; the only way to have a friend is to be one."[33] In other words, virtue is its own reward just as we gain friendship in life by being a friend to someone else. In accounting, integrity is its own reward because it builds trust in client relationships and helps to honor the public trust.

Discussion Questions

1. Select one of the world's religions and give a concrete example of how the Golden Rule applies in that religion.

2. In his account of Aristotelian virtue, MacIntyre states that integrity is the one trait of character that encompasses all others. What do you think he meant by that statement? How does integrity relate to, as MacIntrye said, "The wholeness of a human life"?

3. Do you think "enlightened self-interest" is a contradiction in terms, or is it a valid basis for all action?

4. Recall the last time you acted solely in your own best interests without considering the interests of others. If you had it to do over again, would you change how you acted? Why or why not?

5. Do you think it is the same to act in your own-self interest as it is to act in a selfish way? Why or why not?

6. Describe the facts of a situation in your life when you had to balance the harms and benefits to stakeholders prior to making a decision. What was the outcome of the decision? In retrospect, do you think it was the right decision? Why or why not?

7. Describe a situation in your life when you acted based on the ends that you wanted to achieve and you did not pay enough attention to the means to achieve that end. Where you satisfied with the results? Why or why not?

8. What (who) has had the most influence on your personal ethics to this point in your life? Do you believe that your ethics is still evolving? What would cause you to change your ethics positively or negatively?

9. Think of a situation when you faced a crisis of conscience. Briefly describe the facts. What did you do to resolve the ethical dilemma? Why?

10. What is the most selfish act you can imagine? What makes it selfish? If you found the act morally objectionable, what specifically was objectionable about it?

11. Can a person recover from an unethical act? Explain how. What are the most likely reactions to such an act, and how might it affect that person?

12. Your best friend is from a country outside the United States. One day after a particularly stimulating lecture on the meaning of ethics by your instructor, you and your friend disagree about whether culture plays a role in ethical behavior. You state that good ethics is good ethics and it doesn't matter where you live and work. Your friend tells you that in her country, it is common to pay bribes to gain favor with important people. Comment on both positions. What do you believe?

13. Distinguish between personal ethics and business ethics. Should there be separate standards for each? Explain.

14. What is the relationship between the ethical obligation of honesty and truth telling?

15. a. One day you are walking to the local grocery store when you spot your younger 16-year-old brother in an alley drinking wine with two friends. You are more than 21 years old. You hide from him, take a second look from around the corner, and walk on. You are quite sure he didn't see you walking by. What would you do? Discuss the alternatives available to you and provide support for your chosen action by reference to the Six Pillars of Character discussed in this chapter.

    b. Now assume that your brother is older than you but below the minimum drinking age, and you are 16 years old. Would that change what you do? Why or why not?

16. In the discussion of loyalty in this chapter, a statement was made that "your ethical obligation is to report what you have observed to your supervisor and let him take the appropriate action." We point out that you may want to take your concerns to others. Do you think there are any circumstances when you should go outside the company to report "cooking the books"? If so, to what organization would you go? Why? If not, why would you not take the information outside your CPA firm-employer?

17. There is a statement in the Scope and Organization section of the text in this chapter: "The philosophy of this text is that accounting ethics is best discussed in the context of professional obligations." Explain what is meant by this statement.

18. While writing this book, your authors decided to do a Google search on "ethics papers." Would it surprise you to know that the first Web reference is to an organization that claims to have more than 46,000 nonplagiarized papers available? Have you ever used an Internet service to obtain a paper for a high school or college class? (Remember that this is an ethics class.) If so, how did you feel after doing it? Did you feel justified in doing it? Why or why not? If you have not done it, why not? What motivates your action in this instance?

19. Sir Walter Scott (1771–1832), the Scottish novelist and poet, wrote, "Oh what a tangled web we weave, when first we practice to deceive." Comment on what you think Scott meant by this phrase.

20. David Starr Jordan (1851–1931), educator and writer, served as a president of Indiana University and of Stanford University. His claim to fame, however, was as one of the world's leading ichthyologists. In his writings, Jordan said, "Wisdom is knowing what to do next; virtue is doing it." Explain the meaning of this phrase as you see it.

Endnotes

1. Teaching Values, "The Golden Rule in World Religions," n.d., www.teachingvalues.com/goldenrule.html.

2. William J. Prior, *Virtue and Knowledge: An Introduction to Ancient Greek Ethics* (London: Routledge Publishing, 1991).

3. O. C. Ferrell, John Fraedrich, and Linda Ferrell, *Business Ethics: Ethical Decision Making and Cases* (Boston: Houghton Mifflin, 2005), p. 97.

4. David J. Fritzsche, *Business Ethics: A Global and Managerial Perspective* (New York: McGraw-Hill/Irwin, 2005), p. 47.

5. Ferrell et al., p. 97.

6. Fritzsche, p. 48.

7. Ferrell, p. 98.

8. Fritzsche, p. 49.

9. Ferrell et al., p. 99.

10. Fritzsche, p. 50.

11. Immanuel Kant, *Foundations of Metaphysics of Morals,* trans. Lewis White Beck (New York: The Liberal Arts Press, 1959), p. 39.

12. Fritzsche, p. 50.

13. Kant, p. 39.

14. Fritzsche, p. 50.

15. William Styron, *Sophie's Choice* (London: Chelsea House Publications, 2001).

16. Steven M. Mintz, "Virtue Ethics and Accounting Education," *Issues in Accounting Education* 10, no. 2 (Fall 1995), p. 257. American Accounting Association; full text of the article is available at http://aahq.org/ic/browse.htm.

17. Kurt Baier, *The Rational and Moral Order: The Social Roots of Reason and Morality* (Oxford, England: Oxford University Press, 1994).

18. Aristotle, *Nicomachean Ethics,* trans. W. D. Ross (Oxford, England: Oxford University Press, 1925).

19. Michael Josephson, *Making Ethical Decisions,* rev. ed. (Los Angeles: Josephson Institute of Ethics, 2002). http://www.charactercounts.org, p. 7.

20. Alasdair MacIntyre, *After Virtue,* 2nd ed. (Notre Dame, IN: University of Notre Dame Press, 1984).

21. Josephson, p. 11.

22. George Washington, *George Washington's Rules of Civility and Decent Behavior in Company and Conversation* (Bedfordd, Maine: Applewood Books, 1994), p. 9.

23. Washington, p. 30.

24. Cognitive Sciences Laboratory at Princeton University, *WordNet,* n.d., http.wordnet.princeton.edu.

25. Martin Luther King, Jr., *The Peaceful Warrior* (New York: Pocket Books, 1968).

26. Josephson, p. 11.

27. Josephson, p. 12.

28. Edmund L. Pincoffs, *Quandaries and Virtues against Reductivism in Ethics* (Lawrence, KS: University Press of Kansas, 1986).

29. Josephson, p. 13.

30. Josephson, p. 14.

31. American Institute of Certified Public Accountants, *Code of Professional Conduct* (New York: AICPA, 2002).

32. Mintz, p. 260.

33. Ralph Waldo Emerson, *Essays: First and Second Series* (New York: Vintage Paperback, 1990).

Chapter 1 Cases

Case 1-1

A Student's Dilemma

Helen Kanell has a 4.0 grade point average and is in her last semester of college at Empire State University. Helen has already accepted a position to join the accounting firm of Big & Apple LLC. Still, she is determined to complete her career at Empire State and graduate with at least a 3.90 average to qualify for summa cum laude, the highest academic honor. However, she has a B average in all five courses going into the final exam. It seems as though Helen was distracted from her studies this semester because she agreed to be the president of Beta Alpha Psi, the accounting student honor society, and it has required a great deal more work than anticipated. Helen is quite certain she will maintain her B average in four of the five courses but she knows she must get an A grade in at least one course to qualify for summa cum laude.

Prior to the final exam in Accounting 544, Accounting, Law & Governance, Helen is approached by her best friend who works in the Accounting Department office. Her friend is sensitive to Helen's situation, and she had an opportunity to take a copy of the final exam from the professor's mailbox. She gives it to Helen and says, "You can thank me later."

Questions

1. Discuss Helen's responsibilities to each of the following groups in this situation:

   a. The Accounting Department and University.
   b. Other students in the class and in the department.
   c. Big & Apple LLC.
   d. The professor of Accounting 544.
   e. Her best friend.
   f. Herself.

2. From an integrity perspective, what should Helen do? Why?

3. If you were Helen, what would you do? Include in your answer to whom you might go for advice and the steps you would take to resolve the dilemma. Be specific.

4. Assume that Empire State University provides a $5,000 award to all students who graduate summa cum laude. Would this change your decision? Why or why not?

5. Should there be any consequences for the student who provided the exam to Helen? Why or why not?

6. Would your answer to Question 5 change if Empire State had an honor code? Why or why not?

7. As a fellow student in Accounting 544 with Helen, how would you feel if you found out about what Helen did? Why might you feel that way?

Case 1-2

Giles and Regas

Ed Giles and Susan Regas have never been happier than during the past four months since they have been dating each other. Giles is a 35-year-old CPA and a partner in the medium-size accounting firm of Saduga & Mihca. Regas is a 25-year-old senior accountant in the same firm. Both Giles and Regas know the firm's policy on dating. Although it is acceptable for peers to date, the firm does not permit two members of different ranks within the firm to date. A partner should not date a senior in the firm anymore than a senior should date a junior staff accountant. If such dating does occur and eventually leads to marriage, one of the two must resign because of the conflict of interests. Giles and Regas have tried to be discreet about their relationship because they don't want to create any suspicions.

While most of the staff seem to know about Giles and Regas, it is not common knowledge among the partners that the two of them are dating among the partners. Perhaps that is why Regas was assigned to work on the audit of CAA Industries for a second year even though Giles is the supervising partner on the engagement.

As the audit progresses, it becomes clear to the junior staff members that Giles and Regas are spending personal time together during the workday. On one occasion, they were observed leaving for lunch together. Regas did not return to the client's office that day for three hours. On another occasion, Regas seemed distracted from her work, and later that day she received a dozen roses from Giles. A friend of Regas's, Ruth Revilo, inadvertently discovered this fact when she happened to see the card that accompanied the flowers. It was signed, "Love, Poochie." Regas had once told Revilo that it was the nickname Regas gave to Giles.

Revilo pulls Regas aside at the end of the day and says, "We have to talk."

"What is it?" Regas asks.

"I know the flowers are from Giles," Revilo says. "Are you crazy?"

"It's none of your business," Regas responds.

Revilo goes on to explain that others on the audit are aware of the relationship between Regas and Giles. Revilo cautions Regas about jeopardizing her future with the firm by getting involved in a serious dating relationship with someone of a higher rank. Regas does not respond to this comment. Instead, she admits to being distracted lately because of an argument she had with Giles. She points out that the flowers are his way of saying he is sorry for some of the comments he had made about her. It all started when Regas had suggested to Giles that it might be best if they did not go out during the workweek because she was having a hard time getting to work on time. Giles was upset at the suggestion and called her ungrateful. He said, "I've put everything on the line for you. There's no turning back for me."

Regas promises to talk to Giles and thanks Revilo for her concern. That same day, Regas telephones Giles and tells him she wants to temporarily put aside her personal relationship with him until the CAA audit is complete in two weeks. She suggests that, at the end of the two-week period, they get together and thoroughly examine the possible implications of their continued relationship. Giles reluctantly agrees, but he conditions his acceptance on having a "farewell" dinner at their favorite restaurant. Regas agrees to the dinner.

Giles and Regas have dinner that Saturday night. As luck would have it, CAA Industries's controller, Mark Sax, is at the restaurant with his wife. Sax is startled when he sees Giles and Regas together. He wonders about the possible seriousness of their relationship, while reflecting on the recent progress billings of the accounting firm. Sax believes the number of hours billed is out of line with work of a similar nature and the fee estimate. He had planned to discuss the matter with Herb Morris, the managing partner of the firm. He decides to call Morris on Monday morning.

"Herb, you son of a gun, it's Mark Sax."

"Mark. How goes the audit?"

"That's why I'm calling," Sax responds. "Can we meet to discuss a few items?"

"Sure," Morris replies. "Just name the time and place."

"How about first thing tomorrow morning?" asks Sax.

"I'll be in your office at 8 a.m.," says Morris.

"Better make it at 7 a.m., Herb, before your auditors arrive."

Sax and Morris meet to discuss Sax's concerns about seeing Giles and Regas at the restaurant and the possibility that their relationship is negatively affecting audit efficiency. Morris asks whether any other incidents have occurred to make him suspicious about the billings. Sax says that he is aware of only this one instance, although he sensed some apprehension on the part of Regas last week when they discussed why it was taking so long to get the audit recommendations for adjusting entries. Morris listens attentively until Sax finishes and then asks him to be patient while he sets up a meeting to discuss the situation with Giles. Morris promises to get back to Sax by the end of the week.

Questions

1. Assess the personal responsibility of Ed Giles and Sue Regas for the relationship that developed between them.
2. Analyze the situation as it exists between the two from the perspective of the Six Pillars of Character.
3. Assume that you are the best friend of Sue Regas. What would your advice be to her assuming that Giles calls and informs her that he has been asked to meet with Herb Morris?

4. If Giles were a person of integrity but just happened to have a "weak moment" in starting a relationship with Regas, what do you think he would say when he meets with Herb Morris? Why?

5. What would you do if you were in Herb Morris's position when you meet with Giles? In your response, consider how you would resolve the situation in regard to both the completion of the CAA Industries audit and the longer term issue of the continued employment of Giles and Regas in the accounting firm.

6. Would your decision change in response to Question 5 if Ed Giles was the biggest "Rainmaker" in the firm? Why or why not?

7. Assume that Herb Morris fires Ed Giles. Two days later, Morris gets a call from one of the firm's largest clients who is extremely upset by the firing of his auditor, Ed Giles. The client tells Herb Morris that he intends to leave the firm and go with Giles, who is starting his own practice unless Morris rehires Giles. What should Morris do? Why?

Case 1-3

Jason Tybell

Jason Tybell has been employed as a junior accountant by the professional accountancy corporation of Rodgers & Philips for two years. He graduated with a bachelor's degree in accounting from State University. He became a CPA after passing all parts of the computerized CPA exam in one sitting. Jason is on the fast track with Rodgers & Philips, and he receives high evaluations from his seniors. He hopes to make partner in eight years. However, something just happened during an audit in his second year that makes him question whether that will ever happen—at least at Rodgers & Philips.

Jason is concerned about a meeting he will have later in the day with his mentor, William Jackson. The meeting concerns the fact that Jason was not asked to work on the current year's audit of two clients that he worked on during his first year. It is unusual for a second-year staff accountant not to continue unless something went wrong the first year. Jason is not aware of any such occurrence, but he is preparing for the worst.

At a recent meeting of the partners of Rodgers & Philips, Jackson was informed that a third client had complained about Jason. As a result, his mentor will tell Jason that he will not serve on the audit engagement of this client as well. Jackson discovered that Jason was given a good evaluation on the audit by the senior. However, the manager in charge of the audit requested that Jason not serve on the engagement team again because of complaints about Jason's inappropriate comments in meetings with client personnel. For example, Jason made a sarcastic comment to the office manager about the lack of organization of the computer files and records. Jason said, "Who set up this system, a five year old?" The comment was relayed to the indignant controller who informed the manager of the audit.

Jason enters William Jackson's office at 4 p.m.

"Come in, Jason."

"Thanks, Bill. I gotta tell you I'm nervous about this meeting."

Jackson hesitated. He hadn't expected Jason to be so blunt. Jackson decided to do the same.

"Jason, you've managed to upset some of our biggest clients."

"How so?" Jason responded.

"For starters, Cindi Laramie said that you made an inappropriate comment to her office manager last week and the controller was furious when he found out."

"Oh, you mean the comment about a five year old?" Jason asked.

"That's exactly what I mean," answered Jackson. "If you're aware that it was inappropriate, why did you make it?"

Jason said nothing.

"More important," Jackson said, "why didn't you apologize to the office manager and controller?"

Silence ensued for over a minute while Jason poured a glass of water and collected his thoughts. His mentor started to become impatient. Jackson walked over to Jason, put his hand on Jason's shoulder and asked, "Is everything OK at home?"

"Of course," Jason responded.

"Well, can you explain to me why you made the comment?" Jackson asked.

"I was just kidding. I thought the office manager had a good sense of humor."

At this point, Jackson began to realize there was a big problem with Jason. Client contact is an important part of the responsibilities of all staff members in public accounting. Jackson now senses that Jason might not have what it takes. He decides to end the meeting by making an excuse that he had to go somewhere. Jackson did this to stall so that he could schedule an appointment with other key people in the firm to discuss Jason Tybell's future.

Questions

1. Have you ever been in a similar situation as Jason? If so, explain the circumstances and be prepared to discuss it in class.

2. Do you think it's ever appropriate for a staff accountant to joke around with a member of the client's organization? Why or why not?

3. Is it OK for an accountant to be judged on skills other than technical skills? If so, what might be some of those skills. If not, why not?

4. Is it right for a CPA firm or any other employer to give good evaluations to an employee and then turn around and fire that employee for something that should have been noted in the evaluation? What's wrong with doing it? What might the firm have done to be fairer to Jason before the matter came to a head? What blame, if any, do you attribute to the firm's action or inaction? Or is Jason solely to blame because of the inappropriate comments? Explain.

5. One important aspect of success in public accounting—for that matter, in any area of business—is to understand the culture of the organization that you work for and the culture in the client's organization. Given the facts of this case, write a brief description characterizing what you

believe to be the expectations of Rodgers & Philips in dealings with client personnel.

6. Assume that you are Jason Tybell. What thoughts go through your mind after the brief meeting with your mentor? What would you consider doing, if anything, after the meeting?

7. Assume that after the meeting with other key members of the CPA firm, William Jackson decides to lay down the law to Jason and tell him he has one last chance to stay with the firm. If you were Jason, how would you react to such an admonition? What do you think should be the appropriate time frame for the last chance?

Case 1-4

Lone Star School District

Jose and Emily work as auditors for the State of Texas. They have been assigned to the audit of Lone Star School District. There have been some problems with audit documentation for the travel and entertainment reimbursement claims of the school district's manager. The manager knows about the concerns of Jose and Emily, and he approaches them about the matter. The following conversation takes place.

Manager: "Listen, I've requested the documentation you asked for but the hotel says it's no longer in its system."

Jose: "Don't you have the credit card receipt or credit card statement?"

Manager: "I paid cash."

Jose: "What about a copy of the hotel bill?"

Manager: "I threw it out."

Emily: "That's a problem. We have to document all of your travel and entertainment expenses for the city manager's office."

Manager: "Well, I can't produce documents that the hotel can't find. What do you want me to do?"

Questions

1. Do you think Emily was rude to the manager? Why or why not?

2. Do you think Jose and Emily have a right to question the manager's integrity? Why or why not?

3. Analyze the manager's position and statements from the perspective of trustworthiness.

4. What do you think should be Jose's and Emily's concerns about the situation? Be specific.

5. Assume that Jose and Emily report to Sharon, the manager of the school district audit. Should they inform her of their concerns? If so, what should they say? If not, why not?

6. Assume that they do inform Sharon. What would you do if you were in Sharon's position?

7. Assume that they don't inform Sharon but she finds out from another source. What would you do if you were in her position? Consider in particular your reaction about finding out from another source, not from Jose and Emily.

Case 1-5

Reneging on a Promise

Part A

Billy Tushoes recently received an offer to join the accounting firm of Tick and Check LLP. Billy would prefer to work for Foot and Balance LLP but has not received an offer from the firm the day before he must decide whether to accept the position at Tick and Check. Billy has a friend at Foot and Balance and is thinking about calling her to see if she can find out whether an offer is forthcoming.

Questions

1. Should Billy call his friend? Provide reasons why you think he should or should not.
2. Is there any other action you suggest Billy take prior to deciding on the offer of Tick and Check? Why do you recommend that action?

Part B

Assume that Billy calls his friend at Foot and Balance and she explains that the delay is due to the recent merger of Vouch and Trace LLP into Foot and Balance. She tells Billy that the offer should be forthcoming. However, Billy gets nervous about the situation and decides to accept the offer of Tick and Check. A week later, he receives a phone call from the partner at Foot and Balance who had promised to contact him about the firm's offer. Billy is offered a position at Foot and Balance at the same salary as Tick and Check. He has one week to decide whether to accept that offer. Billy isn't sure what to do. On one hand, he knows it's wrong to accept an offer and then renege on it. On the other hand, Billy hasn't signed a contract with Tick and Check, and the offer with Foot and Balance is his clear preference because he has many friends at that firm.

Questions

1. What should Billy do? Why? Include in your discussion whether Billy should accept the offer at Foot and Balance. Be sure to evaluate the integrity of your recommended action.
2. Assume that Billy accepts the offer at Foot and Balance. How should he handle the situation with Tick and Check?
3. Would your answer change if Billy had accepted the offer of Tick and Check in writing? Why or why not?
4. Imagine that two years after going to work for Foot and Balance, Billy becomes active in the local CPA chapter. He has just been asked to serve on the scholarship committee of the chapter. The partner from Tick and Check is also serving on this committee. How do you think Billy will feel at the first scholarship meeting?
5. Assume instead that Billy accepts the offer with Tick and Check. How long should he work for that firm before changing jobs?
6. Assume that after Billy accepts the offer from Tick and Check, the recruiting partner of that firm informs other student candidates that the firm will not be offering them positions. Three days later, Billy reneges on the offer and joins the firm of Foot and Balance. What effect do you think Billy's reneging on the offer would have on the recruiting partner of Tick and Check, the firm itself, and the candidates who were not given an offer?
7. Having answered the previous six questions, assume that you are one of the student candidates not given an offer. What feelings would go through your mind, assuming that you accepted another offer for $8,000 less the day after being turned down by Tick and Check? What if the offer was for the same salary as Tick and Check but was from a local CPA firm rather than a Big-Four firm such as Tick and Check? Personalize your answer as much as possible in answering this question.

Chapter  2

Ethical Reasoning

When men are pure, laws are useless; when men are corrupt, laws are broken.

Benjamin Disraeli (1804–1881)

The quote by Disraeli, an English novelist, debater, and former prime minister, highlights the important point that ethics is all about how we act when no one is looking. As the ancient Greeks believed, reason and thought precede the choice of action and we deliberate about things we can influence with our decision. In making decisions, most people want to follow the laws and rules. However, rules are not always clear. Laws may not cover every situation. Therefore, it is the ethical foundation we develop and nurture that will determine how we react to unstructured situations that challenge our sense of right and wrong. In the end, we need to rely on moral principles to guide our decision making.

A person of good will honors and respects the rules and laws and is willing to go beyond them when circumstances warrant. As indicated by Disraeli's quote, such people do not need rules and laws to guide their actions. They always try to act in the best interests of others and not to violate anyone's rights.

Rest's Four-Component Model of Morality

The noted researcher and writer in ethical development, James R. Rest (1941–1999), identified a four-component model of how moral behavior occurs.[1] Rest's model provides a useful framework to study the importance of ethical reasoning and decision making.

Moral Sensitivity

The first stage of moral behavior requires that the individual should interpret the situation as moral. A moral situation exists whenever your actions affect others and yourself. For example, let's assume that you go into a store to order a pizza. You go to the counter and place your order. As you move down to the cashier, you notice a $50 bill in the open refrigerated area that contains cold sodas just below the counter. It spans the distance from the order line to the payment area. You notice that two people are ahead of you at the cashier and wonder whether either of them dropped the money. What would you do? Why?

This is an ethical situation because if you decide to keep the money, someone is $50 poorer. You, of course, are $50 richer. Should you act in your own self-interest? If so, how will you justify it? Will you say to yourself, "Finders keepers, loser's weepers?" Or, will you say, "If I had dropped the $50, then I would hope the money would be returned to me."

Our ability to identify an ethical situation enables us to focus on how alternative courses of action might affect ourselves and others. If you simply acted without reflecting on the ethics of the situation in the store, you probably would have looked around, made sure no one was watching, and then pocketed the money. The important point once again is to remember that ethics is all about how we act when no one is looking.

Moral Judgment

This stage requires judging which of the available actions is most ethically justified. A person's ability to make such judgment depends on her stage of moral development. This will be explained later in the chapter.

Moral Motivation

One must have the desire to be a moral person in order to make an ethical decision. A problem that arises is that we face a variety of relationships with other people and pressures exist both internally—in our minds—and externally from outside influences that might lessen the desire to act morally.

A good example is the case of Sherron Watkins, the internal whistle-blower at Enron. Watkins was particularly savvy about accounting issues. She had worked for the accounting firm of Arthur Andersen prior to joining Enron. She was the first person in Enron to point out to top management that the accounting maneuvers conducted over a number of years until the time when the company went bankrupt in December 2001 had jeopardized its ability to remain in business. In a now famous memo to the former chair of Enron's board of directors, Ken Lay, Watkins commented on the sudden resignation of the company's CEO, Jeff Skilling, by stating, "Skilling's departure…[will] raise suspicions of accounting improprieties and valuation issues."[2] Watkins went on to say that she was "incredibly nervous that [Enron] will implode in a wave of accounting scandals."[3]

Watkins clearly identified the ethical issues in the Enron debacle. She was motivated to do the right thing and managed to get the company to review its accounting and valuation treatments although it was to no avail. Still, Watkins put her future in jeopardy both at Enron (somewhat of a moot point at the time) and possibly with other employers. She did not know how her actions would affect her ability to work and earn a living in the future.

It is difficult to hypothesize whether Watkins used proper moral judgment. As you will see later in the chapter, she may not have carefully considered the interests of all of the stakeholders in deciding on a course of action. One statement Watkins made in the memo to Lay appears to emphasize her own self-interests: "My 8 years of Enron work history will be worth nothing on my resume, the business world will consider the past successes as nothing but an elaborate accounting hoax."[4] You should notice that she thinks of herself, not the interests of thousands of stockholders who lost millions of dollars from a decline in Enron stock and thousands of employees who lost their jobs and most of their retirement money if it was invested in 401-K plans that included Enron stock.

We don't mean to be too critical of Watkins. She took an important step that no one else at Enron was willing to take. She became somewhat of an outcast at the company. Still, her actions do illustrate the difference between blowing the whistle internally and external whistle-blowing. Had Watkins gone to the Securities and Exchange Commission (SEC) with her story on or around August 15, 2001, the day Skilling resigned, instead of writing the internal memo to Lay, her actions might have saved thousands of people millions of dollars because the stock price was at $36 on that day and ultimately, when all the dust settled on December 2, 2001, the stock sold for less than $1 a share.

Moral Character

Once a moral person has considered the ethics of the alternatives, that person must construct an appropriate course of action, avoid distractions, and maintain the courage to continue.[5] As noted in Chapter 1, a person of integrity will act out of moral principle, not expediency.

The components of Rest's model are interactive. In other words, a person might know exactly what the right thing to do is and have the desire to do it, but there exists a strong pressure preventing that person from acting in accordance with the moral point of view. One can understand how Sherron Watkins would have felt disloyal had she gone to outside regulators with her concerns. However, we want to emphasize once again that honesty and integrity are more important virtues than loyalty.

How does a person develop the courage to withstand pressures that challenge one's commitment to act in an ethical manner? An important element is to have a supportive environment in the organization. An ethical tone must be set by top management. When an organization attempts to foster an ethical culture, the employees believe they will be supported if they bring matters of concern out into the open. The notion of creating an ethical organization environment will be explored in the next chapter.

Moral Development

An individual's ability to make reasoned judgments about moral matters develops in stages. The psychologist Lawrence Kohlberg concluded, on the basis of 20 years of research, that moral development occurs in a specific sequence of six stages that may be divided into three levels of moral reasoning.[6] Kohlberg's views on ethical development are helpful in understanding how individuals may internalize moral standards and, as they become more sophisticated in their use, apply them more critically to resolve ethical conflicts (see Table 2.1). The examples in the table demonstrate the application of Kohlberg's model of cognitive development to possible decision making in business.

Kohlberg's model suggests that people continue to change their decision priorities over time and with additional education and experience. They may experience a change in values and ethical behavior.[7] In the context of business, an individual's moral development can be influenced by corporate culture, especially ethics training.[8] Ethics training and education have been shown to improve managers' moral development as indicated by an instrument, the Defining Issues Test (DIT), developed by James Rest.[9]

The results of published studies during the 1990s by accounting researchers indicate that CPAs reason primarily at Stages 3 and 4. One possible implication of these results is that a higher percentage of CPAs may be overly influenced by their relationship with peers, superiors, and clients (Stage 3) or by rules (Stage 4). A CPA who is unable to critically apply the technical accounting standards and rules of conduct when these requirements are unclear is likely to be influenced by others in the decision-making process.[10]

An auditor who reasons at the postconventional level could refuse to give in to the pressure applied by the supervisor to overlook the client's failure to follow GAAP. While this would be an ethical position to take, it could go against the culture of the firm and put the continued relationship between the audit firm and the client in jeopardy. As an example, Andersen went along with Enron's efforts to hide debt and inflate profits by establishing special-purpose entities allegedly because the firm did not want to lose Enron as a client. In the last year in which the firm did work for Enron, it had received $52 million in fees: $27 million for nonaudit services and $25 million in audit fees.

Heinz and the Drug

Kohlberg's justice orientation has been criticized by Carol Gilligan, a noted psychologist and educator,[11] claiming that it ignores the care-and-response orientation that characterizes

TABLE 2.1 **Kohlberg's Stages of Moral Development**

<table>
<tr><td align="center">Level 1—Preconventional</td></tr>
</table>

At the preconventional level, the individual is very self-centered. Rules are seen as something external imposed on the self.

Stage 1. Obedience to Rules; Avoidance of Punishment

At this stage what is right is judged by one's obedience to rules and authority.

Example: A company forbids making payoffs to government or other officials to gain business. Susan, the company's contract negotiator, might justify refusing the advances of a government official to make a payment to gain a contract as being contrary to company rules, or she might make the payment if she believes there is no chance of being caught and punished.

Stage 2. Satisfying One's Own Need

At Stage 2, the rules and authority are important only if acting in accordance with them satisfies one's own needs.

Example: Susan might make the payment even though it is against company rules if she perceives that such payments are a necessary part of doing business. She views the payment as essential to gain the contract. Susan may believe that competitors are willing to make payments and that making such payments is part of the culture of the host country. She concludes that if she does not make the payment, it might jeopardize her ability to move up the ladder with the organization and possibly forgo personal rewards of salary increases and/or bonuses.

<table>
<tr><td align="center">Level 2—Conventional</td></tr>
</table>

At the conventional level, the individual becomes aware of the interests of others and one's duty to society. Personal responsibility becomes an important consideration in decision making.

Stage 3. Fairness to Others

At this stage, an individual not only is motivated by rules but also seeks to do what is in the best interests of others, especially those in a family, peer group, or work organization.

Example: Susan might be reluctant to make the payment but agrees to do so not because it benefits her interests but in response to the pressure imposed by her supervisor who claims the company will lose a major contract and employees will be fired if she refuses to go along.

Stage 4. Law and Order

Stage 4 behavior emphasizes societal norms. One's duty to society, respect for authority, and maintaining the social order become the focus of decision making.

Example: Susan might refuse to make the payment even though it leads to a loss of jobs in her company because she views it as her duty to do so in the best interests of society.

Let's return to the receivables example in Chapter 1 for a moment. An auditor who reasons at Stage 3 might go along with the demands of a client or the CPA firm that wants to retain the client. At Stage 4, the auditor would place the needs of society or, in accounting, the public interest, above all else, and certainly question if not refuse to go along with deliberate understatement of the receivables.

<table>
<tr><td align="center">Level 3—Postconventional</td></tr>
</table>

At the postconventional level, the individual looks to basic principles to guide decision making. Integrity would be an important component of deciding what the right thing to do is.

Stage 5. Social Contract

At this stage, an individual is motivated by upholding the basic rights, values, and legal contracts of society. That person recognizes that in some cases, legal and moral points of view may conflict. To reduce such conflict, individuals at this stage base their decisions on a rational calculation of benefits and harms to society.

Example: Susan might weigh the alternatives by evaluating how each of the groups is affected by her decision to make the payment. For instance, the company might benefit by gaining the contract. Susan might even be rewarded for her action. The employees are more secure in their jobs. The official in the other country gets what he wants. On the other hand, if the U.S. government finds out, the company may have violated the Foreign Corrupt Practices Act that prohibits payments to foreign government officials to secure a contract. While application of the act is a more complicated matter that will be discussed in Chapter 6, suffice it to say that if Susan weighs the consequences of making an illegal payment, she might very well conclude that the harms of prosecution, fines, other sanctions, and the loss of one's reputational capital are greater than the benefits.

Stage 6. Universal Ethical Principles

A person at this stage believes that right is determined by universal ethical principles that everyone should follow. The most important ethical principles deal with justice, equality, and the dignity of all people. If a law conflicts with an ethical principle, an individual should act in accordance with the principle.

An example of such a principle is Immanuel Kant's categorical imperative, the first formulation of which can be stated as: "Act only according to that maxim [reason for acting] by which you can at the same time will that it should become a universal law."[12] Kant's categorical imperative creates an absolute, unconditional requirement that exerts its authority in all circumstances and is both required and justified as an end in itself. Kant's moral philosophy will be discussed further in the next section.

Example: Susan would go beyond the norms, laws, and authority of groups or individuals. She would act without regard to the company's best interests or those of her fellow employees. Her action would be guided only by universal ethical principles that would apply to others in a similar situation.

female moral judgment. The classic moral dilemma that Kohlberg used to develop the six stages of moral development illustrates the difference.

In Europe, a woman was near death from a very bad disease, a special kind of cancer. There was one drug that the doctors thought might save her. It was a form of radium that a druggist in the same town had recently discovered. The drug was expensive to make, but the druggist was charging 10 times what the drug cost him to make. He paid $200 for the radium and charged $2,000 for a small dose of the drug. The sick woman's husband, Heinz, went to everyone he knew to borrow the money, but he could gather only about $1,000, which was half of what it would cost. He told the druggist that his wife was dying and asked him to sell it cheaper or let him pay later. But the druggist said, "No, I discovered the drug and I'm going to make money from it." Heinz got desperate and broke into the man's store to steal the drug for his wife.[13]

Should the husband have done that? Was it right or wrong? Most people say that Heinz's theft was morally justified, but Kohlberg was less concerned about whether they approved or disapproved than with the reasons they gave for their answers. Kohlberg monitored the reasons for judgments given by a group of 75 boys ranging in age from 10 through 16 and isolated the six stages of moral thought. The boys progressed in reasoning sequentially with most never reaching the highest stages. He concluded that the universal principle of justice is the highest claim of morality.

Gilligan believes that women need more information before answering the question: Should Heinz steal the drug? Females look for ways to resolve the dilemma so that no one—Heinz, his wife, or the druggist—will experience pain. Gilligan sees the hesitation to judge as a laudable quest for nonviolence, an aversion to cruel situations in which someone will get hurt. However, much of her theories have been challenged in the literature. For example, Kohlberg considered it a sign of ethical relativism, a waffling that results from trying to please everyone (Stage 3).

Heinz's dilemma illustrates the challenge of evaluating the ethics of a decision. If we justify his stealing the drug in this instance, is it right for someone who has no money to steal bread when his family is starving? This is the dilemma in the classic story *Les Miserables* by Victor Hugo. The main character, Jean Valjean, a Frenchman imprisoned for stealing bread, is paroled after serving 19 years at hard labor. Even though he reforms and becomes the mayor and head businessman in a small town, his past comes back to haunt him when a former prison guard, Javert, becomes a police captain and recognizes Valjean. Javert struggles with the ethics of pursuing Valjean in light of how he has reformed his life.

Ethical Relativism

Ethical relativism is the theory that holds that morality is relative to the norms of one's culture. That is, whether an action is right or wrong depends on the moral norms of the society in which it is performed. The same action may be morally right in one society but be morally wrong in another. For the ethical relativist, there are no universal moral standards—standards that can be universally applied to all peoples at all times. The only moral standards against which a society's practices can be judged are its own. If ethical relativism is correct, there can be no common framework for resolving moral disputes or for reaching agreement on ethical matters among members of different societies.

Most ethicists reject the theory of ethical relativism. Some claim that while the moral practices of societies may differ, the fundamental moral principles underlying these practices do not. For example, in the 1990s, a young American in Singapore spray painted graffiti on several cars. The Singaporean government's penalty was to "cane" the youngster. In the United States, some said it was cruel and unusual punishment for such a minor offense. In Singapore, the issue is that in order to protect the interests of society, the government treats harshly those who commit relatively minor offenses. After all, it does send a message that in Singapore, such behavior will not be tolerated. While such a practice might be condemned in the United States, most people would agree with the underlying moral principle—the duty to protect the safety and security of the public (life and liberty concerns). Societies, then, can differ in their application of fundamental moral principles but agree on the principles.

Moral Philosophy

Moral philosophy refers to the principles or rules that people use to decide what is right or wrong. The philosophies present guidelines for determining how conflicts in human interests are to be settled and for optimizing the mutual benefit of people living together in groups.

Moral philosophies provide moral perspectives in the form of abstract principles that guide decision making. They can help a business decision maker to formulate strategies for dealing with ethical dilemmas and resolve them in a morally appropriate way. In Chapter 1, we discussed *teleology* including the utilitarian point of view that recognizes that trade-offs may be necessary in balancing the harms and benefits to the stakeholders. The other major philosophy, *deontology,* emphasizes the rights of stakeholders and duties of decision makers to honor those rights.

Ethicists suggest that the elements of each philosophy may be appropriate in dealing with ethical and moral dilemmas that, by their very nature, have no right or wrong answers. The methods are useful in providing a framework to analyze ethical issues and guide decision making.

There is no single moral philosophy that everyone accepts. Some managers, for example, view profits as the ultimate goal of an enterprise and therefore may not be concerned about the effects of their firms' decisions on society. In his seminal article on the social responsibilities of business, the noted economist Milton Friedman stated that expenditures to benefit society, such as to reduce pollution "beyond the amount that is in the best interests of the corporation or that is required by law" so that the corporation can pursue the social objective of improving the environment, should be made by the "stockholders or the customers or the employees" separately if that is what they wish to do. In his classic book, *Capitalism and Freedom,"* Freedman clarified his position by stating, "There is one and only one social responsibility of business—to use its resources and engage in activities designed to increase profits so long as it stays within the rules of the game, which is to say, engages in open and free competition without deception or fraud."[14]

Adam Smith, the father of modern economics, set out in his 1776 book *An Inquiry into the Nature and Causes of the Wealth of Nations* a philosophy that the pursuit of one's own interest led by the invisible hand of a free marketplace often leads to promoting the interests of society "more effectually than when [one] really intends to promote it."[15]

Smith knew that a considerable structure was required in society before the invisible hand mechanism could work efficiently. For example, property rights must be strong, and there must be widespread adherence to moral norms, such as prohibitions against theft and misrepresentation. Therefore, laws and moral values such as honesty and integrity are a prerequisite for the invisible hand to work in the public interest.

Justice as Fairness

Justice is usually associated with issues of rights, fairness, and equality. A just act respects your rights and treats you fairly. Formulations of *justice theories* date back to Aristotle and Plato in the fifth century BC. An important modern contributor to the theory of justice is John Rawls (1921–2002). He developed a qualified egalitarian theory of justice in his work *A Theory of Justice.*[16]

Rawls uses an innovative conceptual device called the *veil of ignorance* to develop his theory. He argues that valid principles of justice could be agreed on if we could meet for this purpose outside the influence of any society. This would remove the effect of societal pressure from the decision process. Stepping behind the veil of ignorance, we would be in what Rawls called the *original position,* not knowing what characteristics we would possess when we reappeared from behind the veil. We would not know our race, gender, age, education level, or social connections. Being in the original position would prevent us from arguing for principles of justice for personal benefit because we would not know what would benefit us.[17]

Rawls believes we would agree on two principles while in the original position:

1. Each person should be permitted the maximum amount of basic liberty compatible with similar liberties for others.
2. Social and economic inequalities are allowed only if they benefit everyone.

Rawls does not argue that all persons should benefit equally. He believes that, if inequalities do occur, the least advantaged person must end up better off than before.[18]

Questions of *distributive justice* arise when conflicts of interest exist over the fair distribution of goods and services. Aristotle suggests that questions of distributive justice consist of treating equals equally and unequals unequally.[19] This interpretation of justice is sometimes referred to as *impartiality.* It has important implications in accounting because financial information is supposed to be recorded in an unbiased manner.

The problem with this interpretation is in determining which criteria are morally relevant to distinguish between those who are equal and those who are not. It can be a difficult theory to apply in business if, for example, a chief executive officer of a company decides to allocate a larger share of the resources than is warranted (justified) to promote one operation over another because the former is judged to have more short-term expansion potential. If I am the manager in charge of the operation getting fewer resources but producing equal results, then I may believe that I need a raise or bonus. However, if I am the manager getting fewer resources but expected to produce equal results, then I may believe that I am being treated unfairly.

Virtue Principles

As pointed out in Chapter 1, virtue theory dates back to the ancient Greek philosophers, especially Plato and Aristotle. *Virtue theorists* place less emphasis on learning rules and instead stress the importance of developing *good habits of character,* such as benevolence. Plato emphasized four virtues in particular, which were later called *cardinal virtues:* wisdom, courage, temperance, and justice. Other important virtues are fortitude, generosity, self-respect, good temper, and sincerity. In addition to advocating good habits of character, virtue theorists hold that we should avoid acquiring bad character traits, or vices, such as cowardice, insensibility, injustice, and vanity. Virtue theory emphasizes moral education because virtuous character traits are developed in one's youth. Adults, therefore, are responsible for instilling virtues in the young.

The philosopher Alasdair MacIntyre states that the exercise of virtue requires "a capacity to judge and to do the right thing in the right place at the right time in the right way." Judgment is exercised not through a routinizable application of the rules but as a function of possessing those dispositions (tendencies) that enable choices to be made about what is the good for people and by holding in check desires for something other than what will help to achieve this goal.[20]

MacIntyre relates virtues to the internal rewards of a practice. He differentiates between the external rewards of a practice (such as money, fame, and power) and the internal rewards, which relate to the intrinsic value of a particular practice. MacIntyre points out that every practice requires a certain kind of relationship between those who participate in it. The virtues are the standards of excellence that characterize relationships within the practice. To enter into a practice is to accept the authority of those standards, obedience to the rules, and the commitment to achieve the internal rewards. Some of the virtues that MacIntyre identifies are truthfulness and trust, justice, courage, and honesty.[21]

Mintz points out that the accounting profession is a practice with virtues inherent in that practice that enable accountants to meet their ethical obligations to clients, employers, the government, and the public at large. For instance, for auditors to render an objective opinion on a client's financial statements, the main goal of auditing, auditors must be committed to perform such services without bias and to avoid conflicts of interest. Impartiality is an essential virtue for judges in our judicial system. CPAs render judgments on the fairness of financial statements. Therefore, they should act impartially in carrying out their professional responsibilities.[22]

Imagine that you were auditing a client's financial statements and the client's controller was your brother. Could you be objective in making decisions whether the financial statements have been prepared (by the controller) in accordance with GAAP? You might say that you can. After all, you are not about to risk your reputation and violate the ethics of your profession by not pointing out a significant problem that exists in the financial statements just because your brother is the controller. The fact is that it does not matter what you believe you would do. In auditing, there is a strict requirement that the auditor should be *independent* of any interest or entanglement with the client *in fact* and *appear* to be lacking any such potential conflict. In other words, a "reasonable observer" might conclude that you could be influenced by the fact that your brother is the controller. You might not point out problems that exist in the statements because of the subtle bias that develops in one's reasoning when a close relative or member of one's immediate family is involved. The virtues of impartiality and open-mindedness enable an accountant to act with objectivity and independence when auditing a client's financial statements. The ethical principle of independence will be discussed at greater length in Chapter 4.

The virtues enable accounting professionals to resolve conflicting duties and loyalties in a morally appropriate way. They provide accountants the inner strength of character to withstand pressures that might otherwise overwhelm and negatively influence their professional judgment in a relationship of trust.[23] For example, if the client's CEO pressures you to overlook a material misstatement in the financial statements, it is the virtue of honesty that leads you to place your obligation to the public above your client's interest (loyalty to the client). It is the virtue of integrity that enables you to withstand the client's pressure to look the other way, a problem for Andersen in its audit of Enron.

Virtue considerations apply both to the decision maker and to the act under consideration by that party. This is one of the differences between virtue theory and the other moral philosophies that focus on the act. To make an ethical decision, I must internalize the traits of character that make me an ethical (virtuous) person. Virtue ethics has particular appeal in accounting because of the ethical principles that exist in the profession's codes of conduct that will be discussed in Chapter 4.

Application of Ethical Reasoning in Accounting

In this section, we discuss the application of ethical reasoning to a common dilemma faced by accountants and auditors. The case deals with the pressure that can be imposed by top management on internal accountants and external auditors to ignore material misstatements in the financial statements. Accountants and auditors have ethical obligations under the AICPA Code of Conduct that obligate them to place the public interest ahead of all other interests including their own self-interest and that of an employer or client. It is within this context that the following case takes place.

DigitPrint Case

DigitPrint was formed in March 2007 with the goal of developing an outsourcing business for high-speed digital printing. The company is small and does not yet have a board of directors. The comparative advantage of the company is that its founder and president, Henry Higgins, owned his own print shop for several years before starting DigitPrint and made many contacts in the medical and pharmaceutical industries. Higgins recently hired Liza Doolittle to run the start-up business. Wally Wonderful, a CPA with an impeccable reputation for diligence, was hired to help set up a computerized system to track incoming purchase orders, sales invoices, cash receipts, and cash payments.

DigitPrint received $2 million as venture capital to start the business. The venture capitalists were given an equity share interest. From the beginning, they were concerned about management's inability to bring in customer orders and earn profits. In fact, only $200,000 net income was recorded during the first year. Unfortunately, Wonderful had just discovered that $1 million of accrued expenses had not been recorded at year-end. Had that amount been recorded, DigitPrint's $200,000 net income would have changed to an $800,000 loss.

Wonderful approached his supervisor, Liza Doolittle, with what he had uncovered. She told him in no uncertain words that the $1 million of expenses and liabilities could not be recorded. Doolittle warned Wonderful of the consequences of pursuing the matter any further. The reason for this was that the venture capitalists might pull out from financing DigitPrint because of the reduction of net income, working capital, and the higher level of liabilities. Wonderful is uncertain whether to inform Higgins. On the one hand, he feels a loyalty obligation to go along with Doolittle. On the other, he believes he has an ethical obligation to the venture capitalists and other financiers that might help fund company operations.

Using ethical reasoning with reference to the obligations of a CPA, analyze what you think Wonderful should do.

Rights Theory

The venture capitalists have an ethical right to know about the higher level of payables, lower income, and the effect of the unrecorded transactions on working capital. It would be wrong of Wonderful to deny them this information. In fact, he may be open to a lawsuit for denying access to this important information.

Utilitarianism

Although it could be in Wonderful's self-interests to go along with Doolittle, a CPA should never place self-interest or the interests of an employer ahead of the public interest. The consequences of failing to inform the venture capitalists about the outstanding debt are severe not only for Wonderful but also for DigitPrint. These include a possible lawsuit, investigation by regulators for failing to record the information, and most important, a loss of reputational capital in the market place.

Justice (Virtue Considerations)

The virtue of integrity requires Wonderful to not subordinate his judgment to that of Doolittle. This is also required by the AICPA Code. Because he is the accounting expert, it would not be fair for Wonderful to let Doolittle make the final call on whether to record the obligations. The public relies on Wonderful's ethics and integrity to ensure that the financial statements are free of material misstatement.

What Should Wonderful Do?

This is a classic case in which one's loyalty obligation to an employer clashes with what is the right thing to do. As pointed out in Chapter 1, loyalty should never be placed ahead of other ethical obligations such as honesty and integrity. To do otherwise would subvert the ethics of the accounting profession.

Wonderful should inform Doolittle that he will take his concerns to Higgins. That may force Doolittle's hand and cause her to back off placing pressure on Wonderful. Nevertheless, Higgins has a right to know as the president of the company.

Higgins may decide to disclose the matter immediately and cut his losses. This is the right thing to do. On the other hand, if Higgins persists in covering up the matter, Wonderful must decide whether to go outside the company. To do so requires whistle-blowing, and that is prohibited by the confidentiality standard for CPAs. However, if Wonderful reasons at Stage 6, he could decide to disclose the matter out of a sense of obligation to the venture capitalists and a desire to do the right thing.

Conclusion

As you can tell from the DigitPrint case, ethical matters in accounting are not easy to resolve. On the one hand, accountants feel an ethical obligation to their employers or clients. On the other hand, the profession has a strong code of ethics that requires CPAs to place the public interest ahead of all other interests. It is the ethical virtue of integrity that enables a CPA to withstand the pressures that might otherwise lead him to violate ethical norms.

We conclude this chapter by emphasizing the need to analyze conflicting situations and evaluate the ethics by considering all of the principles and carefully applying logical reasoning to resolve the dilemma. Remember that there is a difference between what you have a right to do and what is the right thing to do.

Discussion Questions

1. What do you think Disraeli meant when he said, "When men are pure, laws are useless; when men are corrupt, laws are broken"?

2. What is the significance of moral motivation to ethical decision making?

3. With regard to the third quote from Sherron Watkins on page 26, do you think it exhibits a dog or cat loyalty mentality? Why?

4. Do you think Sherron Watkins should have informed someone or some organization outside Enron about the manipulation of financial statement numbers in the company's financial statements? Why or why not? Be specific about who should have been informed if that is what you say.

5. How do you assess at what stage of moral development in Kohlberg's model you reason in making decisions? Are you satisfied with that stage? Do you believe there are factors or forces preventing you from reasoning at a higher level? If so, what are they?

6. Assume that you are driving to campus for a final exam with your best friend. Your college is in a big city, and you are a commuter. The day of the final there is a transportation workers strike that has shut down all bus and metro service. It has taken you 2 hours to drive 30 miles. You look at your watch and see that it is 8:58 a.m., 2 minutes before the starting time of your final exam. You are one and one-half blocks from the entrance to the parking structure. At this rate, you will not make it for at least 10 minutes. Your friend who is in the same class is panicking because

he has a marginal C grade and fears that any delay in starting the final will cost him points and perhaps lead to a final course grade of less than C. Here are your options:

a. Continue at the same pace and arrive 15 minutes late (it is a 2-hour final).

b. Abandon your car and run the rest of the way. You and your friend will arrive 2 minutes after the exam begins.

c. Drive on the sidewalk for the last one and one-half blocks assuming no one is walking on the sidewalk at that time. You will get to class at 9 a.m.

d. Some other alternative you identify.

What will you do and why?

7. Do you agree with Milton Friedman's assessment that the social responsibility of business is to increase profits for the shareholders so long as it plays by the rules of the game and does not deceive or commit fraud? What is the basis for your opinion? Explain.

8. Do you think "enlightened self-interest" is a contradiction in terms, or is it a valid basis for all action?

9. Recall the last time you acted solely in your own best interests without considering the interests of others. If you had it to do over again, would you change how you acted? Why or why not?

10. a. Assume that you have been hired by the head of a tobacco industry group to do a cost-benefit analysis of whether the tobacco firms should disclose that nicotine is addictive. Assume that this was before the federal government's requirement of such disclosure on all packages of cigarettes. Explain how you would go about determining the potential harms and the potential benefits of disclosing this information voluntarily. Is there any information you believe cannot be included in the evaluation? What is it? Why can't you include it? If you could include it, would it impact your recommendation to the head of the industry group?

b. Analyze the situation from a rights perspective, justice, and virtue theory. How might it change your recommendation to the head of the industry group?

11. Felix Morley (1894–1982), the so-called "journalist philosopher," said, "A right without an attendant responsibility is as unreal as a sheet of paper which has only one side." Explain what you think Morley meant by the statement.

12. Former associate justice of the U.S. Supreme Court, Potter Stewart (1915–1985), said, "Fairness is what justice really is." How would you interpret this statement in the context of business decision making?

13. How does virtue theory apply both to the decision maker and the act under consideration by that party? Explain.

14. Do you agree with Carol Gilligan that Kohlberg's model of moral development fails to adequately consider the way in which women confront ethical dilemmas? Can you identify a situation in the past when you and a friend of the opposite gender differed in reasoning out what should be the decision to a difficult problem? How was the matter resolved? Were you happy with the resolution? Why or why not?

15. Was Heinz right to steal the drug? Justify your position using ethical reasoning.

16. Distinguish between ethical rights and obligations.

17. Have you ever been asked to hide important information from another person who may have had a right to know about it? Describe the situation. What did you do? Why?

18. Is it ever proper *not* to tell someone something he or she has a right to know? If so, describe the circumstances when this could be the case. If not, explain why not.

19. In the DigitPrint case, what stage of ethical reasoning did Doolittle seem to use to get Wonderful to change his position on the disclosure matter?

20. In the DigitPrint case, Wonderful was obligated to follow the AICPA Code of Conduct. Assume that he was not a CPA. Should he have done something else? If you were in Wonderful's position, what would you have done? Why might you have chosen this course of action?

Endnotes

1. James R. Rest, "Morality," in *Handbook of Child Psychology: Cognitive Development, Vol. 3 ed.* J. Flavell and E. Markman (New York: John Wiley, 1983), pp. 556–629.

2. Mimi Swartz and S. Watkins, *Power Failure: The Inside Story of the Collapse of Enron* (New York: Doubleday, 2003), p. 275.

3. Swartz and Watkins, p. 275.

4. Swartz and Watkins, p. 275.

5. Muriel J. Bebeau and S. J. Thoma, " 'Intermediate' Concepts and the Connection to Moral Education," *Educational Psychology Review* 11, no. 4 (1999), p. 345.

6. Lawrence Kohlberg, "Stage and Sequence: The Cognitive Developmental Approach to Socialization," in *Handbook of Socialization Theory and Research,* ed. D. A. Goslin (Chicago: Rand McNally, 1969), pp. 347–480.

7. O. C. Ferrell, John Fraedrich, and Linda Ferrell, *Business Ethics: Ethical Decision Making and Cases* (Boston: Houghton Mifflin Company, 2005), p.109.

8. Clare M. Pennino, "Is Decision Style Related to Moral Development among Managers in the U.S.?" *Journal of Business Ethics* 41 (December 2002), pp. 337–47.

9. See Michael K. Shaub, "An Analysis of the Association of Traditional Demographic Variables with the Moral Reasoning of Auditing Students and Auditors," *Journal of Accounting Education* (Winter 1994), pp. 1–26; and Lawrence A. Ponemon, "Ethical Reasoning and Selection Socialization in Accounting," *Accounting, Organizations and Society* 17 (1992), pp. 239–58.

10. James C. Lampe and Don W. Finn, "A Model of Auditors' Ethical Decision Process," *Auditing: A Journal of Practice and Theory,* II Supplement (1992), pp. 33–66.

11. Carol Gilligan, *In a Different Voice: Psychological Theory and Women's Development* (Cambridge, MA: Harvard University Press, 1982).

12. Immanuel Kant, "Fundamental Principles of the Metaphysics of Morals," in *Problems in Moral Philosophy: An Introduction,* 2nd ed., ed. Paul W. Taylor (Encino, CA: Dickenson, 1972), p. 229.

13. Ferrell et al., p. 95.

14. Milton Friedman, *Capitalism and Freedom* (Chicago: University of Chicago Press, 1982).

15. Adam Smith, *An Inquiry into the Nature and Causes of the Wealth of Nations,* 5th ed., ed. Edwin Cannan (London: Methuen and Co., 1904).

16. John Rawls, *A Theory of Justice* (Cambridge, MA: Harvard University Press, 1971).

17. David J. Fritzsche, *Business Ethics: A Global and Managerial Perspective* (New York: McGraw-Hill Irwin, 2005), p.53.

18. Fritzsch, p. 53.

19. Aristotle, *Nicomachean Ethics,* trans. J.E.C. Weldon (Buffalo, NY: Prometheus Books, 1987).

20. Alasdair MacIntyre, *After Virtue,* 2nd ed. (Notre Dame, IN: University of Notre Dame Press, 1984), pp. 149–50.

21. MacIntyre, pp. 187–92.

22. Steven M. Mintz, *Cases in Accounting Ethics & Professionalism,* 3rd ed. (New York: McGraw-Hill Co., 1997), p. 26.

23. Mintz, p. 26.

Chapter 2 Cases

Case 2-1

A Faulty Budget

Jackson Daniels graduated from Lynchberg State College two years ago. Since graduating from the College, he has worked in the accounting department of Lynchberg Manufacturing. Daniels was recently asked to prepare a sales budget for the year 2008. He conducted a thorough analysis and came out with projected sales of 250,000 units of product. That represents a 25 percent increase over 2007.

Daniels went to lunch with his best friend, Jonathan Walker, to celebrate the completion of his first solo job. Walker noticed that Daniels seemed very distant. He asked what the matter was. Daniels stroked his chin, ran his hand through his bushy, black hair, and looked straight into the eyes of his friend of 20 years.

"Jon, I think I made a mistake with the budget."

"What do you mean?" Walker asked.

"You know how we developed a new process to manufacture soaking tanks to keep the ingredients fresh?"

"Yes," Walker answered.

"Well, I projected twice the level of sales for that product than will likely occur."

"Are you sure?" Walker asked.

"I checked my numbers. I'm sure. It was just a mistake on my part," Daniels said.

"So, what are you going to do about it?" asked Walker.

"I think I should report it to Pete. He's the one who acted on the numbers to hire additional workers to produce the soaking tanks."

"Wait a second," Walker said. "How do you know there won't be extra demand for the product? You and I both know demand is a tricky number to project, especially when a new product comes on the market. Why don't you sit back and wait to see what happens?"

"But what happens if I'm right and the sales numbers were wrong? What happens if the demand does not increase beyond what I now know to be the correct projected level?" Daniels asks.

"Well, you can tell Pete about it at that time. Why raise a red flag now when there may be no need?" Walker states.

As the lunch comes to a conclusion, Walker pulls Daniels aside and says, "Jack, this could mean your job. If I were in your position, I'd protect my own interests first."

Questions

1. What should an employee do when he or she discovers that there is an error in a projection? Why do you suggest that action?

2. Would your answer to Question 1 change if the error was not likely to affect other aspects of the operation such as employment? Why or why not?

3. Identify the stakeholders potentially affected by what Daniels decides to do. How might each stakeholder be affected by his decision and action?

4. What do you think about the role of Jonathan Walker in this case? Did he provide good advice to Daniels?

5. What would you do if you were in Jackson Daniels's position? Be sure to support your answer using ethical reasoning.

Case 2-2

Better Boston Beans

Better Boston Beans is a coffee shop located in the Faneuil Hall Marketplace near the waterfront and Government Center in Boston. The coffee shop specializes in exotic blends of coffee including Sumatra dark roast black, India mysore gold nuggets, and Guatemala antigua. It also serves blended coffees including reggae blend, Jamaican Blue Mountain blend, and Marrakesh blend. For those with more pedestrian tastes, the shop serves French vanilla, hazelnut, and Hawaiian macadamia nut. The coffee of the day varies, but the most popular is Colombia supremo. The coffee shop also serves a variety of cold blended coffees.

Cindie Rosen has worked for Better Boston Beans for six months. She took the job right out of college because she wasn't sure whether she wanted to go to graduate school before beginning a career in financial services. Cindie hoped that by taking a year off before starting her career or going on to graduate school, she would experience "the real world" and find out first hand what it is like to work a 40-hour week. She did not have a full-time job during college because her parents helped to pay for the tuition.

Because Cindie is the "new kid on the block," she is often asked to work the late shift from 4 p.m. to midnight. She works with one other person, Jeffrey Lyndell, who is the assistant shift supervisor. Lyndell has been with Boston Beans for three years but recently was demoted from shift supervisor.

For the past two weeks, Lyndell has been leaving before 11 p.m., when most of the stores in the marketplace close, and he has asked Cindie to close up by herself. Cindie felt this was wrong and it was starting to concern her, but she hasn't spoken to Lyndell and has not informed the store manager. However, something happened one night that caused Cindie to consider taking the next step.

At 11 p.m., 10 Japanese tourists came into the store for coffee. Cindie was alone and had to rush around to make five different cold blended drinks and five different hot blended coffees. While she was working, one of the Japanese tourists who spoke English very well approached her and said that he was shocked that such a famous U.S. coffee shop would have only one worker in the store at any time during the workday. Cindie didn't want to ignore the man's comments, so she answered that her co-worker had to go home early because he was sick. That seemed to satisfy the tourist.

It took Cindie almost 20 minutes to make all of the drinks and field two phone calls that came in during that time. After she closed for the night, Cindie reflected on the experience.

She realized it could get worse before it gets better because Jeffrey Lyndell was now making it a habit to leave work early. She had to either approach him about it or speak with the store manager. She felt much more comfortable talking to the store manager. In fact, in Cindie's own words: "Lyndell gives me the creeps."

Questions

1. Do you think Cindie has an obligation to speak with Lyndell before taking the matter to the store manager? Why or why not?

2. Consider Kohlberg's six stages of moral development; analyze the options open to Cindie if she reasons at each of the three levels.

3. Assume that Cindie approached Lyndell about her concerns. He tells her that he has an alcohol problem. Lately, it's been really bad. That's why he's left early: to get a drink and calm his nerves. Lyndell also said that this is the real reason he was demoted. He was warned that if one more incident occurred, the store manager would fire him. He pleaded with Cindie to work with him through these hard times.

   How would you react to Lyndell's request if you were Cindie? Would you honor his request for confidentiality and support? Why or why not? Be sure to consider the implications of your decision on other parties potentially affected by your actions.

4. Is it a virtue to keep the confidences of a co-worker who trusts you, relies on your discretion, and may have his future determined by what you do or say, or don't do and don't say? Answer the question with regard to the matter at Better Boston Beans and consider, among other ethical issues, the fairness of the situation to those affected by Lyndell's behavior.

5. Assume that Cindie keeps quiet. The following week, another incident occurred. Cindie got into a shouting match with a customer who was tired of waiting for his coffee after 10 minutes. Cindie felt terrible about it, apologized to the customer after serving his coffee, and left work that night wondering if it was time to apply to graduate school. If you were in Cindie's position, would you now approach the store manager? What would you say? If you still choose to remain quiet, justify your action from an ethical perspective.

Case 2-3

Eating Time

Kevin Lowe is depressed. He has been with the CPA firm, Stooges LLP, for only three months. The partners in charge of the firm, Bo Chambers and his brother Moe Chambers, have asked for a "sit down." Here's how it goes:

"Kevin, we asked to see you because your time reports indicate that it takes you 50 percent longer to complete audit work than your predecessor," Moe said.

"Well, Bo and Moe, I'm new and still learning on the job," replied Lowe.

"That's true," Bo responded, "but you have to appreciate that we have fixed budgets for these audits. Every hour over the budgeted time costs us money."

"Are you asking me to cut down on the work I do?" Lowe asked.

"We would never compromise the quality of our audit work," Moe said. "We're trying to figure out why it takes you so much longer than other staff members."

At this point Lowe started to perspire. He wiped his forehead and took a drink of water.

He asked, "Would it be better if I took some of the work home at night and on weekends, completed it, but didn't charge the firm or the client for my time?"

Bo and Moe were surprised by Kevin's openness. On the one hand, they valued that trait in their employees. On the other, they couldn't answer with a "yes." The Chambers brothers did not want to set an example. They feared that other employees would feel pressured to do the same and a culture of hiding information to protect one's self-interests might develop in the firm. Moe looked at Bo, and then turned to Kevin.

"It's up to you to decide how to increase your productivity on audits," he said. "As you know, this is an important element of performance evaluation."

Kevin cringed. He wondered if this was the handwriting on the wall in terms of his future with the firm.

"I understand what you're saying," Kevin said. "I will do better in the future; I promise."

"Good," responded Bo and Moe. "Let's meet in 30 days and we'll discuss your progress on the matters we've discussed today and your future with the firm."

Questions

1. Prior to reading this case, were you aware that in public accounting pressure exists to complete jobs within specified time constraints and that this could affect your performance evaluations and future growth with a firm? Does it surprise you that such an expectation exists? Why or why not?

2. Do you think it is ethical for the firm to have the policy described in this case? Why or why not? In answering this question, describe how those parties potentially affected by the policy might be benefited or harmed.

3. Kevin Lowe has an ethical dilemma. Describe that dilemma in one paragraph. What tools might he use to analyze the situation? Why did you select these means of analysis?

4. Assume that on Kevin's very next audit, he exceeds the budgeted time allowed for substantiating all capital expenditures. That is, he's already spent the allotted time to gather evidence, such as invoice descriptions, and he's only 50 percent through with the analysis. Given the facts of this case, what would you do if you were in Kevin's position? Why?

5. Assume that Kevin takes home the remaining 50 percent of the work, works through the night, and completes the job by 8 a.m. How does his action potentially affect the parties you mentioned in answering Question 2? Do you think Kevin did the right thing? Why or why not?

Case 2-4

Is Internal Whistle-Blowing "Right"?

In 2005, the U.S. Supreme Court heard arguments in the case *Garcetti v. Ceballos* (docket 04-473). The facts of the case are that Bonnie I. Robin-Vergeer of Washington was representing a deputy prosecutor in Los Angeles who claimed he was disciplined in retaliation for an internal memo to his supervisor complaining about a deputy sheriff's misconduct in obtaining a search warrant. Her client, Richard Ceballos, sued his supervisors, claiming a violation of his First Amendment rights. Ceballos sought clarification from the Court on the standard to be used when public employee speech is engaged in internal whistle-blowing but deals with a matter of "public concern."

Prior Court rulings on public employee speech are instructive. For example, in 1983, the Supreme Court ruled in *Connick v. Myers,* that Harry Connick, the district attorney at that time in Orleans Parish and father of jazz musician Harry Connick, Jr., did not violate Sheila Myers' First Amendment rights when he discharged her for distributing a questionnaire to her fellow district attorneys in the office. Myers distributed the questionnaire after being told by the then-first assistant district attorney Dennis Waldron that she was being transferred to another section of the criminal court after working in the district attorney's office for more than five years. Myers believed the transfer to be unjust and complained to Waldron about some other procedures in the office. Waldron informed her that others did not share her concerns.

According to Myers, she told Waldron she would obtain information on these matters. Waldron said "fine," according to Myers, and she took that to mean that she could distribute a questionnaire to fellow staff members about the office transfer policy. Some of the questions asked fellow staffers whether "there should be an office grievance committee" and "whether they ever felt pressured to work in political campaigns on behalf of office-supported candidates." When Waldron found out that the questionnaire was distributed to 15 assistant district attorneys, he phoned Connick and told him Myers was creating a "mini-insurrection" within the office.

Connick called Myers and told her that she was being terminated for refusing to accept the transfer. He also told her that distribution of the questionnaire was an act of insubordination. Myers sued in federal court, contending she was fired in violation of her First Amendment right to free speech. A district court sided with Myers, finding that the real reason for her termination was her constitutionally protected act of distributing the questionnaire about important public issues. The district court determined that the questionnaire had not "substantially interfered" with the workings of the D.A.'s office.

After the U.S. Circuit Court of Appeals for the 5th District affirmed the lower court, Connick appealed to the U.S. Supreme Court, which agreed to review the case. The Supreme Court ruled 5–4 in favor of Connick. Writing for the majority, Justice Byron White phrased the issue as "whether the First and Fourteenth Amendments (Due Process rights) prevent the discharge of a state employee for circulating a questionnaire concerning internal office affairs.

A key to the Court's decision was whether it believed that the speech in question touched on matters of public concern. In this regard, the Court relied on an earlier ruling in *Pickering v. Board of Education.* In that case, the Supreme Court had determined that school board officials in Will County, Illinois, violated the First Amendment rights of high school teacher Marvin Pickering when they fired him for writing a letter to the editor of the local newspaper. In his letter, Pickering criticized the board of education for its allocation of school funds between athletes and education.

The Court ruled in the *Pickering* case that the problem in public employee free-speech cases was balancing "the interests of the [employee], as a citizen, in commenting upon matters of public concern and the interest of the State, as an employer, in promoting the efficiency of the public services it performs through its employees." Unlike the Myers case that had involved mostly private internal matters, the Court ruled in *Pickering* that the speech touched on matters of public importance.

Returning to *Garcetti v. Ceballos,* the discussion in front of the Court prompted mixed reactions from the justices. Justice Anthony M. Kennedy displayed anguish about the "sweeping…intrusive consequences" of broad First Amendment protection for public employees who blow the whistle internally. Other justices supported Kennedy's view. However, an alternative perspective was expressed by Justice John Paul Stevens who said that it seemed odd to suggest that there would be First Amendment protection only if an employee went outside the agency to register a complaint about a public issue instead of making the complaint through internal channels. Justice Kennedy countered that the First Amendment was at its most important when used to protect "speaking out in public," as opposed to doing so in the privacy of the workplace. Ultimately, the Court ruled 5–4 in favor of Ceballos's employer, stating that the action was appropriate and alluding to it as part of his performance evaluation.

Questions

1. How would you define whistle-blowing in a general sense? Do you think it is ever ethical to blow the whistle on internal wrongdoing? Why or why not?

2. In the *Pickering* case, Marvin Pickering signed the letter to the editor as a "citizen, taxpayer and voter." Do you think the Supreme Court would have ruled differently if he had signed the letter as a high school teacher? Why or why not?

3. In the Connick case, the majority of the Supreme Court seemed to believe that Myers's issue was not of public concern. However, if the office of the district attorney routinely fired people for internally speaking out against a policy, wouldn't that affect the public interest?

4. An arbitrator in a whistle-blowing case once told an employee that you cannot "bite the hand that feeds you and insist on staying on for the banquet." Do you agree with the sentiments expressed by this statement? Do you think it is consistent with the ethical notion of justice as fairness?

5. In the case of *Garcetti v. Ceballos*, do you agree with the Supreme Court's linking the speech of Ceballos and his firing with performance evaluation? Why or why not? Use ethical reasoning to support your answer.

6. Chief Justice John G. Roberts tried to bring the issue in the *Ceballos* case close to the Court when he suggested that a ruling for internal whistle-blowing could mean that a justice might face a First Amendment challenge if she fired a law clerk for preparing a memo suggesting that another justice's "jurisprudence was wacky." When Ceballos's lawyer said the clerk would have no First Amendment claim for the exercise of "bad judgment," Roberts countered that, if the public interest were the deciding factor in the calculus, nothing could be "more important than the conduct of justice."

What if Roberts' hypothetical was written by an audit staff member about the partner in charge of the engagement. That is, he wrote a memo that the partner's judgment on audit matters was whacky. If the audit staff member was fired by the firm, do you think he should be able to sue for a violation of his First Amendment rights when he was fired for "whistle-blowing"? Why or why not?

Case 2-5

Play Ball

It's the last game of a long baseball season. The New York Frankees and the Texas Toasties are tied for the division lead. The winner of the game goes on to the division championship series. The loser goes home until next spring when it all starts over again.

Sandy Monson is scheduled to pitch for the Frankees. Monson is a perennial 20-game winner but has fallen back in the past two years since the Frankees signed him. Last year his record was 12-9. This year it is 10-13. Perhaps age is catching up to Monson. He will be 44 next month.

Monson has been worried for the past two months that the Frankees wouldn't renew his contract for next season. He knows that a good performance in this last game will go a long way toward securing that extra year he wants. He's already decided to retire after the next season when he'll be 45.

Lorge Casada is the catcher for the Frankees. Last night, Casada happened to overhear a conversation between the owner of the Frankees and the team's manager. Casada distinctly heard the owner say that the Frankees will not renew Monson's contract. The owner told the manager that "he does not want to pay $40 million for a losing pitcher."

Casada doesn't know what to do. He can wait until after the game and let Monson find out from management that he won't be around next year. However, Casada and Monson room together on the road, and they have become good friends. Casada doesn't feel right about just ignoring what he overheard. Still, he doesn't want to say something that might upset Monson, cause him to lose concentration, and possibly pitch poorly in this all-important game.

Questions

1. To whom does Casada owe his allegiance? Monson? the Frankees? the fans? Be sure to support your position.

2. Casada has an ethical dilemma. Analyze the alternatives available to him using ethical reasoning.

3. What would you do if you were in Casada's position? Why?

4. Would it make a difference to you if Monson were younger and hoped to get a multiyear contract? Why or why not?

5. Assume that Casada does not tell Monson. He pitches a shutout, and the Frankees go to the playoffs. Would you now tell him that the baseball club does not intend to renew his contract? Why or why not?

Case 2-6

Supreme Designs, Inc.

Supreme Designs, Inc., is a small manufacturing company located in Detroit, Michigan. There are three stockholders of the company, Gary Hoffman, Ed Webber, and John Sullivan. Hoffman manages the business including having the responsibility for the financial statements. Webber and Sullivan do most of the sales work, and they cultivate potential customers for Supreme Designs.

Hoffman recently hired his daughter, Janet, to manage the office. She had successfully managed a small clothing boutique in downtown Detroit for the past eight years. She sold the shop to a regional department store that wanted to expand its operations. Gary Hoffman hopes that his daughter will take over as an owner in a few years when he reaches retirement age. Webber and Sullivan are significantly younger than Gary Hoffman.

Janet is given complete control over the payroll, and she approves disbursements, signs checks, and reconciles the general ledger cash account to the bank statement balance. Previously, the bookkeeper was the only employee with such authority. However, the bookkeeper recently left the company, and Gary Hoffman needed someone he could trust to be in charge of these sensitive operations. Hoffman asked his daughter to hire someone as soon as possible to help with these and other accounting functions. Janet hired Kevin Greenberg shortly thereafter based on a friend's recommendation.

Greenberg is a relatively inexperienced accountant, but he was willing to work for less than the amount the company had paid the former bookkeeper. Greenberg holds a bachelor's degree in accounting from Detroit Pistons College. He had been working for Prince Brothers Enterprises for the past 16 months. However, Prince Brothers decided to go public, and the company hired Chauncey Bentley LLP to do the accounting and auditing work.

On April 29, 2007, about one year after hiring Kevin, Janet discovered that she needed surgery. Even though the procedure is fairly common and the risks are minimal, Janet planned to spend five weeks in recovery because of related medical problems that could flare up if she returns to work too soon. She asked Greenberg to approve vouchers for payment and present them to her father during this time, and her father would write the checks during Janet's absence. Janet had previously discussed this plan with her father and they both agreed that Greenberg was ready to assume the additional responsibilities. They did not, however, discuss the matter with either Webber or Sullivan.

The bank statement for April arrived on May 3, 2007. Janet did not tell Kevin to reconcile the bank statements. In fact, she specifically told him to just put all of them aside until she returns. However, Kevin decided to reconcile the April bank statement as a favor to Janet and to lighten her work load after she returns.

Although everything appeared to be in order, Kevin wasn't sure what to make of his finding that Janet approved and signed five checks payable to herself for the same amount during April 2007. Each check appears in correct numerical sequence, one check of every 10 checks written during the month. Kevin was surprised because if these were payroll checks, as he had suspected because they were for the same amount, it was highly unusual because the payroll is processed once a month for all employees of Supreme Designs. In fact, he found only one canceled check for each of the other employees including himself.

Curiosity got the better of Kevin, and he decided to trace the checks paid to Janet to the cash disbursements journal. He looked for supporting documentation but couldn't find any. He noticed that four of the five checks were coded to different accounts including supplies, travel and entertainment, books and magazines, and two to miscellaneous expenses.

After considering what his finding might have meant and whether he should contact Janet, Kevin decided to expand his search. He reviewed the bank statements for January through March of 2007. In all, there were 15 additional checks made payable to Janet, each for the same amount as the five in April. These 20 checks totaled $20,000. Kevin still thought it was possible these amounts represented Janet's salary because he knows her annual salary is $50,000. Perhaps she took out a little more this year.

Kevin doesn't know what to do. He could contact Janet, but he knows she would be unhappy that he opened the bank statement and went so far as to reconcile cash even though she specifically told him not to do it. Perhaps he should contact the three stockholders. Then again, it could be best if he keeps quiet about the entire matter.

Questions

1. Do you think Kevin did the right thing by opening the bank statement and reconciling it to the general ledger? Why or why not?

2. Explain what Kevin should do if he reasons at each of the six stages of Kohlberg's moral reasoning.

3. If you were Janet and Kevin dropped by the hospital to tell you about his discovery, how would you react? Would you discuss it with your father or any of the other shareholders? Why or why not?

4. Assume that Kevin contacts Janet's father because he doesn't want to upset her after the surgery. What should Gary Hoffman do? Why? To whom does he owe an obligation?

5. Assume that Hoffman talks to his daughter, and she informs him that she had a shortage in her personal funds and planned to repay the $20,000 after she returns. What would you do now if you were Gary Hoffman? Why?

6. Assume that Hoffman does nothing because of his daughter's explanation. Janet returns to work and fires Kevin Greenberg. What would you do if you were Kevin? Why? How do you think Kevin's action (or inaction) might affect his opportunity for other jobs? Should that matter in terms of what he decides to do?

Case 2-7

The City of West Buckle

Kile Jalop is the chief of police of the city of West Buckle. Jalop was the chief of a smaller town and decided to move up after three years. He accepted the offer from the mayor of West Buckle to be its police chief effective October 2007.

Jalop decided to talk to the previous police chief and find out why she had left after only six months on the job. She said she couldn't discuss the specifics because of a confidentiality obligation but told Jalop that she left three envelopes for him in the bottom right drawer of her desk. Jalop found that odd but respected the previous police chief's wishes and didn't pursue the matter any further.

Two months after taking over as the police chief, Jalop received a phone call from a local reporter who asked Jalop if he would like to comment about alleged favors being granted to certain vendors in gaining contracts to provide training materials to city workers. Jalop knew nothing about it, so he decided to stall. He told the reporter that he would call her back. Jalop then went to his desk, opened the bottom right drawer, and saw the three envelopes. They were marked: open first, open second, and open last. Jalop opened the first envelope and removed the paper inside. It said: "Tell them you are new to the job and will have to check further before formally responding." Jalop called back the reporter and told her just that. The reporter seemed satisfied because two months on the job isn't very long.

Two months later, several reporters showed up at Jalop's office and asked about alleged kickbacks in the Police Department in fixing traffic tickets for city officials. Once again, Jalop was at a loss to answer. He started to hem and haw. The reporters persisted in their questioning. Finally, Jalop started to scratch his head and said: "Listen, folks. You know I've only been here for four months. I'm just starting to realize that changes need to be made. Give me a day or two and I'll get back to all of you."

Jalop went to his desk and opened the second envelope that said: "Tell them you are reorganizing the Police Department." Jalop did just that. He asked the public liaison to call each reporter and inform each one that he is reorganizing the department. One reporter in particular seemed impressed. He told the public relations person that the prior chief had promised to do that but never got around to it in her six months on the job.

Two months later, the phones in the police station rang off the hook. Everyone wanted to know what Jalop was going to do about the alleged embezzlement of millions of dollars by someone in the mayor's office. Jalop said he was waiting for a call from the mayor and would get back to the reporters. The reporters tell Jalop they are coming over to police headquarters and they won't leave until they get a satisfactory explanation. Jalop said nothing and hung up the phone.

Jalop went to his desk, opened the last envelope, pulled out the paper and read: "Make up your three envelopes!" Jalop put down the paper, picked up the telephone, and called his best friend, Charlie, to ask what he should do.

Questions

1. What's wrong with granting favors to certain vendors to supply materials under a contract with a government entity? Would your answer change if the contract was for a private organization? Why or why not?

2. What is a kickback? When someone gives a kickback, what do you think that person expects in return? What ethical values are violated in offering a kickback and in accepting it?

3. What is embezzlement? Is it possible that a high-ranking government official or someone in the official's office took money from the city for legitimate reasons even though the amount taken was not authorized by anyone in the official's office? Explain your answer. Is it unethical to take money from a government office without proper approval? Why or why not? Would your answer be different if money was taken without approval from a private business? What about taking money without approval from a public company?

4. Assume that you are in Charlie's position and Jalop asked for your advice. What would you say to him? Why? Is there any advice you can give to Jalop to try to prevent accepting a job in the future from an organization that could have a history of problem activities? What would that be?

Case 2-8

The CPA Review Course

The CPA review course, "Results and Performance," or RAP, is coming to the campus of State University to talk to accounting and other interested students about its review program. Daniel Justin is the campus representative for RAP. In that role, he is expected to post brochures about the course, hand out flyers about current and future review programs, talk to students about the course, and keep the directors of the course informed about what is happening on campus that may be of interest to RAP.

The director of the local RAP review program contacted Daniel and asked him to circulate a sheet of paper to gather the e-mail addresses of all accounting students at State University. The director tells Daniel that it is essential that the course communicate with all students before the RAP event on campus. The director also tells Daniel to provide the list 10 days before the scheduled event.

Daniel is also the treasurer of the campus chapter of Beta Alpha Psi (BAP), the accounting student honor society. At a meeting of the officers of BAP, Daniel raises the issue of the list. Denise Sanchez is the president of BAP. She questions Daniel about the propriety of circulating such a list and invading the privacy of students at State University. Daniel responds that he has no choice. The course director said Daniel would be fired if he didn't produce the list at least 10 days before the campus event.

Alice Fraxson points out that other review courses have asked for the same kind of list. "Not while I've been president," Denise responds. A silence ensues during which time Daniel and Alice start a side conversation. Here's how the rest of the meeting goes.

"What are the two of you talking about?" Denise asks.

"Don't get excited, Denise," answers Alice.

"Listen, both of you. It's just wrong to ask students to provide e-mail addresses to an organization that might sell the list or otherwise compromise the anonymity of our students," Denise responds.

"What do you mean 'compromise their anonymity'?" Daniel asks.

"Well," Denise says, "RAP might sell the names to organizations that could send unwanted e-mails to the students, and that could lead to viruses and other intrusions."

"You're paranoid," Alice responds.

"Wake up and smell the coffee," replies Denise abruptly. "You know very well, Alice, that some businesses make side money these days by selling e-mail addresses to others."

"I agree with Denise," says Reggie Willis. "Let's not go down that road. The fact that we might have done it in the past doesn't mean that this group of leaders should sanction it."

"I'm sorry," Daniel says. "I'm doing it with or without the approval of BAP. I owe it to RAP."

At this point, the meeting breaks up because a shouting match ensues between Daniel, Alice, and Denise.

Questions

1. Evaluate the position and reactions of Daniel Justin using Rest's four-component model of morality.

2. What ethical values might have motivated Denise to take such a strong stand on the matter of giving out the e-mail list? Be specific.

3. Evaluate the positions of Daniel and Denise using Kohlberg's model of moral development.

4. To whom does Daniel owe his loyalty? Explain. To whom does Denise owe her loyalty? Explain?

5. Assume that Daniel changes his mind and calls the RAP director to tell him that he has been prevented from gathering a list of the e-mail addresses of accounting students at State University. The director of the review course points out to Daniel that he will be in violation of the contract he signed with RAP if he does not live up to this obligation. Daniel realizes at that point that he did not carefully read the contract before signing it. He asks for more time to think over the matter. Daniel pulls out the agreement that reads in part: "Any failure to live up to the terms of this agreement will lead to the forfeiture of the right to take the RAP program free of charge and the campus representative must return all monies paid by the review course." The agreement further states, "Any differences between the student representative of the course and RAP will be resolved by an arbitrator."

   If you were in Daniel's position, would these contractual matters change your mind about gathering e-mail addresses? Why or why not? Use ethical reasoning to support your decision.

Case 2-9

The Ethics of iPod-ing

Your accounting professor just finished a lecture on why it is unethical to download music to an iPod. According to Professor Goody, it is wrong to download music from iTunes Music Store because the artists who originally recorded the music do not get a royalty each time their song is downloaded. You stand up and argue that it is not unethical because you pay 99 cents to download a song. Your professor answers that it doesn't matter because the money doesn't go to the artist and there is nothing to stop you from burning copies and "sharing" them with your friends.

Another student, Bethel, then points out that in 2003, the Recording Industry Association of America (RIAA) filed lawsuits against 261 peer-to-peer file sharing users for illegally downloading copyrighted music. "This was the Napster era," she proclaims. "Things are different now. An agreement was reached with the RIAA to pay a fee for downloaded music." Bethel finishes by saying, "It is 100 percent legal to download music from the Internet."

Julian responded that it is still wrong because there are no controls on how you use the downloaded music. He made the analogy of buying a video from the store, duplicating it, and then selling the copies on the black market. "It is wrong, and so is selling or even giving away downloaded music," Julian says.

Felicia then politely raised her hand. Professor Goody asked her to voice her opinion. Felicia said, "I'm cheap. I have zero money to spend on music. I'm a struggling college student working at night to pay for my education. I'm not going to pay anything to download music. I just upload my brother's music to my computer."

Professor Goody continued to let the students have their say; eventually, he came to believe that the ethics of the issue wasn't registering. The professor decided to change his approach. He asked the students whether any of them who had an iPod had ever received annoying advertisements. Sharonne said she had "about rock concerts, CDs, and country music events in my area." Billy stood up and added he had too and even "received ads about pop stars' clothing sales." Grace pointed out that she got a virus after downloading music. After continued discussion, Professor Goody looked at his watch and saw class time was up for the day. He ended the period by giving the students a group of questions to be discussed during the next class session.

Questions

1. Do you own an iPod? If so, have you ever stopped to think about whether it is right to download music and use the songs without controls, even though you do pay 99 cents for each song? Do you think that you should be concerned about the ethics of this activity? Why or why not?

2. What could be the implications of Felicia's approach to downloading music on society in general?

3. Given the facts of this case, consider Felicia's statement using the various ethics approaches discussed in this chapter.

4. Do you agree with Julian's analogy? Support your answer with reference to ethical reasoning.

5. Is it right for iTunes Music Store to sell information about you to merchants who then contact you about buying their product? Why or why not?

6. Today it is possible to buy books on tape and play them in your car while commuting to school or work. Is there a difference between buying a song from iTunes Music Store, downloading it on your iPod, and then allowing your friends to burn copies of the song and making copies of the book on tape and giving them away to your family and friends? Explain.

Case 2-10

The Tax Return

Brenda Sells sent the tax return she had prepared for the president of Purple Industries, Inc., Harry Kohn, to Vincent Dim, the manager of the tax department at her accounting firm. Dim asked Sells to come to his office at 9 a.m. on Monday, April 10, 2007. Sells had no idea why Dim wanted to speak to her. The only reason she could come up with was the tax return for Kohn.

"Brenda, come in," Vincent said.

"Thank you, Vincent," Brenda responded.

"Do you know why I asked to see you?"

"I'm not sure. Does it have something to do with the tax return for Mr. Kohn?" asked Brenda.

"That's right," answered Vincent.

"Is there a problem?" Brenda asked.

"I just spoke with Kohn. I told him that you want to report his winnings from the lottery. He was incensed."

"Why?" Brenda asked. "You and I both know that the tax law is quite clear on this matter. When a taxpayer wins money by playing the lottery, that amount must be reported as revenue. The taxpayer can offset lottery gains with lottery losses, if those are supportable. Of course, the losses cannot be higher than the amount of the gains. In the case of Mr. Kohn, the losses exceed the gains so there is no net tax effect. I don't see the problem."

"Let me tell you the problem," Vincent stated sharply. "It's taken me years to gain the trust of Kohn. Our firm now audits his company's books, prepares its annual tax return, prepares Kohn's personal tax return, and provides financial planning services for both. Kohn and Purple Industries together are the largest client in our office. I can't afford to lose any of the business these clients provide for our firm. As you know, we are under increasing competition from larger regional firms that are looking for new clients. If we don't support Kohn, some other firm will step in and do it. Poof, there goes 20 percent of our revenues."

Brenda didn't know what to say. Vincent seemed to be telling her the lottery amounts shouldn't be reported. But that was against the law.

She turns to Vincent and asks: "Are you telling me to forget about the lottery amounts on Mr. Kohn's tax return?"

"I want you to go back to your office and think carefully about the situation. We'll meet again in my office tomorrow at 9 a.m."

Questions

1. Analyze the alternatives available to Brenda using Kohlberg's six stages of moral development. That is, what would Brenda's position be when she meets with Vincent, assuming that it is determined by each of the six different stages of moral development on an independent basis?

2. Assume that Brenda meets with Vincent, who says her future with the firm depends on her willingness to go along with what Kohn wants. Analyze Brenda's options at this point using ethical reasoning. What would you do if you were Brenda? Why?

3. Assume that Brenda decides to go along with Vincent and omits the lottery losses and gains. Next year, the same situation arises but then with gambling losses and gains. If you were Brenda, and Vincent asked you to do the same thing you did last year regarding omitting the lottery losses and gains, what would you do this second year? Why?

4. Assume now that Brenda refuses to go along with Vincent and the firm. She threatens to quit if Vincent forces her hand. Vincent reminds Brenda that she went along with the improper treatment of the lottery losses and gains last year and says, "How do you think it will look if Kohn's tax problems become public and the financial press asks about it and I say that Brenda never informed me of that situation? Remember, he is one of the wealthiest businesspeople in town. The press will jump all over the story—and me." Would this change your mind in terms of going along with the firm a second time? Why or why not?

3

Ethical Decision Making in Business

Capitalism is the astounding belief that the most wickedest of men will do the most wickedest of things for the greatest good of everyone.

John Maynard Keynes (1883–1946)

The scornful remark of John Maynard Keynes, the noted English economist, stands in sharp contrast to Adam Smith's doctrine of the invisible hand of the marketplace guiding how an individual employs capital to promote the interests of society even though the individual's goal may be to promote self-interest. So, which is it? Is capitalism a beacon for individual choice and prosperity for all, or is it an outdated theory that might have been applicable during the period of economic development of the United States when individual decision makers cared about how their decisions affected others even though their ultimate goal may have been to promote their own self-interests?

We can turn to Mahatma Gandhi (1869–1948), the Indian political spiritual leader, for insight into what capitalism really stands for. Gandhi said, "Capitalism as such is not evil; it is its wrong use that is evil. Capitalism in some form or other will always be needed."[1] In short, the way in which capitalism plays out in the real world of business largely depends on the motivation of individual decision makers. So, we are back to the foundational issue of ethical behavior: What should a person of good will do?

As pointed out in Chapter 2, moral motivation is a necessary ingredient to ethical action. It is a necessary but not sufficient condition for ethical decision making to take place. The decision maker also must have the integrity, or moral courage, to follow through with an ethical choice.

Ethical decision making does not occur because a system is based on capitalism any more than unethical decision making takes place for the same reason. It is the decision maker's core ethical values that create a culture for decisions in business that respects the interests of shareholders, creditors, employees, customers, and others who are affected by those decisions. These parties are the *stakeholders* of a corporation along with the government because it is charged with regulating business and the effects of business on society in general, for example, to preserve the environment and promote sustainability.

What Is Business Ethics?

John Maxwell contends there is no such thing as "business" ethics. He believes that a single standard of ethics applies to both our business and to our personal lives. Maxwell identifies the standard as the "Golden Rule." He says in making ethical decisions we should ask the question, "How would I like to be treated in a particular situation?" To Maxwell, the Golden Rule is an integrity guideline for all situations.[2]

Maxwell's perspective implies that we should treat others the way we would like to be treated. His view is consistent with Kant's notion of universality, that is, we should act in ways that we would want others to act for similar reasons in similar situations. Our actions should possess universality so that if another decision maker looked at what we had decided and how we came to that conclusion, that person would also decide the same way for the same reasons.

While most people recognize that business must earn a profit to survive, it is the steps taken in business dealings and financial reporting to make the profit that concerns ethicists. As Kant points out, the ends do not justify the means. If it did, businesses could rationalize not taking the necessary steps to protect the environment based on the excessive costs to comply with the laws of the Environmental Protection Agency. If a company takes such a position, it would be placing its own self-interests, perhaps in the guise of maximizing shareholder wealth, ahead of the interests of society.

In this book, we define *business ethics* as the core values and standards adopted to guide decision making. In the course of developing those principles and making ethical decisions, a business must consider the interests of its stakeholders. These include the owners, stockholders, creditors, employees, suppliers, customers, and government agencies that regulate business.

Ethical Issues in Business

An ethical issue in business is a problem, situation, or opportunity that requires an individual decision maker, group of people, or organization to choose among alternative actions that must be evaluated as (the better) right or (the lesser) wrong, ethical or unethical.[3] We use the ethical reasoning methods explained in Chapter 2 as the primary tool for making that evaluation.

Ferrell, Fraedrich, and Ferrell identify five major ethical issues in business including honesty and fairness, conflicts of interest, fraud, discrimination, and information technology. While all issues affect the practice of accounting, we focus on the first three (separating the discussion of honesty and fairness) because they are most directly related to the goal of producing accurate and reliable financial statements.[4]

Honesty

Abraham Lincoln once said, "No man has a good enough memory to be a successful liar." A person who lies about a matter then has to remember what was said and be sure to provide a consistent response when questioned; otherwise, the story will come apart over time. It's easy to remember something said that is truthful. It's already etched in your mind.

Imagine that you and a friend were sent to a conference in New York City to learn about the growing field of forensic accounting. Forensic accountants utilize accounting, auditing, and investigative skills when conducting an investigation of a matter such as fraud. You and your friend decide to skip out on the afternoon session. You go to the half-price theatre ticket kiosk on Times Square and buy two tickets for the show *Chicago*. After you return to the office, your boss asks what you learned about litigation support. You look at each other somewhat perplexed, but your friend "saves the day." She says, "It's a part of forensic accounting." "That's it?" your boss responds.

Litigation support provides assistance to one or another party in a lawsuit. Forensic accountants provide litigation support on matters related to fraud when people have lost money as a result of a financial wrongdoing. Had you and your friend attended that session, you might have learned that the Association of Certified Fraud Examiners provides extensive education and training in this area and a person can study to become a certified fraud examiner.

Going back to our case, what would happen if you or your friend, but not both of you, is asked by another supervisor in the firm about the forensics session. Did the two of you develop a script to respond consistently? What if one of you forgets his or her lines? Will it implicate that person only? Will the other also be implicated? Are you starting to see how much easier it is simply to tell the truth?

Another problem with lying in this case is that the firm is paying for your registration and, perhaps, one or more nights at a fancy hotel in midtown Manhattan. You have squandered the firm's resources and will be reimbursed for hotel and lodging including the time that you were on "personal" business. It's just as if you had asked to be paid for time you didn't work. It's as wrong to do this as it would be to take office supplies home for your own use or make copies of personal documents on the company copier and on company time. You have an obligation to be honest and trustworthy. Moreover, what kind of example do you set for your son or daughter if you do improper things in business while touting ethical behavior at home in your personal life?

Fairness

Fairness has already been addressed in the context of treating others equally and of fairness as justice in ethical decision making. Fairness also implies objectivity in accounting and auditing. Accounting professionals should approach their roles as preparers of financial statements without bias or predisposition of how transactions should be reported and disclosed. There are two important points. First, the statements should be transparent: accurate, reliable, and reflect full disclosure. Second, and related to the first requirement, is for the statements to be prepared in accordance with GAAP and not be misleading.

It is important to note that the idea of being "fair" is often shaped by vested interests. One or both parties to a business negotiation may view an action as unfair or unethical because the outcome was less beneficial than expected. Fairness relates to utilitarianism in this regard, and it is based on the theory of justice.

Conflict of Interests

A conflict of interest is a situation in which private interests or personal considerations could affect or be perceived to affect an employee's judgment to act in the best interests of the organization. Examples include using an employee's position, confidential information, or personal relationships for private gain or advancement.

Objectivity and integrity are essential qualities for employees of any organization. It is the perception that a person may be influenced by matters or relationships not relevant to a decision that creates many of the conflict of interest problems in business. For example, assume that a purchasing manager for a manufacturing company has to decide which of two suppliers should be given a contract to provide millions of dollars of raw material to the company. The purchasing manager's brother-in-law is the sales manager of one of the two companies. If the purchasing manager selects that company for the contract, the perception may be that his decision was tainted by the existence of a family relationship in awarding the contract.

Does that mean that the purchasing manager should choose the other supplier to avoid any questions about bias in the decision-making process? While that may protect the integrity of the decision, it's not very fair to the brother-in-law or to his company, assuming that it provides the best product at the most reasonable price. So, what should the purchasing manager do? One possibility is to allow someone else to make the decision. He could step aside or recuse himself from the matter and avoid the appearance of bias.

A good example of a conflict of interest policy is that of Johnson & Johnson. Selected sections of that policy appear in Appendix 1 in this chapter. One of the most interesting aspects of the conflict of interest policy is its emphasis on disclosure. Disclosure is an element of honesty. Honest people not only avoid lying but also have as a goal the disclosure of all information that another party has a right to know. This is consistent with rights theory. Those who are honest typically look at disclosure as a positive obligation, not something a person does after being caught violating a law or breaking a rule.

Fraud: Concept and Examples

Fraud can be defined as a deliberate misrepresentation to gain an advantage over another party. For example, on September 25, 1992, Lena Guerrero resigned as the head of the Texas Railroad Commission after it became public knowledge that Guerrero had claimed on her resume that she was a graduate of The University of Texas when, in fact, she never graduated. Worse, she falsely claimed to be a member of Phi Beta Kappa, and she failed classes on Texas government and Mexican-Americans in the Southwest. Guerrero lied about her graduation during the process of running for election to head the Commission having been initially appointed by then Governor Ann Richards.

In 2006, the Association of Certified Fraud Examiners (ACFE) released a follow-up study to its 2002 and 2004 reports, *2006 Report to the Nation on Occupational Fraud and Abuse.* The ACFE defines *occupational fraud* as "the use of one's occupation for personal enrichment through the deliberate misuse or misapplication of the employing organization's resources or assets."[5]

ACFE identifies four key elements of all occupational fraud schemes including these: the activity is clandestine; it violates the perpetrator's fiduciary duties to the victim organization; the act is committed for the purpose of direct or indirect financial benefit to the perpetrator; and it costs the employing organization assets, revenue, or reserves.[6] These schemes occur because of a lack of internal controls and ineffective corporate governance. More will be said about these important systems later in the chapter.

The data for the study were supplied by certified fraud examiners from 1,134 cases they had personally investigated. The median dollar loss caused by fraud schemes was $159,000, representing 5 percent of annual revenues. The ACFE made an estimate of total dollar loss to the U.S. economy because of fraud in 2006 by multiplying the 5 percent by the estimated 2006 $13.037 trillion U.S. gross domestic product; the result was about *$652 billion lost to fraud.*

The frauds occurred at a variety of organizations including private companies (36.8 percent), public companies (31.7 percent), government organizations (17.6 percent), and not-for-profit organizations (13.9 percent). Approximately 36 percent of the frauds occurred at small organizations defined as those that employ fewer than 100 people. The median loss was $100,000. In large organizations, the medium loss ranged from $179,000 (100–999 employees) to $150,000 (10,000+ employees).[7] Clearly, all organizations are fraud targets, and you should learn how fraud could affect your performance of professional services for public, private, government, and not-for-profit organizations.

Perhaps the most interesting finding about fraud is the way in which it occurs and the increase in the median loss. The latter suggests a larger dollar amount of fraud when compared to the 2004 study. The comparative percentages for 2004 are in parenthesis. The most common type of fraud was asset misappropriation. Overall, 91.5 percent (92.7 percent) of the frauds were of this type that includes cash misappropriation and fraudulent disbursements such as false billings, inappropriate expense reimbursements, check tampering, and false payroll payments. The median loss due to asset misappropriation was $150,000 ($93,000). Various forms of corruption such as accepting kickbacks and engaging in conflicts of interest were next, representing 30.8 percent (30.1 percent), and the median loss was $538,000 ($250,000). Finally, fraudulent financial statements accounted for only 10.6 percent (7.9 percent) of the fraud cases, but the median loss was $2 million ($1 million).[8]

Chapter 5 has a discussion of how to prevent and detect fraud in accounting. In Chapter 6, we discuss some of the legal liabilities for auditors who fail to detect fraud. In Chapter 7, we describe the various kinds of financial statement manipulations including earnings management that can lead to fraud investigations by the SEC.

Fraud occurs as a result of a failure in organizational ethics because financial statement fraud cannot occur without the involvement of top management and either a breakdown or override of internal controls. In these organizations, the tone set by top management does not promote ethical behavior, and the result is increased pressure on accountants and auditors to detect and report the fraud.

Foundations of Corporate Governance Systems

The four pillars of corporate governance are responsibility, accountability, fairness, and transparency. To be effective, these principles must be part of the culture of an organization. They should emphasize conducting business and managing the company in a manner that promotes ethical and honest behavior, compliance with applicable laws and regulations, effective management of the company's resources and risks, and accountability of persons within the organization.

The role of the board of directors and executive officers once they have agreed on the principles is to set the appropriate ethical tone for the company and communicate these principles throughout it. As noted by Robert Noyce, the inventor of the silicon chip, "If ethics are poor at the top, that behavior is copied down through the organization." (http://www.josephsoninstitute.org/business-ethics_quotations.html)

Definition of Corporate Governance

A fairly narrow definition of corporate governance given by Shleifer and Vishny emphasizes the separation of ownership and control in corporations. They define corporate governance as dealing with "the ways in which the suppliers of finance to corporations assure themselves of getting a return on their investment."[9]

Goergen, Manjonantolin, and Renneboog compare corporate governance mechanisms in Germany with those in other countries including the United States. They point out that a corporate governance regime typically includes the mechanisms to ensure that the agent (management) runs the firm for the benefit of one or more principals (shareholders, creditors, suppliers, clients, employees, and other parties with whom the firm conducts its business). The mechanisms include internal ones such as the board of directors, its committees, executive compensation policies, internal controls, and external measures that include monitoring by large shareholders and creditors (in particular banks), external auditors, and the regulatory framework of a securities exchange commission, the corporate law regime, and stock exchange listing requirements and oversight.[10]

The Importance of Good Governance

Various survey results in the early 2000s have indicated that the investment community is willing to pay more for a company with strong and effective corporate governance policies. For example, a survey conducted by Economist Intelligence Unit in 2001 indicates that more than 80 percent of European and U.S. institutional investors say they would pay more for companies with good governance.[11]

The importance of good governance to share prices can be seen in the results of a survey of 310 international executives conducted in 2003 by The Economist Intelligence Unit. The results indicate that 70 percent believe that the perception of good governance standards have a positive impact on stock prices and, in a related question, 79 percent state that a negative impact will occur if the perception is poor. These responses are consistent with the finding that 8, 32, and 37 percent, respectively, rate corporate governance as a top priority in their organization, one of the top 3 priorities, and among the top 10 priorities. Only 23 percent indicate it is not a priority.[12]

Agency Theory

In whose interests should corporations be governed? The traditional view in U.S. corporate law has been that the corporate managers and directors (agents) owe their primary allegiance to the shareholders of the corporation (principals).

According to Core, Holthausen, and Larcker, the central problem in corporate governance then becomes to construct rules and incentives (that is, implicit or explicit "contracts") to effectively align the behavior of managers (agents) with the desires of the principals (owners). However, the desires and goals of management and shareholders may not be in accord, and it is difficult for the shareholder to verify the activities of corporate management. This is often referred to as the *agency problem*.[13]

Agency Costs

A basic assumption of the agency theory is that managers are likely to place personal goals ahead of corporate goals, resulting in a conflict of interests between stockholders and management. This is consistent with egoism. An enlightened egoist would emphasize other interests including stockholders and creditors while trying to satisfy that person's own self-interest.

Jensen and Meckling demonstrate how investors in publicly traded corporations incur (agency) costs in monitoring managerial performance. In general, agency costs also arise whenever there is an "information asymmetry" between the insiders (the corporation) and outsiders (investors) because insiders know more about a company and its future prospects than outsiders do.[14]

Agency costs can occur if the board of directors fails to exercise due care in its oversight role of management. Allegedly, Enron's board of directors did not properly monitor the company's incentive compensation plans, thereby allowing top executives to "hype" the company's stock so that employees would add it to their 401(k) retirement plans. While this was occurring, Enron's former CEO Ken Lay sold about 2.3 million shares for $123.4 million.[15]

Overcoming the Agency Problem

The agency problem can never be perfectly solved, and shareholders may experience a loss of wealth due to divergent behavior of managers. Investigations by the SEC and Department of Justice of 20 corporate frauds indicate that $236 billion in shareholder value was lost between the time the public first learned of the Enron fraud and September 3, 2002, the measurement date.

Executive Compensation

One of the most common approaches to the agency problem is to link managerial compensation to the financial performance of the corporation in general and the performance of the company's shares. Typically, this occurs by creating long-term compensation packages and stock option plans that tie executive wealth to an increase in the corporation's stock price. These incentives aim to encourage managers to maximize the market value of shares.

Board of Directors' Actions to Control Management

The stockholders select the board of directors by electing its members. Managers who do not pursue stockholders' best interest(s) can be replaced because the board of directors can hire and fire management. However, the accounting scandals taught us that boards can be controlled by management or be inattentive to their oversight responsibilities. For example, Andy Fastow, the now imprisoned former chief financial officer of Enron, directly or indirectly controlled many of the special-purpose entities that he had established. Enron's board waived the conflict of interest provision in the company's code of ethics to enable Fastow to wear both hats.

The Accounting System as a Monitoring Device

The accounting system should help to prevent and detect fraud including materially false and misleading financial reports, asset misappropriations, and inadequate disclosures in the financial statements. Management establishes internal controls to help prevent and detect fraud. These controls are designed to ensure that management policies are followed. However, even the best internal controls can be overridden by top management. For example, top executives at Tyco and Adelphia used hundreds of millions of dollars from interest-free loans for personal purposes. The board at each company claimed to have been uninformed about the nature and purpose of the loans.

Audited Financial Statements

The accounting statements that management prepares report the company's financial results in accordance with GAAP, and the external auditor renders an independent opinion on those statements. The financial reports can be used to mitigate the conflict between owners and managers posited by agency theory. If owners perceive that accounting reports are reliable, management should be rewarded for their performance and for helping to control agency monitoring costs. While management is responsible for the preparation of the financial reports, publicly owned companies must hire independent auditors to render opinions on the fairness of the presentations in their financial statements. Because the purpose of an audit is to provide "reasonable assurance" to investors and creditors that the financial statements are free of material misstatement, the audit plays an important role in corporate governance.

Stakeholder Theory

Freeman suggests in his seminal book on stakeholder theory that successful managers must systematically attend to the interests of various stakeholder groups.[16] This "enlightened self-interest" position has been expanded on by others who believe that the interests of stakeholders have intrinsic worth regardless of whether these interests advance those of shareholders. Under this perspective, the success of a corporation is not merely an end in itself but should also be seen as providing a vehicle for advancing the interests of stakeholders other than shareholders.[17]

Boatright asserts that the shareholder-management relation is not unique because the fiduciary duties of officers and directors are owed not to shareholders but to the corporation as an entity with interests of its own, which can, on occasion, conflict with those of shareholders. Furthermore, he says, "corporations have some fiduciary duties to other constituencies, such as creditors (to remain solvent so as to repay debts) and to employees (in the management of a pension fund)."[18]

McDonnell supports employee governance as a way to ensure that corporations are governed in part in the interests of employees. He identifies three approaches: employee share ownership, electing employee representatives to the board of directors, and employee involvement in quality circles, work councils, or the like.[19]

Building Ethics into Corporate Governance Systems

A critical issue for an organization that aspires to be ethical is how it should build ethics into its corporate governance systems. For example, how can an organization ensure that its management operates and makes decisions in a manner that promotes ethical behavior among all of those in the organization?

Top management should establish an ethical tone at the top of the organization. Imagine that you just began working in the accounting department of a company and on your first day at work, after the usual meetings about human resource issues, the CEO meets with all new hires. The CEO walks into the conference room, welcomes everyone to the company, hands each one a copy of the code of ethics, and then says make sure you read it. That's not very inspiring, and it may not engender a great deal of enthusiasm for the code or the company's commitment to ethical behavior. Imagine instead that the CEO walks in, greets everyone, holds up the code, and then says:

> This is our code of ethics. We believe in it. It guides our actions. It's not just a piece of paper. In fact, next week, you will go through a two-day ethics training program to learn just what the provisions mean to you in the performance of your services. Don't hesitate to question an action if you think it violates the code. We have an ethics hotline on which you can discuss any matter anonymously with our ethics officer. If all else fails, come to me directly, and we'll discuss it. This organization supports ethical behavior. No cutting of corners. No fudging numbers. No padding expense accounts. And be careful to avoid even the appearance of a conflict of interest.

The expected response from employees probably would be to identify with the company's ethical expectations. Wouldn't you feel proud to work for such a company?

Corporate Values

Recall that values are basic and fundamental beliefs that guide or motivate attitudes or actions. Ethics is revealed through a decision maker's behavior when solving business problems that emerge from carrying out corporate policies and operations. Thus, the underlying antecedents of behavior are values and, as such, values are the foundation of ethical decision making.[20]

Increasingly, companies around the world have adopted formal statements of corporate values, and senior executives now routinely identify ethical behavior, honesty, integrity, and social concerns as top issues on their companies' agendas. In 2004, the consulting firm of Booz Allen Hamilton teamed up with the Aspen Institute, an organization dedicated to promoting values-based leadership and public policy, to survey corporations in 30 countries and five regions. The purpose of the survey was to examine the way that companies define corporate values, to expand the research about the relationship of values to business performance, and to identify best practices for managing corporate values.[21]

The survey's most significant finding was that a large number of companies are making their values explicit. Exhibit 3.1 presents the results of a survey of the frequency of values included in corporate values statements.[22]

To give the reader some examples of how companies instill values into their culture, we turn first to Dell Computer Inc., a global technology company based in Austin, Texas. Beginning in 2002, Dell engaged every employee in the company in a deep, two-year reexamination of its culture that culminated in a new corporate values statement, "The Soul of Dell." This document articulates five corporate values that Dell considers central to its success including customer loyalty, teamwork, direct communication and relationships, global citizenship, and winning.[23]

Dell identifies its ethics and values as indicated in Appendix 2.[24] As you read this statement, notice the importance of integrity to ethics at Dell.

EXHIBIT 3.1
Corporate Values Statements

Source: Reggie Van Lee, Lisa Fabish, and Nancy McGaw, "The Value of Corporate Values," *Strategy + Business,* Spring 2005 (Booz Allen Hamilton Inc.). Reprinted with permission from strategy+business, the award-winning management quarterly published by Booz Allen Hamilton. www.strategy-business.com.

Values	Percentage
Ethical behavior/integrity	90%
Commitment to customers	88
Commitment to employees	78
Teamwork and trust	76
Commitment to shareholders	69
Honesty/openness	69
Accountability	68
Social responsibility/corporate citizenship	65
Innovativeness/entrepreneurship	60
Drive to succeed	50
Environmental responsibility	46
Initiative	44
Commitment to diversity	41
Adaptability	31

Corporate Codes of Conduct

Corporate codes of conduct are formal statements that describe the organization's expectations for its employees. An example of a corporate code with clearly defined principles is that of Kerr-McGee Corporation, a global energy company based in Oklahoma City.

Kerr-McGee begins its "Code of Business Conduct & Ethics" with the statement that it is "committed to legal compliance and upholding high ethical standards. Our culture is bound to a set of principles fundamental to our belief system."[25] The company correctly distinguishes between compliance with laws and ethical behavior. Indeed, laws establish minimum standards of behavior. Laws and regulations can't cover every situation that a businessperson will face. A decision maker needs a strong sense of ethics—right and wrong—to guide decisions when laws or regulations are unclear. The case of Ford Motor Company that will be discussed later in this chapter exemplifies when a company failed to act ethically but instead, relied on compliance with regulations that were clearly too lenient.

Returning to the Kerr-McGee code, the following principles support ethical behavior in the company: respect for the individual, ethical business dealings, safe working practices, responsible corporate citizenship, responsible care for the environment, and continuous improvement. According to the company, "Each employee receives the Kerr-McGee Code of Business Conduct and Ethics upon joining the company, and compliance is a condition of employment."[26]

In addition to a statement of values and a code of ethics, some companies use a credo to instill virtue. A *credo* is an aspirational statement that encourages employees to internalize the values of the company. A good example of a corporate credo is that of Johnson & Johnson (see Exhibit 3.2).[27]

The Johnson & Johnson credo clearly sets a positive ethical tone. Notice that it emphasizes the company's primary obligations to those who use and rely on the safety of its products. The company links earning a fair return for the shareholders to operating in accordance with its ethical values. The company is credited with being an ethical organization in part because of the way it handled the Tylenol poisonings in 1982. This will be discussed later in the chapter.

Code of Ethics for CEOs and CFOs

In virtually all of the frauds discussed later in the text, including those at Enron, WorldCom, Tyco, and Adelphia, the CEOs and CFOs knew about the company's materially misstated financial statements. One important provision of SOX that helps to protect the public

EXHIBIT 3.2
Johnson & Johnson
Credo

Johnson & Johnson Credo

We believe our first responsibility is to the doctors, nurses and patients,
to mothers and fathers and all others who use our products and services.
In meeting their needs everything we do must be of high quality.
We must constantly strive to reduce our costs
in order to maintain reasonable prices.
Customers' orders must be serviced promptly and accurately.
Our suppliers and distributors must have an opportunity
to make a fair profit.

We are responsible to our employees,
the men and women who work with us throughout the world.
Everyone must be considered as an individual.
We must respect their dignity and recognize their merit.
They must have a sense of security in their jobs.
Compensation must be fair and adequate,
and working conditions clean, orderly and safe.
We must be mindful of ways to help our employees fulfill
their family responsibilities.
Employees must feel free to make suggestions and complaints.
There must be equal opportunity for employment, development
and advancement for those qualified.
We must provide competent management,
and their actions must be just and ethical.

We are responsible to the communities in which we live and work
and to the world community as well.
We must be good citizens—support good works and charities
and bear our fair share of taxes.
We must encourage civic improvements and better health and education.
We must maintain in good order
the property we are privileged to use,
protecting the environment and natural resources.

Our final responsibility is to our stockholders.
Business must make a sound profit.
We must experiment with new ideas.
Research must be carried on, innovative programs developed
and mistakes paid for.
New equipment must be purchased, new facilities provided
and new products launched.
Reserves must be created to provide for adverse times.

When we operate according to these principles,
the stockholders should realize a fair return.

against fraudulent financial statements is the requirement that the CEO and CFO must certify that to the best of their knowledge, there are no material misstatements in the financial statements.

Another requirement of SOX is that public companies must have a code of ethics for its CEO and principal financial officers. This code must be separate from the company's code of ethics. Appendix 3 at the end of the chapter presents the code of ethics of Kerr-McGee Corporation for its CEO and principal financial officers. Notice that the code refers to honesty and integrity and emphasizes avoiding conflicts of interest and full disclosure.

Employees' View of the Ethics of Their Organizations

The famous U.S. investment entrepreneur, Warren Buffet, once said, "Earnings can be pliable as putty when a charlatan heads the company reporting them." ("Guide One Governance," International Labor Organization, 2005) The CEOs of Tyco and Adelphia used company resources for their own benefit without getting proper authority from the board of directors and without proper disclosure. We can assume that each company had a series of internal controls in place to prevent such an occurrence. However, the CEOs circumvented their own controls to accomplish their self-interest-oriented wrongdoing. The tone at the top of these organizations apparently was that employees should do what the CEO says, not what the CEO does. This is a sure way to encourage a cynical attitude on the part of employees who could come to view the organization as not following its own ethical standards while expecting its employees to adhere to them.

The 2005 Ethics Resource Center (ERC) national business ethics survey, *How Employees View Ethics in Their Organizations 1994–2005,* released in 2005 provides a perspective on whether employees believe the tone at the top is ethical and whether actions of top company officials support that tone. Exhibit 3.3 presents some of its more interesting findings.[28]

As a result on a composite finding developed from the responses to the ERC survey, it was determined that supervisors clearly set an ethical tone. The finding is that "nearly three in four employees agree that their supervisor takes appropriate action in four areas related to business ethics: Talking about the importance of ethics, keeping promises and commitments, supporting employees and setting a good ethical example." (Ethics Resource Center. *Natonal Business Ethics Survey: How Employees View Ethics in Their Organizations 1994–2003,* p. 48.)

Overall, the results of the ERC survey show a positive trend in ethical behavior by top management between 2000, 2003, and 2005. In all likelihood, some of the improvement can be attributed to the response of business and regulators to the Enron and WorldCom scandals and the passage of SOX. However, the results that pertain to supervisors are mixed. In only one question (promise keeping) did the results go up from 2000 to 2005. In two areas (talks about importance of ethics and disciplines employees who violate the

EXHIBIT 3.3
How Employees View Ethics in Their Organizations: 2005 Business Ethics Survey

Reproduced with permission from the Ethics Resource Center, Washington, D.C.

Questions	Percentage of employees strongly agreeing or agreeing		
	2005	2003	2000
1. Head of organization/top management sets a good example of ethical behavior	87%	88%	83%
2. Management talks about the importance of ethics	89	89	87
3. Top management keeps promises and commitments	81	84	79
4. Supervisor sets a good example of ethical behavior (modeling)	91	89	87
5. Supervisor talks about the importance of ethics	90	86	85
6. Supervisor keeps promises and commitments	88	87	86
7. Supervisor disciplines employees who violate ethical standards	68	77	84
8. Supervisor supports me in following ethics standards	93	93	N/A

standards), they went down. The latter is of particular importance in light of the decline in the numbers of those who strongly agree and agree from 84 percent to 77 percent. Perhaps top management has not done a sufficient job in communicating a more ethical tone in the organization.

The importance of the tone at the top is evident in the 2005 ERC national business ethics survey, *How Employees View Ethics in Their Organizations 1994–2005.* A key finding is that "formal ethics and compliance programs do have an impact [on ethics], but organizational culture, which has changed little over the years of the . . . study, is more influential in determining outcomes."[29]

Detection of Occupational Fraud

The *2006 Report to the Nation on Occupational Fraud and Abuse* by the Association of Certified Fraud Examiners (ACFE) details how fraud was initially detected. See Exhibit 3.4.[30]

The ACFE survey also indicates that about 75.0 percent of the organizations that had a fraud occurrence in both 2004 and 2006 had had an external audit. This is interesting in that only 12.0 percent (10.9) percent of the frauds were detected by external audits. The obvious conclusion is that external audits do not discover fraud or at least should not be relied on to do so. In fact, the purpose of an external audit is to provide "reasonable assurance" that the financial statements are free of material misstatement. This is a far cry from saying that the external audit is designed to detect fraud. Indeed, for an external audit to better detect fraud, the amount of time and resources devoted to the audit would have to increase substantially. The client company typically would not want to pay the extra audit fee for this purpose. Nevertheless, the auditing profession has made progress in developing better procedures to help identify fraud. These will be discussed in Chapter 5.

The ACFE survey indicates that 59.0 percent (57.2 percent) of the organizations experiencing fraud had internal audits. Surprisingly, the percentage of fraud identified by internal audits decreased in 2006 to 20.2 percent from 23.8 percent in 2004. This result could be due to the increase in percentage of frauds caught through internal controls: 19.2 percent in 2006 versus 18.4 percent in 2002. These results support the heightened awareness given by SOX to the importance of having strong internal controls to provide a foundation for internal and external audits.

Of particular note in the 2006 study is that 479 organizations had fraud hotlines or other anonymous reporting mechanisms when the frauds occurred compared to 581 that did not. Moreover, organizations with hotlines had a median loss of $100,000 per scheme and detected their frauds within 19 months of inception. By contrast, organizations without hotlines suffered twice the median loss—$200,000 —and it took 24 months to detect their frauds.[31]

These results might account for the relatively high percentage of frauds being detected by tips (34.2 percent) and accident (25.4 percent). It would appear that the whistle-blowing

EXHIBIT 3.4   **Association of Certified Fraud Examiners Survey of Initial Detection of Fraud, 2006 vs. 2004 (in parentheses)**

Reproduced with permission from the Association of Certified Fraud Examiners, Austin, Texas.

Year	Tip	Internal Audit	By Accident	Internal Controls	External Audit	Notified by Police
2006	34.2%	20.2%	25.4%	19.2%	12.0%	3.8%
2004	(39.6)	(23.8)	(21.3)	(18.4)	(10.9)	(0.9)

provisions in SOX may have contributed to the anonymous reporting. SOX contains a whistle-blower protection provision that says if an employee contacts the hotline or reports fraud overtly and then is fired, that employee can bring a wrongful dismissal lawsuit against the company. The government will investigate the charges and if it concurs, the Department of Labor will help to support the employee in his lawsuit.

Ethics Officers

In 1992, a dozen ethics officers got together and formed the Ethics Officers Association. Today, the EOA has more than 1,250 members including more than one-half of the following: Fortune 100, government organizations, and not-for-profits. In 2006, the organization changed its name to the Ethics and Compliance Officer Association (ECOA) to denote the increased responsibilities for ethics officers that result from passage of the Sarbanes-Oxley Act. The mission of the ECOA is to promote "ethical business practices and [serve] as a global forum for the exchange of information and strategies among organizations and individuals responsible for ethics, compliance and business conduct programs."[32]

The ECOA plays a critical role in helping to create a positive ethical tone in organizations. Ethics officers should take the lead in ensuring that the organization is in compliance with laws and regulations, including SOX, and they should serve as a sounding board for management to try out new ideas to see whether it passes the ethics "sniff" test. That is, can the ethics officer detect (smell) any perceived or real violation of the code of ethics?

Ethical Reflection and Decision Making

Reflection can be seen as consciously thinking about and analyzing what one has done (or is doing). In virtue theory, the moral virtues are affected by and affect the intellectual virtues. Taken together, reflective learning is a technique that when combined with Aristotelian virtue provides a strong foundation for teaching ethics to accounting students.

A decision-making process can help to organize the various elements of ethical analysis and reasoning. A good model should be based on the core values described in Chapter 1, should incorporate ethical reasoning as discussed in Chapter 2, and should consider the interests of shareholders and other stakeholders as explained in this chapter. The recommended decision-making model follows.

1. **Frame the ethical issue.**

   What is the primary ethical issue in this case?

2. **Gather all of the facts.**

   Specify the relevant facts, including differences of opinion, disagreements, and other conflict situations.

3. **Identify the stakeholders and obligations.**

   Determine the obligations of the decision maker to each of the *primary stakeholders.*

4. **List the relevant core values involved in the situation.**

   Use the ethical issue to identify the most important *ethical values* to be considered in evaluating the alternative courses of action.

5. **Identify the operational issues.**

   These might include, for example, communication in the organization, lines of reporting, internal controls, and corporate governance.

6. **Identify the accounting issues.**

   These might include revenue recognition, expense recognition, disclosure, and conformity with GAAP.

7. **List all of the possible alternatives of what you can or cannot do.**

   Be creative in identifying alternative courses of action. Most ethical issues are not black or white—there are shades of gray and the alternatives should account for that uncertainty.

8. **Reflect on how alternative courses of action affect others.**

   Have all stakeholders and obligations been considered or addressed?   Have any stakeholders been forgotten?

9. **Make an ethical analysis of the alternatives.**

   Is it *legal* (in conformity with laws and rules)?

   Is it *consistent with professional standards*? (to be discussed in the next chapter).

   Is it consistent with *in-house rules* (i.e., codes of conduct)?

   Is it right?

   What are the potential *harms and benefits* to the stakeholders?

   Is it *fair* to the stakeholders?

   Is it consistent with *virtue considerations*?

10. **Decide on a course of action.**

    After evaluating the ethics of the alternatives, select the one that best meets the ethical requirements of the situation.

11. **Reflect on your decision.**

    Before taking action, think about what you are about to do and why. Double check the correctness of your proposed action by asking: How would I feel if my decision were made public and I had to defend it?

Figure 3.1 presents the ethical decision-making process. It is designed to facilitate an understanding of the issues in a case study. One way to go through the steps is for the instructor to form student teams and then assign each student to analyze one or two steps in the process.

Some may view the model as onerous. However, making ethical decisions is not an easy task. Perhaps this is why so many decision makers fail to adequately consider the ethical issues before acting. Some just "fly by the seat of their pants."

In using the model to analyze ethical issues, you should keep in mind that not every step needs to be addressed. The information given may limit the analysis. Also, there is some justification for simply explaining the rationale for using the ethical reasoning method that was chosen rather than analyzing the ethical issues from all perspectives unless that is what is asked at the end of the case or required by your instructor.

Making ethical decisions is a thought-provoking, reflective exercise. It should bring us to the very core of our being. For example, if a company manufactures a product that the public seems to want but questions arise about its safety, what should the company do? How should it analyze the situation? Two real-life examples follow.

Ethical Decision Making in Business

We conclude this chapter by describing two situations in which the ethics of major companies was tested. The first is Johnson & Johnson. This case provides a positive example of how to deal with a crisis situation in an ethical, responsible manner. We use the Tylenol poisonings to analyze the company's reaction using the ethical decision-making model.

The second case involves Ford Motor Company. We will describe the facts of how the company reasoned through its ethical dilemma after vehicle crashes involving the Ford Pinto caused people to be burned and some died. The Pinto situation illustrates how a company can use inappropriate reasoning and suffer significant consequences as a result.

FIGURE 3.1
An Ethical Decision-Making Model

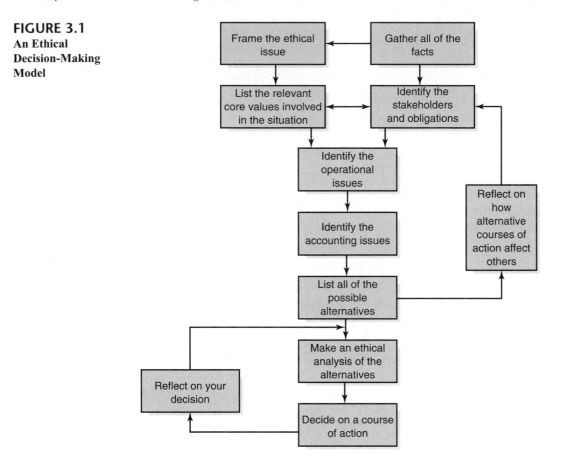

Tylenol

In the fall of 1982, seven people in the Chicago area collapsed suddenly and died after taking Tylenol capsules that had been laced with cyanide. These five women and two men became the first victims ever to die from what came to be known as *product tampering.*

McNeil Consumer Product, a subsidiary of Johnson & Johnson, was confronted with a crisis when it was determined that each of the seven people had ingested an Extra-Strength Tylenol capsule laced with cyanide. The news of this incident traveled quickly and was the cause of a massive, nationwide panic.[33]

Tamara Kaplan, a professor at Penn State University, contends that Johnson & Johnson used the Tylenol poisonings to launch a public relations program immediately to save the integrity of both its product and its corporation as a whole. We find this to be a vacuous position. By Kaplan's own admission, "Johnson & Johnson's top management put customer safety first, before they worried about their companies' profit and other financial concerns."[34] This hardly sounds like a company that used a catastrophic event to boost its image in the eyes of the public.

Johnson & Johnson's stock price dropped precipitously after the initial incident was made public. In the end of the Tylenol crisis, the stock price recovered because the company's actions gained the support and confidence of the public. Johnson & Johnson acted swiftly to remove all of the product from the shelves of supermarkets, provide free replacements of Tylenol capsules with the tablet form of the product, and make public statements of assurance that the company would not sell an unsafe product. To claim that the company was motivated by a public relations agenda, even though in the end its actions did provide a public relations boon for the company, is to ignore a basic point that Johnson & Johnson's management may have known all along: Good ethics is good business. But don't be fooled by this expression. If a company benefits as a result of an ethical action, so much the better. The main reason to make ethical decisions, as did Johnson & Johnson, is that it is the right way to act—in one's personal life as well as in business.

Let's analyze Johnson & Johnson's actions from the perspective of the ethical decision-making model starting with the first public disclosure of the poisoning and how the company should have (and did) act in response.

1. Frame the ethical issue.   *How should the company react to protect the public interest?* According to the company, its reaction was guided by its Credo.[35] If you read the Credo, you'll notice that the company places the interests of the people who rely on the safety of the product ahead of its own self-interest. In fact, it links making a "fair profit" to its ethical action and social responsibility. Johnson & Johnson's actions during the Tylenol crisis today are viewed as a model of business ethics.

2. Gather all of the facts.   Typically, these would be presented in summary or bullet form. Because the facts have already been described, they will not be repeated, although you should be prepared to do the summary in analyzing discussion questions and ethics cases in this book.

3. Identify the stakeholders and obligations.   This was arguably the most important step for Johnson & Johnson. The Credo clarifies the stakeholders. In addition to the company's obligations to doctors, nurses, patients, and parents, to provide a safe and reliable product, the company has an obligation to its employees to "walk the talk" of the Credo. If it did not act in accordance with the company's written statement of core values, employees might wonder about the company's commitment to its own Credo. This would send a negative message concerning the tone at the top of the organization.

The company also has an important obligation to its investors. As noted earlier, even though the company's stock price declined at first, it ultimately recovered all of that loss. The point is that by acting ethically, the company retained the trust of its stockholders, many of whom are parents and can probably relate to the parents of children who might accidentally ingest a tainted product.

Finally, Johnson & Johnson has an obligation to the government because the Federal Drug Administration regulates pharmaceutical products and is concerned about its role in protecting the public health. The issue of product tampering is one that has grown in importance since the Tylenol event as more and more companies including automobile manufacturers, tire manufacturers, tobacco companies, and makers of silicon gel breast implants have been questioned about the safety of their products.

4. List the relevant core values involved in the situation.   Virtually all of Josephson's six pillars of character are involved in the Tylenol situation. Honesty exists because the company has an obligation to fully disclose all of the information that the public has a right or need to know. Integrity requires that the company should have the courage to stand up for the values in its Credo regardless of the consequences. The company demonstrated accountability and responsibility by acting to remove the tainted form of Tylenol from the shelves of all supermarkets. At first, Johnson & Johnson acted only to remove the product from Chicago-area markets, but it eventually recalled the capsule form of the product nationally. By assuring the public that it would not allow a tainted product to be sold, the company garnered the public's trust. Finally, because the company acted in a socially responsible manner, its commitment to citizenship was clearly established.

5. Identify the operational issues.   Johnson & Johnson's application of its Credo in handling the Tylenol incident was an operational issue. The company indicated that it turned to the Credo immediately for guidance. This means that it was guided operationally by the one internal control—the Credo—that enabled it to respond in an ethical manner.

Additional facts of the Tylenol poisoning indicate that the company established a toll-free hotline for consumers to call for any inquiries about the safety of Tylenol. Operationally, this was another positive step to assure the public of the company's concern for its safety.

The company acted swiftly and responsibly to develop a safer packaging for Tylenol. It was a triple safety seal packaging: a glued box, a plastic sear over the neck of the bottle, and a foil seal over the mouth of the bottle.[36] This is the industry standard today.

6. Identify the accounting issues. The main accounting issues were how to disclose information about the Tylenol poisonings and the ultimate legal liability of the company. Because the Tylenol incident was the first of its kind, it would have been difficult for the accountants to determine the potential monetary liability in any lawsuit brought against the company. Still, the event itself should have been disclosed in the footnotes as a contingent liability because it was reasonably possible that there would have been a material liability for the company.

7. List all of the possible alternatives of what you can or cannot do.

a. Ignore the poisonings and let the government dictate what the company should do.

b. Do the minimum. Recall the tainted product.

c. Do all that the company can do to assure the public by acting in a responsible and ethical manner.

Of course, the company chose the last alternative as explained earlier. Undoubtedly, other alternatives can be identified.

Imagine the public outcry if the company had ignored or downplayed the severity of the situation as so many companies have since the Tylenol incident. For example, in May 1988, the Ford Motor Company reacted to safety concerns of its Pinto brand by conducting a cost-benefit analysis of whether the company should fix the apparently unsafe placement of Pinto gas tanks behind the rear axle. The Pinto case is presented next.

8. Make an ethical analysis of the alternatives. *Is it legal* (in conformity with laws and rules)? Johnson & Johnson did not violate any laws. The company did not cause the poisoning.

Is it consistent with professional standards? Because accounting issues were not involved, the accounting profession's standards are not relevant. However, other professional standards may be relevant. Engineering ethics standards would be relevant when, for example, the safety of a building is in question.

Is it consistent with in-house rules (i.e., codes of conduct)? Yes, the "rules" were the company's Credo, and they were diligently followed.

Is it right? This is the strength of the actions taken by Johnson & Johnson. The company respected the rights of the parties that used and relied on the safety of Tylenol in crafting a response to the crisis.

What are the potential harms and benefits to the stakeholders? It is difficult to see how a stakeholder would have benefited by any response other than the one developed by the company. The shareholders were harmed initially when the stock lost market value. However, in the long run, they were better off both monetarily and from the perspective of being connected with a company that became highly regarded by the public for its actions in the Tylenol poisonings.

Is it fair to the stakeholders? The users of Tylenol should not have their health placed in jeopardy by a company that ignores its ethical obligations. Clearly, Johnson & Johnson did not do this. The company acted in accordance with its Credo that emphasizes fair treatment for its stakeholders, especially the "doctors, nurses and patients, to mothers and fathers, and all those who use [company] products and services."

Is it consistent with virtue considerations? There is an expression that virtue is its own reward. This implies that a person who acts out of virtue will be rewarded by the internal feeling of having done the right thing. It does seem to apply to Johnson & Johnson.

9. Decide on a course of action.   We know what Johnson & Johnson did and why. Imagine if it had ignored the situation. The number of deaths could have risen before the government stepped in and forced a recall. The company's reputation might have suffered irreparable harm. The lawsuits would have been flowing.

10. Reflect on your decision.   We know that the company did the right thing. The chairman of its board of directors at the time, James E. Burke, was quoted as saying in regard to questions about the company's survivability after the poisonings were publicly reported:

> It will take time, it will take money, and it will be very difficult; but we consider it a moral imperative, as well as good business, to restore Tylenol to its preeminent position.

The Ford Pinto

The public in the late 1980s was shocked to find out that Pinto cars could engulf the passengers in flames in accidents at speeds of only 30 miles per hour or less. As remarkable as it may seem today, in May 1988, the Ford Motor Company reacted to safety concerns regarding its Pinto brand by conducting a cost-benefit analysis to determine whether the company should fix the apparently unsafe placement of Pinto gas tanks behind the rear axle. It did this because the National Highway Traffic Safety Administration had a policy that excused a defendant from being penalized if the monetary costs of making a production change were greater than the "societal benefit" of that change. The analysis followed the same approach modeled after Judge Learned Hand's ruling in *United States v. Carroll Towing* in 1947 that boiled the theory of negligence down to the following:[37]

> If the expected harm exceeded the cost to prevent against it, the defendant was obligated to take the precaution, and if it did not, would be held liable.

> If the cost was larger than the expected harm, the defendant was not expected to take the precaution. If there was an accident, the defendant would not be found guilty.

A summary of the Ford analysis follows:[38,]

Ford's Cost-Benefit Analysis

Benefits of Fixing the Pintos

Savings: 180 burn deaths, 180 serious burn injuries, 2,100 burned vehicles

Unit cost: $200,000 per death (figure provided by the government); $67,000 per burn injury and $700 to repair a burned vehicle (company estimates).

Total benefits: 180 × ($200,000) + 180 × ($67,000) + 2,100 × ($700) = **$49.5 million**

Costs of Fixing the Pintos

Sales: 11 million cars, 1.5 million light trucks

Unit cost: $11 per car, $11 per light truck

Total cost: 11,000,000 × ($11) + 1,500,000 × ($11) = **$137 million**

Based on this analysis and other considerations, such as the fact that at the time of the Pinto product design and crash tests, the law had not required the redesign of the fuel system, Ford decided not to change the placement of the fuel tank. It used as a justification for its inaction that the Pinto met all of the prevailing safety standards at that time.

Ford's decision turned out to be a huge mistake and illustrates the dangers of using compliance with laws instead of ethical behavior as a guiding force in making business decisions. Ford used act-utilitarian reasoning, focusing only on costs and benefits, an approach that ignores the rights of various stakeholders. A rule-utilitarian approach might have led Ford to follow this rule: "Never sacrifice public safety." A rights theory approach also would have led to the same result based on the reasoning that the driving public has an ethical right to expect that their cars will not blow up if there is a crash at low speed.

The other danger of act-utilitarian reasoning is that an important factor can be omitted from the analysis. Ford did not include as a potential cost the lawsuit judgments against the company that might be awarded to the plaintiffs. For example, in May 1972, Lily Gray was traveling with 13-year-old Richard Grimshaw when their Pinto traveling approximately 30 miles per hour was struck by another car. The impact ignited a fire in the Pinto, which killed Lily Gray and left Richard Grimshaw with devastating injuries. A judgment was rendered against Ford, and the jury awarded the Gray family $560,000 and Matthew Grimshaw, the father of Richard Grimshaw, $2.5 million in compensatory damages. The surprise came when the jury also awarded $125 million in punitive damages as well. This was subsequently reduced to $3.5 million.[39]

Conclusion

An ethical tone must be set by top management supported by a commitment to core values embodied in the code of ethics. The company should appoint an ethics officer to oversee compliance with the code and SOX. A hotline should be established and the anonymous reporting of fraud should be encouraged.

The failure of ethics in an organization usually occurs because of systemic problems such as a lack of trust. There is an adage that it takes a long time to build up trust but only minutes to lose it. The best protection is for ethical behavior to filter through the organization at all levels supported by an ethical tone at the top.

Discussion Questions

1. To whom do managers owe their allegiance? Is it to the shareholders? To other stakeholders? Be sure to support your answer with ethical thought and examples in the text from discussions about corporate governance.

2. Ambrose Bierce (1842–1914?) was the author of supernatural stories that have secured his place in both the weird tradition and in Americana letters at large. In 1913, at the age of 71, Bierce joined Bandit Pancho Villa and allegedly perished in the battle of Ojinaga on January 11, 1914. One of Bierce's "notable" accomplishments was *The Unabridged Devil's Dictionary.* In it he defines a corporation as follows:

   Corporation, n., An ingenious device for obtaining profit without individual responsibility.

   Comment on this definition. Do you agree with some or all of it? Why or why not?

3. Five major ethical issues in business were identified in the chapter. One of these issues is information technology. Discuss how information technology might create an ethical challenge for a business.

4. The four pillars of corporate governance are responsibility, accountability, fairness, and transparency. Discuss how each of these pillars helps to create an ethical corporate governance system.

5. The ACFE identifies four key elements of occupational fraud schemes including the fact that the act is committed for the direct or indirect benefit of the perpetrator of the fraud. What do you think this statement means?

6. Steroid use in baseball is an important societal issue. Many members of society are concerned that their young sons and daughters may be negatively influenced by what apparently has been done at the major league level to gain an advantage. The possibility of severe health problems for young children from continued use of the body mass enhancer now and in the future also concerns them. Others wonder whether players such as Barry Bonds and Mark McGuire, two future hall-of-famers for their accomplishments in home run productivity, should be listed in the record book with an asterisk after their names and an explanation that their records were established at a time when baseball productivity might have been positively affected by the use of steroids. Some even believe they should be denied entrance to the baseball Hall of Fame. What do you think about these issues? Be sure to use ethical reasoning to support your position.

7. In 2005, a group of concerned shareholders of Johnson & Johnson requested the board of directors establish a policy of, whenever possible, separating the roles of the chairman and CEO so that an independent director who has not served as an executive officer of the company serves as the chair of the board of directors. Do you think such a policy would improve corporate governance? Why or why not?

8. On August 9, 2005, Chancellor William B. Chandler III of the Delaware Chancery Court[40] ruled that the directors of the Walt Disney Co. had acted in good faith when Michael Ovitz was hired in 1995 to be the CEO of Disney and then allowed to walk away 15 months later after being fired by Michael Eisner, the chair of the Disney's board of directors, with a severance package valued at $130 million. Discuss the role and responsibilities of a board of directors. How do agency costs relate to the Ovitz decision?

9. Briefly describe what you think is the link between ethics in business and ethics in accounting.

10. Marvin Bower, the former managing partner of McKinsey & Co., said, "There is no such thing as business ethics. There is only one kind—you have to adhere to the highest standards." (http://www.josephsoninstitute.org/business-ethics_quotations.html) What does this statement mean to you?

Mini-Cases and Research

11. "It ain't no trick to get rich quick," the Seven Dwarfs sang in their "Heigh-Ho" song, "if you dig dig dig with a shovel or a pick." An editorial by the *New York Times* titled "Regulating Fantasyland" published on August 12, 2005, three days after the decision by the Delaware Chancery Court referred to in Question 8, points out that while the legal decision may appear to be a victory for Disney board members, it also makes clear that "corporate governance rules are changing—and that the next board sued for being so profligate with shareholders' money may not get off as easily." Former Disney finance chief Stephen Bollenbach testified during the trial, "The high hopes for Michael Ovitz quickly faded as the former super agent struggled to adjust to the Walt Disney Co. corporate culture."

    Comment on these views from the perspective of good governance practices in regard to the importance of due diligence. That is, can it be possible that Disney did its due diligence in hiring Ovitz as the CEO given that he was fired from that position less than 16 months after being hired?

    Selected Resources

    James B. Stewart, *Disney War* (New York: Simon & Shuster, 2005).

    Bob Tourtelotte, "Eisner leaves mixed legacy as Disney chief," September 29, 1995 (www.redorbit.com/news/entertainment/255971/eisner_leaves_mixed_legacy_as_disney_chief/)

    Graef Crystal, "Mike Ovitz Got Away With Murder…And I Helped Him," December 22, 1996 (www.slate.msn.com/id/2408/).

    "Roy E. Disney, Eisner take stand in Ovitz case," *Los Angeles Business Journal,* November 15, 2004 (www.bizjournals.com/losangeles/stories/2004/11/15/daily10.html).

    Michael Learmonth, "Ovitz: Bonus, then the boot," October 13, 2004 (www.variety.com/index.asp?layout=print_story&articleid=VR1117912801&catego).

12. In 1974, Congress created the Pension Benefit Guaranty Corporation as part of the Employment Retirement Income Security Act to protect workers from pension failures. The PBGC currently protects the pensions of about 45 million U.S. workers and retirees in 32,000 private single-employer and multiemployer defined benefit pension plans. The PBGC receives no funds from general tax revenues. Operations are financed by insurance premiums set by Congress and paid by sponsors of defined benefit plans, investment income assets from pension plans trusteed by PBGC, and recoveries from the companies formerly responsible for the plans. The PBGC collects premiums from U.S. pension plans and uses the money to pay partial retirement benefits if a plan cannot meet its pension obligations to workers. For example, the maximum monthly guarantee for plans terminated in 2005 for people at age 65 was $3,801. That may seem like a lot of money. However, in many cases, it makes up less than two-thirds of the amount a senior-level worker would have been paid as a monthly benefit had her company not failed to meet its pension obligations.

In 2001, the PBGC had a $7.7 billion surplus. By the end of 2004, the corporation had a $23.4 billion deficit. This may be just the tip of the iceberg. In May of 1995, United Airlines was granted permission by the bankruptcy court to terminate its $9.8 billion in pension obligations. The PBGC will cover about $6.6 of the shortfall with retirees bearing the burden of reduced benefits of about $3.2 billion. The agency estimates that total underfunding of traditional pensions is about $450 billion, including $96 billion for defaults it calls "reasonably possible."

Who should be responsible for honoring the promises that companies make to their workers? Why? Should workers at companies that walk away from their pension benefits be forced to just accept their fate? What, if anything, can or should they do about it?

Selected Resources

Josh Weitzman, "Pension Plight," The Blue Chip Review, September 2005 (www.bluechipreview.com/Weitzman_September_2005.html).

Tim Gray, "Pension Roulette: Millions of Americans Are Losing Promised Benefits: How Secure Is Your Future?" AARP Bulletin, July–August 2005 (www.aarp.org/bulletin/yourmoney/pension_roulette,html/?print).

"Pension Tension," *New York Times*, editorial, August 8, 2004.

David C. John, "Senate Pension Agreement Paves the Way for a Taxpayer Bailout," The Heritage Foundation, January 27, 2004 (www.heritage.org/Research/Regulation/?wm4-5.cfm)

The Pension Benefit Guaranty Corporation (www.pbgc.gov/).

"The S&L Crisis: A Chron-Bibliography," Federal Deposit Insurance Corporation (www.fdic.gov/bank/historical/s&l/).

13. On the evening of January 27, 1986, the temperature outside the Kennedy Space Center in Florida dropped below freezing. The National Aeronautics and Space Administration (NASA) had a dilemma. In discussions with executives from the Morton Thiokol Corporation that produced the solid rocket boosters for the space shuttle program, it was decided there was insufficient evidence and specific testing about how the cold weather would affect the rocket booster seals. The temperature had dropped to 27 degrees at launch time. It took only 75 seconds after the launch for tragedy to strike. Eleven miles above the earth, fire leaked from one of the booster seals, and the Challenger erupted into flames, killing all aboard including schoolteacher Christa McAuliffe, America's first private citizen in space.

Research the Challenger tragedy. Analyze the decision making by NASA using the model presented in this chapter. Did NASA do the right thing by allowing the launch to go on? Be sure to support your answer with ethical reasoning.

Selected Resources

Space Shuttle Challenger Disaster— A NASA Tragedy (space.about.com/cs/challenger/a/challenger_p.html).

Roger Boisjoly, "Professional Integrity and Accountability," *Accounting Horizon*, March 1993.

Randy Avera, *The Truth About Challenger* (Good Hope, Georgia: Randolph Publishing, 2003).

Diane Vaughn, *The Challenger Launch Decision: Risky Technology, Culture, and Deliverance at NASA,* (Chicago: University of Chicago Press, 1996).

14. "Give me the 'McFacts,' mam, nothing but the McFacts!" So argued the defense attorney for McDonald's Corporation as she questioned Stella Liebeck, an 81-year-old retired sales clerk, two years after her initial lawsuit against McDonald's claiming it served dangerously hot coffee. Liebeck had bought a 49-cent cup of coffee at the drive-in window of an Albuquerque, New Mexico, McDonald's, and while removing the lid to add cream and sugar, she spilled the coffee and suffered third-degree burns of the groin, inner thighs, and buttocks. Her suit claimed the coffee was "defective." During the trial, it was determined that testing of coffee at other local restaurants found that none came closer than 20 degrees to the temperature at which McDonald's coffee is poured, about 180 degrees. The jury decided in favor of Liebeck and awarded her compensatory damages of $200,000, which they reduced to $160,000 after determining that 20 percent of the fault belonged with Liebeck for spilling the coffee. The jury then found that McDonald's had engaged in willful, reckless, malicious, or wanton conduct, the basis for punitive damages. It awarded $2.7 million in punitive damages. That amount was ultimately reduced

by the presiding judge to $480,000. The parties then settled out of court for an amount reported to be less than the $480,000.

For its part, McDonald's had suggested that Liebeck may have contributed to her injuries by holding the cup between her legs and not removing her clothing immediately after the spill. The company also argued that Liebeck's age may have made the injuries worse than they might have been in a younger individual "since older skin is thinner and more vulnerable to injury."

Who is to blame for the McSpill? Be sure to support your answer with a discussion of personal responsibility, corporate accountability, and ethical reasoning.

Selected Resources

Andrea Gerlin. "McDonald's Callousness Was Real Issue, Jurors Say, in Case of Burned Woman," *The Wall Street Journal,* September 1, 1994.

Liebeck v. McDonald's Restaurants, No. CV-93-02419, 1995 (N.M. Dist. Aug. 18, 1994).

"Legal Myths: The McDonald's 'Hot Coffee' Case" (citizen.org/print_article.cfm?ID=785).

Morgan S. Reed, "Verdict against McDonald's Is Fully Justified," *The National Law Journal* 17, no. 8 (October 24, 1996), A20.

"McDonald's Settles Lawsuit of Woman Burned by Coffee, *Liability Week* 9, no. 47 (December 5, 1994).

Endnotes

1. (http://www.quotationsbook.com/quotes/5302/view.

2. John C. Maxwell, *There's No Such Thing as "Business" Ethics* (New York: Warner Business Books, 2003).

3. O.C. Ferrell, John Fraedrich, and Linda Ferrell, *Business Ethics: Ethical Decision Making and Cases* (Boston: Houghton Mifflin Company, 2005), p. 31.

4. Ferrell et al., pp. 31–40.

5. Association of Certified Fraud Examiners. *2006 Report to the Nation on Occupational Fraud and Abuse* (Austin: ACFE, 2006).

6. ACFE, p. 6.

7. ACFE, pp. 23–24.

8. ACFE, p.10.

9. Andrei Shleifer and Robert Vishny, "A Survey of Corporate Governance," *Journal of Finance,* 1997, pp. 737–82.

10. Marc Goergen, Miguel C. Manjonantolin, and Luc Renneboog, *Recent Developments in German Corporate Governance,* ECGI- Finance Working Paper Series No. 41/2002, Center Discussion Paper Series No. 2004-123.

11. Economist Intelligence Unit, "A Survey of Corporate Governance: A White Paper," *The Economist,* 2001.

12. Economist Intelligence Unit, "Corporate Governance: Business under Scrutiny: A White Paper," *The Economist,* 2003.

13. John E. Core, Robert W. Holthausen, and David F. Larcker, "Corporate Governance, Chief Executive Officer Compensation, and Firm Performance," *Journal of Financial Economics,* 1999, pp. 371–406.

14. Michael Jensen and William H. Meckling, "Theory of the Firm: Managerial Behavior, Agency Costs, and Ownership Structure," *Journal of Financial Economics,* 1976, pp. 305–60.

15. Bethany McLean and Peter Elkind, "No More Mr. Nice Guy," *Fortune,* May 15, 2006, Vol. 153, Iss. 9, pp. 72–76.

16. R. Edward Freeman, *Strategic Management: A Stakeholder Approach* (Boston: Pitman, 1984).

17. Oliver Hart, *Firms, Contracts, and Financial Structure* (Cambridge, England: Oxford University Press, 1995).

18. James R. Boatright, "Fiduciary Duties and the Shareholder-Management Relation: Or What's So Special about Shareholders?" *Business Ethics Quarterly,* 1994, pp. 393–407.

19. Brett H. McDonnell, *Corporate Constituency Statutes and Corporate Governance,* Minnesota Public Law Research Paper No. 02-13 (University of Minnesota Law School, October 2002).

20. Milton Rokeach, *The Nature of Human Values* (New York: The Free Press, 1973).

21. Reggie Van Lee, Lisa Fabish, and Nancy McGaw, "The Value of Corporate Values," *Strategy + Business,* Spring 2005 (Booz Allen Hamilton Inc.). Reprinted with permission from strategy+business, the award-winning management quarterly published by Booz Allen Hamilton. www.strategy-business.com.

22. Van Lee et al., p. 5.

23. Lawrence M. Fisher, "How Dell Got Soul," *Strategy + Business,* Fall 2004 (Booz Allen Hamilton Inc.), pp. 46–59.

24. www.dell.com/content/topics/global.aspx/corp/diversity/en/commitment?c=us&l=en&s=corp.

25. www.dell.com/content/topics/global.aspx/corp/diversity/en/commitment?c=us&l=en&s=corp or www.anadarko.com/investor_relations/governance.asp.

26. www.kerr-mcgee.

27. www.jnj.com/our_company/our_credo/.

28. Ethics Resource Center, *National Business Ethics Survey: How Employees View Ethics in Their Organizations* (Washington, D.C: ERC, 2003).

29. Ethics Resource Center, *National Business Ethics Survey: How Employees View Ethics in Their Organizations 1994–2005* (Washington, D.C: ERC, 2005).

30. ACFE, p. 28.

31. ACFE, p. 35.

32. Ethics and Compliance Office Association. www.eoa.org.

33. Tamara Kaplan, "The Tylenol Crisis: How Effective Public Relations Saved Johnson & Johnson," www.personal.psu.edu/users/w/x/wxk116/tylenol/crisis.html.

34. Kaplan.

35. U.S. Department of Defense, *Case Study: The Johnson & Johnson Tylenol Crisis.* Crisis Communication Strategies. www.ou.edu/deptcomm/dodjcc/groups/02C2/Johnson%20&%20Johnson.htm.

36. U.S. Department of Defense.

37. *United States v. Carroll Towing,* 159 F.2d 169 (2d Cir. 1947).

38. Douglas Birsch and John H. Fiedler, *The Ford Pinto Case: A Study in Applied Ethics, Business and Technology* (Albany, New York: State University of New York, 1994).

39. *Grimshaw v. Ford Motor Co.,* 1 19 Cal. App.3d 757, 174 Cal. Rptr. 348 (1981).

40. The Delaware Court of Chancery is widely recognized as the preeminent forum in the United States for the determination of disputes involving the internal affairs of thousands of Delaware corporations and other business entities. The court has jurisdiction to hear all matters related to equity. Its decisions can be appealed to the Delaware Supreme Court.

Appendix 1

Johnson & Johnson: *Selected Sections from Conflict of Interest Policy*

Every employee has a duty to avoid business, financial or other direct or indirect interests or relationships which conflict with the interests of the Company or which divides his or her loyalty to the Company. Any activity which even appears to present such a conflict must be avoided or terminated unless, after disclosure to the appropriate level or management, it is determined that the activity is not harmful to the Company or otherwise improper.

A conflict or the appearance of a conflict of interest may arise in many ways. For example, depending on the circumstances, the following may constitute an improper conflict of interest:

- Ownership of or an interest in a competitor or in a business with which the Company has or is contemplating a relationship (such as a supplier, customer, landlord, distributor, licensee/ licensor, etc.) either directly or indirectly, such as through family members.

- Profiting, or assisting others to profit, from confidential information or business opportunities that are available because of employment by the Company.

- Soliciting or accepting gifts, payments, loans, services or any form of compensation from suppliers, customers, competitors or others seeking to do business with the Company.

- Influencing or attempting to influence any business transaction between the Company and another entity in which an employee has a direct or indirect financial interest or acts as a director, employee, partner, agent or consultant.

- Buying or selling securities of any other company using non-public information obtained in the performance of an employee's duties, or providing such information so obtained to others.

Disclosure is the key [when a conflict exists]. Any employee, who has a question about…a conflict of interest or the appearance of one, should disclose the pertinent details, preferably in writing, to his or her supervisor. Each supervisor is responsible for discussing the situation with the employee and arriving at a decision after consultation with or notice to the appropriate higher level of management. Each President, General Manager and Managing Director is responsible for advising his or her Company Group Chairman or International Vice President, as the case may be, in writing, of all disclosures and decisions made under this Policy. The Law Department should be consulted for advice as necessary.

To summarize, each employee is obligated to disclose her own conflict or any appearance of a conflict of interest. The end result of the process of disclosure, discussion and consultation may well be approval of certain relationships or transactions on the grounds that despite appearances those relationships are not harmful to the Company. But all conflicts and appearances of conflicts of interest are prohibited, even if they do not harm the Company, unless they have gone through this process.

Appendix 2

Dell Computer Inc.: *Statement on Ethics and Values*

The Board and management are jointly responsible for managing and operating Dell's business with the highest standards of responsibility, ethics and integrity. In that regard, the Board expects each director, as well as each member of senior management, to lead by example in a culture that emphasizes trust, integrity, honesty, judgment, respect, managerial courage and responsibility.

Furthermore, the Board also expects each director and each member of senior management to act ethically at all times and to adhere to the policies, as well as the spirit, expressed in Dell's Code of Conduct. The Board will not permit any waiver of any ethics policy for any director or executive officer.

Kerr-McGee Corporation: *Code of Ethics for the Chief Executive Officer and Principal Financial Officers*

This Code of Ethics for the Chief Executive Officer and Principal Financial Officers governs the conduct of the Chief Executive Officer, Chief Financial Officer, and Controller of Kerr-McGee Corporation. This Code of Ethics supplements—but does not replace—the Code of Business Conduct and Ethics applicable to all employees, officers, and directors and is designed to deter wrongdoing and to promote ethical and legal behavior by the Company's Chief Executive Officer, Chief Financial Officer, and Controller.

Each of the Chief Executive Officer, Chief Financial Officer, and Controller are responsible for:

- Acting with honesty and integrity, and avoiding actual or apparent conflicts of interest involving personal and professional relationships, as described in the Company's Code of Conduct;

- Disclosing to the general counsel any material transaction or relationship that reasonably could be expected to give rise to such a conflict;

- Ensuring that the Company's disclosure controls and procedures function properly and providing officials of the Company information that is full, fair, accurate, complete, objective, timely, and understandable for inclusion in filings the Company makes with the Securities and Exchange Commission and in other public communications made by the Company;

- Complying with laws, rules, and regulations of all U.S. and non-U.S. governmental entities, as well as other private and public regulatory agencies to which the Company is subject; and

- Reporting to the general counsel any violations of this Code of Ethics of which each such person is aware.

The waiver of any duty or responsibility set forth in this Code of Ethics must be made by the Board of Directors of the Company and will be reported in a public filing with the SEC within two business days after such waiver is granted.

ACKNOWLEDGMENT

This is to acknowledge receipt of the Code of Ethics for the Chief Executive Officer and Principal Financial Officers. I understand that failure to adhere to the principles and responsibilities set forth in this Code of Ethics may result in disciplinary action, including reprimand, warnings, suspension, demotion, salary reduction, restitution and/or discharge, as well as possible legal penalties.

Name (please print) _____

Signature _____

Date _____

Chapter 3 Cases

Case 3-1

Bhopal, India: A Major Case Study

You are not here merely to make a living. You are here in order to enable the world to live more amply, with greater vision, with a finer spirit of hope and achievement. You are here to enrich the world, and you impoverish yourself if you forget the errand.

Woodrow T. Wilson (1856–1924)
28th president of the United States

At five past midnight on December 3, 1984, 40 tons of the chemical Methyl Isocynate (MIC), a toxic gas, started to leak out of a pesticide tank at the Union Carbide plant in Bhopal, India. The leak was first detected by workers about 11:30 p.m. on December 2, 1984, when their eyes began to tear and burn. According to AcuSafe,[1] "in 1991 the official Indian government panel charged with tabulating deaths and injuries counted more than 3,800 dead and approximately 11,000 with disabilities." However, estimates now range as high as 8,000 killed in the first three days and more than 120,000 injured.[2] There were 4,000 deaths officially recorded by the government, although 13,000 death claims were filed with the government, according to a United Nations report, and hundreds of thousands more claim injury as a result of the disaster.[3] While the numbers may be debatable, there can be no doubt that the Bhopal incident raises a variety of interesting ethical questions including these:

- Did the company knowingly sacrifice safety at the Bhopal plant?
- Did the Indian government properly oversee the functioning of the plant consistent with its regulatory authority?
- Did the company react quickly enough to avoid sustained health problems to those injured by the leak of toxic fumes?
- In the aftermath of the disaster, were the disclosures made by Union Carbide sufficiently transparent to enable a concerned public to understand the causes of the leak and the steps the company was taking to address all of the issues?
- Did the company and the Indian government reach a fair resolution for the thousands of claims filed by Indian citizens?

Make up your own mind as you read about the tragedy that is Bhopal.

In the Beginning

On May 4, 1980, the first factory exported from the West to make pesticides using MIC began production in Bhopal, India. The company planned to export the chemicals from the United States to make the pesticide, Sevin. The new CEO of Union Carbide had come over from the United States especially for the occasion.[4]

As you might expect, the company seemed very concerned about safety issues. "Carbide's manifesto set down certain truths, the first being that 'all accidents are avoidable provided the measures necessary to avoid them are defined and implemented.'" The company's slogan was "Good safety and good accident prevention practices are good business."[5]

Safety Measures

The Union Carbide plant in Bhopal was equipped with an alarm system with a siren that was supposed to be set off whenever the "duty supervisor in the control room" sensed even the slightest indication that a possible fire might be developing "or the smallest emission of toxic gas." The "alarm system was intended to warn the crews working on the factory site." Even though thousands of people lived in the nearby bustees,[6] "none of the loudspeakers pointed outward" in their direction. Still, they could hear the sirens coming from the plant. The siren went off so frequently that it seemed as though the population had become used to it and weren't completely aware that one death and several accidental poisonings had occurred before the night of December 2, and there was a "mysterious fire in the alpha-naphtol unit."[7]

In May 1982, three engineers from Union Carbide came to Bhopal to evaluate the plant and confirm that everything was operating according to company standards. The investigators identified more than 60 violations of operational and safety regulations. An Indian reporter managed to obtain a copy of the report that noted "shoddy workmanship," warped equipment, corroded circuitry, "the absence of automatic sprinklers in the MIC and phosgene production zones," a lack of pressure gauges, and numerous other violations. The severest criticism was in the area of personnel. There was "an alarming turnover of inadequately trained staff,

[1] According to CorpWatch **www.corpwatch.org.**

[2] United Nations, "United Nations University Report on Toxic Gas Leak." See www.unu.edu/unupress/unupbooks/uu21le/uu21le0c.htm#5%20long%20term%20recovery%20from%20the%20bhopal%20crisis

[3] Dominique LaPierre Javier Moro, *Five Past Midnight in Bhopal* (New York: Warner Books, 2002).

[4] Moro, p. 145.

[5] Moro, pp. 161; 173–181.

[6] A small settlement or area of makeshift housing in India similar to a shantytown and resembling a slum.

[7] Moro, pp. 187–188.

unsatisfactory instruction methods and a lack of rigor in maintenance reports."[8]

The reporter wrote three articles proclaiming the unsafe plant. The third article was titled "If You Refuse to Understand, You Will Be Reduced to Dust." Nothing seemed to matter in the end because Union Carbide and government representatives had assured the population that no one "need be concerned because the phosgene produced at the plant was not a toxic gas."[9]

The Accident

The accident occurred when a large volume of water entered the MIC storage tanks and triggered a violent chain reaction. Normally, water and MIC were separated, but on the night of December 2, "metal barriers known as slip blinds were not inserted and the cleaning water passed directly into the MIC tanks." It is possible that additional water entered the tanks later on in trying to control the reaction. Shortly after the introduction of water, "temperatures and pressures in the tanks increased to the point of explosion."[10]

The report of consultants[11] that reviewed the facts surrounding the accident indicates that workers made a variety of attempts to save the plant, including these:

- They tried to turn on the plant refrigeration system to cool down the environment and slow the reaction, but the system had been drained of coolant weeks before and had never been refilled as a cost-savings measure.
- They tried to route expanding gases to a neighboring tank, but the tank's pressure gauge was broken and indicated the tank was full when it was really empty.
- They tried other measures that didn't work due to inadequate or broken equipment.
- They tried to spray water on the gasses and have them settle to the ground, but it was too late because the chemical reaction was nearly complete.

The Workers and Their Reaction

It was reported that the maintenance workers did not flush out the pipes after the factory's production of MIC stopped on December 2. This was important because the pipes carried the liquid MIC produced by the plant's reactors to the tanks. The highly corrosive MIC leaves chemical deposits on the lining of the tanks that can eventually get into the storage tanks and contaminate the MIC. Was it laziness, as suggested by one worker?[12]

Another worker pointed out that the production supervisor of the plant left strict instructions to flush the pipes but it was late at night and neither worker really wanted to do it. Still, they followed the instructions for the washing operation but the supervisor had omitted the crucial step of placing solid metal discs at the end of each pipe to ensure that the tanks were hermetically sealed.[13]

The cleansing operation began when one worker connected a hosepipe to a drain cock on the pipe work and turned on the tap. After a short time, it was clear to the worker that the injected water was not coming out of two of four drain cocks. The worker called the supervisor, who walked over to the plant and instructed the worker to clean the filters in the two clogged drain cocks and turn the water back on. They did that but the water did not flow out of one drain. After informing the supervisor, who said just to keep the water flowing, the workers left for the night. It would now be up to the night shift to turn off the tap.[14]

The attitude of the workers as they started the night shift was not good because Union Carbide had started to cut back on production and lay off workers. They wondered if they might be next. The culture of safety that Union Carbide had tried to build was largely gone as the workers typically handled toxic substances without protective gear. The temperature readings in the tanks were made less frequently, and it was rare when anyone checked the welding on the pipe work in the middle of the night.[15]

Even though the pressure gauge on one of the tanks increased beyond the "permitted maximum working pressure," the supervisor ignored warnings coming from the control room because he was under the impression that Union Carbide had built the tanks with special steel and walls thick enough to resist even greater pressures. Still, the duty head of the control room and another worker went to look directly at the pressure gauge attached to the three tanks. They confirmed the excessive pressure in one tank.

The duty head climbed to the top of that tank, examined the metal casing carefully, and sensed the stirring action. The pressure inside was increasing quickly, leading to a popping sound "like champagne corks." Some of the gas then escaped, and a brownish cloud appeared. The workers returned to where the pipes had been cleaned and turned off the water tap. They smelled the powerful gas emissions. They heard the fizzing sound as if someone was blowing into an empty bottle. One worker had a cool enough head to sound the general alarm, but it was too late for most of the workers and many of those living in the shanty towns below the plant.[16]

The Political Response

Union Carbide sent a team to investigate the catastrophe, but the Indian government had seized records and denied the

---

[8] Moro, p. 189.

[9] Moro, p. 194.

[10] Ron Graham, "FAQ on Failures: Union Carbide Bhopal," Barrett Engineering Consulting. See www.tcnj.edu/rgraham/failures/UCBhopal.html.

[11] United Nations.

[12] Moro, p. 272.

[13] Moro, pp. 274–75.

[14] Moro, pp. 273–274.

[15] Moro, pp. 279–80.

[16] Moro, pp. 291–292.

investigators access to the plant and the eyewitnesses. The Madhya Pradesh state government tried to place the blame squarely on the shoulders of Union Carbide. It sued the company for damages on behalf of the victims. The ruling Congress party was facing national parliamentary elections three weeks after the accident and it "stood to lose heavily if its partners in the state government were seen to be implicated or did not deal firmly with Union Carbide."[17]

The government thwarted early efforts by Union Carbide to provide relief to the victims in its attempt to gain the goodwill of the public. The strategy worked because the Congress party won both the state legislative assembly and the national parliament seats from Madhya Pradesh by large margins.[18]

Economic Effects

The economic impact of a disaster like the one that happened in Bhopal is staggering. The $25 million Union Carbide plant in Bhopal was shut down immediately after the accident, and 650 permanent jobs were lost. The loss of human life means a loss of future earning power and a loss of economic production. The thousands of accident victims had to be treated and in many cases rehabilitated. The closure of the plant had peripheral effects on local businesses and the population of Bhopal. It is estimated that "two mass evacuations disrupted commercial activities for several weeks, with resulting business losses of $8 to $65 million."[19]

In the year after the accident, the government paid compensation of about $800 per fatality to relatives of dead persons. About $100 was awarded to 20,000 victims. Beginning in March 1991, new relief payments were made to all victims who lived in affected areas and a total of $260 million was disbursed.[20]

Union Carbide's Response

Shortly after the gas release, Union Carbide launched what it called "an aggressive effort to identify the cause." According to the company, the results of an independent investigation conducted by the engineering consulting firm Arthur D. Little were that "the gas leak could only have been caused by deliberate sabotage. Someone purposely put water in the gas storage tank, causing a massive chemical reaction. Process safety systems had been put in place that would have kept the water from entering the tank by accident."[21]

In a 1993 report prepared by Jackson B. Browning (the Browning Report), the retired vice president of Health, Safety, and Environmental Programs at Union Carbide

Corporation, he stated that he didn't find out about the accident until 2:30 a.m. on December 3. He claims to have been told that "no plant employees had been injured, but there were fatalities—possibly eight or twelve—in the nearby community."

A meeting was called at the company's headquarters in Danbury, Connecticut, for 6 a.m. The chairman of the board of directors of Union Carbide, Warren M. Anderson, had received the news while returning from a business trip to Washington, D.C. He had a "bad cold and a fever" so Anderson stayed at home and designated Browning as his "media stand-in" until Anderson could return to the office.[22]

At the first press conference called for 10 p.m. on December 3, the company acknowledged that the disaster had occurred at its plant in Bhopal. The company reported that it was sending "medical and technical experts to aid the people of Bhopal, to help dispose of the remaining [MIC] at the plant and to investigate the cause of the tragedy." Notably, Union Carbide halted production at its only other MIC plant in West Virginia and it stated its intention "to convert existing supplies into less volatile compounds."

Warren Anderson traveled to India and offered aid of $1 million, and the Indian subsidiary of Union Carbide pledged the Indian equivalent of $840,000. Within a few months, the company offered an additional $5 million in aid that the Indian government rejected. The money was then turned over to the Indian Red Cross and used for relief efforts.[23]

The company continued to offer relief aid with "no strings attached." However, the Indian government rejected the overtures and it didn't help the company to go through third parties. Union Carbide believed that the volatile political situation in India—Prime Minister Indira Gandhi had been assassinated—hindered its relief efforts, especially after the election of Rajiv Gandhi on a government reform platform. It appeared to the company that Union Carbide was to be made an example of as an exploiter of Indian natural resources and the government may have wanted to "gain access to Union Carbide's financial resources."[24]

Union Carbide had a contingency plan for emergencies, but it didn't cover the "unthinkable." The company felt compelled to show its "commitment to employee and community safety and specifically, to reaffirm the safety measures in place at their operation." Andersen went to West Virginia to meet with the employees in early February 1985. At that meeting, as "a measure of the personal concern and compassion of Union Carbide employees," the workers established a "Carbide Employees Bhopal Relief Fund and collected more than $100,000 to aid the tragedy's victims."[25]

---

[17] United Nations.

[18] United Nations.

[19] United Nations.

[20] United Nations.

[21] Union Carbide started a Web site, www.bhopal.com, after the leak to provide its side of the story and details about the tragedy. In 1998, the Indian state government of Madhya Pradesh took full responsibility for the site.

[22] Jackson B. Browning, *The Browning Report*, Union Carbide Corporation, 1993. See www.bhopal.com/pdfs/browning.pdf.

[23] Browning, pp. 4–5, 9.

[24] Browning, pp. 9–10.

[25] Browning, p. 8.

Analysis of Union Carbide's Bhopal Problems

Documents uncovered in litigation (*Bano et al. v. Union Carbide Corp & Warren Anderson, 99cv11329 SDNY*, filed on 11/15/99) and obtained by the Environmental Working Group of the Chemical Industry Archives, an organization that investigates chemical company claims of product safety, indicate that Union Carbide "cut corners and employed untested technologies when building the Bhopal Plant." The company went ahead with an unproven design even though it posed a "danger of polluting subsurface water supplies in the Bhopal area." The following is an excerpt from a document numbered UCC 04206 and included in the Environmental Working Group Report on Bhopal India.[26] It also reveals the indifferent attitude of the Indian government toward environmental safety.

> The systems described have received provisional endorsement by the Public Health Engineering Office of the State of Madhya Pradesh in Bhopal. At present there are no State or Central Government laws and/or regulations for environmental protection, though enactment is expected in the near future. It is not expected that this will require any design modifications.
>
> ### Technology Risks
>
> The comparative risk of poor performance and of consequent need for further investment to correct it is considerably higher in the [Union Carbide-India] operation than it would be had proven technology been followed throughout…the MIC-to-Sevin process, as developed by Union Carbide, has had only a limited trial run. Furthermore, while similar waste streams have been handled elsewhere, this particular combination of materials to be disposed of is new and, accordingly, affords further chance for difficulty. In short, it can be expected that there will be interruptions in operations and delays in reaching capacity or product quality that might have been avoided by adoption of proven technology.
>
> [Union Carbide-India] finds the business risk in the proposed mode of operation acceptable, however, in view of the desired long term objectives of minimum capital and foreign exchange expenditures. As long as [Union Carbide-India] is diligent in pursuing solutions, it is their feeling any shortfalls can be mitigated by imports. Union Carbide concurs.

As previously mentioned, there had been one death and several accidental poisonings at the Bhopal plant before December 3, 1984. The International Environmental Law Research Center prepared a Bhopal Date Line that showed the death occurred on December 25, 1981, when a worker was exposed to phosgene gas. On January 9, 1982, 25 workers were hospitalized as a result of another leak. On October 5, 1982, another leak from the plant led to the hospitalization of hundreds of residents.[27]

It is worth noting that the workers had protested unsafe conditions after the January 9, 1982, leak, but their warning went unheeded. In March 1982, a leak from one of the solar evaporation ponds took place, and the Indian plant expressed its concern to Union Carbide headquarters. In May 1982, the company sent its U.S. experts to the Bhopal plant to conduct the audit previously mentioned.

The reaction to newspaper allegations that Union Carbide-India was running an unsafe operation was for the plant's works manager to write a denial of the charges as baseless. The company's next step was, to say the least, bewildering. It rewrote the safety manuals to permit the switching off of the refrigeration unit and the shut down of the vent gas scrubber when the plant was not in operation. The staffing at the MIC unit was reduced from 12 workers to 6. On November 29, 1984, three days before the disaster, Union Carbide had completed a feasibility report, and the company had decided to dismantle the plant and ship it to Indonesia or Brazil.

India's Position

The Indian government has itself acknowledged that 521,262 persons, well over half the population of Bhopal at the time of the toxic leak, were "exposed" to the lethal gas.[28] In the immediate aftermath of the accident, most attention was devoted to medical recovery. The victims of the MIC leak suffered damage to lung tissue and respiratory functions. The lack of medical documentation affected relief efforts. The absence of baseline data made it difficult to identify specific medical consequences of MIC exposure and to develop appropriate medical treatment. Another problem was that malnourishment of the poor Indians affected by the tragedy added to the difficulty because they already suffered from many of the postexposure symptoms such as coughing, breathlessness, nausea, vomiting, chest pains, and poor sight.[29]

Pratima Ungarala, a student at Hindu University, wrote a paper on the Bhopal tragedy in which he analyzed the Browning Report and characterized the company's response as a public relations effort. He noted that the report identified the media and other interested parties such as customers, shareholders, suppliers, and other employees as most important to pacify. Ungarala criticized this response for its lack of concern for the people of India or the people of Bhopal. Instead,

---

[26] Environmental Working Group, *Chemical Industry Archives.* See www.chemicalindustryarchives.org/dirtysecrets/bhopal/index.asp.

[27] S. Muralidhar, "The Bhopal Date Line," International Environmental Law Research Centre. See www.ielrc.org/content/n0409.htm.

[28] Vinay Lal and Jamie Cassels, "Sovereign Immunity: Law in an Unequal World," *Social and Legal Studies* 5, no. 3 (1996), pp. 421–36.

[29] Paul Shrivastava, "Long-Term Recovery from the Bhopal Crisis," *The Long Road to Recovery: Community Responses to Industrial Disaster* (New York: United Nations University, 1996).

the corporation saw the urgency to assure the people of the United States that such an incident would not happen there.[30]

Browning's main strategy to restore Union Carbide's image was to distance the company from the site of the disaster. He points out early in the document that Union Carbide had owned only 50.9 percent of the affiliate, the Union Carbide India Ltd. He notes that all of the employees in the company were Indians and that the last American employee had left two years before the leak.

The report contended that the company "did not have any hold over its Indian affiliate." This seems to be a contentious issue because while "many of the day to day details, such as staffing and maintenance, were left to Indian officials, the major decisions, such as the annual budget, had to be cleared with the American headquarters." In addition, by both Indian and U.S. laws, a parent company (United Carbide in this case) holds full responsibility for any plants they operate through subsidiaries and in which they have a majority stake. Ungarala concluded that Union Carbide was trying to avoid paying the $3 billion that India demanded as compensation and was looking to find a "scapegoat" to take the blame.[31]

After the government of Madhya Pradesh had taken over the information Web site from Union Carbide, it began to keep track of applications for compensation. Between 1985 and 1997, more than 1 million claims for personal injury were filed. In more than half of those cases, the claimant was awarded a monetary settlement. The total amount disbursed as of March 31, 2003, was about $345 million.[32] An additional $25 million was disbursed through July 2004, at which time the Indian Supreme Court ordered the government to pay to the victims, and families of the dead, the remaining $330 million in the compensation fund.

Lawsuits

The inevitable lawsuits began in December 1984 and March 1985, when the government of India filed against Union Carbide in India and in the United States, respectively. Union Carbide asked for the case filed in the Federal District Court of New York to be moved to India because that was where the accident had occurred and most of the evidence existed. The case went to the Bhopal District Court, the lowest level court that could hear such a case. During the next four years, the case made "its way through the maze of legal bureaucracy" from the state high court up to the Supreme Court of India.[33]

The legal disputes were over the amount of compensation and the exoneration of Union Carbide from future liabilities.

The disputes were complicated by a lack of reliable information about the causes of the event and its consequences. The government of India had adopted "Bhopal Gas Leak Disaster Ordinance—a law that appointed the government as sole representative of the victims." It was challenged by victim activists who pointed out that the victims had not been consulted about legal matters or settlement possibilities. The result was, in effect, to dissolve "the victims' identity as a constituency separate and differing from the government."[34]

In 1989, India had another parliamentary election, and it seemed a politically opportune time to settle the case and win support from the voters. It had been five years since the accident, and the victims were fed up with waiting. By that time, "hundreds of victims had died and thousands had moved out of the gas-affected neighborhoods." Even though the Indian government had taken Union Carbide to court asking for $3 billion, in January 1989, the company reached a settlement with the government for $470 and it gave Union Carbide immunity from future prosecution.

In October 1991, India's Supreme Court upheld the compensation settlement but canceled Union Carbide's immunity from criminal prosecution. The money was held in a court-administered account until 1992, while claims were sorted out. By early 1993, there had been 630,000 claims filed of which 350,000 had been substantiated on the basis of medical records. The numbers were larger than previously mentioned because the extent of health problems increased continuously after the accident, and hundreds of victims continued to die. Despite challenges by victims and activists to the settlement with Union Carbide, at the beginning of 1993, the government of India began to distribute the $470 million that had increased to $700 million as a result of interest earned on the funds.[35]

What Happened to Union Carbide?

The lawsuits and bad publicity affected Union Carbide's stock price. Before the disaster, the company's stock had traded between $50 and $58 a share. In the months immediately following the accident, it traded at $32 to $40. In the latter half of 1985, the GAF Corporation of New York made a hostile bid to take over Union Carbide. The ensuing battle and speculative stock trading ran up the stock price to $96 and forced the company into financial restructuring.[36]

The company's response was to fight back. It sold off its consumer products division and received more than $3.3 billion for the assets. It took on additional debt and used the funds from the sale and borrowing to repurchase 38.8 million of its shares to protect the company from further threats of a takeover.

The debt burden had accounted for 80 percent of the company's capitalization by 1986. At the end of 1991, the

[30] Pratima Ungarala, Bhopal Gas Tragedy: An Analysis, Final Paper HU521/Dale Sullivan 5/19/98. See www.hu.mtu.edu/hu_dept/tc@mtu/papers/bhopal.htm.

[31] Ungarala.

[32] Madhya Pradesh Government, Bhopal Gas Tragedy Relief and Rehabilitation Department. See www.mp.nic.in/bgtrrd-mp/facts.htm.

[33] United Nations.

[34] Michael R. Reich, *Toxic Politics: Responding to Chemical Disasters* (Ithaca, New York: Cornell University Press, 1991).

[35] United Nations.

[36] United Nations.

debt levels were still high, 50 percent of capitalization. The company sold its Linde Gas Division for $2.4 billion, "leaving the company at less than half its pre-Bhopal size."[37]

The Bhopal disaster "slowly but steadily sapped the financial strength of Union Carbide and adversely affected" employee morale and productivity. The company's inability to prove its sabotage claim affected its reputation.[38] In 1994, Union Carbide sold its Indian subsidiary, which had operated the Bhopal plant, to an Indian battery manufacturer. It used $90 million from the sale to fund a charitable trust that would build a hospital to treat victims in Bhopal.

Two significant events occurred in 2001. First, the Bhopal Memorial Hospital and Research Centre opened its doors. Second, the Dow Chemical Company purchased Union Carbide for $10.3 billion in stock and debt. Union Carbide became a subsidiary of Dow Chemical.

Questions

1. These questions relate to the Browning Report.
   a. The report indicates that the results of an independent investigation by the consulting firm Arthur D. Little point to sabotage as the cause of the gas leak. Do you think that was possible given the facts of the case? Why or why not?
   b. Because Arthur D. Little was hired for $700,000 by Union Carbide to investigate the incident, do you consider it to be an "independent" investigation? Why or why not?
2. From an ethical perspective, how do you evaluate the attitude and actions taken by Union Carbide in the aftermath of the tragedy in Bhopal?

[37] United Nations.
[38] United Nations.

3. Union Carbide seemed to be primarily concerned with the effects of the disaster on its image, especially in the United States, and the reaction of the media, customers, shareholders, suppliers, and employees. Is there anything "wrong" with this approach in the Bhopal case? Why or why not? Be sure to use ethical reasoning in responding to the question.
4. What degree of responsibility does the government of India bear for Bhopal? Did it act ethically? Was the government justified in taking a hard line with Union Carbide? Why or why not?
5. The document uncovered by the Environmental Working Group Report refers to the acceptable "business risk" in the Bhopal operation due to questions about the technology. Is it ethical for a company to use business risk as a measure of whether to go ahead with an operation that may have safety problems? Why or why not?
6. Compare the decision-making process used by Union Carbide to deal with its disaster and those of Ford Motor Co. and Johnson & Johnson as described in this chapter.
7. Do you think Dow Chemical has an ethical obligation to revisit the issue of the adequacy of the $470 million settlement made with the Indian government in January 1989 in light of knowledge gained since then about the extent of medical problems from the leak of toxic gas? Be specific in responding to this question.
8. How do you assess blame for the tragedy that is Bhopal?

We are citizens of the world. The tragedy of our times is that we do not know this.

Woodrow T. Wilson

Case 3-2

Bubba Tech, Inc. (BTI)

Willie Carson and Waylon Boone are friends who grew up in Dallas, Texas. They both attended the University of Texas at Austin and graduated with degrees in accounting and computer sciences, respectively. They moved back to Dallas after graduation. Carson went to work for the accounting and assurances services firm of Randy Burnham & Co., one of the largest accounting firms in the world. It is considered to be an expert in accounting for companies in the high-tech industry. Boone went to work for Alorotom, Inc., which is one of the largest manufacturers of high-tech products in the world.

Carson and Boone worked for these companies for seven years. During this time, Carson became a certified public accountant, and Boone successfully completed a master's degree program in information systems at Southern Methodist University. In 2001, they decided to strike out on their own, and they formed a manufacturing company, Bubba Tech, Inc. (BTI), in Austin. Boone became the chief executive officer (CEO) and Carson the chief financial officer (CFO). BTI was privately owned by Carson, Boone, and a venture capital firm. The firm had complete confidence in the abilities of Boone and Carson, so there was no board of directors. Moreover, the venture capitalists built a provision into their agreement with Boone and Carson that the two would receive a 10 percent return on their investment for five years and then, after the company went public, they would be repaid the amount of their investment.

Because BTI planned to go public within five years, it hired Randy Burnham & Co. to audit its December 31, 2002, financial statements. Burnham completed its audit for that year and the following four years and rendered unqualified opinions on the audited financial statements. In 2007, Bubba Tech decided to go public. During a meeting with the auditors from Randy Burnham, Waylon Boone asked the partner in charge of the BTI audit, Clint Strait, to prepare a list of operational issues to consider as the company went from being privately held to a publicly held corporation.

Strait called a meeting of the audit engagement team to discuss how to proceed. Shania Hill suggested that as the manager in charge of the audit, she should head the effort to prepare a list for discussion with BTI management. Strait agreed, and he asked Hill whom she wanted on her team. Hill said she would like to have Faith Twain join the team because Faith had been in charge of the consulting services engagement for BTI. Faith agreed to join the team and suggested adding Garth Chesney from the tax department. Garth agreed and suggested that Kenny Brooks also should be on the team because Kenny is responsible for the information technology work related to the audit of BTI. Brooks agreed, and the team was finalized.

Questions

1. Based on the limited facts of this case, prepare a list of the operational issues to present to top management at BTI. Include in your list any corporate governance issues of importance in relation to the management of BTI after it becomes a public company and any issues related to the relationship between BTI and Randy Burnham & Co.

2. Do you think there are any ethical issues that should have been addressed by Carson and Boone before they hired Randy Burnham & Co. as their auditors? Are there any ethical issues that arise because of Carson's relationship with Randy Burnham prior to becoming the CFO of BTI? Be specific and discuss why these issues are ethical issues.

3. A *fiduciary* is a person who occupies a position of trust in relation to someone else so that this person is required to act for the latter's benefit within the scope of that relationship. Discuss what fiduciary relationships exist in BTI and between BTI and its stakeholders. Also address the relationship between BTI and Randy Burnham & Co. Be sure to include an explanation of the specific relationship of trust.

Case 3-3

Hot & Cold Inc.

Hot & Cold Inc. manufactures an extensive variety of temperature-measuring equipment and pressure gauges. The company has been a leader in its field for almost 20 years, and it has never been too concerned with cost control. Whenever its raw material, labor, or overhead costs increased, Hot & Cold simply passed it along to the consumer by raising prices. That strategy had worked quite well until the past two years. During that time, less expensive products made in Mexico put pressure on Hot & Cold to cut costs to reduce prices 20 percent to remain competitive.

Stan Bonner is the chief executive officer (CEO) of Hot & Cold. Jon Smith is the chief financial officer (CFO). Frank Lumin is the chief operating officer (COO). The three top executives are meeting to discuss the cost-cutting measures required to maintain the company's competitive position.

"Listen Frank, we have to cut some workers. That's the only way to reduce costs sufficiently to match the 20 percent price reduction," Smith said.

"I agree with Jon," Bonner added.

"I won't abandon the workers like that," Lumin said. "We have a responsibility to them and their families."

"Where else can we save $800,000?" Smith asked.

"We have been very generous with the stockholders in paying out higher dividends each year. The stockholders now get a 6 percent return on their investment, and they're common stockholders. We could reduce the annual dividends," Lumin responded.

"I'll have my head chopped off if we do that," Bonner said. "Our primary responsibility is to the stockholders, not the employees."

Lumin had a disgusted look on his face. He scratched his forehead, took a deep breath, and then began to lecture both Bonner and Smith.

"The workers are this company. They haven't had a raise in two years. We threatened the union with layoffs and got their agreement to cut the pension and health benefits last year. How much longer do you think they will stand for it before they strike? Do you really want a union fight on your hands?" Lumin asked rhetorically.

Bonner glanced at Smith, expecting him to answer Lumin, but Smith was silent. Bonner got up, poured himself a cup of hot coffee, and began to respond. Looking straight at Lumin, who had a chilling expression on his face, Bonner said, "I'm giving you one week to come up with a proposal to cut $800,000 from operating costs. I don't care how you do it. You can hire cheaper labor if you want. Just get it done."

Questions

1. To which party or parties does management owe its ultimate allegiance? How should it balance that obligation with other responsibilities of managing a company with $4 million in annual sales?

2. What should be the workers' expectations for fair treatment by management? Be specific. Do workers have a right to lifetime employment? Do they have a right to pensions? To health benefits? Are these considerations all part of good governance?

3. Do you think the ultimatum Bonner gave to Lumin was ethical? Why or why not?

4. Assume that Lumin came back with a proposal to save $800,000 through the following operational changes:

   a. Not replacing five workers who are scheduled to retire within the next six months. The savings on salaries and benefits would be $400,000.

   b. Changing raw material suppliers for a savings of $200,000.

   c. Reducing the number of quality control inspectors from three to two. This would produce another $100,000 savings.

   d. Reducing paid vacations for all hourly workers from three weeks to two weeks for another $100,000 savings.

Using ethical reasoning, evaluate each of the proposed cuts. If the proposed cuts went through and enabled Hot & Cold to maintain its competitive position for the next two years, do you think the cuts will have been worth it? That is, what might be the long-term effects of the cuts? Be sure to include union considerations.

Case 3-4

Lupeville Senior Care

Lupeville Senior Care serves adults over 60 years of age by providing in-home nursing care and residential facilities. The center in Lupeville, Indiana, can accommodate up to 50 residents. Lupeville is owned by the Garton Group, which owns 25 facilities in Indiana and Illinois.

The Garton Group was recently investigated for failing to meet required standards in its residential facility in Indiana. The investigators noted the following problems that needed to be addressed:

Work Environment

- Nurses and other personal care staff are sometimes harassed by administrators who put undue pressure on employees to serve more and more patients in less and less time. The average number of patients served by one nurse increased from 10 to 15 between 2004 and 2007.
- Nurses complain that doctors treat them like second-class citizens and don't appreciate the one-on-one attention nurses give to their patients.
- Nurses and other staff sometimes cover for each other when one takes personal time. This is not properly recorded and supervisors are not informed.

Patient Care

- Patients have complained that nurses are curt with them and downplay patient health problems.
- Doctors have complained that nurses leave certain tasks undone such as recording blood pressure and pulse readings on a daily basis.
- Staff members have complained that nurses expect them to do more than is required by their job description. For example, two staff members said that the nurses expected them to fill out reports indicating everything is fine with patient care even though patients consistently complain.

Administrative Oversight

- Doctors have complained that administrators are typically too busy to speak to them when they ask for an appointment to discuss patient care.
- Some doctors have pointed out that they are expected to visit more and more patients each time they visit the facility without any increase in their professional fees.

Abel Bodey is the executive director of Lupeville Senior Care. He has just met with representatives of the doctors, nurses, and staff to decide how to respond to the problems noted in the investigators' report. Lupeville has been given six months to describe how it plans to improve the operations of the facility. If the state accepts the plan, the facility will be removed from the "watch" list, a designation that will certainly negatively influence future demand by seniors for the facility.

Abel asked the head of internal auditing, Helen Hoosier, to sit in on the meeting. Hoosier realized early that one problem was that the facility had no written policies on the behavioral expectations for those who work at Lupeville. She suggested that a starting point would be to develop a written code of ethics. As is often the case, the reward for a good suggestion was for Helen to be assigned the task of developing a draft of the code of ethics.

Helen returned to her office and called in her assistants. They agreed to help develop the code and set a meeting in two weeks to develop the first draft. At that meeting, the following code of ethics was developed.

Code of Ethics
Lupeville Senior Care

Purpose

Lupeville's Code of Ethics guides us in all that we do. It does not replace the more specific policies and practices established by management. Each employee is responsible for reading the Code and complying with its provisions.

Work Environment

We strive to create a supportive work environment. The basis for our working together and with patients is *respect*.

- Respect differences in position and rank in the workplace.
- Respect our patients who have come to us for care and treatment.
- Respect deadlines and meet your obligations to management.
- Conflicts should be resolved by reporting differences to your supervisor who will resolve the conflict in a way that respects all parties.

Patient Care

We strive to provide the best possible care consistent with our resources. The basis for that level of care is *empathy*.

- Empathize with our patients. Often what's required to provide good service is to offer to listen to their "story."
- Be understanding when they act forgetfully or ask naïve questions.
- Smile when you see them and say "hello."

Administrative Oversight

You must complete all required forms on a timely basis and do your own work. If another worker is a slacker, you should inform your supervisor. The basis for your obligations to the administrative staff is to be *responsible.*

- Be responsible about coming to work on time, taking breaks in the morning and afternoon for 10 minutes and a one-hour lunch.
- Listen to the doctors when they tell you something about patient care and ask questions if you are not sure what to do.
- Uphold the confidentiality of patient information. We rely on your discretion.

Questions

1. Describe how the Lupeville case emphasizes the importance of internal auditors' examining operational efficiency and gathering qualitative instead of quantitative data.

2. Evaluate the draft code of ethics from the perspective of the values in Exhibit 1 in the chapter. Do you think the proposed code meets the standards expressed by the values in the exhibit? Why or why not?

3. Select one section of the proposed code and rewrite it in a way that better reflects what you think should be the values of a facility like Lupeville Senior Care.

4. What do you think about the "tone at the top" set by top management of Lupeville Senior Care as evidenced by its operating issues and the draft code of ethics?

5. Comment on the following statement: "Meaningful conflict is a cornerstone in healthy, successful organizations. Adherence to your business ethics depends on it."

Case 3-5

Milton Manufacturing Company

Milton Manufacturing Company produces a variety of textiles for distribution to wholesale manufacturers of clothing products. The company's primary operations are located in Long Island City, New York, with branch factories and warehouses in several surrounding cities. Milton Manufacturing is a closely held company. Irv Milton is the president of the company. He started the business in 1995, and it grew in revenue from $500,000 to $5.0 million in 10 years. However, the revenues declined to $4.5 million in 2006. Net cash flows from all activities also were declining. The company was concerned because it planned to borrow $20 million from the credit markets in the fourth quarter of 2007.

Irv Milton met with Ann Plotkin, the chief accounting officer (CAO), on January 15, 2007, to discuss a proposal by Plotkin to control cash outflows. She was not overly concerned about the recent decline in net cash flows from operating activities because these amounts were expected to increase in 2007 as a result of projected higher levels of revenue and cash collections.

Plotkin knew that if overall capital expenditures continued to increase at the rate of 26 percent per year, Milton

Manufacturing probably would not be able to borrow the $20 million. Therefore, she suggested establishing a new policy to be instituted on a temporary basis. Each plant's capital expenditures for 2007 would be limited to the level of capital expenditures in 2005. Irv Milton pointedly asked Plotkin about the possible negative effects of such a policy, but in the end, he was convinced it was necessary to initiate the policy immediately to stem the tide of increases in capital expenditures. A summary of cash flows appears in Exhibit 1.

Sammie Markowicz is the plant manager at the headquarters location in Long Island City. He was informed of the new capital expenditure policy by Ira Sugofsky, the vice president for operations. Markowicz told Sugofsky that the new policy could negatively affect plant operations because certain machinery and equipment, essential to the production process, had been breaking down more frequently during the past two years. The problem was primarily with the motors. New and better models with more efficient motors had been developed by an overseas supplier. These were expected to be available by April 2007. Markowicz said that he planned

---

EXHIBIT 1
MILTON MANUFACTURING COMPANY
Summary of Cash Flows
For the Years Ended December 31, 2005 and 2006 (000 omitted)

2005	December 31, 2006	December 31, 2005
Cash Flows from Operating Activities		
Net income	$ 372	$ 542
Adjustments to reconcile net income to net cash provided by operating activities	1,350	1,383
Net cash provided by operating activities	$ 1,722	$ 1,925
Cash Flows from Investing Activities		
Capital expenditures	$(2,420)	$(1,918)
Other investing inflows (outflows)	176	84
Net cash used in investing activities	$(2,244)	$(1,834)
Cash Flows from Financing Activities		
Net cash provided (used in) financing activities	$ 168	$ (376)
Increase (decrease) in cash and cash equivalents	**$ (354)**	**$ (285)**
Cash and cash equivalents— beginning of the year	$ 506	$ 791
Cash and cash equivalents— end of the year	$ 152	$ 506

to order 1,000 of these new motors for the Long Island City operation, and he expected that other plant managers would do the same. Sugofsky told Markowicz to delay the acquisition of new motors for one year after which time the restrictive capital expenditure policy would be lifted. Markowicz reluctantly agreed.

Milton Manufacturing operated profitably during the first six months of 2007. Net cash inflows from investing activities exceeded outflows by $250,000 during this time period. It was the first time in three years that there had been a positive cash flow from investing activities. Production operations accelerated during the third quarter as a result of increased demand for Milton's textiles. An aggressive advertising campaign initiated in late 2006 seemed to bear fruit for the company. Unfortunately, the increased level of production put pressure on the machines, and the degree of breakdown was increasing. A big problem was that the motors wore out prematurely.

Markowicz was concerned about the machine breakdowns and increasing delays in meeting customer demands for the shipment of the textile products. He met with the other branch plant managers, who complained bitterly to him about not being able to spend the money to acquire new motors. Markowicz was very sensitive to their needs. He told them that the company's regular supplier had recently announced a 25 percent price increase for the motors. Other suppliers had followed suit and Markowicz saw no choice but to buy the motors from the overseas supplier. That supplier's price was lower, and the quality of the motors would significantly enhance the machines' operating efficiency. However, the company's restrictions on capital expenditures stood in the way of making the purchase.

Markowicz approached Sugofsky and told him about the machine breakdowns and concerns of other plant managers. Sugofsky seemed indifferent. He reminded Markowicz of the capital expenditure restrictions in place and that the Long Island City plant was committed to making expenditures at the same level as it had made in 2005. Markowicz argued that he was faced with an unusual situation and he had to act now. Sugofsky hurriedly left, but not before he said to Markowicz, "A policy is a policy."

Markowicz reflected on the comment and his obligations to Milton Manufacturing. He was conflicted because he viewed his primary responsibility, and that of the other plant managers, as ensuring that the production process operated smoothly. The last thing the workers needed right now was a production stoppage because of machine failure.

At this time, Markowicz learned of a 30-day promotional price offered by the overseas supplier to gain new customers by lowering the price for all motors by 25 percent. Coupled with the 25 percent increase in price by the company's supplier, Markowicz knew he could save the company $1,500, or 50 percent of cost, on each motor purchased from the overseas supplier.

After carefully considering the implications of his intended action, Markowicz contacted the other plant managers and informed them that while they were not obligated to follow his lead because of the capital expenditure policy, he planned to purchase 1,000 motors from the overseas supplier for the headquarters plant in Long Island City.

Markowicz made the purchase in the fourth quarter of 2007 without informing Sugofsky. He convinced the plant accountant to record the $1.5 million expenditure as an operating (not capital) expenditure because he knew the higher level of operating cash inflows would mask the effect of his expenditure. In fact, Markowicz was proud that he had "saved" the company $1.5 million and had done what was necessary to ensure that the Long Island City plant continued to operate.

The acquisitions by Markowicz and the other plant managers enabled the company to keep up with the growing demand for textiles, and the company finished the year with record high levels of net cash inflows from all activities. Markowicz was lauded by his team for his leadership. The company successfully executed a loan agreement with Second Bankers Hours & Trust Co. The $20 million borrowed was received on January 3, 2008.

During the course of an internal audit on January 21, 2008, Beverly Wald, the chief internal auditor, discovered that there was an unusually high level of motors in the inventory. A complete check of inventory determined that $1.0 million of motors remained on hand.

Wald reported her findings to Ann Plotkin and together they went to see Irv Milton. After being informed of the situation, Milton called in Ira Sugofsky. When Wald told him about her findings, Sugofsky's face turned beet red. He paced the floor, poured a glass of water, drank it quickly, and then began his explanation. Sugofsky told them about his encounter with Sammie Markowicz. Sugofsky stated in no uncertain terms that he had told Markowicz not to increase plant expenditures beyond the 2005 level. "I left the meeting believing that he understood the company's policy. I knew nothing about the purchase," he stated.

At this point, Wald joined in and explained to Sugofsky that the $1 million is accounted for as inventory and not an operating cash outflow. "What we do in this case is transfer the motors out of inventory and into the machinery account once they are placed into operation because, according to the documentation, the motors added significant value to the asset." Sugofsky had a perplexed look on his face. Finally, Irv Milton took control of the accounting lesson by asking: "What's the difference? Isn't the main issue that Markowicz didn't follow company policy?" The three officers in the room shook their heads simultaneously, perhaps in gratitude for being saved the additional lecturing. Milton then said he wanted the three of them to brainstorm some alternatives on how best to deal with the Sammie Markowicz situation and present the alternatives to him in one week.

Question

1. Use the 10-step decision-making model explained in the chapter and develop the alternatives to be presented to Milton. Be sure to select the optimum alternative.

Case 3-6

Taking Care of Business

Francine Fried graduated from State University with a degree in accounting five years ago. She was promoted to manager last week by the local CPA firm of Reed & Dent LLP. The firm has two partners, Charlie Cain, the managing partner and Gary Grey.

Francine feels guilty about the promotion because for the past six months, she has been moonlighting at night and weekends, trying to develop her own base of clients that would enable her to leave the firm and strike out on her own. She's one big client away from making her dream come true.

One day Francine was having lunch with Gary Grey when Harry Wall, president of Wall Construction, dropped by to say hello.

"Hey, Harry. Long time no see," Gary said.

"Gary. What's it been—five years?" Harry responded.

"That sounds about right," Gary answered. "Let me introduce you to our newest manager, Francine Fried. Francine is an expert in construction accounting."

"Wow. I just fired my outside auditor," responded Harry. "Could I meet with you, Francine, at a convenient time to see if you'd like to come on board?"

Gary looked shocked. He stared at Harry and said, "I just told you she works for our firm. You know the drill, Harry. We might be able to assign Francine to an engagement with you, but it starts with your formally requesting the firm's help and then we decide whether to pursue the audit opportunity. I'm assuming you aren't looking for competitive bids from other firms?"

"No, no, no. I'm sorry. You misunderstood. " Harry said. "I would never…."

At this point, Gary cuts off Harry and says that he understands. Meanwhile, Francine is wondering whether this might be the opportunity she was looking for to provide enough of a client base to hang out her shingle.

"Listen, Gary," Harry said. "I'm interested in having Reed & Dent serve our needs. You know I'm a small construction company right now, a family-owned business. But we intend to grow and go public one day."

"Sounds great," Gary responds. "How about if I speak to Charlie Cain about coming down to see you and we can go from there?"

"It's a deal," responds Harry.

Questions

1. Do you think it is right for Francine to moonlight on the side while she works full-time for Reed & Dent? Why or why not? Be sure to support your response with ethical reasoning.

2. Does Francine have a conflict of interest? If so, describe it. If not, explain why not.

3. Assume that you are Francine Fried and you decide to contact Harry Wall to follow up on the lunch discussion. What would you do, if anything, about telling Grey of your intended contact with Wall? The firm does not have a noncompete clause in its employment agreement with staff CPAs.

4. Assume that you are Francine and decide not to tell Grey. Consider the possible consequences of your action for the stakeholders.

5. Assume that Francine contacts Wall and tells him she will quit Reed & Dent and will gladly audit Wall's financial statements as an independent contractor. She informs Wall that whatever Reed & Dent quotes as the fee for the audit engagement, she will charge one-third less. Wall hires Francine, and she quits Reed & Dent without any explanation.

   a. What values are illustrated by Francine's decision that cause you concern?

   b. From Charlie Cain's perspective, what would be your reaction if six months after Francine quit, you run into Harry Wall at a social function, and he tells you how happy he is with Francine's audit work. Would you discuss the matter with Wall? Why or why not? Would you contact Francine? Why or why not?

Case 3-7

Telecommunications, Inc.

Telecommunications, Inc. is a U.S. company and a global leader in information technology and it specializes in building data network systems. It pioneered local area network (LAN) and wide area network (WAN) systems. Today's technology for global enterprises demands WAN and metropolitan area network (MAN) systems.

LANs were the rage of the 1980s and 1990s. They cover a relatively small area such as a home, office, or small group of buildings such as a college. WANs span a larger geographical area. Typically, a WAN consists of two or more local area networks. Computers connected to a WAN are often connected through public networks, such as the telephone system. They can also be connected through leased lines or satellites. The largest WAN in existence is the Internet.

A MAN is a relatively new class of network. It serves a role similar to an Internet service provider in providing access to the Internet for others through a connectivity service. The difference is that a MAN serves corporate users with large LANs. A MAN network is typically owned by a consortium of users or by a single network provider that sells the service to the users.

Telecommunications, Inc. is a major player in the industry, although it is no match for companies like Cisco Systems. Recently, however, it has been more successful in securing contracts to build and support data network systems outside the United States. In one recent competitive bidding situation with companies from two other countries, the Latin American country of Bolumbia awarded Telecommunications a multimillion-dollar contract to develop a MAN network for the corporate community. The job went so well that Telecommunications believes it will have a leg up on other companies in bidding for future contracts.

Telecommunications was the prime contractor on that job. It was responsible for selecting subcontractors to perform the work that Telecommunications didn't want to do or for which the company believed it was advantageous to use a local contractor. According to the company's contract with Bolumbia, only Latin American companies could be selected for subcontract work. In a recent competitive bidding selection process, Bolumbia National Communications (BNC), S.A.,[1] was chosen to assist in infrastructure connectivity. BNC wasn't as well established as other companies such as Telefonica, the Spanish multinational company that operates throughout the Spanish- and Portuguese-speaking world, but it had submitted a bid that met all of the job's specifications including some that were unusual requests. Telefonica did not include these items in its subcontractor bid.

Ed Keller is employed as an engineer for Telecommunications, Inc. He recently graduated with a master's degree in

engineering and joined the company six months ago. Keller had a 3.92 grade-point-average and could have worked for a variety of engineering firms. He chose Telecommunications because of the opportunity it afforded to travel around the world and of its reputation for quality service and high moral standards.

During lunch at the office one day, Keller was talking to several of the more senior members of the engineering staff of Telecommunications, who told him about their recent trip to Bolumbia. They visited four cities and a resort in one week, and BNC paid all of their expenses. Keller knew that BNC had just completed its work on the contract for infrastructure connectivity. Out of curiosity, he questioned the engineering staff about the propriety of accepting an all-expense paid trip from a major subcontractor. Keller was told that it was common practice for Latin American companies to make gestures of gratitude, such as free travel and entertainment. One of the senior engineers, Mike Stone, said, "There's nothing wrong with accepting such an offer. After all, the offer of free travel was made after the decision to accept BNC's bid and the completion of the job. We weren't responsible for making the selection decision. All we did was to establish the engineering specifications for the job."

Keller viewed this as an opportunity to learn more about the bidding process, so he approached Sam Jennings, the head of the internal audit department of Telecommunications. Keller grew up with Jennings' son, and Jennings had been a close friend of the Keller family for many years.

Keller asked Jennings to have lunch with him one day. Jennings was curious about the request since they hadn't had lunch during the six months that Keller had worked for Telecommunications. Keller said he had some questions about reporting expenses on trips that he might be assigned in the future. Because it was a work-related request and their families went back a long time, Jennings cleared his calendar and agreed to have lunch with Keller.

During the lunch, Keller raised the issue of whether there was a conflict of interest when a member of the senior engineering staff, such as those who worked on developing specifications for the BNC job, accepted free travel and entertainment from a subcontractor. At first, Jennings was furious because Keller had misled him about the purpose of the lunch, but he gave Keller the benefit of the doubt and proceeded to answer the question.

Jennings told Keller that the relationship between the engineers in question and BNC and whether there was any inappropriate influence one way or the other had been examined because of the company's concern about a possible violation of the Foreign Corrupt Practices Act (FCPA). Jennings went on to explain that the act prohibits U.S. multinationals or their agents from making payments that improperly influence

[1] S.A., Sociedad Anonima, is the designation for a Spanish company.

government officials or their representatives in another country in the normal course of carrying out their responsibilities. Jennings told Keller that no evidence existed that the awarding of the contract was a prepayment for the promise of later free travel and entertainment, as Keller had expected. Moreover, explained Jennings, the decision to accept the BNC bid was made by Richard Kimble, the engineering division manager, and Bob Gerard, the vice president for engineering, and neither of them received any free travel or lodging. The fact was, according to Jennings, that while the rejected bids were lower than BNC's, they were inadequate and did not meet the contract specifications. Only BNC's proposal could do that.

Keller felt better about the situation after discussing it with Jennings. Still, he wondered about the values of a company that condones accepting free travel and entertainment from a subcontractor and of the engineers who should be beyond reproach in carrying out their responsibilities.

Questions

1. Based on the facts of this case, do you think there may have been a "quid pro quo," something given for something gained, in the way in which the contract was awarded to BNC? If so, explain what the "equal exchange or substitution" might have been. If you do not believe there was a tacit agreement between the senior engineers and those who developed the proposal at BNC, support your belief with references to the facts of the case.

2. Assume that the Telecommunications engineers influenced the decision-making process and received free travel and lodging from BNC in return for their actions but only after the job was completed. Is there anything wrong with that?

3. Would your answer to Question 2 be different if the free travel were awarded during the decision-making process by Richard Kimble and Bob Gerard? Why or why not?

4. Do you think that Ed Keller is right to be concerned about the values of Telecommunications and the senior engineers who accepted the offers of free travel and lodging? Why or why not? If you believe that Keller's concerns are warranted, which values should be of concern to him?

5. Do you think that Keller violated ethical standards when he told Jennings the purpose of the meeting was to find out more about how to report expenses related to business travel? Why or why not? If you believe that his actions were improper, briefly describe what was wrong with the way that he approached Sam Jennings.

Case 3-8

The Federal False Claims Act

Introduction

The Federal False Claims Act permits a person with knowledge of fraud against the U.S. government, referred to as the "qui tam plaintiff," to file a lawsuit on behalf of the government against the person or business that committed the fraud (the defendant). The False Claims Act's "qui tam" provision[1] authorizes people to file suit on behalf of the United States against those who falsely claim federal funds. The government then reviews the case and decides whether to take part in the suit. If the action is successful, the qui tam plaintiff is rewarded with a percentage of the recovery.

According to the Department of Justice (DOJ), the federal government obtained more than $1.4 billion in settlements and judgments for fraud committed against the government in fiscal 2004–2005, with health care claims accounting for much of the total. One of the biggest recoveries in the 12 months that ended September 30, 2005, was $327 million from HealthSouth Corp.

The United States is cracking down on health care fraud as state and federal governments attempt to rein in spiraling medical costs. Of the 2004–2005 total, $1.1 billion was recovered through lawsuits by so-called whistle-blowers under the Federal False Claims Act, which were mainly health care related. Of particular note are the $41.9 million settlement with PricewaterhouseCoopers LLP for alleged false claims for travel expenses in contracts with numerous federal agencies and the $30.5 million recovered from Harvard University in connection with a U.S. Agency for International Development agreement to advise Russia in its transition to a market economy.

If the government intervenes in a qui tam action, the person who filed the suit is eligible to receive as much as 25 percent of any judgment. During the 12 months ended September 30, 2005, whistle-blowers were awarded $166 million. The fiscal 2005 total brings total recoveries since 1986, when Congress strengthened the civil False Claims Act, to $15 billion, according to the Justice Department.

Exhibit 1 at the end of this case presents background information about the act, amendments to it, and recent lawsuits that were successful.

[1] The phrase *qui tam* is a shortened version of the Latin term " *qui tam pro domino rege quam pro se ipson in hac parte sequitur*," which means "he who brings the action for the King as well as for himself." Under the act, a person bringing a *qui tam* action is referred to as a "relator," or, in more common parlance, this party is known as the plaintiff filing on behalf of the government.

The Case

Charlie Henneson shook his head in disbelief as he saw his dream to be the administrator of a local medical facility disappearing before his eyes. He couldn't believe it was all happening because one of his best friends, Francis Lundon, had blown the whistle on something that Henneson felt was standard practice in the industry. He knew of three other facilities in the state that did the same thing that Rolliter Medical Center was accused of doing. What's worse, Henneson didn't personally benefit by any of the alleged wrongdoings. Why me, he wondered?

On October 24, 2007, the Rolliter Medical Center agreed to pay an $80 million fine without admitting any wrongdoing in connection with compliance and conflict of interest charges brought by Francis Lundon with the aid of the DOJ. The payments would be stretched over four years with interest at 5 percent accruing after the first year on unpaid amounts. The total payments would consume 60 percent of the medical center's reserves. Rolliter Medical Center officials said the facility would still have enough cash on hand to cover 62 patient days (more than $50 million). However, this is a relatively low amount by customary standards, and some current patients and residents of the small southeastern town of Rolliter are concerned about the long-term viability of the center and the potential effects on the local community. Trustees of the center said that they had agreed to the settlement to avoid a time-consuming, drawn-out, and potentially even more costly legal battle with the federal government.

The primary issue in the case is the allegation that beginning in 1997, Rolliter agreed to pay remuneration to induce physicians to use its facility. Allegedly, Rolliter paid millions of dollars into a Physicians Professional Development Plan and entered into a number of physician service agreements including medical administrator contracts, joint lease agreements with a variety of medical specialists associations, and a travel fund. The government contends that the remuneration was paid directly to physicians affiliated with the medical specialists' associations or funneled to the physicians through third parties.

According to the government's lawsuit, the medical center submitted false claims to Medicare for inpatient and outpatient hospital and home health services referred or ordered by physicians that were included in the professional development plan payments. The settlement that was entered into on October 24, 2007, said that the claims were false because the Stark Law[2] prohibited Rolliter from billing Medicare for items or services referred or ordered by physicians with whom it had such financial relationships.

An attorney for Rolliter responded to questions from the press after the settlement by explaining that the federal government had "gotten some sensitive information" about inner workings of the medical center from a source within the medical center. The fact is that Francis Lundon, a disgruntled physician who had been passed over for chief of surgery, had kept covert records about the Physicians Professional Development Plan using information from files left open by other physicians at the medical center and about conversations that he had overheard. He went to the government with his information, and the DOJ brought a lawsuit against Rolliter Medical Center. The whistle-blower stands to receive $16 million from the settlement.

[2] The Stark statute applies only to physicians who refer Medicare and Medicaid patients for specific services to entities with which they (or an immediate family member) have a "financial relationship." Referrals under the law include any physician request for a service, item, or good payable under Medicare or Medicaid; a referral for consultation and all services ordered as a result of the consultation; and a prescription for a course of treatment. Referrals within a physician group are included. Services included, known as "designated health services," are clinical laboratory services; durable medical equipment and supplies; occupational therapy services; outpatient prescription drugs; home health care; radiation therapy; prosthetics, orthotics, and prosthetic devices; and supplies.

Questions

1. Do you think it was disloyal for Lundon to bring a lawsuit and serve as the government's whistle-blower in this case? Why or why not? To whom does Lundon owe primary responsibility?

2. Do you think it was ethical for Lundon to do what he did? If you answer yes, support your answer with ethical reasoning. If no, be sure to give specific reasons.

3. If you were in Francis Lundon's position, is there something else you might have done that Lundon didn't do? Be specific and include what you would have done differently if you believe that your actions would have taken a different path.

4. Given that the medical center's financial position is threatened by the settlement and that it might affect long-term care at the facility, not to mention the economic well-being of the town, do you think the government should have considered this in going after Rolliter Medical Center? Why or why not?

5. Did the medical center fail in its social responsibilities to the doctors, nurses, and staff at the facility? What about to the patients? To the town of Rolliter?

6. Some critics of the Federal False Claims Act contend that it encourages whistle-blowers to gather evidence, bring a lawsuit against the employer, and get a big pay day in the future. Do you agree with this claim? Is it "wrong" for a person to do such a thing? Why or why not?

Exhibit 1
The Federal False Claims Act

Background of the Act

The Federal False Claims Act (Title 31 of the U.S. Code Sections 3729-3733) was enacted in 1863 during the Civil War to deter fraud by contractors who were supplying the Union Army. The act provided a civil cause of action and sanctions of double damages and penalties of $2,000 per false claim for those found to have defrauded the government.

The 1986 Amendments

Prior to 1986, very few cases were brought under the act in part because a 1943 amendment to it act barred *qui tam* actions if the government had knowledge of the relator's allegations prior to the filing of the suit. A number of suits were dismissed under this provision because the relator was the original source of the allegations in the filing but that person had disclosed the allegations to the government prior to filing the suit. This fact, coupled with widespread media coverage throughout the 1970s and 1980s of rampant government fraud caused Congress, in 1986, to enact revisions to enhance the provisions of both the act and its *qui tam* provision.

The 1986 amendments had substantially strengthened the act and its enforcement. The 1943 bar regarding information in the possession of the government was eliminated and replaced with language that allows such cases to be brought so long as the relator is an "independent source" of the allegations in a complaint. The amendments also clarified the level of intent necessary to establish a violation. With the amendments, it is not necessary that a defendant be proven to have intentionally defrauded (had knowledge of the fraud) the government. Rather, it is sufficient to establish that the defendant acted with "reckless disregard" for the truth of the information in its claim or in "deliberate ignorance" of the information provided, a lesser standard sometimes referred to as "constructive fraud."

The amendments also clarified that the burden of proof to sustain an action brought against the defendant is the same as that in a typical civil action (i.e., the "preponderance of the evidence"), not the higher burden of "clear and convincing evidence," as some courts had ruled. These amendments significantly aided a relator's cause in bringing an action and sustaining a victory under the act.

The 1986 amendments also significantly increased the penalties. From the enactment of the act in 1863 until 1986, the act provided for the recovery of double damages and $2,000 per false claim. The penalties were increased in 1986 to treble (triple) damages and a per claim assessment of between $5,000 and $10,000 to be determined by the court. Under the 1986 amendments, a government contractor submitting 100 false claims and overbilling the government by $100,000 may be liable for as much as $1,300,000.

Of particular note is that prior to 1986, the act provided that a successful *qui tam* relator was entitled to up to 25% of the proceeds to the government in an action prosecuted by the relator. The 1986 amendments changed the relator's percentage to not less than 25% nor more than 30%. **The percentage now stands at between 15% to 25%.** Moreover under the amendments, if a relator is successful, that party is entitled to recover attorneys' fees as well as costs and expenses.

The 1986 amendments also contained a whistle-blower provision that protects an employee from retaliation by his employer in the event the employee becomes involved in the filing or investigation of an action under the act against his employer. In the event an employer retaliates, the act provides for the employee's reinstatement, double the back pay plus interest, and any "special damages."

Recent Settlements

Two cases stand out in recent times above all others as examples of the magnitude of these cases: The Northrop Grumman case and the HCA settlement with the government.

Northrop Grumman

On June 9, 2003, Northrop Grumman agreed to pay $111.2 million to the federal government in an out-of-court settlement to end a whistle-blower lawsuit alleging that TRW Inc., which was acquired by Northrop, padded bills submitted to the government under space and technology contracts.

The *qui tam* lawsuit, which the federal government joined, charged that TRW defrauded the government through deceitful accounting practices from 1990 to 1997, including billing the government for work done on nongovernment contracts.

At the time, Daniel S. Goldin, the former NASA administrator, was general manager of TRW's space and technology group, which was at the center of the fraudulent scheme. The lawsuit said that Goldin approved mischaracterizing at least some of the charges to the government.

As part of the litigation, the whistle-blower, Richard Bagley, and the government won a series of rulings, known as "summary judgments," in which the court essentially said the undisputed evidence showed that TRW had overcharged the government. The collaboration between Bagley's attorneys and the government led to the successful action and settlement of the case. The government agreed to pay Bagley $27.2 million, which was 24.5% of the settlement.

Bagley and the government said TRW defrauded the government in several ways, including:

- Charging to government contracts in 1995 virtually all of the $11 million in costs to develop a proposal to build and operate a satellite-based telephone system Odyssey, a purely commercial project that TRW later abandoned.
- Inflating overhead costs charged to the government to recoup certain nonreimburseable costs to develop its Universal Spacecraft Bus, the part of a spacecraft that delivers satellites into space, a project that also was abandoned.
- Allocating certain research and development costs of its Center for Automotive Technology to unrelated contracts the government had with TRW's Space and Electronics Satellite Systems.

HCA

On June 26, 2003, HCA Inc. (formerly known as Columbia/HCA and HCA — the Healthcare Company) agreed to pay the government $631 million in civil penalties and damages arising from false claims that the government alleged it had submitted to Medicare and other federal health programs. It was the most comprehensive health care fraud investigation ever undertaken by the Justice Department, working with the Departments of Health and Human Services and Defense, the Office of Personnel Management, and the states. The settlement resolves HCA's civil liability for false claims resulting from a variety of allegedly unlawful practices, including cost report fraud and the payment of kickbacks to physicians.

Robert D. McCallum, Jr., assistant attorney general for the Civil Division said, "Health care providers and professionals hold a public trust, and when that trust is violated by fraud and abuse of program funds, and by the payment of kickbacks to the physicians on whom patients and the programs rely for uncompromised medical judgment, health care for all Americans suffers."

Case 3-9

The State of Nirvana

The State of Nirvana was formed as the 51st state of the United States of America in 2007 after California decided to split in two. The northern part of the state became the State of Nirvana and chose San Francisco as its capital city. In what was perceived as a "slap in the face," Sacramento, the former capital of California, seceded from the old California and became part of Nevada. To the south, California retained its status as a state with Los Angeles as its capital. The then governor Arnold Schwarzenegger remained the governor of California while the activist leader Blissful Peace became the governor of the State of Nirvana.

It wasn't long after Blissful Peace took office that scandal emerged in the state legislature. It was reported that a state senator used a private aircraft for personal trips and accepted a payment for a speech to an antiwar group. One state representative was accused of using her office to benefit family members financially and promote business for family members. A second state representative allegedly used favoritism in awarding a contract to provide organically grown fruits and vegetables to all schools in Nirvana as part of its healthy lunch program.

Blissful was not very peaceful when she heard about the charges. She ordered her ethics officer to conduct a full investigation and submit a written a report in in one month. During that month, an investigator for the ethics office discovered the following:

- State Senator Dubious Dan had traveled to the Redwood Forest using a private helicopter provided by Friends of the Earth.
- Dubious Dan received $10,000 for his speech to the group End War 4ever.
- State Representative Connie Conniver solicited funds from the pro-nuclear power group Nukes in Nirvana that were paid to her husband, Harold Helpless, to fund his vegetarian restaurant in the Haight-Ashbury district of San Francisco. In all, $55,000 was paid to Helpless, and some reporters for the *San Francisco Sunshine* alleged that the payment was to influence Conniver's vote to build a nuclear power plant along the Mendocino county coast.
- State Representative Bill Bias in his role as chair of the Food and Nutrition Committee made final recommendations to the entire legislature on contracts for food supply to the schools in Nirvana. Bias reviewed state agency recommendations and either supported them or independently sought alternative proposals on which he based the selection of the primary food contractor. Bias allegedly overturned the Department of Health's recommendation to award the contract to Bristolite Farms to supply fresh

fruit and vegetables to Nirvana schools. Bias awarded the contract to a start-up fresh fruit and vegetable business owned by his sister-in-law.

To assist in writing its report to Governor Blissful Peace, the state's ethics office gathered the following information from the State Ethics Code.

Travel Payments

The term "travel payment" includes payments, advances, or reimbursements for travel, including actual transportation and related lodging and subsistence.

The following types of travel are prohibited:

1. Transportation provided to legislators directly in connection with an event at which a legislator gives a speech, participates in a panel or seminar, or provides similar service.
2. Free admission, refreshments, and similar noncash nominal benefits provided to a legislator during the entire event at which the legislator gives a speech, participates in a panel or seminar, or provides a similar service.
3. Necessary lodging and subsistence, including meals and beverages, provided to a legislator directly in connection with an event at which the legislator gives a speech, participates in a panel or seminar, or provides a similar service. However, in most cases, the exclusion for meals and beverages is limited to those provided on the day of the activity.
4. Reimbursements for travel expenses provided to a legislator by a bona fide nonprofit, tax-exempt entity for which the legislator provides equal or greater consideration.

Honoraria

An "honorarium" is any payment made in consideration for any speech given, article published, or attendance at any public or private conference, convention, meeting, social event, meal, or like gathering.

No state elected official or a candidate for state office may accept honoraria payments.

Gifts

A "gift" is any payment or other benefit provided to a legislator that confers a personal benefit for which the legislator does not provide goods or services of equal or greater value. You have received or accepted a gift when you know that you have actual possession of the gift or when you take any action exercising direction or control over the gift, including discarding the gift or turning it over to another person.

Elected state legislators and heads of a state government agency may not accept gifts from any single source of more than $200 in any calendar year. This includes passes or tickets that provide admission or access to facilities, goods, services or other benefits.

Lobbyists

A "lobbyist" is a person who is paid a salary, fee, or is otherwise compensated for seeking to influence the governmental decision making. The influence may be seeking a gift, honorarium, or payment of expenses related to an honorarium event. The influence of governmental decision making includes the making of, encouragement of, passage of, defeat, or modification of any proposal or recommendation by state legislator or agency head in an official capacity or governmental agency.

A "lobbyist" also means any person who is paid a salary, fee, or was otherwise compensated for seeking and sought to influence governmental decision making within the 12 months preceding the payments. Those payments include a gift, honorarium, or the payment of expenses related to an honorarium event, which were intended to influence the making of, encouragement of, passage of, defeat, or modification of any proposal or recommendation by state legislator or agency head in an official capacity or governmental agency.

One is seeking to influence or seeking to encourage when one has the intent to affect a decision, proposal, or recommendation and takes any action that directly or indirectly furthers or communicates one's intention. A purely informational request made to a state legislator or agency head and not included in any way to directly or indirectly affect a decision, proposal, or recommendation of a legislator or officer or employee of an agency, does not constitute seeking to influence government decision making or seeking to encourage the passage, defeat, or modification of a proposal or recommendation. The following are prohibited in dealing with lobbyists:

1. A legislator or procurement employee is prohibited from soliciting any gift, food, or beverage from a lobbyist who lobbies the individual or from a political action committee, where such gift, food, or beverage is for the personal benefit of the legislator or an employee connected with that person's function, another procurement employee, or any parent, spouse, child, or sibling of the legislator or employee.

2. This prohibition does not apply to gifts solicited from a relative of the legislator or procurement employee, regardless of whether the relative is a lobbyist or the partner, employer, or principal of a lobbyist.

3. A legislator or procurement employee, or any other person on the legislator's or procurement employee's behalf, is prohibited from knowingly accepting, directly or indirectly, a gift from a lobbyist who lobbies the individual or from a political action committee, or directly or indirectly on behalf of the lobbyist or partner, firm, principal or employer of such lobbyist, if the individual knows or reasonably believes the gift has a value in excess of $200.

Nepotism

Nepotism is favoritism shown by elected officials to relatives, especially in hiring, awarding of contracts, or related activities. Those included in prohibited nepotism relationships are any business associate, parent, spouse, child, or sibling of the legislator or employee.

Nepotism must be avoided in the award and administration of procurement actions. In some cases it can be avoided through recusal or similar means. In other cases it may be difficult to mitigate at all, and officials should ensure that the procurement process is not used in a manner that would subject the integrity of elected officials to any question on the basis of nepotism.

Questions

1. Sir Isaac Newton (1643–1727), the famous British mathematician, is best known for his three laws of motion. Newton's third law of motion has been formally stated as: "For every action, there is an equal and opposite reaction." Consider this law in light of ethics standards for government legislators and other officials. What do you interpret it to mean?

2. What is the purpose of the state's ethics restrictions on travel imposed on members of the legislature? Do you think that Dubious Dan violated the state's restrictions on travel? If so, what would you recommend that Dan do to make things right? Why do you suggest that action? If you think Dan did not violate the travel policy, support your answer with ethical reasoning.

3. What is the danger of accepting an honorarium for making a speech, publishing an article, attending a public or private convention, meeting, or social gathering? Be specific and identify the ethical issues surrounding such an activity. Did Dan violate the state's honorarium policy? Why or why not?

4. Why do you think the State of Nirvana has a gift acceptance limitation of $200? Why not $100 or $500 dollars? What is it that the state is trying to protect by having such a monetary limitation on the acceptance of gifts? Would it be better to simply prohibit the acceptance of any gift no matter how much its value? Why or why not? Be specific and incorporate the ethical values discussed in Chapter 1 in answering this question.

5. What is the purpose of the state's ethics restrictions on accepting payments from lobbyists and political action groups? Why do you think the prohibition extends to the

legislator's parent, spouse, child, and sibling? Do you think Connie Conniver violated the state's restrictions on accepting payments from lobbyists? Why or why not? What is the ethical danger of allowing a member of a state legislature or state agency head, in that person's official capacity, to accept payments or other favors from lobbyists?

6. What is the ethical danger of awarding a contract to a family member? Do you think Bill Bias violated the state's nepotism rules? Why or why not? What is the ethical danger of allowing a member of a state legislature or state agency head to award a contract to a family member even if that family member can provide the product or service as well as or better than any other vendor?

Case 3-10

Wi-Fi Security: We Spy for U

In 2006 the start-up company, We Spy for U, located in the Research Triangle Park in North Carolina, developed a Wi-Fi security system that prevents unauthorized users from hacking into a computer laptop as long as the system is activated. The system became an overnight success, but certain accounting issues have caused Wi-Fi not to go forward with more advanced systems. Exhibit 1 at the end of this case presents background information on the evolution of Internet connectivity leading up to Wi-Fi.

Problems with Wi-Fi Access

No doubt we have moved from the information age to the connectivity age. The information is, of course, still out there, and some cities have gone completely wireless. However, wireless access and related security issues have opened an entire new area for ethics, legal boundaries, and responsibilities.

The convenience of going to wireless technology has made life easier for high-tech criminals because it provides near anonymity for them. Each online connection generates an Internet protocol address, a unique set of numbers that can be traced back to a house or business.

That's still the case with Wi-Fi, but if criminals tap into a network, their actions would lead to the owner of that network. Anything a criminal does can be traced back to the owner's address and investigated. By the time authorities show up to investigate, the hacker would probably be long gone.

Some contend that the person who opened up access to the hacker is unlikely even to know, let alone mind, that someone else has used it. If that person does object, the answer is to use the password protection built into the wireless setup.

Security Certifications

We Spy for U created security certifications for Wi-Fi systems. The current generation of security system was developed as an intermediary step toward enhanced security measures. Since 2006, We Spy for U has been working on the next generation of security support for Wi-Fi to stay one step ahead of hackers and the spoofers. However, the company needs additional financing to continue with research and development of new state-of-the-art security systems.

Accounting Issues

We Spy for U has relied on venture capital funding during its start-up years, 2004 through 2006. In 2007, the company exhausted all funds available and started to apply for a loan at a bank in North Carolina. The banks in general were skeptical about why the venture capitalists stopped funding We Spy for U, but one bank was willing to look at the financial statements prepared by management for the years ending on December 31, 2004, 2005, and 2006, and then make a funding decision.

The financials had already been prepared by Bella Lagoosi, the chief accounting officer of We Spy for U. When Lagoosi presented them to Horace Frankenstone, the CEO of We Spy for U, Frankenstone protested. Here's how the conversation went between Lagoosi and Frankenstone.

"Forget it, Bella," Frankenstone said. "If we show $10 million due to the venture capitalists in our short-term payables, the bank won't lend us the money. Our current ratio will be .8:1."

"It is what it is," responded Lagoosi. "I can't change the numbers."

"You can and you will. If you put the payables into the long-term category, then our current ratio will be 1.33:1. That should clinch the loan from First Weirdoo Bank & Trust."

"What if the bank asks for loan documentation and sees that the loan is due on June 30, 2007?" Lagoosi asked.

"Let me worry about the bankers," Frankenstone responded. "I can tap dance around the issue."

Bella Lagoosi considered himself to be an ethical person. He knew what Frankenstone asked him to do was wrong. However, he also knew that it wouldn't be changing the overall liability numbers, there would be no effect on net income, and probably no one would be the wiser. Lagoosi thought to himself, who would get hurt with this one change?

Questions

1. The case starts out by pointing out the new "ethical issues and responsibilities" created by the wireless phenomenon and security matters. Describe those issues using virtue, values, and the ethical reasoning models discussed in previous chapters.

2. Refer to the 10-step ethical decision-making model, analyze the alternatives available to Bella Lagoosi, and discuss which one you would recommend. You do not have to address the operating issues.

Exhibit 1
Background Information

The various forms of Internet connectivity have evolved over a short period of time as follows.

Dial-Up Internet

Once the world standard for Internet network connections, dial up is slowly being replaced with higher speed options. Dial-up uses ordinary telephone lines, but, unlike more sophisticated systems such as DSL, dial-up connections occur over telephone wires, so they prevent simultaneous voice calls.

DSL—Digital Subscriber Line

DSL is one of the most prevalent forms of Internet connection today. DSL provides high-speed networking over ordinary phone lines using digital modems. DSL connection sharing can be easily achieved with either wired or wireless, and the user can still receive incoming phone calls over conventional phone lines.

Cable—Cable Modem Internet

Like DSL, cable modem is a form of broadband Internet connection. Cable uses neighborhood cable television conduits rather than telephone lines, but the same broadband routers that share DSL Internet connections also work with cable.

Satellite Internet

A few enterprises offer satellite Internet service. With an exterior mounted mini-dish and a proprietary digital modem inside the home, Internet connections can be established over a satellite link similar to satellite television services. Satellite Internet can be particularly troublesome to a network. Satellite modems may not work with broadband routers, and some online services and online games may not function over satellite connections.

BPL—Broadband over Power Line

BPL supports Internet connections over residential power lines. The technology behind power line BPL works the same as phone line DSL, employing unused signaling space on the wire to transmit the Internet traffic. However, BPL is a controversial Internet connection method. BPL signals generate significant interference in the vicinity of power lines, affecting other licensed radio transmissions. BPL requires specialized (but not expensive) equipment to join to a home network.

Wireless Broadband Internet

The current rage, wireless fidelity, or Wi-Fi technology, supports high-speed wireless Internet via base stations like cellular networks. So-called Wi-Fi community or "mesh" networks serve a similar function using different technologies. One notable problem with Wi-Fi systems is the possibility that another laptop user might hack into your wireless Internet network. The good news is that wireless mooching is easily preventable by turning on encryption or requiring passwords. The problem, security experts say, is that many people do not take the time or are unsure how to secure their wireless access from intruders.

Chapter

Ethics in Accounting: Ethical Obligations and Decision Making

By certifying the public reports that collectively depict a corporation's financial status, the independent auditor assumes a public responsibility transcending any employment responsibility with the client. The independent public accountant performing this special function owes ultimate allegiance to the corporation's creditors and stockholders, as well as to the investing public. This "public watchdog" function demands that the accountant maintain total independence from the client at all times and requires complete fidelity to the public trust.[1]

Chief Justice Warren Burger

Writing the unanimous opinion of the Supreme Court in United States v. Arthur Young & Co.

This important ruling of the U.S. Supreme Court reminds us that the independent audit provides the foundation for the existence of the accounting profession in the United States. Even though independent audits were common before the passage of the landmark legislation of the Securities Act of 1933 and the Securities Exchange Act of 1934, there is no doubt that CPAs derive their franchise as a profession to perform independent audits from these two pieces of legislation.

The Burger Court opinion emphasizes the trust placed by the public in the independent auditor's opinion. The basis for that trust is the strong set of ethical standards that distinguishes the accounting profession as the only one that places the public interest ahead of the interests of one's employer, client, and self-interests.

The medical profession recognizes the primacy of the physician's responsibility to a patient. The legal profession emphasizes the lawyer's responsibility to the client. The Public Interest Principle in the Code of Professional Conduct of the American Institute of CPAs (AICPA Code) states, "In discharging their professional responsibilities, members (of the AICPA) may encounter conflicting pressures from each of these groups [clients, employers…]. In resolving those conflicts, members should act with integrity, guided by the precept that when members fulfill their responsibility to the public, clients' and employers' interests are best served."[2]

Background of the Code of Professional Conduct of the AICPA

The AICPA Code is generally recognized as a model for the accounting profession. However, only members of this voluntary professional organization are subject to its ethics rules. About 350,000 CPAs in the United States belong to the AICPA. Each of the 50 states as well as Washington, D.C., Puerto Rico, the Virgin Islands, and Guam have independent professional societies for CPAs. The state CPA societies also have codes of conduct for their membership that often mirror the AICPA Code.

CPAs are granted a license to practice in a given state by that state's board of accountancy. This board carries out the intent of the state legislature stated in its statutes, and the board promulgates its own rules of professional conduct. It is important to remember that the state board of accountancy grants the right to practice accounting in a given state, establishes standards of professional conduct including ethics rules, investigates allegations that a CPA violated the rules, and issues sanctions against CPAs that can include a suspension or revocation of one's license to practice.

Rules of professional conduct, whether issued by the AICPA or a state board of accountancy, apply to all CPAs in performing professional services including those in public accounting, private industry, government, and education. The rules apply to a variety of professional services including accounting, auditing and other assurance services, taxation, financial advisory services, and consulting services.

Ethical Foundations of Accounting

A textbook on ethical obligations and decision making in accounting must, of necessity, emphasize the AICPA Code because it is impractical to discuss the rules of all 50 states and four jurisdictions. However, we emphasize that differences can exist between the AICPA rules and state board requirements. CPAs who are licensed by a state board must be familiar with those rules and remember to emphasize state board rules in providing services if conflicts exist with the AICPA rules.

From time to time we will refer to the rules of conduct in Texas. The Public Accountancy Act directs the Texas State Board of Public Accountancy to promulgate rules of professional conduct for licensed CPAs "in order to establish and maintain high standards of competence and integrity in the practice of public accountancy and to insure that the conduct and competitive practices of licensees serve the purposes of the Act and the best interest of the public."[3]

One reason for using Texas as an example is the forward-looking ethics education requirement passed by that state's board of accountancy that took effect on July 1, 2005. To qualify to take the CPA Exam in Texas, individuals who hold a baccalaureate degree from a recognized educational institution must demonstrate, as part of the educational requirements, that they have passed a three-semester-hour course in ethics that includes "ethical reasoning, integrity, objectivity, independence and other core values."[4] You should note that even if they are educated in another state, to be eligible to take the Exam in Texas, that state's ethics requirement must be meet.

Link to the Philosophy of Ethics

In previous chapters, we have emphasized the need to be ethical both in one's personal as well as professional life. Remember that ethical behavior is not like a faucet that you can just turn on or off. It requires a deep commitment to do the right thing in all situations.

The noted philosopher Kurt Baier argues that one's practical reasoning should consider both individual and social considerations in deciding "what is the best thing to do" in particular circumstances. He contends that we are moral because it is rational to be so even when our private interests are outweighed by the welfare of others. Baier refers to this belief as "The Moral Point of View."[5] The discussion of the ethical standards for CPAs in Chapter 1 clearly links expected CPA behavior to the moral point of view in placing the public interest ahead of one's own self-interest.

Kohlberg's six stages of moral reasoning that were discussed in Chapter 2 incorporate a social perspective in each stage of reasoning. In the sixth stage that is guided by universal ethical principles, the reason for doing right is that, as a rational person, one takes the perspective of a moral point of view from which social arrangements derive or on which they are grounded.

It is important to emphasize that the moral point of view is aided by having moral motivation and moral character as noted in Chapter 2. In other words, one must have the desire to do the right thing in addition to acting on rational thought informed by the moral point of view.

Ethical reasoning and judgment are critical to ethical decision making. These are skills that can be learned through the application of philosophical reasoning methods in resolving ethical dilemmas. CPAs are required to utilize these techniques when the accounting rules are unclear, when there is a difference of opinion with an employer or client, and when there are conflicts between the interests of stakeholder groups. The Integrity Principle best illustrates the ethical requirements of CPAs that are embodied in the AICPA Code of Professional Conduct.

"Integrity" is measured in terms of what is right and just. In the absence of specific rules, standards, or guidance, or in the face of conflicting opinions,

> a [CPA] should test decisions and deeds by asking: "Am I doing what a person of integrity would do? Have I retained my integrity?" Integrity requires a [CPA] to observe both the form and the spirit of technical and ethical standards; circumvention of those standards constitutes subordination of judgment.[6]

Auditing and Ethics Standards

The cornerstone of the ethical obligation of CPAs to society is to render an opinion on the financial statements of an entity. An opinion is rendered after auditing or examining the financial statements of that entity. The opinion provides "reasonable assurance" that the financial statements are free of material misstatement including fraud. The nature and scope of audits and audit opinions will be discussed more fully in Chapter 5. However, a brief overview of audit and other attest-related (opinion-related) responsibilities is in order before we discuss the ethical obligations of CPAs when performing these and other professional services.

All publicly owned companies that sell stock on an established exchange such as the New York Stock Exchange and NASDAQ are required by the SEC to have their financial statements audited annually, and their quarterly reports must be reviewed by CPAs. A *review* is a less involved examination of financial statements than an audit because the auditor doing the review provides only limited assurance as compared to the reasonable assurance provided by an audit. We explore the concept of reasonable assurance in more depth in the next chapter.

Independence, Integrity, and Objectivity

A CPA also could compile financial statements based on data provided by the client. Because a compilation entails putting together the statements from accounting data, both internal and external, accountants can perform this service. Unlike the audit and review service that cannot be performed by an external CPA unless that person is independent of the client, a compilation can be performed when independence is lacking as long as that fact is disclosed. The reason for not requiring independence with a compilation is that the CPA does not provide an opinion with the compiled statements.

Auditors do not prepare the financial statements for an entity under audit because it would be a conflict of interests that impairs independence and violates the profession's ethical standards. The client's management prepares the financial statements. Typically, this means that the accounting department prepares the statements with the controller's oversight. In most publicly owned companies, the controller reports to the CFO.

Recall that the Integrity Principle links to moral behavior by emphasizing the rights of the stakeholders in decision making. A CPA cannot maintain integrity without judging situations with objectivity. Consider, for example, that a sole practitioner-CPA borrowed a significant amount of money from a friend who happened to be the CEO of a client entity under audit. This CPA lacks objectivity because of the possible influence of that relationship over the CPA's ability to be independent in decision making. In other words, will the CPA be able to withstand client pressure when there is a difference of opinion with top management over how to properly account for or report a financial transaction?

An auditor must be independent *in fact,* that is, actually be objective, and avoid actions that may *appear* to affect independence. Because it is difficult for the public to know whether a CPA has acted independently in providing professional services, the CPA must avoid creating the perception that independence could be impaired as would exist when a CPA borrows money from a client or members of top management.

Armadillo Foods, Inc.: An Example of Integrity and Objectivity

Let's assume that you are the controller (and a CPA) of Armadillo Foods, Inc., a large southwestern processor of armadillo-based food products. One day the CFO comes to you and says the earnings results for the quarter ending June 30, 2007, are 20 percent below financial analysts' estimates. As a public company, you know the stock price is likely to decline, perhaps significantly, after public disclosure of the earnings reduction for the second straight quarter in 2007. The CFO tells you that the CEO insists the company must "make the numbers" this quarter. You are told to find a way to make it happen. What would you do? Why?

This is a hypothetical situation but one that occurred all too often during the accounting scandals of the 1990s and 2000s. The pressure that is applied by the CFO and CEO on the controller tests that person's commitment to act ethically. A controller who gives in to the pressure when the financial statements are not prepared in accordance with GAAP violates the Integrity Principle because the controller has subordinated professional judgment to the (biased) judgment of superiors.

Due Care in the Performance of Professional Responsibilities

Whereas independence, integrity, and objectivity relate to the virtues of the individual CPA who performs professional services, the Principle of Due Care addresses the quality of services performed by the CPA. In a study of enforcement actions against CPAs between 1987 and 1997, Beasley, Carcello, and Hermanson point out that in 80 percent of the cases, the CPA failed to gather sufficient audit evidence. In 71 percent of the cases, the CPA failed to exercise due professional care. Other violations also relate to the absence of proper care in performing professional services including failing to appropriately apply GAAP (49 percent).[7]

A study by John Raspante, a manager with a large insurance firm that deals with professional liability claims against CPAs, reported that the three most common complaints made against small- to mid-size CPA firms involve (1) failure to return client records on a timely basis, (2) failure to exercise due professional care, and (3) conflicts of interest.[8]

AICPA Ethics Rules and Interpretations

The rules of conduct are the enforceable provisions of the AICPA Code. Interpretations of the rules provide guidance on the applicability of the rules in specific situations. The rules and interpretations apply to CPAs in public practice, private industry, government, and education.

The *practice of public accounting* is defined as the performance of specific services for a client while "holding out" as a CPA. *Holding out* generally occurs by informing the public that a person is a CPA. The services include accounting, auditing, tax, personal financial planning, litigation support, and those services for which standards are established by authoritative organizations. The latter include, for example, Statements of Financial Accounting Standards, Statements on Auditing Standards, Statements on Standards for Tax Services, Statements on Standards for Accounting (Compilation) and Review Services, Statements on Standards for Consulting Services, Statements of Governmental Standards, and Statements on Standards for Attestation Engagements.[9]

You are likely to be most familiar with financial accounting standards established by the FASB and auditing standards established by the AICPA. We remind you that the Public Company Accounting Oversight Board (PCAOB) now establishes auditing standards for public companies while the AICPA continues to establish auditing standards for privately held companies. Subsequent to its formation under the Sarbanes-Oxley Act, the PCAOB adopted AICPA auditing standards as its interim standards.

The rules and interpretations are divided into four sections for purposes of our discussion: (1) independence, integrity, and objectivity, (2) professional standards and quality of work, (3) responsibilities to clients, and (4) other responsibilities and practices. While we discuss all four sections, we emphasize independence, integrity, and objectivity because they represent the core values of the profession and are directly related to the virtues that enable a CPA to act ethically and in accordance with all of the standards in the AICPA Code.

Conceptual Framework for AICPA Independence Standards

To meet the independence standard, the CPA should avoid certain relationships that could impair his or her ability to be independent. Generally, these fall into three categories: (1) financial relationships, (2) business relationships, and (3) family relationships.

Given the breadth and complexity of independence standards, we emphasize situations that could create an unacceptable risk to the CPA's independence. The AICPA uses this risk-based approach in its conceptual framework for analyzing threats to independence.

Independence in fact is defined as the state of mind that permits the performance of an attest service without being affected by influences that compromise professional judgment, thereby allowing an individual to act with integrity and professional skepticism. To *appear to be independent,* the CPA should avoid circumstances that would cause an informed third party to reasonably conclude that the integrity, objectivity, or professional skepticism of a firm or member of the audit (attest) engagement team had been compromised.

Threats to independence are situations that arise in the context of the relationships that could impair independence without the necessary countervailing steps to prevent a loss of independence.[10] For example, an intimidation threat exists when the client attempts to influence the CPA's judgment on a GAAP matter by threatening to change auditors if the CPA does not go along with the client's demands. Other threats are discussed below.

Financial Relationships That Impair Independence

Under Rule 101 of the AICPA Code, independence is required when performing audit and other attest-related services. To avoid violating the independence standard, a CPA should not own a direct financial interest in the client. This would create a financial self-interest threat. The ownership of even one share of stock precludes independence. The CPA also should not own a material indirect financial interest in a client such as through ownership of a mutual fund that includes the client entity's stock. The problem with owning direct and material indirect financial interests is that these arrangements could create the impression in the mind of an outside observer that the CPA cannot make decisions without being influenced by the stock ownership. The logical conclusion is that the auditor's opinion would be tainted by the existence of either of these relationships.

Another example of a financial self-interest threat is when a CPA becomes involved in a loan transaction to or from a client including home mortgage loans from financial institution clients. This type of loan is prohibited under Interpretation 101-5. Permitted loans include automobile loans collateralized by the automobile, loans fully collateralized by cash deposits at the same financial institution (e.g., "passbook loans"), and aggregate credit card balances from credit cards and overdraft reserve accounts that are reduced to $10,000 or less on a current basis taking into consideration the payment due and any available grace period.[11]

Perhaps no other situation illustrates the danger of a CPA accepting loans from a client than that of Jose Gomez, the lead partner of Alexander Grant (now Grant Thornton) during its audit of ESM Government Securities from 1977–1984. Over the eight-year period, ESM committed fraud and in the process used its leverage against Gomez from $200,000 in loans to gain his silence even though Gomez knew ESM's financial statements did not present fairly its financial position and the results of operations. Top management of ESM also threatened to pull the audit from Gomez's firm if he spoke out about the fraud. Gomez compromised his integrity, and the event ruined his reputation. Ultimately, Gomez was sentenced to a 12-year prison term and served 4 and one-half years, and Gomez's firm, Alexandar Grant, made approximately $175 million in civil payments.[12]

Family Relationships That Impair Independence

AICPA Interpretation 101-1 extends the independence rule to certain family members of the CPA. The detailed provisions of this Interpretation are beyond the scope of this book, but we do want to emphasize two points to provide examples of familiarity threats to independence. First, when a CPA is part of the attest engagement team that includes employees and contractors directly involved in an audit and those who perform concurring and second partner reviews, the rules extend to that CPA's immediate family members and close relatives. The former include the CPA's spouse, spousal equivalent, and dependents (whether or not related). These family members come under the Independence rules.

Second, the CPA's close relatives, including a parent, sibling, or nondependent child, come under the Independence rule if they hold a key position with the client, that is, one that involves direct participation in the preparation of the financial statements or a position that gives the CPA the ability to exercise influence over the contents of the financial statements. Close relatives also are subject to the Independence rule if they own a financial interest in the client that is material to that person's net worth and of which the CPA has knowledge, or if they own a financial interest in the client that enables the close relative to exercise significant influence over the client.[13] Of course, the potential danger in these family relationships is that the family member's financial or employment relationship with the client could influence the perception that the CPA can be independent in fact or appearance.

Other relationships will bring a CPA under scrutiny under the Independence rules including when a partner or manager provides 10 hours or more of nonattest services to the attest client. The problem here is that it could appear to an outside observer that the partner or manager could influence the attest work because of the significant number of hours devoted to the nonattest services.

Let's stop at this point and consider the Independence rule as a challenging standard for the CPA and family members, one that could present some interesting dilemmas. For example, assume that a CPA knows that his or her father owns a financial interest in a client entity but does not know if that interest is material to the father's net worth. Should the CPA contact the father to find out? Or could the CPA reason that it is better not to know because the Independence rule applies only if the CPA has knowledge of the extent of the father's financial interest in the client? From an ethical perspective, the CPA should make a good faith effort to determine the extent of the father's financial interest in the client entity.

Business Relationships That Impair Independence

Providing Nonattest Services to an Attest Client The issue of when a CPA is permitted to provide nonattest services to an attest client has been examined for many years because certain nonattest services could create the impression of potential bias due to a conflict of interests. For example, a CPA should not perform management functions or make management decisions for the attest client. That presents a management participation threat and places the CPA in the compromising position of making decisions for the client and then auditing those decisions. On the other hand, the CPA may provide advice and recommendations to assist the client's management in performing its functions and making decisions.

Interpretation 101-3[14] establishes requirements that must be met during the period covered by the financial statements and the period of the attest engagement by the CPA to conduct nonattest services for the client without impairing audit independence. The client must agree to perform the following functions in connection with the nonattest engagement: (1) Make all management decisions and perform all management functions, (2) designate an individual who possesses suitable skill, knowledge, and/or experience to oversee the services, (3) evaluate the adequacy and results of the services performed, (4) accept responsibility for the results of the services, and (5) establish and maintain internal controls, including monitoring ongoing activities.

Sarbanes-Oxley Prohibitions

HR 3763—The Sarbanes-Oxley Act of 2002 (SOX)—prohibits CPAs and CPA firms from providing certain nonattest services for public company attest clients. The potential for a conflict of interest exists because of a self-review threat to independence that occurs when a CPA reviews, as part of an attest engagement, evidence that results from the CPA's own (nonattest) or the attest firm's work.[15]

As will be discussed later, the accounting profession successfully fought off past challenges to restrict nonattest services for attest clients. However, the Enron scandal changed the dynamics. Arthur Andersen's revenue from Enron in its last year was $25 million in audit fees and $27 million in nonaudit fees. The firm had performed significant internal audit work for Enron, creating a self-review threat. Because the firm seemed to have adopted a hands-off approach on certain accounting issues, the impression is that the firm had lost its audit independence. Perhaps the close relationship between Andersen professionals and Enron employees was attributable to the internal audit services, and that relationship may have affected Andersen's ability to approach the audit issues with the independence and objectivity of mind that underlie professional skepticism as will be discussed in the next chapter.

Section 201 of SOX provides that the following nonattest services may *not* be performed for attest clients in addition to bookkeeping or other services related to the accounting records or financial statements of the audit client;[16]

1. Financial information systems design and implementation.
2. Appraisal or valuation services, fairness opinions, or contribution-in-kind reports.
3. Actuarial services.

4. Internal audit outsourcing services.

5. Management functions or human resources.

6. Broker or dealer, investment adviser, or investment banking services.

7. Legal services and expert services unrelated to the audit.

8. Any other service that the board of directors determines, by regulation, is impermissible.

SOX also requires that tax services provided for the audit client should be preapproved by the audit committee. Tax services are not restricted under SOX, but an audit committee may decide not to permit the audit firm to do taxes to help gain the public trust. As will be mentioned later, the PCAOB does restrict certain kinds of tax services and fee payment arrangements.

The PeopleSoft Case

On April 16, 2004, the SEC sanctioned Ernst & Young LLP because it was not independent in fact or appearance when it audited the financial statements of PeopleSoft for fiscal years 1994–1999. The SEC's sanctions included a six-month suspension from accepting new SEC audit clients, disgorgement of audit fees (which were more than $1.6 million), an injunction against future violations, and an independent consultant report on its independence and internal quality controls.

The SEC found independence violations arising from Ernst & Young's business relationships with PeopleSoft while auditing the company's financial statements. These relationships created a mutuality of interests between the firm and PeopleSoft, creating a financial self-interest threat.

The SEC action against Ernst & Young (EY)[17] indicates that the firm violated independence standards in its business dealings with the audit client as a result of the relationship that developed between the two entities relating to a system developed by EY for PeopleSoft. EY's Tax Group developed an in-house software program to assist clients with the tax consequences of managing employees with international assignments. The EY global expatriate management system (EY/GEMS) was enhanced with the use of PeopleTools, a software product created by EY's audit client, PeopleSoft. A business relationship was created whereby a license to use PeopleTools was granted to EY in return for a payment to PeopleSoft of 15 percent of each licensee fee it received from outside customers purchasing the new software, 30 percent of each license renewal fee, and a minimum royalty of $300,000, payable in 12 quarterly payments of $25,000 each.

The SEC found that EY and PeopleSoft had a "symbiotic relationship" engaging in joint sales and marketing efforts, sharing considerable proprietary and confidential business information, and EY had partnered with PeopleSoft to accomplish increased sales and boost consulting revenues for EY. The findings of the SEC indicate that EY and PeopleSoft entered into a direct business relationship and shared a mutual interest in the success of EY/GEMS for PeopleSoft and acted together to promote the product so that a reasonable investor with knowledge of all of the facts would conclude that EY was closely identified in fact and appearance with its audit client.

Investigations of the Profession

Concerns about whether nonaudit services impair auditor independence have existed in the accounting profession for many years. Congress has investigated the profession three times during the past 30 years including after the Enron and WorldCom scandals. To the profession's credit, it has organized its own self-review groups as well and has adopted several important recommendations on internal controls.

Metcalf Committee and Cohen Commission, 1977–1978

As CPA firms have become global entities, the profession's concern about ethics and regulation has increased. In 1977, a major study examined the relationship between auditors and clients and the provision of nonaudit services for those clients. The Metcalf (Moss) Report was the first real investigation of the accounting profession since the 1930s. An investigation was conducted between 1975 and 1977 by Senator Lee Metcalf and Representative John Moss.[18] The Metcalf Report issued four recommendations, two of which are described here. The report did not lead to any new legislation at the time, but since then, all four recommendations have been adopted in one form or another.

The first recommendation of the Metcalf Committee was to establish a self-regulatory organization of firms that audit publicly owned companies. It led to the AICPA's formation of a two-tier voluntary peer review program in 1977, one for firms with public company clients and one for smaller firms with only private company clients. In 2004, the PCAOB assumed the AICPA's responsibilities relating to firms that audit public clients, ending the period of self-regulation by the profession, at least for public companies. PCAOB instituted a mandatory quality inspection program for CPA firms that audit public companies. The AICPA assists private companies in meeting state licensing and AICPA membership requirements.[19]

The second recommendation of the Metcalf Committee was to limit types of management services to those relating directly to accounting. The accounting profession was upset at the implication that somehow the provision of management consulting services tainted the audit. It was left to the Cohen Commission to conduct an in-depth study of the issue. In the meantime, the SEC followed up the concern with a requirement that public companies should disclose in their annual reports the aggregate fees they paid to their accountants for nonaudit services.[20]

The profession's own Cohen Commission Report on auditors' responsibilities examined a variety of issues that are still debated today, including the auditor's responsibility for detecting fraud and the expectation gap that exists between the profession's goals for the audit and what the public expects an audit to accomplish.[21] Beyond that, the Cohen Commission recommended that management should report on its internal controls to the users of the financial statements and that the auditor should evaluate management's report. This recommendation was ultimately enacted into legislation as part of SOX.

The events that eventually led to change were two rounds of major scandals, one in the 1980s including the failures of savings and loan institutions and the second in the late 1990s and early 2000s led by Enron and WorldCom. After Enron and WorldCom, the profession agreed to go along with the change in the form of the provisions passed by SOX and the creation of the new public oversight board, the PCAOB.

The Cohen Commission headed by Manny Cohen, a former SEC commissioner, was important for two reasons. First, its final report included an instance that demonstrates the potential conflict when a CPA provides nonattest service(s) for an audit client. The Cohen Commission discovered that the audit of Westec Corporation had been compromised because of a consulting project. Second, it decried the lowballing of audit fees that raised the possibility of a decline in audit quality.[22] The latter concern in addition to "opinion shopping" has contributed over the years to a shift in the environment of professionalism that has existed in the accounting profession to one emphasizing the commercialization of accounting services.

The practice of *lowballing* consists of deliberately underbidding for an audit engagement to obtain the audit client with the hope of securing more lucrative management advisory or other consulting services from that client in the future. *Opinion shopping* occurs when a client seeks the views of various accountants until it finds one that will go along with the client's desired—not necessarily most ethical—accounting treatment. This practice can lead to pressure being applied on the auditor to remain silent or lose the account, an intimidation threat to independence.

The House Subcommittee on Oversight and Investigations

Representative Ron Wyden had introduced a bill in May 1986 to hold the accounting profession responsible for the detection of fraud in light of the failure at ESM Government Securities and bank failures in the early 1980s at Continental Illinois National Bank and Trust and Penn Square Bank.[23] The former received a $4.5 billion federal bailout and dismissed its then Big Eight CPA firm-auditor Ernst & Whinney, and the latter was liquidated by the Federal Deposit Insurance Corporation (FDIC) just four months after receiving an unqualified opinion on its audit by Peat Marwick. The cry in Congress heard during the investigation was "Where were the auditors?"

Wyden eventually changed his proposed legislation because of criticisms by the AICPA and SEC, the latter under then Chairman John Shad who believed the system was "working well" to protect the public from major financial fraud. The new legislation called once again for internal control reports and emphasized the need for auditors to detect material illegalities or irregularities.

Representative John Dingell was chair of both the House Committee on Energy and Commerce and its Subcommittee on Oversight and Investigations. In January and February 1988, the Subcommittee held two hearings concerning the failure of ZZZZ Best Co., a corporation that had "created" 80 percent or more of its total revenue in the form of fictitious revenue from the restoration of carpets, drapes, and other items in office buildings after fires and floods. Chairman Dingell characterized the fraud as follows:[24]

> The fact that auditors and attorneys repeatedly visited make-believe job sites and came away satisfied does not speak well for the present regulatory system. The fact that the audit firm discovering the fraud resigned the engagement without telling enforcement authorities is even more disturbing. . . .Cases such as ZZZZ Best demonstrate vividly that we cannot afford to tolerate a system that fails to meet the public's legitimate expectations in this regard.

Savings and Loan Industry Failures

By the late 1980s, the savings and loan (S&L) industry failures became the focus of Congressional hearings as a $300 million failure at Beverly Hills Savings & Loan and a $250 million failure at Sunrise Savings, a Florida S&L institution, engulfed Deloitte & Touche. In addition, Arthur Young, the firm that was to merge with Ernst & Whinney, had run into deep trouble in its S&L audits. In particular, it certified the financial statements of Western Savings Association in 1984 and 1985 that were overstated by $400 million. If Arthur Young had not merged with Ernst & Whinney, the firm may have been forced out of business. Eventually, Arthur Young paid the federal government $400 million to settle claims that the company's auditors had failed to warn of disastrous financial problems that caused some of the nation's biggest thrift failures.

Perhaps the most publicized failure was that of Lincoln Savings & Loan. Thousands of California retirees lost their life savings after buying uninsured subordinated debentures issued by Lincoln's parent company, American Continental, and sold through Lincoln branches. Arthur Young, the auditors of American Continental, issued unqualified opinions on the entity's financial statements for fiscal years 1986 and 1987. The audit opinions were part of the annual reports of American Continental that were furnished to prospective buyers of the worthless debentures.

The cost to the public to clean up 1,043 failed thrift institutions with total assets of more than $500 billion during the 1986–1995 period was reported to be $152.9 billion including $123.8 billion of U.S. taxpayer losses. The balance was absorbed by the thrift industry itself. It was the greatest collapse of U.S. financial institutions since the Great Depression.[25]

The accounting issues in failed S&Ls centered on three issues: (1) the failure to provide adequate allowances for loan losses, (2) the failure to disclose dubious deals between the S&Ls and some of their major customers, and (3) the existence of inadequate internal controls to prevent these occurrences.[26] The profession was already considering ways to address the large number of business failures in the 1980s when the savings and loan debacle occurred. The profession's response to deal with this new pressure was to form the Tread way Commission, and its work was given a new sense of urgency.

Internal Accounting Environment

Treadway Commission Report

The National Commission on Fraudulent Financial Reporting, referred to as The Treadway Commission after its chairman, James C. Treadway, was formed in 1985 to study and report on the factors that can lead to fraudulent financial reporting. This independent private sector initiative was sponsored by five professional associations called the Committee of Sponsoring Organizations (COSO). The work of the Treadway Commission and COSO since 1985 has been extremely valuable to those who study how to enhance the ethics of an organization and strengthen its internal control environment. The Treadway Commission and COSO have emphasized the need to change the corporate culture and establish the systems necessary to prevent fraudulent financial reporting. It starts with the "tone at the top"; that is, top management should set an ethical tone that filters throughout the organization and influences everything and everyone.

While Metcalf-Moss and Dingell and Wyden focused mainly on the role of the external auditor including independence matters, Treadway and COSO extended its review to include the role and responsibilities of internal accountants and auditors and the board of directors in preventing and detecting fraud. Exhibit 4.1 presents the framework for financial reporting that supports a strong control environment.[27]

AICPA Rules on Integrity and Objectivity

An important part of a strong control environment is for the internal auditors to have direct and unrestricted access to the audit committee of the board of directors. If top management

EXHIBIT 4.1
Internal Control Environment: "Corporate Culture"

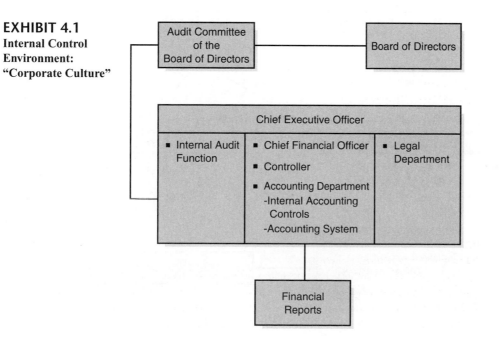

(i.e., the CEO and CFO) attempts to manipulate earnings or use company assets for inappropriate reasons, the internal auditors supported by strong internal controls should detect and report the wrongdoing to the audit committee. The audit committee's responsibility is to do whatever is necessary to reverse top management's action.

The controller and other financial officials have a critical role to play in preventing fraud. If the controller is a CPA, the ethical requirements of Integrity and Objectivity in the AICPA Code (Rule 102) provide that the controller should not knowingly misrepresent facts or subordinate judgment to others.

Returning to the Armadillo Foods example, you can see that the controller has an ethical dilemma. The controller has been told by the CFO to manipulate earnings amounts to meet financial analysts' projections. The question is what the controller should do. Ethics Interpretation 102-4 provides guidance for the controller.[28] Exhibit 4.2 illustrates the steps that should be taken to avoid subordinating judgment to the CFO and CEO in violation of the rules of conduct.

Notice that the process is clearly defined for the controller who should bring any concerns to higher ups in the organization including the audit committee and prepare an informative memorandum that would summarize the various positions including that of members of top management. The memo should help to provide a defense of due care and compliance with ethical standards in case it becomes a regulatory or legal matter.

If all parties refuse to support the controller, the question is whether to inform the external auditors who, after all, rely on the objectivity and integrity of the controller in performing external audit services. The relationship of trust that exists between the controller and the external auditors can be compromised if the controller is silent.

EXHIBIT 4.2
Ethical Responsibilities of Industry CPAs to Avoid Subordinating Judgment[a]

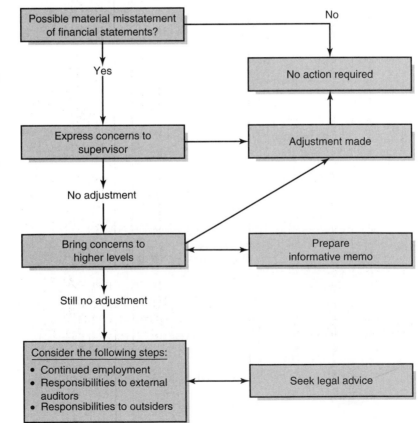

[a]Depiction of the requirements of Interpretation 102-4 developed by Steven Mintz.

Beyond informing the external auditors, the controller has no responsibility to bring accounting matters of concern to outsiders, and to do so violates confidentiality. As for considering the controller's continued employment with the company, that could be a moot issue at this time because the controller could have been fired. In all seriousness, the situation portrayed is a difficult one for the controller. However, it is important to emphasize that studies such as that cited in Chapter 3 by the ACFE indicate that if fraud does not get by the internal accountants, the external auditors' responsibility to find fraud is lessened. The external auditors' responsibilities to detect fraud will be discussed in Chapter 5.

Professional Standards and Quality of Work

AICPA Rule 201 establishes standards for the quality of work performed by CPAs including professional competence, due professional care, planning and supervision, and sufficient relevant data. The frequency of due care violations of the AICPA Code has already been addressed. Interpretation 201-1 of the rule also requires that a CPA should gain the competence to perform services, if necessary, by consulting with experts in the area of those services.[29] An option exists to turn down the opportunity to provide services. In that case, as noted in Rule 501.74 of the Texas Administrative Code, the CPA should "suggest to the client the engagement of someone competent to perform the needed professional service, either independently or as an associate."[30]

A CPA who strives to meet the ethical standards should be sensitive to limitations of her or his capabilities and recommend another practitioner perform professional services for the potential client. After all, if you were doing a group project with other students to develop a business plan, you could feel comfortable working on the financial plan but, presumably, you would not want to be responsible for developing the marketing plan. You would expect the marketing students to assume that responsibility.

Rule 203 of the AICPA Code obligates CPAs to ensure that the financial statements and disclosures are in conformity with GAAP before rendering an opinion that the statements comply with those accounting standards.[31] Interpretation 203-4 emphasizes that this requirement applies equally to internal and external accountants.[32]

At the conclusion of an audit, the CEO and CFO sign a letter or other communication to the external auditor on behalf of the client about the financial statements' conformity with GAAP. This management representation is similar to the requirement in Section 302 of SOX for the CEO and CFO to certify the financial statements filed with the SEC.[33]

The first major test case of Section 302 occurred in 2003 when the SEC charged the CEO of HealthSouth Corporation, Richard Scrushy, and the CFO, William T. Owens, with certifying financial statements filed with the SEC on August 14, 2002, that they knew, or were reckless in not knowing, contained materially false and misleading information. Other accounting personnel also were charged with participating in the falsification of HealthSouth's financial statements during the 1999–2002 reporting periods. The alleged fraud led to an earnings restatement of about $2.7 billion.[34]

Scrushy was acquitted of all charges that he participated in the fraud and cover-up. He had served as chairman of the board at HealthSouth from 1984 through early 2003. He also served as CEO during that time except for periods in late 2002 and early 2003. The Birmingham, Alabama, jury chose to believe Scrushy's claims of ignorance even though five HealthSouth financial and accounting officers had admitted to their role in the fraud and had accused Scrushy of knowing about it. As U.S. District County Judge Sharon Lovelace Blackburn stated on December 9, 2005, before sentencing William Owens to five years in prison for his part in the financial scandal, "life is not always fair" and the sentence "should be sufficient to serve as a deterrent and provide just punishment."[35]

Responsibilities to Clients

Two rules provide important standards that directly address a CPA's responsibilities to clients. The first, Rule 301 on Confidential Client Information, emphasizes the CPA's obligation not to divulge client information. The second, Rule 302 on Contingent Fees, clarifies when contingent fees can and cannot be accepted as a form of payment for services.

Confidentiality

A CPA should not divulge confidential client information unless the client specifically agrees. The client may consent, for example, when there is a change of auditor and the successor auditor approaches the client for permission to discuss matters related to the audit with the predecessor. This step is required by GAAS. Of course, the client can always deny permission and cut off any such contact in which case the successor probably should run in the opposite direction of the client as quickly as possible. In other words, the proverbial "red flag" will have been raised. The CPA should be skeptical and wonder why the client refused permission.

Rule 301 also permits the CPA to discuss confidential client information without violating the rule in the following situations: (1) in response to a validly issued subpoena or summons, or to adhere to applicable laws and government regulations, (2) to provide the information necessary for a review of the CPA's professional practice under AICPA or state CPA society or board of accountancy authorization, and (3) to provide the information necessary for one's defense in any investigation initiated by the groups mentioned in (2).[36]

Conflicts of interest can arise in the course of deciding confidentiality issues. A classic case occurred in *Fund of Funds Ltd. v. Arthur Andersen & Co.* in the early 1980s. In that case, Arthur Andersen had issued an unqualified opinion on the audit of Funds of Funds and then essentially the same audit team began the audit of King Resources, a natural resource company whose stock was part of Fund of Funds mutual funds holdings. Andersen learned during its audit of King Resources that King's natural resource holdings were overvalued, affecting the investment's value as it related to Fund of Funds. Rather than withdrawing from the audit on learning that there was a relationship between two of Andersen's clients, the firm decided not to tell Fund of Funds. Andersen was probably concerned about a lawsuit if it had told the mutual fund company and, instead, gambled that the company would not find out that King's natural resource properties were overstated, thereby rendering the company's investment much less valuable.[37]

King Resources went bankrupt, and the investors in Fund of Funds sued Andersen, claiming the auditors should have disclosed that the properties were overvalued. The firm claimed a confidentiality obligation to King Resources in its defense, but the court did not buy it. The court found that the auditors were liable for, among other things, failing to use information they had obtained from another client (King) to determine which of the two clients' financial statements accurately portrayed the facts of the same transaction.[38] Thus, a legal precedent could exist for holding an auditor liable for failing to disclose and use information obtained from services rendered to one client that is relevant to the audit of another client.

Contingent Fees

In January 1985, the Federal Trade Commission (FTC) began an investigation of AICPA rules and interpretations that banned the acceptance of commissions and contingent fees. Around the same time, the profession formed the Anderson Committee that would issue A Plan to Restructure the Profession. In its report, the committee recommended modification of the rules prohibiting contingent fees and the possibility of future changes relating to commissions. The profession was sharply divided over these issues, and eventually the AICPA Ruling Council voted 98 to 97 to defeat the two recommendations.[39]

The AICPA acted to end the investigation in 1990 by signing a Final Order with the Federal Trade Commission (FTC) narrowing AICPA's ability to prohibit the acceptance of commissions and contingent fees. The AICPA amended Rule 302 to prohibit the acceptance of contingent fees (and commissions) only with respect to clients for whom the CPA performs attest services.

The AICPA Rule 302 also prohibits the acceptance of contingent fees when preparing original or amended tax returns or claims for tax refunds. Interpretation 302-1 provides that contingent fees in tax engagements can be accepted when the fee is determined based on the findings of governmental agencies.[40] In other words, a governmental agency, such as the Internal Revenue Service, must either initiate a review of the client's tax return or review the return because of some automatic trigger such as exceeding the amount for a tax refund ($1 million at March 1991). A contingent fee can be accepted in a claim for a tax refund as long as it is based on a tax issue that is either the subject of a tax case (involving a different taxpayer) or the taxing authority is developing a position on a matter.[41]

The change in AICPA rules to permit a contingent fee unless the CPA performs audit or other attest-related services for the client is noteworthy because it reflects the higher level of ethics required when attest services are performed for a client. These services require independence, and an auditor who accepts a contingent fee for performing an attest service is not independent. A contingent fee arrangement creates a self-review threat to independence because it provides that no fee will be charged unless a specified finding or result is attained or when the amount of fee depends on the finding or result of the service.

The PCAOB recently issued Rule 3521 that prohibits contingent fees in tax engagements performed for an audit client.[42] This would not affect the acceptance of contingent fees in tax-only engagements that the AICPA permits because the PCAOB rules apply only to audits of public companies.

Assume that an auditor (or audit firm) agrees to do the audit of an entity's financial statements and agrees to file its income tax return and will be paid a 10 percent contingent fee based on the amount of the tax refund. A reasonable observer could conclude that the auditor could be biased in conducting the audit. After all, an auditor who identifies a $500,000 overstatement of revenue by the client could decide to let it go because an adjustment of this size will lead to a fee for the tax return that is $50,000 less than it would be. Remember that it is the *appearance* of a bias or a conflict of interests that impairs independence.

Other Responsibilities and Practices

Commissions

We have already talked about the FTC challenge to the contingent fee rule. A similar challenge occurred with AICPA Rule 503 that contained a complete ban on commissions. The rule was changed to permit the acceptance of commissions except from those clients for which the CPA also provided attest services. In the case of commissions, the rule change also requires the CPA to disclose the fact to the nonattest client that a commission is being paid to that CPA. For example, if the CPA gets a commission from a software company if clients buy the software, then the CPA must disclose the commission to the nonattest client.[43]

Commission payments typically are made to a CPA for recommending a product to the client. CPAs can also accept referral fees for recommending or referring any service of a CPA or pay a referral fee to obtain a client as long as such acceptance or payment is disclosed to the client.[44]

The interplay of other ethics rules can be seen with the contingent fee and commission rules. Even though a CPA is not prohibited from accepting a commission, for example, for recommending a financial or investment product to a nonattest client, there still exists an obligation to use due care in identifying the best products for the client and to act objectively in the decision-making process.

FTC Challenges to Ethics Rules: Advertising and Solicitation

Even before the FTC challenge on contingent fees and commissions, the AICPA had acted to head off FTC legal challenges to its ethics rules as being too prohibitive. In 1978, the U.S. Supreme Court ruled in *National Society of Professional Engineers v. U.S.*[45] that the engineering profession's canon of ethics violated the Sherman Antitrust Act because its competitive bidding rule was an unreasonable restraint of trade. Following this decision, the AICPA decided to drop its ban on competitive bidding in the AICPA Code by reasoning that the 1978 decision affecting professional engineers was also meant to apply to other professions.

The advertising and solicitation rules also came under attack when in 1977 the Supreme Court ruled in *Bates v. State Bar of Arizona* that the free flow of commercial information protects the public interest. The Court ruled that the ban on attorney advertisements in newspapers violated the First Amendment because it inhibited free (commercial) speech.[46] This led to the end of the ban on CPA advertising.

The Court followed with a ruling in *Edenfeld v. Fane* that Florida's ban on "direct, in-person, uninvited solicitation" to obtain new clients violated the First and Fourteenth (due process) Amendments. The CPA in the case, Scott Fane, had alleged that Florida's ban prevented him from soliciting new clients. The Court sided with Fane, and in his opinion for the Court, Justice Kennedy noted the considerable value of solicitation in facilitating communication between a buyer and seller of professional accounting services. Kennedy pointed out that Florida's ban on uninvited solicitation "threatens societal interests in broad access to complete and accurate commercial information that the First Amendment coverage of commercial speech is designed to safeguard."[47]

The *Edenfeld* ruling led the AICPA to end its complete ban on uninvited solicitation. However, while the advertising and solicitation rules now permit these practices, the rules include guidelines to protect the public against certain forms of commercialization that could be false, misleading, or deceptive.[48]

To be fair to the accounting profession, it was the government's intervention into the ethics standards that lighted the fuse igniting the practice of commercialization in the profession. Most professionals were against these changes and sensed they could lead accounting down the road of putting commercial interests ahead of the public's interest.

The profession did hold its ground on advertising by issuing Interpretation 502-2 that identifies examples of advertising practices that are not in the public interest because they create false and unjustified expectations of favorable results or imply the ability to influence official bodies, and/or they make deceptive and misleading statements about fees.[49] Rule 502 also prohibits solicitation by the use of coercion, overreaching, or harassing conduct.[50]

Ethical Standards in Operating a CPA Practice

Ethics rules apply not only to individual CPAs who are licensed by state boards but also to accounting firms and certain members of alternative practice structures. State boards need to have regulatory authority over practice units as well as CPAs because the members of a CPA firm could pressure an individual CPA within that firm to do something unethical. The firm should be sanctioned for the inappropriate behavior, and so should the CPA if he or she gives in to the pressure.

Rule 505 of the Code provides that CPAs may practice public accounting only in a form of organization permitted by state law or regulation. For example, in Texas the legal forms of ownership must contain the names of a corporation, professional corporation, limited liability partnership, or professional limited liability company. Sole proprietor CPA firms must contain the name of the sole proprietor.[51] Both the AICPA and Texas rules prohibit the use of a firm name that is misleading.

The right of an entity to call itself a CPA firm has changed over the years. There was a time when all partners had to be licensed CPAs. However, over the years, the profession has expanded its consulting services, and firms have hired specialists who have not always held the CPA designation. These experts wanted an ownership interest in the firm, so over time, the rules have changed to permit an entity to call itself a CPA firm as long as "a majority of the ownership of the firm in terms of financial interests and voting rights...belong to CPAs."[52]

One of the recent changes in the way CPA services have been provided to the public is through the formation of alternative practice structures (APS). Typically, a CPA firm is purchased by an entity that is not majority owned by CPAs, a so-called APS. The latter assumes the nonattest services while the CPA firm continues, sometimes as a shell entity, to provide attest services. The CPA firm may be making payments to the APS for leasing space and payments for the use (in audit work) of former CPA firm members who now perform nonattest services for the APS.[53]

Imagine, for example, that a tax preparation entity purchased a small CPA firm. The tax entity (now called an APS) cannot do audit work because it is not majority CPA owned. It can, however, perform all nonattest services while the original CPA firm does the audit work. The CPA firm and the APS have a relationship as a result of the sale, and that can cause some problems. A potential danger is when the APS performs its services for the same client that uses the related CPA firm for audit services. Independence of CPA firm members can be impaired by virtue of the relationship because the APS has some control over the CPA firm and its members as a result of the acquisition.

To control for the possibility that a top management official of the APS could attempt to influence the decision making of a member of the CPA firm, the AICPA rules extend to direct superiors of the APS who can directly control the activities of those in the CPA firm and indirect superiors who could influence the decisions made by the CPA in its audit work for mutual clients. Interpretation 101-14 subjects direct superiors to Rule 101 and its interpretations while indirect superiors are included only if they have material financial relationships as defined under Rule 101 and its interpretations.[54]

Ethics and Tax Services

The AICPA has issued eight Statements on Standards for Tax Services (SSTS) that explain CPAs' responsibilities to their clients and the tax systems in which they practice. The statements demonstrate a CPA's commitment to tax practice standards that balance advocacy and planning with compliance. At the federal level, the Internal Revenue Code and Treasury Department Circular 230 apply to those practicing before the Internal Revenue Service (IRS).[55] We focus only on the tax statements issued by the AICPA.

Tax services differ from audit services in two important respects. First, the independence requirement for an auditor does not pertain to the tax practitioner although a CPA firm that performs both services would be required to be independent to conduct the audit. Under SOX requirements, the audit committee of a public client must approve the tax services. This is a check in the system to ensure that the board of directors is comfortable with the audit firm also performing tax services.

The second difference is due to the way in which objectivity relates to tax services. Auditors must maintain an unbiased attitude in conducting the audit. An auditor should never do what the audit client asks just because the client asks it. The final decision must be made by the CPA based on ethical considerations and using her or his professional judgment. However, in tax practice, CPAs sometimes serve as advocates for the client's tax position. If a reasonable level of support exists for that position, as will be discussed, the CPA should support that position. The tax practitioner still must be objective in determining the supportability of that position. However, once supportability has been affirmed, the

CPA can advocate that position in tax and legal proceedings. The relationship between the CPA and tax client as just explained creates an advocacy threat to independence, and it is particularly worrisome when the CPA represents the client in U.S. Tax Court.

Tax Advocacy Positions   Tax practitioners offer tax advice, prepare tax returns, and represent taxpayers before the IRS. Taxpayers are responsible for the information they provide. The decisions made by a CPA in providing advice, preparing returns, and representing clients are the product of following the Statements on Standards for Tax Services (SSTS) and ethics rules (i.e., objectivity, due care, confidentiality, and contingent fees) of the accounting profession.

Interpretation 102-6 of the AICPA Code recognizes the potential advocacy position. The interpretation reiterates the requirement to follow the ethics rules and notes that in certain cases, the tax services could go beyond "sound and reasonable practice, or may compromise credibility, and therefore pose an unacceptable risk of impairing the reputation" of the CPA or CPA firm "with respect to independence, integrity, and objectivity." In such cases, the CPA/firm should "consider whether it is appropriate to perform the service."[56]

Statements on Standards for Tax Services   SSTS No. 1, "Tax Return Position," and Interpretation No. 1-1 are the most important standards with respect to the goals of this book. These standards provide that tax return information is "primarily a taxpayer's representation of facts" and as client advocates, "CPAs have the duty to assist taxpayers in lawfully minimizing the tax burden, as long as any tax return position satisfies the 'realistic possibility' standard." Taxpayers have the final responsibility for any tax position taken on a return.[57] The ethical "control," so to speak, is the realistic possibility standard.

Tax positions are taken because the tax rules are not always clear. A tax practitioner is required by SSTS No. 1 to "have a good faith belief that the tax return position is warranted in existing law or can be supported by a good-faith argument for an extension, modification, or reversal of existing law."[58]

This good faith belief requirement in taking a tax position is further explained in Interpretation No. 1-1. It links a good faith belief with the notion that "the tax return position being recommended has a realistic possibility of being sustained administratively or judicially on its merits, if challenged." Absent the realistic possibility requirement, the CPA still can recommend the position to the taxpayer if it is not frivolous and the practitioner recommends appropriate disclosure of the position. If the tax client does not disclose the position, the CPA should not "prepare or sign the tax return containing the position."[59] SSTS No. 1 points out that "a frivolous position is one that is knowingly advanced in bad faith and patently improper."[60]

Other constraints exist in SSTS No. 1 such as that the practitioner should not recommend a tax return position or prepare or sign a return reflecting a position that the CPA knows "exploits the audit selection process of the taxing authority."[61] In other words a CPA should not adopt a tax position with the hope the client's tax return will not be audited by the IRS.

Recall from the discussion in Chapter 2 that when rules are not clear, individuals should utilize moral principles to decide on the proper course of action. In tax practice, the CPA applies the realistic possibility standard. A critical evaluation of these approaches reveals that the ethical requirement to use moral reasoning conflicts with the realistic possibility standard. Ethically speaking, we should not make decisions based on whether "reasonable support" exists for that position. To be an ethical person is an absolute requirement for the CPA, and ethical decision making is not relative to the situation or a tax position. Having said that, it is important that the CPA not be influenced by the tax client in determining what should be the tax position. Moreover, once that position is adopted, the CPA should resist client pressures to deviate from the strict requirements of the SSTSs.

To illustrate the interplay of ethics and tax standards, assume that a tax practitioner decides to recommend a tax position to a client because it minimizes the client's tax liability even though the CPA is not sure it is the right thing to do. The tax statements do not say to recommend another position if it is (ethically) better. As long as there is support for the first position, it is acceptable to adopt it in a tax situation. The CPA recommends the first position because there is sufficient support for it in a court of law, assuming that the position was to be challenged, and it is the position desired by the client. The CPA's task is to gather enough evidence to support the position if challenged in court. The fact that the alternative position could seem to be fairer or the right one does not matter.

Tax Shelters

One of the most controversial aspects of the Enron collapse was the alleged involvement of Arthur Andersen in marketing aggressive tax-planning ideas that the IRS and the courts subsequently found to be abusive. The accounting profession received a second serious blow after the Enron scandal when in 2005 KPMG settled a criminal tax case with the Department of the Treasury and the IRS for $456 million to prevent the firm's prosecution over tax shelters sold between 1996 and 2002. This is the largest criminal tax case ever filed.[62]

The creation of tax shelter investments to help wealthy clients avoid paying taxes has been part of tax practice for many years. The difference in the KPMG case, according to the original indictment, is that tax professionals in the firm prepared false documents to deceive regulators about the true nature of the tax shelters. There appears to have been a clear *intent to deceive* the regulators, and that makes it fraud.

The indictment claims that the tax shelter transactions broke the law because they involved no economic risk and were designed solely to minimize taxes. The firm had collected about $128 million in fees for generating at least $11 billion in fraudulent tax losses, and it resulted in at least $2.5 billion in taxes evaded by wealthy individuals. On an annual basis, KPMG's tax department was bringing into the firm nearly $1.2 billion of its $3.2 billion total U.S. revenue. Ultimately, the $128 million in fees were forfeited as part of the $456 million settlement.[63]

Perhaps the most interesting aspect of the KPMG tax shelter situation is the apparent culture that existed in the firm's tax practice during the time the tax shelters were sold. In 1998, the firm had decided to accelerate its tax services business. The motivation probably was the hot stock market during the 1990s and the increase in the number of wealthy taxpayers. The head of the KPMG's tax department, Jeffrey M. Stein, and its CFO, Richard Rosenthal, created an environment that treated those who didn't support the growth at all costs effort as not being team players. From the late 1990s, KPMG established a telemarketing center in Fort Wayne, Indiana, that cold-called potential clients from public lists of firms and companies. KPMG built an aggressive marketing team to sell the tax shelters, with names like Blips, Flip, Opis, and SC2, that it had created.[64]

PCAOB Rules

Following the KPMG case, the PCAOB adopted new rules for tax services that are designed to prevent auditors from providing (1) certain aggressive tax shelter services to their public company audit clients, (2) any other service for a contingent fee, and (3) tax services to members of the audit client's management who serve in financial reporting oversight roles or to their immediate family members.[65] The PCAOB rule prohibits public company executives from calling on their audit firms for tax preparation and planning services. Second, the PCAOB does not make an exception in its contingent fee rule for certain tax services (when it is subject to tax review) as do the SEC and AICPA. All contingent fees paid to audit clients would be banned. Third, the new rule provides that an audit firm is not independent if it provides services to an audit client on specified classes of tax-motivated transactions. The suspect categories are transactions with a confidentiality requirement imposed by a tax adviser on a client and any transaction recommended by an auditor or tax adviser that has as its main purpose tax avoidance unless the proposed tax treatment is at least more likely than not to be allowable under relevant tax laws.[66]

Conclusion

You have seen in this chapter that the ethics of CPAs is frequently challenged because of the pressure imposed on CPAs by superiors (employers) and by top management (clients). The dilemma is whether the CPAs should risk losing their job or an audit client and its future revenue source or to give in to superiors' or clients' demands. This ethical dilemma presents a clash between what may be in the CPA's self-interest and doing the right thing.

The chapter gave examples of when performing nonattest services for attest clients poses an independence threat because of relationships that develop between the auditor and the client or its top management. The marketing of professional services creates other challenges to avoid such as accepting forms of payment in commissions and contingent fees that can, under certain circumstances, impair objectivity.

The increase in tax services and expansion into providing tax-advantaged investments such as tax shelters tests the CPA's commitment to the accounting profession's ethics standards in tax practice. In general, to keep up with the competition, a CPA could sell certain services to clients that may not be in the client's best interests but that helps to grow the CPA's business. The ethical test here is for the CPA to ask whether he or she would buy the same service from someone else.

To avoid taking the first step down the proverbial ethical slippery slope when you began your careers, you must constantly work on developing personal integrity and taking responsibility for your actions. Once you go along with the nefarious demands of a superior or client, it is difficult to go back and climb up the (ethical) ladder. By going along to get along, you would create a relationship in which the client or your superior expects a certain type of behavior. You give the green light to that person who feels supported in the wrongdoing and will not hesitate to blame you if the situation and cover-up explodes in everyone's face.

Discussion Questions

1. The opening quote in this chapter includes the statement: "By certifying the public reports that collectively depict a corporation's financial status, the independent auditor assumes a public responsibility transcending any employment responsibility with the client." Discuss what it means for the auditor to have a public responsibility that transcends any employment responsibility with the client.

2. In their landmark book that was published in 1966, *Ethical Standards of the Accounting Profession,* John Carey and William Doherty state,[67] "The code [of ethics] in effect is an announcement that, in return for the faith which the public reposes in [CPAs], members of the profession accept the obligation to behave in a way that will be beneficial to the public." Comment on the meaning of this statement as you understand it.

3. Describe the role of the state board of accountancy in your state. Does it have an ethics requirement similar to that of Texas? Do you believe that such a requirement would help to improve ethics in the accounting profession? Why or why not?

4. The accounting profession has been investigated by Congress over a number of years. However, none of the investigations or recommendations for change seems to have made a difference because fraud cases continued into the early 2000s. Why do you think instances of accounting fraud will continue to occur?

5. Think of a time when you sacrificed your own interests for the interests of another. What motivated you to make that decision? Can you draw an analogy between your motivations and the ethical responsibilities of CPAs?

6. Have you ever agreed to do something when you weren't sure that you had the skills to accomplish the job? Why did you agree to do it? Can you draw an analogy between your motivations and the ethical responsibilities of CPAs?

7. What does it mean to observe both the form and the spirit of ethical standards?

8. Assume that the CPA firm of Bolsing & Jets LLP audits Timin Systems Inc. The controller of Timin happens to be a tax expert. During the current tax season, Bolsing & Jets gets far behind in processing tax returns for wealthy clients. It does not want to approach them and ask permission to file for an extension to the April 15 deadline. One alternative is for the firm to hire Timin's controller as a consultant just for the tax season. Discuss the ethical issues that should be

considered by Bolsing & Jets before deciding whether to hire the controller, including possible threats to independence.

9. The managing partner of the CPA firm of Bolsing & Jets LLP is approached by the CEO of a major client in the firm's headquarters office in Chicago. The CEO can't use two tickets to the Super Bowl between the Indianapolis Colts and the New York Giants. The CEO knows the partner is a huge Colts fan and is looking forward to the Peyton Manning versus Eli Manning match. Therefore, the CEO offers the tickets to the partner. At first, the partner is excited about the prospects of going to the Super Bowl but then realizes that there may be some ethical issues to be considered before deciding whether to accept the tickets. Assume that the partner asks for your help. You are a CPA and a long-time friend of the partner. Considering parts (a) and (b) separately, what would your advice be? Be sure to describe your feelings and personal integrity issues as well as ethics rules in the AICPA Code of Professional Conduct to support your answers.

   a. You were asked by the partner to accompany him to the game and are able to do so.

   b. You were asked by the partner to go but declined because you had a conflicting appointment that day.

10. Can a CPA be independent without being objective? Why or why not?

11. Can a CPA be objective without being independent? Why or why not?

12. Integrity is said to be the backbone of ethical behavior. How does the integrity requirement of CPAs affect the performance of professional services by (1) a controller of a corporation and (2) the external auditor of a company? Give an example of how integrity influences the ability of a CPA to make objective decisions.

13. In the consideration of the Armadillo Foods case in this chapter, let's assume that the controller is being asked to make the numbers by a difference of $.01 EPS (to make accounting entries such that EPS is $.01 higher). This sounds innocent enough. However, doing this could be enough for the stock market to reward the company by an increase in share price or at least not decrease the share price.

   a. Would it matter that the officers of the company all had stock options in the company?

   b. Would it matter if the $.01 EPS represented a misstatement in net income of $1,000,000?

   c. Would it matter if the $.01 EPS difference meant that the company would not be in default on a loan covenant?

14. What is the danger from an ethical perspective of having a CPA firm that conducts the audit of a public company also engaged in consulting with the company on the installation of a new financial information system?

15. What's wrong with a CPA accepting a commission for the recommendation of an investment product to an audit client?

16. Read the following advertisement that appeared in the community newspaper where you live. Do you think the advertisement violates any of the ethics rules? Explain the reasons for your answer.

IRS TAX TERMINATOR, A Professional Services Corporation

We have 10 CPAs on staff and provide a full range of tax services. We guarantee a tax refund or you pay nothing for our services. Call us at 999-777-7711. Your call will be routed to one of our tax experts who will take down all relevant information and inform you of our fee structure that includes a fixed amount regardless of the service provided and a variable amount that is based on the type of service provided.

---

17. Assume that you are a CPA and the controller of a Fortune 500 company. On January 2, 2008, your boss, the CFO, comes into your office with a sales invoice and tells you to backdate the document that is for a $20 million shipment of merchandise to a customer to December 30, 2007. The shipment will go out today and the invoice will be mailed at the same time. You tell the CFO that the request is highly unusual. The CFO admits that but tells you about his

chewing out by the CEO because the company did not make its numbers for the 12 months ended December 31, 2007. What ethical issues should you consider in deciding whether to agree to the request? Who are the stakeholders in your decision? Using ethical reasoning, explain how you would handle the situation and why.

18. Ruth Moss is an associate with the CPA firm of Bolsing & Jets LLP. She graduated from Oklexas State University. She has been working for the firm for two years. Ruth is assigned to run her first audit. In preparing for the audit, what ethical issues that pertain to the quality of her professional work do you think should be important to Ruth?

19. Lew Walls is a CPA and a sole practitioner. He serves a small client base in the city of Tuscaloosa, Alabama. A potential client comes into Walls's office one day and asks to discuss the possibility of Walls preparing her 1040 tax return for the year 2007. Walls asks questions about the client's hair salon business and personal investments. Everything sounds all right to him, so he agrees to do the tax return. Four days before the April 15 deadline. the client comes into Walls's office with a shoebox filled with tax receipts. Walls asks, "What's this?" The client answers, "All the information you need to do my taxes." After drinking two glasses of water and doing some yoga exercises, Walls calmly tells the client he can't work with a shoebox full of tax information. The client assures Walls everything is in order, each taxable item or tax deduction category has been separated out, and there are explanations at the bottom of the shoebox for everything. Out of curiosity Walls removes the stacks and picks up the paper at the bottom which is a receipt for a $200 pair of Nike shoes. Walls finds the explanation sheet for that purchase which says: "Required for comfort on the job." Later that day, after the client has left, Walls goes through the separate stacks and notices there is no W-2 form for earnings from the salon. Walls calls the client, who explains that it is strictly a cash business and Walls should pick a number after looking at all the other tax information and then decide on the earnings amount from the business. She conditions the statement by saying she wants a $2,000 tax refund in 2007.

    a. What would you do if you were Lew Walls? Why?

    b. Assume that this scenario occurs on April 14, and you know the client will not have enough time to find someone else to do her taxes in time if you decide to walk away from the engagement. Would that change your decision? Why or why not?

    c. Assume that the client was your sister. Would that change what you do? Why or why not?

20. A large, national accounting firm decides it is time to outsource the preparation of income tax returns to an organization in India that has performed outsource services for other U.S. CPA firms. The firm will transmit income tax information necessary to prepare the returns electronically and staff accountants in India will prepare the return. The return will then be transmitted back to the United States for final review and approval and then will be given to clients. Explain the ethical concerns of outsourcing income tax returns. Assume that the cost savings to the CPA firm are significant because of the lower salaries paid to chartered accountants in India and that the quality of work in India is as good or better than that of U.S. tax accountants. Would you recommend the practice to the U.S. firm? Why or why not? Be sure to address the ethical issues of concern that influence your decision.

Endnotes

1. *United States v. Arthur Young,* 465 US 805, www.usm.maine.edu/~gramlich/caltex/USvArthur Young1984.pdf.

2. American Institute of CPAs. *AICPA Professional Standards Volume 2: As of June 1, 2005* (New York: AICPA, 2005).

3. Texas State Board of Public Accountancy, *Texas Administrative Code Title 22, Part 22, Chapter 501, Subchapter A, Rule 501.51,* http://info.sos.state.tx.us/pls/pub/readtac$ext. TacPage?sl=R&app=9&p_dir=&p_rloc=&p_tloc=&p_ploc=&pg=1&p_tac=&ti=22&pt=22& ch=501&rl=51.

4. *Texas Administrative Code Title 22, Part 22, Chapter 501, Subchapter A, Rule 501.51,* http:// info.sos.state.tx.us/pls/pub/readtac$ext.TacPage?sl=R&app=9&p_dir=&p_rloc=&p_tloc=&p_ ploc=&pg=1&p_tac=&ti=22&pt=22&ch=501&rl=51.

5. Kurt Baier, *The Moral Point of View* (New York: McGraw-Hill College, 1965).

6. AICPA, *Professional Standards Volume 2,* Section 54.04. AICPA Professional Standards by AICPA. Copyright 2005 by AMERICAN INSTITUTE OF CERTIFIED PUBLIC

ACCOUNTANTS. Reproduced with permission of American Institute of Certified Public Accountants in the format Textbook via Copyright Clearance Center.

7. Mark S. Beasley, Joseph V. Carcello, and Dana R. Hermanson, "Top 10 Audit Deficiencies," *Journal of Accountancy*, April 2001, www.aicpa.org/pubs/jofa/apr2001/beasley.htm.

8. John F. Raspante, "Common Ethical Problems for CPAs," *The Trusted Professional,* April 2003 www.nysscpa.org/trustedprof/archive/0403/1tp13a.htm.

9. AICPA, *Professional Standards Volume 2,* Sections 92.11 and 92.25.

10. AICPA, "A Conceptual Framework for AICPA Independence Standards—January 22, 2004," www.aicpa.org.

11. AICPA, *Professional Standards Volume 2,* Section 101.06-.07.

12. Association of Certified Fraud Examiners, "Cooking the Books: What Every Accountant Should Know about Fraud," www.acfe.org.

13. AICPA, *AICPA Professional Standards Volume 2,* Section101.02.

14. AICPA, Section 101.5.

15. HR 3763, 107th Congress of the United States of America: The Sarbanes-Oxley Act, www.findlaw.com.

16. HR 3763.

17. Securities and Exchange Commission, Release No. 249; File No. 3-10933. *In the matter of Ernst & Young LLP:* Initial Decision, April 16, 2004, www.sec.gov/litreleases.

18. Mike Brewster, *Unaccountable: How the Accounting Profession Forfeited a Public Trust* (Hoboken, NJ: John Wiley, 2003).

19. William F. Messier Jr., Steven M. Glover, and Douglas F. Prawitt, *Auditing & Assurance Services: A Systematic Approach* (New York: McGraw-Hill/Irwin, 2006).

20. American Institute of CPAs, *Journal of Accountancy: AICPA Centennial Issue 1987,* May 1987.

21. Brewster, pp. 153–54.

22. Brewster, pp. 155–56.

23. Jeff Baily, "Continental Illinois Dismisses Ernst & Whinney," *Wall Street Journal,* November 2, 1984, D1.

24. "Hearings Focus on ZZZZ Best," *Journal of Accountancy,* April 1988, p. 80. Copyright © 1988 from the Journal of Accountancy by the AICPA. Opinions of the authors are their own and do not necessarily reflect policies of the AICPA. Reprinted with permission of AMERICAN INSTITUTE OF CERTIFIED PUBLIC ACCOUNTANTS in the format Textbook via Copyright Clearance Center.

25. Timothy Curry and Lynn Shibut, "The Cost of the Savings and Loan Crisis: Truth and Consequences," www.fdic.gov/bank/analytical/banking/2000dec/brv13n2_2.pdf.

26. National Commission on Fraudulent Financial Reporting (Treadway Commission Report), Report of the National Commission on Fraudulent Financial Reporting, October 1987. Copyright © 1987, 2004 by the Committee of Sonsoring Organizations of the Treadway Commission. Reproduced with permission from the AICPA acting as authorized copyright administrator for COSO.

27. Treadway Commission Report.

28. AICPA, *Professional Standards Volume 2,* Section 102.04.

29. AICPA, Section 201.01.

30. Texas Administrative Code Part 22, Chapter 501, Subchapter C, Rule 501.74: Competence, www.tsbpa.state.tx.us.

31. AICPA, *Professional Standards Volume 2,* Section 202.01.

32. AICPA, Section 203.05.

33. HR 3763.

34. Securities and Exchange Commission (SEC), Accounting and Auditing Enforcement Release (AAER) No. 1744, March 20, 2003, www.sec.gov/litigation/litreleases/lr18044.htm.

35. Michael Tomberlin, "Owens Sentenced to 5 years in Prison," *The Birmingham News,* December 10, 2005.

36. AICPA, *Professional Standards Volume 2,* Section 302.02.

37. 545 F. Supp. 1314 (S.D.N.Y. 1982).

38. 545 F. Supp. 1314.

39. Mary Beth Armstrong, *Ethics and Professionalism for CPAs* (Cincinnati, OH: South-Western Publishing, 1993).

40. AICPA, *Professional Standards Volume 2,* Section 302.02.

41. AICPA, Section 302.02.

42. Public Company Accounting Oversight Board, Rule 3521, www.pcaobus.org.

43. AICPA, *Professional Standards Volume 2,* Section 503.01.

44. AICPA, Section 503.01.

45. *National Society of Professional Engineers,* 435 U.S. 679 (1978).

46. *Bates v. Arizona State Bar Association,* 433 U.S. 350 (1977).

47. *Edenfeld v. Fane,* 507 U.S. 761 (1993).

48. AICPA, *AICPA Professional Standards Volume 2,* Section 502.01.

49. AICPA, Section 502.02.

50. AICPA, Section 502.01.

51. Texas State Board of Public Accountancy. *Texas Administrative Code Title 22, Part 22, Chapter 501, Subchapter D, Rule 501.83,* http://info.sos.state.tx.us/pls/pub/readtac$ext. TacPage?sl=R&app=9&p_dir=&p_rloc=&p_tloc=&p_ploc=&pg=1&p_tac=&ti=22&pt=22&ch=501&rl=83.

52. AICPA, "Council Resolution Regarding Rule 505—Form of Organization and Name," *Professional Standards Volume 2,* Appendix B.

53. AICPA, *Professional Standards Volume 2,* Section 505.3.

54. AICPA, Section 101.14.

55. John C. Gardner, Susan L. Willey, and Barbara J. Eide, "Statements on Standards for Tax Services: An Examination and Overview, *CPA Journal,* December 2000.

56. AICPA, *Professional Standards Volume 2,* Section 102.07.

57. AICPA Tax Executive Committee, Statement on Standards for Tax Services (SSTS) No. 1, Tax Return Positions, *AICPA Professional Standards Volume 2: As of June 1, 2005* (New York: AICPA, 2005).

58. Gardner et al.

59. AICPA Tax Executive Committee, Interpretation No. 1-1, "Realistic Possibility Standard" of SSTS No. 1, Tax Return Positions, *AICPA Professional Standards Volume 2: As of June 1, 2005* (New York: AICPA, 2005).

60. AICPA Tax Executive Committee, SSTS No. 1.

61. AICPA Tax Executive Committee, SSTS No. 1.

62. "KPMG Settles IRS Tax-shelter Case for $456 million," *International Tax Review,* www.internationaltaxreview.com/?Page=9&PUBID=210&ISS=20252&SID=578917&SM=&SearchStr=KPMG%20Settles%20Tax%20Shelter%20case.

63. Lynnley Browning, Corporate Watch, "How an Accounting Firm Went from Resistance to Resignation," www.corpwatch.org/article.php?id=12575.

64. IRS Commissioner Mark V. Everson, "KPMG to Pay $456 Million for Criminal Violations," IR-2005-83, August 29, 2005, www.irs.gov/newsroom/article/0,,id=146999,00.html.

65. Public Company Accounting Oversight Board (PCAOB), Ethics and Independence Rules, www.pcaobus.org.

66. A. Michael Hirsh, "New PCAOB Rules Affect Personal Tax Services for Key Management, *CPA Journal,* December 2005.

67. John L. Carey and William O. Doherty, *Ethical Standards of the Accounting Profession* (New York: AICPA, 1966).

Chapter 4 Cases

Case 4-1

Beauda Medical Center

Lance Popperson woke up in a sweat. He felt an anxiety attack coming on. Popperson popped two anti-anxiety pills, lay down to try to sleep for the third time that night, and thought again about his dilemma.

Popperson is an associate with the accounting firm of Scoop and Shovel LLP. He recently discovered, through a casual conversation with Brandy Snow, a friend of his on the audit staff, that one of the firm's clients she manages recently received complaints that its heart monitoring equipment was malfunctioning. Cardio-Systems Monitoring, Inc. (CSM) called for a meeting of the lawyers, auditors, and top management to discuss what to do about the complaints from health care facilities that had significantly increased between the first two months of 2007 and the last two months of that year. Doctors at these facilities claim the systems shut off for brief periods and, in one case, the hospital was unable to save a patient who went into cardiac arrest.

Popperson got out of bed, went for a glass of water, looked at the clock that said 2:58 a.m., and tried to sleep for the fourth time. He tossed and turned and wondered what he should do about the fact that Beauda Medical Center, his current audit client, planned to buy 20 units of Cardio-Systems heart monitoring equipment for its brand new medical facility in the outskirts of Beauda, Texas.

Questions

1. Assume that both Popperson and Snow are CPAs. Do you think Snow violated her confidentiality obligation under the AICPA Code of Professional Conduct? Why or why not?

2. Popperson has not told anyone on the Beauda Medical Center audit about the situation at CSM. What are his ethical obligations under the AICPA Code? What do you suggest he do when he arrives at work that morning? Why?

3. Assume that Popperson says nothing. Do you think he has violated the ethical standards of the accounting profession? Why or why not?

4. Assume instead that Popperson informs the senior in charge of the Beauda audit and the senior informs the manager, Kelly Korn. A meeting is held the next day with all parties in the office of Iceman Cometh, the managing partner of the firm. Here's how it goes:

Iceman: If we tell Beauda about the problems at CSM, we will have violated our confidentiality obligation as a firm to CSM.

Kelly: Lance, you're the closest to the situation. How do you think Beauda's top hospital administrators would react if we told them?

Lance: They wouldn't buy the equipment.

Iceman: Once we tell them, we're subject to investigation by our state board of accountancy for violating the confidentiality obligation we have to CSM.

Kelly: Who would report us? I mean, the Beauda people are going to be happy that we prevented them from buying what may be faulty equipment.

Senior: I agree with Kelly. We'd be doing the right thing.

Iceman: I don't like it. I think we should be silent and find another way to warn Beauda Medical without violating confidentiality.

Lance: What about contacting the state board for advice?

a. Discuss all matters of concern for the firm of Scoop and Shovel LLP in deciding whether to do as Iceman Cometh suggests and not tell the administrators at Beauda Medical Center.

b. Are there alternatives to handle the situation from the firm's perspective that could help it avoid violating confidentiality?

c. What do you think about Lance's suggestion to contact the state board for advice on the matter? Is that the function of a state board of accountancy?

Case 4-2

Campus Sports & Fitness Health Club

Campus Sports & Fitness Health Club (The Club) advertises primarily on college campuses to attract students to become members while they go to school. The club's management figures that students have the time for fitness, want to stay in good shape, need energy for their daily and weekly activities, and are gullible.

The Club recently sent 10 sales agents to campuses in Philadelphia. The Club was running a promotional sales offer through which students could sign up for membership and receive two years of membership for the price of one year. The students who agreed to join were contacted by managers at the Club and invited to try out the equipment free of charge for that day and then sign their contract at the end of the day.

The Club reported a 50 percent rate of signed membership from the free days. The promotional events helped The Club to increase its earnings by 20 percent over prior year levels. One accounting issue of concern is how The Club should record the advertising costs for the campus promotions. The Club decided to capitalize all of the costs and write them off over the two-year membership period. This is where Dina and Yossi Caufman come in to the picture.

Dina and Yossi have been married for 12 years. They met in college, studied and passed the CPA Exam at the same time, and got married after the grades were reported. They respect each other's opinions, are sensitive to each other's feelings, and contribute to their partner's happiness. However, the current conflict has all the markings of destroying their relationship.

It all started yesterday when Yossi came home without even saying hello to his wife. He went to the den, closed the door, and proceeded to make a phone call that lasted almost two hours. He left the den, went up to the bedroom, and said goodnight to his wife. She couldn't believe it. He hadn't even said "hello." He didn't eat with her. Worst of all, Yossi did not ask Dina how her day was. He had always done that in the past. His caring about what was important to her was one thing Dina loved about her husband.

Yossi arrived at the accounting firm the following day for a 7 a.m. breakfast meeting with his partner, Lou Wolf. Yossi is in charge of the audit of Campus Sports & Fitness Health Club. Wolf found out about Yossi's dilemma with respect to the client during the two-hour phone call the night before.

During that call, Yossi told Wolf that accounting principles require the immediate expensing of all advertising costs.

Dina Caufman is the chief accounting officer of Campus Sports & Fitness Health Club. She made the final decision to capitalize the advertising costs after the Club's president, Tom Lion, ordered her to change the initial accounting for the costs from expensing to capitalization. Lion told Dina that the company needed to maximize its earnings this year in anticipation of a private stock offering to wealthy residents in Philadelphia to help expand the Club's operations throughout the state.

"Listen, Yossi," Lou Wolf said. "I understand the agony you feel because Dina made the final decision, but we both know that Lion forced her hand."

"I know, Lou, but I thought Dina was more principled than that. I guess I was wrong."

"Yossi, we have to resolve the matter by the end of the week. The Club needs the final financial statements to prepare its stock offering."

"I hear you, Lou. Give me tonight to discuss it with Dina, and I'll get back to you tomorrow. I think we'll be able to wrap it up at that time."

Questions

1. Explain the independence rules in the AICPA Code. In particular, differentiate between independence in fact and in appearance.

2. Do you think the independence rules were violated in this case? Why or why not?

3. Describe the rule(s) of accounting for determining whether a cost should be capitalized or expensed. Do you think that The Club properly accounted for the advertising costs? Why or why not?

4. Comment on the independence of Yossi Caufman in this case. Has he done the right thing? If so, why? If not, explain what he should have done.

5. If you were in Yossi Caufman's position, what would you say to your wife when you arrive home that evening with respect to the accounting issues? How do you think Dina will respond?

Case 4-3

Cleveland Custom Cabinets

Cleveland Custom Cabinets (CCC) is a specialty cabinet manufacturer for high-end homes in the Cleveland Heights and Shaker Heights areas. The company manufactures cabinets built to the specifications of homeowners and employs 125 custom cabinet makers and installers. There are 30 administrative and sales staff members working for the company.

James Leroy owns CCC. His accounting manager is Marcus Sims. Sims manages 15 accountants. The staff is responsible for keeping track of manufacturing costs by job and preparing internal and external financial reports. The internal reports are used by management for decision making. The external reports are used to support bank loan applications.

The company applies overhead to jobs based on direct labor hours. For 2008, it estimated total overhead to be $9,600,000 and 80,000 direct labor hours. The cost of direct materials used during the first quarter of the year is $1,100,000 and direct labor cost is $900,000 (based on 20,000 hours worked). The company's accounting system is old and does not provide actual overhead information until about four weeks after the close of a quarter. As a result, the applied overhead amount is used for quarterly reports.

On April 10, 2008, Leroy came into Sims's office to pick up the quarterly report. He looked at it aghast. He had planned to take the statements to the bank the next day and meet with the vice president to discuss a $1 million expansion loan. He knew the bank would be reluctant to grant the loan based on the following income numbers.

EXHIBIT 1
CLEVELAND CUSTOM CABINETS
Net Income for the Quarter Ended March 31, 2008

Sales	$6,400,000
Cost of goods manufactured	4,400,000
Gross margin	$2,000,000
Selling and administrative expenses	1,910,000
Net income	$ 90,000

Leroy asked Sims to explain how net income could have gone from 14.2 percent of sales for the year ended December 31, 2007, to 1.4 percent for March 31, 2008. Sims pointed out that the estimated overhead cost had doubled for 2008 when compared with the actual cost for 2007. He explained to Leroy that rent had doubled and the cost of utilities had skyrocketed. In addition, the custom-making machinery was wearing out more rapidly, so the company's repair and maintenance costs also doubled from 2007.

Leroy understood but wouldn't accept Sims's explanation. Instead, he told Sims that as the sole owner of the company, there was no reason not to "tweak" the numbers on a one-time basis. Sims asked Leroy just how he expected that to happen. Leroy flinched, held up his hands, and said, "I'll leave the creative accounting to you."

Questions

1. Do you agree with Leroy's statement that it doesn't matter what the numbers look like since he is the sole owner? Support your answer with reference to the ethical reasoning methods and virtues discussed in Chapters 1 and 2.

2. Assume that Sims is a CPA. What are the ethical considerations for him in deciding on a course of action?

3. Assume that Sims decided to reduce the estimated overhead for the year by 50 percent. How would that change the net income for the quarter? What would it be as a percentage of sales? Do you think Leroy would like the result?

4. Assume instead that you are in Sims's position and refuse to go along with Leroy's request. Leroy threatens to fire you unless you change your mind. Discuss what would be the ethical issues of concern to you in deciding whether to back off from your position.

5. Assume instead that you back off from your position and agree to make the change described in Question 3. Evaluate the possible long-term consequences of your decision.

Case 4-4

Family Games, Inc.

"Yeah, I know the negotiations weren't completed until January 2, 2008, but we started to discuss the matter on December 30. By my way of reasoning, it's a continuation transaction, and the $12 million revenue belongs in the results for 2007."

This comment was made by Carl Land, the chief financial officer of Family Games, Inc. The company has sales of about $50 million each year from a variety of manufactured board and electronic games that are designed for use by the entire family. However, during the past two years, the company had a net loss due to cost-cutting measures that were necessary to compete with overseas manufacturers and distributors.

Land made the comment to Helen Strom, the controller of Family Games, after Strom had expressed her concern that because the lawyers didn't sign off on the transaction until January 2, the revenue should not be recorded in 2007. She emphasized that the product was not shipped until January 2 and there was no way of justifying its inclusion in the previous year operating results.

"Listen, Helen, this comes from the top. The big boss said we need to have the $12 million recorded in the results for 2007."

"I don't get it," Helen said to Land. "Why the pressure?"

"The boss wants to increase his performance bonus, and he wants the cash now. Apparently, he lost some money in Vegas last weekend and left a sizeable 'I Owe U,'" Land responded.

Helen just shook her head. She didn't like the idea of operating results being manipulated based on the personal needs of the chief executive officer. She knew that the CEO has a gambling problem. It had happened before. The difference this time is that appears to have affected company operations, and she is being asked to do something that she knows is wrong.

"I can't change the facts," said Helen.

"All you have to do is backdate the sales invoice to December 30," Land responded. "As I said before, just think of it as a revenue-continuation transaction that started in 2007 and, but for one minor technicality, should have been recorded in 2007."

"You're asking me to 'cook the books,'" Helen said. "I won't do it."

"I hate to play hardball with you, Helen, but the boss authorized me to tell you he will cut off reimbursement payments in the future that the company makes so that your kid can have a live-in nanny unless you are a team player on this issue."

Helen was surprised to hear the threat. She slowly sat down in her chair and reflected on the fact that the reimbursement payments are $35,000, 35 percent of her annual salary. She is a single working mother. Helen knows there is no other way that she can afford to pay for the full-time care needed by her autistic son.

Questions

1. Briefly discuss the rules for revenue recognition in accounting. How does the proposed handling of the $12 million violate those rules? Be specific.

2. Assume that both Carl Land and Helen Strom are CPAs. What ethical issues exist for them in this situation? How does the ethical value of integrity relate to their professional responsibilities?

3. To what extent should Helen consider the gambling problems of her boss in deciding on a course of action?

4. To what extent should Helen consider her child care situation and the threatened cut off of reimbursements in deciding on a course of action?

5. Considering all the facts in this case including those in both Questions 3 and 4, who are the stakeholders that Helen should consider in deciding on a course of action, and what are their interests?

6. If you were Helen Strom, what would you do? Why?

Case 4-5

First Community Church

First Community Church is the largest church in the city of Perpetual Happiness. Yes, it's in California!

A meeting was held on Friday, November 16, to address the fact that money had been stolen from the weekly collection box during the course of the year and church leaders were getting quite concerned. At first, no one paid much attention because the amounts were small and could have been attributed to inadvertent errors due to discrepancies between the actual count and what really was collected. However, after 45 weeks of the continuous discrepancies, the total amount of differences had become alarming. Eddie Wong, the controller for the church, estimated that the total was now $23,399. That represents well over 5 percent of the church's annual collections from members totaling about $400,000.

The meeting began at 9 a.m., a time that was early for the church leaders who often had late evening calls to make. The church staff brought donuts, bagels, and coffee to help get the meeting off to a good start—but that's not the way it happened.

"I want an explanation," said Allen Yuen, the executive director of the church.

"I can't explain it, Allen," responded Eddie Wong.

"Jennie, how about you?" Yuen asked. He was addressing Jennie Lin, the member of the executive committee of the board of trustees who was directly responsible for the count each week.

Jennie seemed uncomfortable. She hesitated before saying, "I think my count is correct. I take the money given to me by Joey, put it in the safe, and then Eddie opens the safe on Monday morning. He records the cash receipts and makes a bank deposit."

Eddie said, "That's right. My deposit always matches the amount of money reported by Jennie."

"That doesn't make sense," Yuen said. "Someone is getting his or her hands on the money between the collection process and recording the amount."

"Perhaps the tally amount record independently submitted by the church volunteers has been overstated," Jennie said.

"Why would that happen?" Yuen asked. "I mean, while it could happen and it would be an honest mistake, it seems unlikely."

Jennie was starting to sweat. She decided a diversion was in order. "Maybe someone gets their hands on the collection box after the tally and before Joey gives it to me."

Joey Ching is the accounting manager who delivers the collection box and tally sheet to Jennie after each service. Joey goes to church on a regular basis and volunteered to do the job to establish a control in the process.

At this point, Jennie lowered her head while she waited for a response. It came from Alex Yuen. "Jennie, are you accusing Joey of stealing money from the church collection box?"

Jennie shook her head as if to say no. She was visibly upset. Yuen was called to the phone, and the meeting had to break up. The group agreed to continue the discussion in two days. In the meantime, Alan Yuen said he'd call Joey Ching and ask him to attend the next meeting.

Jennie went back to her office, closed the door, and started to reflect on what she had just done. The truth is that Jennie had been taking the money each week and giving it to a homeless shelter two blocks from the church. Some of the homeless attend church services, and Jennie has befriended many of them. She knew it was wrong to take money from the collection box, but she thought it was for a very good cause and that the church clergy would approve. She never thought about getting caught because she told the bookkeeper to record the lower amount. Now she feels guilty about bringing Joey into the picture.

Questions

1. Evaluate Jennie's actions from an ethical perspective. Did she do the right thing? Is there any way to justify what she has done with ethical reasoning?

2. Eddie Wong and Jennie Lin are both CPAs. Because they work for a not-for-profit organization, do they come under the AICPA Code of Professional Conduct? Why or why not? Support your answer with reference to the relevant provisions in the Code. Should the fact that the CPAs are working for a not-for-profit organization change their ethical obligations?

3. Comment on the internal controls at the church. Do you think the controls are to blame for the problem, or are they effective within the constraints of the system? Explain your answer with reference to the facts of the case.

4. Evaluate the alternatives available to Jennie from an ethical and professional perspective. What would you do if you were Jennie Lin?

5. Regardless of your answer to the previous question, assume that Jennie called Joey and explained the situation. She asked that Joey not come to the meeting so she could explain what she had done without his involvement. If you were Joey, would you stay away from the meeting? Why or why not?

6. Assume that Jennie went to the meeting and explained what she had done and why. Eddie Wong got angry at Jennie. He told her that she had been disloyal to him and the church. Allen Yuen, on the other hand, commended Jennie for her community awareness. He did tell Jennie, however, that she would have to replace the money from personal funds. Evaluate the positions taken by Wong and Yuen. What do you think Jennie should do? Why?

Case 4-6

Juggyfroot

"I'm sorry, Lucy. That's the way it is," Ricardo Rikey said.

"I just don't know if I can go along with it, Ricardo."

"We have no choice. Juggyfroot is our biggest client, Lucy. They've warned us that they will put the engagement up for bid if we refuse to go along with the reclassification of marketable securities to trading."

"Have you spoken to Fred and Ethel about this?" Lucy asked.

"Are you kidding? They're the ones who made the decision to go along with Juggyfroot," Ricardo responded.

This scene took place in the office of Deziloo LLP, a large CPA firm in Beverly Hills, California. Lucy Spheroid is the partner on the engagement of Juggyfroot, a global manufacturer of pots and pans. Ricardo Rikey is the managing partner of the office. Fred and Ethel are the two members of the firm who make final judgments on difficult accounting issues, especially when there is a difference of opinion with the client. All four are CPAs.

Ricardo is preparing for a meeting with Norman Baitz, the CEO of Juggyfroot. Ricardo knows that the company expects to borrow $5,000,000 next quarter and it wants to put the best face possible on its financial statements to impress the banks. That would explain why the company had reclassified a $2,000,000 market gain on an available-for-sale investment from stockholder's equity to current income. The investment now shows up in the balance sheet as "trading" and, as a result, the reclassification led to an increase in earnings by 8 percent over the first quarter of 2007. Ricardo also knows that without the change, the earnings would have declined by 2 percent and the company's stock price would have taken a hit.

In the meeting, Ricardo points out to Baitz that the investment in question was made in an affiliate company that Juggyfroot had owned for six years. Ricardo adds that there is no justification under generally accepted accounting principles to change the classification from available-for-sale to trading securities.

Questions

1. Briefly discuss the rules in accounting for investments in trading securities and available-for-sale securities. Does it appear from the facts of the case that Juggyfroot was correct in making the reclassification? Why or why not?

2. Who are the stakeholders in this case? What expectations should they have, and what are the ethical obligations of Deziloo and its CPAs to the stakeholders? Use ethical reasoning and virtue theory to answer this question.

3. Using the AICPA Code of Professional Conduct as a reference, what ethical issues exist for Ricardo, Lucy, Fred, and Ethel, and Deziloo LLP in this matter?

4. Regardless of your answers to Questions 1–3, assume that the CPAs were able to convince Juggyfroot to go back to its original classification of the investment, and this resulted in a 2 percent decline in quarterly earnings. After the news became public, the stock price of Juggyfroot declined 10 percent. Norman Baitz stormed into the Deziloo office that day at 5 p.m. and asked to speak with Lucy and Ricardo. They met in a conference room where the CEO informed them he had just lost $12 million on his investment in the company's stock. He demanded an explanation. Ricardo asked for 24-hours to prepare written comments. The CEO agrees to the delay; they are to meet the next day at the same time.

   Describe how you feel about what Norman Baitz has said and done.

5. Draft a one-page memorandum to explain the firm's position to the CEO.

Case 4-7

Phar-Mor

The Dilemma

The story of Phar-Mor shows how quickly a company that built its earnings on fraudulent transactions can dissolve like an Alka-Seltzer tablet.

One day Stan Cherelstein, the controller of Phar-Mor, discovered cabinets stuffed with held checks totaling $10 million. Phar-Mor couldn't release the checks to vendors because it did not have enough cash in the bank to cover the amount. Cherelstein wondered what he should do.

The Background

Phar-Mor was a chain of discount drug stores, based in Youngstown, Ohio, that had been founded in 1982 by Michael Monus and David Shapira. The company grew from 15 to 310 stores in less than 10 years and had 25,000 employees. According to Litigation Release No. 14716 issued by the SEC,[1] Phar-Mor had cumulatively overstated income by $290 million between 1987 through 1991. In 1992, prior to disclosure of the fraud, the company overstated income by an additional $238 million.

The Cast of Characters

Mickey Monus personifies the hard-driving entrepreneur who was bound and determined to make it big whatever the cost. He served as the president and chief operating officer of Phar-Mor from its inception until a corporate restructuring was announced on July 28,1992.

David Shapira was the chief executive officer of Phar-Mor and the CEO of Giant Eagle, Phar-Mor's parent company and majority stockholder. Giant Eagle also owned Tamco, which was one of Phar-Mor's major suppliers. Shapira left day-to-day operations of Phar-Mor to Monus until the fraud became too large and persistent to ignore.

Patrick Finn was the chief financial officer of Phar-Mor from 1988 to 1992. Finn initially brought Monus the bad news that following a number of years of eroding profits, the company faced millions in losses in 1989.

John Anderson was the accounting manager at Phar-Mor. Hired after completing a college degree in accounting at Youngstown State University, Anderson became a part of the fraud.

Coopers & Lybrand, prior to its merger with Price Waterhouse, was the auditor firm for Phar-Mor. The firm failed to detect the fraud as it was unfolding.

[1] Securities and Exchange Commission, Litigation Release No. 14716, November 9, 1995, *SEC v. Michael Monus, Patrick Finn, John Anderson and Jeffrey Walley, Case No. 4:95, CV 975, (N.D., OH)* www.sec.gov/litigation/litreleases/lr14716.txt.

How It Started

The facts of this case are taken from SEC filings in the matter and a Public Broadcasting System Frontline program, "How to Steal $500 Million." The interpretation of the facts is consistent with reports, but some literary license has been taken to add intrigue to the case.

Finn approached Monus with the bad news. Monus reacted by taking out his pen, crossing off the losses, and writing in higher numbers to show a profit. Monus couldn't bear the thought of his hot growth company that had been sizzling for five years suddenly flaming out. In the beginning, it was to be a short-term fix to buy time while the company improved efficiency, put the heat on suppliers for lower prices, and turned a profit. Finn believed in Monus's ability to turn things around, so he went along with the fraud. Finn prepared the reports and Monus changed the numbers for four months before turning the task over to Finn. These reports with the false numbers were faxed to Shapira and given to Phar-Mor's board. Basically, the company was lying to its owners.

The fraud occurred by dumping the losses into a "bucket account" and then reallocating the sums to one of the company's hundreds of stores in the form of increases in inventory amounts. Phar-Mor issued fake invoices for merchandise purchases and made phony journal entries to increase inventory and decrease cost of sales. The company overcounted and double counted merchandise in inventory.

The fraud was helped by the fact that the auditors from Coopers observed inventory in only four of 300 stores, which allowed the finance department at Phar-Mor to conceal the shortages. Moreover, Coopers had informed Phar-Mor in advance which stores they would visit. Phar-Mor executives fully stocked the four selected stores but allocated the phony inventory increases to the other 296 stores. Regardless of the accounting tricks, Phar-Mor was heading for collapse, and its suppliers threatened to cut the company off for nonpayment of bills.[2]

Stan Cherelstein's Role

Cherelstein was hired to be the controller of Phar-Mor in 1991 long after the fraud had begun. One day, John Anderson, Phar-Mor's accounting manager, called Cherelstein into his office and explained that the company had been keeping two sets of books, one that showed the true state of the company with the losses and the other, called the subledger, that showed the falsified numbers that were presented to the auditors.

Cherelstein and Anderson discussed what to do about the fraud. Cherelstein was not happy about it at all and demanded

[2] Joseph T. Wells,"Ghost Goods: How to Spot Phantom Inventory," Association of Certified Fraud Examiners, www.acfe.com/fraud/view.asp?ArticleID=18.

to meet with Monus. Cherelstein did get Monus to agree to repay the company for the losses from his investment of company funds in the World Basketball League, but Monus never kept his word. In the beginning, Cherelstein felt compelled to give Monus some time to turn things around through increased efficiencies and by using a device called *exclusivity fees* that were paid by vendors to get Phar-Mor to stock their products. Over time, Cherelstein became more and more uncomfortable as the suppliers called more frequently demanding payment on their invoices.

Accounting Fraud

Misappropriation of Assets

The unfortunate reality of the Phar-Mor saga was that it involved not only bogus inventory but also the diversion of company funds to feed Monus's personal habits. One example was the movement of $10 million in company funds to help start a new basketball league, the World Basketball League (WBL) that limited player participation to those six feet tall and under.

False Financial Statements

According to the ruling by the U.S. Court of Appeals that heard Monus's appeal of his conviction on all 109 counts of fraud,[3] the company had submitted false financial statements to Pittsburgh National Bank, which increased a revolving credit line for Phar-Mor from $435 million to $600 million in March 1992. It also defrauded Corporate Partners, an investment group that had bought $200 million in Phar-Mor stock in June 1991. The list goes on including the defrauding of Chemical Bank, which served as the placing agent for $155 million in 10-year senior secured notes issued to Phar-Mor; Westinghouse Credit Corporation, which had executed a $50 million loan commitment to PharMor in 1987; and Westminster National Bank, which served as the placing agent for $112 million in Phar-Mor stock sold to various financial institutions in 1991.

Tamco Relationship

The early financial troubles experienced by Phar-Mor in 1988 can be attributed to at least two transactions. The first was that the company provided deep discounts to retailers to

[3] *United States of America v. Michael I. Monus,* 1997 FED App. 0311P (6th Cir.)

stock its stores with product. There was concern early on that the margins were too thin. The second was that its supplier, Tamco, was shipping partial orders to Phar-Mor while billing for full orders. Phar-Mor had no way of knowing because it was not logging in shipments from Tamco.

After the deficiency was discovered, Giant Eagle agreed to pay Phar-Mor $7 million in 1988 on behalf of Tamco. Phar-Mor later bought Tamco from Giant Eagle in an additional effort to solve the inventory and billing problems. However, the losses just kept on coming.

Back to the Dilemma

Cherelstein looked out the window at the driving rain storm. He thought about the fact that he didn't start the fraud or the cover-up. Still, he knew about it later and felt compelled to do something. Cherelstein thought about the persistent complaints by vendors that they were not being paid and their threats to cut off shipments to Phar-Mor. He knew that without any product in Phar-Mor stores, the company could not last much longer.

Questions

1. How do you assess blame for the fraud? That is, to what extent was it caused by Pat Finn's willingness to go along with the actions of Mickey Monus? What about David Shapira's lax oversight? What responsibilities exist for John Anderson and Sam Cherelstein that contributed to the fraud. Finally, should the blame all go to Mickey Monus?

2. Using the decision-making model discussed in Chapter 3, identify the alternative courses of action for Stan Cherelstein.

3. Assume that Stan Cherelstein is a CPA. If you were in his position, what would you do? Support your decision using ethical reasoning.

4. Discuss the due care standard in the AICPA Code of Conduct. What are the ethical obligations of a CPA or CPA firm under this standard? Given the limited facts of the case, do you think Coopers and Lybrand violated the due care standard? Why or why not?

5. What is the ethical message of Phar-Mor? That is, explain what you think is the "moral of the story."

Case 4-8

The New CEO

Liza Perky was recently selected to be the CEO of a small company in Oklahoma City. The company distributes paper products and office machines to businesses in the Oklahoma, Texas, and Arkansas tristate area. Texarkoma Products had planned to go public after five years of growth in sales from $200,000 to $1,500,000. However, increased competition from Kanecola, a start-up paper company in the Kansas, Colorado, and Nebraska tristate area, forced Texarkoma to cut prices, and the losses started to mount. In 2005, Texarkoma lost $500,000, and in 2006, it lost $700,000. For the first nine months of 2007, the company lost $600,000. That's when it fired the former CEO and hired Perky.

Perky knows the company will soon turn things around because Kanecola was recently taken over by Clips, Inc., a national office paper products company that is located in 40 states. Texarkoma now has a competitive advantage in the local tristate area because small businesses in the area tend to be loyal to local and regional distributors because of the personal service and long-standing ties to the community.

During the last three months of 2007, the company reported a preliminary loss of $250,000. On January 8, 2008, Perky took a look at the results and didn't like them. She summoned her chief accounting officer, Joe Boreing. He asked Perky what the problem was. The following conversation took place.

Perky: Joe, I've been looking over the results for the last three months and the supporting numbers and I can't understand why you only put through a $200,000 write-down of the Gobble line of fax machines.

Boreing: I think we can salvage something from a discount sale of the machines.

Perky: How so, Joe? We haven't sold very many of these machines during the past three months.

Boreing: We've sold 50 machines.

Perky: And what was our loss?

Boreing: It was 50 percent of the cost of each machine. That amounted to $25,000.

Perky: And your numbers indicate there are still 500 machines in stock.

Boreing: That's right.

Perky: Well, you're the math wiz, but I figure that means a potential loss of at least $250,000.

Boreing: That's right, but I cut it to $200,000 because I have a potential buyer. It's the Texas School District. The superintendent wants to buy the faxes for all K-12 schools, and she doesn't care that it's not the latest model with all the bells and whistles.

Perky: Do you have a signed contract?

Boreing: No, I expect that to happen by the end of January.

Perky: Well, aren't you always preaching conservatism to me in terms of the numbers?

Boreing: Not always but in general; the accounting rules require that we provide for all potential losses immediately.

Perky: Right. So I want you to do that with the Gobble faxes.

Boreing: OK. I'll add $50,000 to the write-down.

Perky: That's not enough. I want you to double the amount.

Boreing: You want me to increase the write-down to $300,000?

Perky: No. I want you to record a total write-off of the Gobble inventory.

Boreing: You want me to write-off all $500,000?

Perky: That's what I said.

Boreing started to resist but after 10 more minutes of discussion, he knew it was no use. Perky cut him off and told him she had given a direct order and expected it to be obeyed, or else.

Questions

1. What do you think is Perky's motivation? What is she trying to accomplish by having Joe record a $500,000 write-down? To support your answer, use the various possible loss figures for the 9 months and 12 months ended September 30, 2007, and December 31, 2007, respectively, when compared with the losses in 2005 and 2006.

2. Is it unethical to knowingly increase an estimated loss in a year beyond the one that appears to be justified by the events? Why or why not?

3. Assume that Boreing is a CPA and member of the AICPA. If he goes along with Perky's demand, will he be violating any of the rules of conduct in the AICPA Code? Be specific.

4. Using the ethical decision-making model discussed in Chapter 3, identify the alternatives available to Boreing. What would you do if you were in his position? Why?

Case 4-9

The New Staff Member

Pavzi Abbadoola is of Middle Eastern descent. He recently graduated from state university with a master's degree in accountancy. His grade point average was 3.92. Pavzi had earned all *A*'s in his undergraduate degree before moving to the United States to undertake the MAcy program at the university.

Pavzi is understandably a very shy person. His language skills are excellent, but he doesn't feel completely comfortable being in the United States because of cultural differences. However, he has worked hard to be more outgoing and recently received an offer to join a Big-Four CPA firm. He started working for the firm in January 2008.

On his first audit, Pavzi came across an unusual transaction. The client had recorded $1 million in operating revenue that represented a payment from a customer who had backed out of a contract to buy a product from the client. Pavzi discovered that the customer had decided to buy a different information system network from a competitor. The contract with the client stated that customers could be released from purchase contracts by paying $1 million. That represented 5 percent of the overall contract price.

Pavzi had tried to question the senior on the job, but every time he approached her, she was too busy with other things. She told him after several attempts that she trusted his judgment and that the $1 million probably had been recorded in the proper account.

The audit was completed on February 15. The staff members on the audit were to report to the office the next day for their new assignments. Pavzi just didn't feel right about the fact that he couldn't fully discuss the disclosure of the $1 million with the senior on the job and it seemed to be a material amount. He also knows that the client's income from operations for the 12 months ended December 31, 2007, is reported as $895,000.

Questions

1. Why is it important to have self-confidence when working for a CPA firm? How can one develop the level of self-confidence needed to be successful, assuming that it is not an innate quality?

2. What are the professional responsibilities of a new staff member when faced with an accounting issue that appears to have been improperly recorded or reported?

3. Assume that the senior on the audit is a CPA. Do you believe she has violated any ethical standards based on the limited information in the case? If so, explain which rules may have been violated. If not, explain why you feel that way.

4. Given the facts of the case, where do you think the $1 million should be recorded? Why? What difference does it make whether the item is recorded in one category in the income statement versus another? Consider the possible implications of the disclosure for future operating results.

Case 4-10

ZZZZ Best

The story of ZZZZ Best is one of greed and audaciousness. It is the story of a 15-year-old boy from Reseda, California, who was driven to be successful regardless of the costs. His name is Barry Minkow.

Minkow had high hopes to make it big—to be a millionaire very early in life. He started a carpet cleaning business in the garage of his home. Minkow realized early on that he was not going to become a millionaire cleaning other people's carpets. He had bigger plans than that. Minkow was going to make it big in the insurance restoration business. In other words, ZZZZ Best would contract to do carpet and drapery cleaning jobs after a fire or flood. Because the damage from the fire or flood probably would be covered by insurance, the customer would be eager to have the work done. The only problem with Minkow's insurance restoration idea was that it was all a fiction. There were no insurance restoration jobs, at least for ZZZZ Best. In the process of creating the fraud, Minkow was able to dupe the auditors, Ernst & Whinney,[1] into thinking the insurance restoration business was real. In fact, more than 80 percent of his revenue was allegedly from this work. The auditors never caught on until it was too late.

How Barry Became a Fraudster[2]

Minkow wrote a book, *Clean Sweep: A Story of Compromise, Corruption, Collapse, and Comeback,*[3] that provides some insights into the mind of a 15-year-old kid who was called a "wonder boy" on Wall Street until the bubble burst. He was trying to find a way to drum up customers for his fledgling carpet cleaning business. One day, while he was alone in the garage-office, Minkow called Channel 4 in Los Angeles. He disguised his voice to sound like an adult and told a producer that he had just had his carpets cleaned by the 16-year-old owner of ZZZZ Best and was very impressed that a high school junior was running his own business. He sold the producer on the idea that it would be good for society to hear this success story. The producer bought it lock, stock, and carpet cleaner. Minkow gave the producer the phone number of ZZZZ Best and waited. It took less than 5 minutes for the call to come in. Minkow answered the phone and when the producer asked to speak with Mr. Barry Minkow, Minkow said: "Who may I say is calling?" Within days, a film crew

was in his garage shooting ZZZZ Best at work. The story aired that night, and it was followed by more calls from radio stations and other television shows wanting to do interviews. People called demanding that Barry Minkow personally clean their carpets.

As his income increased in the spring of 1983, Minkow found it increasingly difficult to run the company without a checking account. He managed to find a banker that was so moved by his story that the banker would agree to allow someone underage to open a checking account. Minkow used the money to buy cleaning supplies and other necessities. Even though his business was growing, he ran into trouble paying back loans and interest when due.

Minkow developed a plan of action. He was tired of worrying about not having enough money. He went to his garage, where all his great ideas first began, and looked at his bank account statement, which showed that he had more money than he thought he had based on his own records. Minkow soon realized it was because some checks he had written had not been cashed, so they hadn't yet shown up on the bank statement. Voila! Minkow started to kite checks between two or more banks. He would write a check on one ZZZZ Best account and deposit it into another. Because it could take a few days for the check written on Bank 1 to clear that banks' records—back then, checks weren't always processed in real time— Minkow could pay some bills out of an account with another bank and the first bank would not know, at least for a few days, that Minkow had written a check on his account when he had a negative balance in it. The bank didn't know this because some of the checks that Minkow had written before the visit to Bank 2 had not cleared his account in Bank 1.

It wasn't long thereafter that Minkow realized that he could kite checks big-time. Not only that, he also could make the transfer of funds at the end of a month or a year and show a higher balance than really existed in Bank 1 and carry it on to the balance sheet. Because Minkow did not count the check written on his account in Bank 1 as an outstanding check, he was able to double count.

Time to Expand the Fraud

Over time, Minkow moved on to bigger and bigger frauds, such as having his trusted cohorts confirm to banks and other interested parties that ZZZZ Best was doing insurance restoration jobs. Minkow used the phony jobs and phony revenue to convince bankers to make loans to ZZZZ Best. He had cash remittance forms made up from nonexistent customers with whatever sales amount he wanted to appear on the document. He even had a coconspirator write on the bogus remittance form, "job well done." Minkow could then show a lot more revenue that he was really making.

---

[1] Ernst & Whinney and Arthur Young were two of the Big 8 CPA firms that existed before the 1990s. The two firms merged and are now known as Ernst & Young.

[2] The facts are derived from a video by the ACFE, *Cooking the Books: What Every Accountant Should Know about Fraud.*

[3] Barry Minkow, *Clean Sweep: A Story of Compromise, Corruption, Collapse, and Comeback* (Nashville, TN: Thomas Nelson, 1995).

Minkow's phony financial statements enabled him to borrow more and more money and expand the number of carpet cleaning outlets. However, his personal tastes had become increasingly more expensive, including the purchase of a Ferrari with the borrowed funds and a down payment on a 5,000-square foot home. So, the question was how he solved a perpetual cash flow problem. He went public! That's right, Minkow made a public offering of stock in ZZZZ Best. Of course, he owned a majority of the stock to maintain control of the company.

Minkow had made it to the big leagues. He was on Wall Street. He had investment bankers, CPAs, and attorneys all working for him. The 15-year-old kid from Reseda had turned a mom and pop operation into a publicly owned corporation.

Barry Goes Public

Minkow's first audit was for the 12 months ended April 30, 1986. A sole practitioner performed the audit. Minkow had established two phony front companies that allegedly placed insurance restoration jobs for ZZZZ Best. He had one of his cohorts make out invoices for services and respond to questions about the company. There was enough paperwork to fool the auditor into thinking the jobs were real and the revenue was supportable. However, the auditor never visited any of the insurance restoration sites. If he had done so, there would have been no question in his mind that ZZZZ Best was a big fraud.

Pressured to get a big-time CPA firm to do his audit as he moved into the big leagues, Minkow hired Ernst & Whinney to perform the April 30, 1987, fiscal year-end audit. Minkow continued to be one step ahead of the auditors—that is, until the Ernst & Whinney auditors insisted on going to see an insurance restoration site. They wanted to confirm that all of the business—all of the revenues—that Minkow had said was coming in to ZZZZ Best was real.

The engagement partner drove to an area in Sacramento, California, where Minkow did a lot of work—supposedly. The partner looked for a building that seemed to be a restoration job. Why he did that isn't clear, but he identified a building that seemed to be the kind that would be a restoration job in process.

At around the same time, Minkow sent one of his cohorts to find a large building in Sacramento that appeared to be a restoration site. As luck would have it, Minkow's associate picked out the same site as the engagement partner had.

Prior to the visit of the partner later that weekend, Minkow's cohorts went to Sacramento and found the leasing agent for the building. They convinced the agent to give them the keys so that they could show the building to some potential tenants over the weekend. Minkow's helpers went to the site before the arrival of the partner and placed placards on the walls that indicated ZZZZ Best was the contractor for the building restoration. In fact, the building was not fully constructed at the time, but it looked as if some restoration work would have been going on at the site.

Minkow was able to pull it off in part due to luck and in part because the Ernst & Whinney auditors did not want to lose the ZZZZ Best account. It had become a large revenue producer for the firm, and Minkow seemed destined for greater and greater achievements. Minkow was smart, and he used the leverage of the auditors not wanting to lose the ZZZZ Best account as a way to complain when they became too curious about the insurance restoration jobs. He would threaten to take his business away from Ernst & Whinney and give it to other auditors.

Minkow also took a precaution with the site visit. He had the auditors sign a confidentiality agreement that they would not make any follow-up calls to any contractors, insurance companies, the building owner, or other individuals involved in the restoration work. This prevented the auditors from corroborating the insurance restoration contracts with independent third parties.

The Fraud Starts to Unravel

It was a Los Angeles housewife who started the problems for ZZZZ Best that would eventually lead to the demise of the company. Because Minkow was a well-known figure and flamboyant character, the *Los Angeles Times* did an article about the carpet cleaning business. The Los Angeles housewife read the story about Minkow and recalled that ZZZZ Best had overcharged her for services in the early years by increasing the amount of the credit card charge for carpet cleaning services.

Minkow had gambled that most people don't check their monthly statements so he could get away with the petty fraud. However, the housewife did notice the overcharge, complained to Minkow, and eventually he returned the overpayment. She couldn't understand why Minkow would have had to resort to such low levels back then if he was as successful as the *Times* article made him out to be. So, she called the reporter to find out more, and that ultimately led to the investigation of ZZZZ Best and future stories that weren't so flattering.

Because Minkow continued to spend lavishly on himself and his possessions, he always seemed to need more and more money. It got so bad over time that he was close defaulting on loans and had to make up stories to keep the creditors at bay, and he couldn't pay his suppliers. The complaints kept coming in, and eventually the house of cards that was ZZZZ Best came crashing down.

During the time that the fraud was unraveling, Ernst & Whinney decided to resign from the ZZZZ best audit. The firm never issued an audit report. It had started to doubt the veracity of Minkow and the reality of business at ZZZZ Best.

The procedure to follow when a change of auditor occurs is for the company being audited to file an 8-K form with the SEC and the audit firm to prepare an exhibit commenting on the accuracy of the disclosures in the 8-K. The exhibit is attached to the form that is sent to the SEC within 30 days of the change (currently a 4-day filing requirement). Ernst & Whinney waited the full 30-day period, and the SEC released the information to the public 45 days after the change had occurred. Meanwhile, ZZZZ Best had filed for bankruptcy. During the interim period, Minkow had borrowed more than $1 million dollars, and the lenders never were repaid. Bankruptcy laws protected Minkow and ZZZZ Best from having to make those payments.

Legal Liability Issues

The ZZZZ Best fraud was one of the largest of its time. ZZZZ Best reportedly settled a shareholder class action lawsuit for $35 million. Ernst & Whinney was sued by a bank that had made a multimillion-dollar loan based on the financial statements for the three-month period ending July 31, 1986. The bank claimed that it had relied on the review report issued by Ernst & Whinney in granting the loan. However, the firm had indicated in its review report that it was not issuing an opinion on the ZZZZ Best financial statements. The judge ruled that the bank was not justified in relying on the review report because Ernst & Whinney had expressly disclaimed issuing any opinion on the statements.

Barry Minkow was charged with engaging in a $100 million fraud scheme. He was sentenced to a term of 25 years but was paroled after serving 8 years in jail.

Questions

1. Do you believe that auditors should be held liable for failing to discover fraud? Why or why not?

2. What are the criteria for audit independence? Comment on the independence and objectivity of Ernst & Whinney in conducting its audit of ZZZZ Best.

3. Auditors are expected to exercise due care in the performance of professional services. Explain the purpose of the due care standard. Based on the facts of the case, do you think the sole proprietor-auditor and Ernst & Whinney met their due care obligations? Why or why not?

4. Assume that you had been involved in the ZZZZ Best audit. You have discovered a bogus invoice for restoration work. The amount is material. You go to the partner in charge of the engagement who tells you to forget about it. What are the ethical considerations that would be important to you in deciding on a course of action? What would you do?

5. These are selected numbers from the financial statements of ZZZZ Best for fiscal years 1985 and 1986.

	1985	1986
Sales	$1,240,524	$4,845,347
Cost of goods sold	576,694	2,050,779
Accounts receivable	0	693,773
Cash	30,321	87,014
Current liabilities	2,930	1,768,435
Notes payable—current	0	780,507

What calculations or analyses would you make with these numbers that could help you assess whether the financial relationships are "reasonable"? Given the facts of the case, what inquiries could you make of management based on your analysis?

Chapter 5

Professional Responsibilities and Ethical Obligations in Auditing

Under the old world order, senior executives of companies that were most aggressive were the ones that won most often. We have to be able to convince the senior executives at companies that the world has changed and that under the new rules you are going to consistently lose if you are using accounting tricks. . . .

Howard Schilit

The quotation by Howard Schilit, president of the Center for Financial Research and Analysis (CFRA) and a leading authority on detecting accounting gimmicks, emphasizes the role of senior executives in pushing a company to commit accounting fraud in the financial statements. The goal of this chapter is to explain the techniques in auditing that exist to help auditors live up to their professional and ethical obligations, including risk assessment and internal control evaluation, and to avoid the types of legal liabilities discussed in Chapter 6.

What Is an Audit?

An *audit* is an examination of the financial statements of a company prepared by management in accordance with generally accepted accounting principles (GAAP). To enhance the reliability of the statements to investors and creditors, the Securities and Exchange Commission (SEC) requires that all public companies must have an independent auditor examine the statements and issue an opinion on its conformity with GAAP. The exact wording of the audit report appears in Exhibit 5.1.

EXHIBIT 5.1
**The Auditor's
Standard Report**

Source: Public Company
Accounting Oversight Board,
Auditing Standard No. 1,
*References in Auditors' Report
to the Standards of the Public
Company Accounting Oversight
Board* (Washington, D. C.:
PCAOB, May 14, 2004).

Report of Independent Registered Public Accounting Firm

We have audited the accompanying balance sheet of X Company
as of December 31, 2008 and 2007, and the related statements of
income, retained earnings, and cash flows for each of the three years
in the period ended December 31, 2008. These statements are the
responsibility of the Company's management. Our responsibility
is to express an opinion on these financial statements based
on our audit.

We conducted our audit in accordance with the standards of the
Public Company Accounting Oversight Board (United States). Those
standards require that we plan and perform the audit to obtain
reasonable assurance [italics added for emphasis] about whether the
financial statements are free of material misstatement. An audit
includes examining, on a test basis, evidence supporting the amounts
and disclosures in the financial statements. An audit also includes
assessing the accounting principles used and significant estimates
made by management, as well as evaluating the overall financial
statement presentation. We believe that our audit provides a
reasonable basis [italics added for emphasis] for any opinion.

In our opinion, the financial statements referred to above *present
fairly* [italics added for emphasis], in all *material* [italics added for
emphasis] respects, the financial position of X Company as of [at]
December 31, 2008 and 2007, and the results of its operations
and its cash flows for each of the three years in the period ended
December 31, 2008, in conformity with accounting principles
generally accepted in the United States of America.

[Signature]
[City and State or County]
[Date]

Explanation of the Audit Report

Introductory Paragraph

The three important elements in the introductory paragraph follow:

1. Identifies the financial statements being examined.
2. Clarifies management's responsibilities for the statements.
3. States the auditor's responsibility to express an (independent) opinion on those statements.

In most companies, the financial statements are prepared under the direction of the controller who reports to the chief financial officer (CFO). The CFO reports to the chief executive officer (CEO). In virtually all of the frauds that occurred in the late 1990s and early 2000s, the CFO either gave in to the CEO's pressure to prepare materially false or misleading financial statements or, as in the case of Enron, the CFO personally directed the fraud.

The controller's position is a difficult one because of the dual obligations of loyalty to one's employer and adherence to ethical standards. As a CPA, the controller should be aware of the ethical obligation not to stand idly by while false statements are issued. A controller who does remain silent violates the AICPA Code of Conduct as was initially discussed in Chapter 4 and is reviewed here later. The controller also may become a party to a lawsuit brought for constructive or actual fraud.

The controller can avoid violating the Integrity Rule (Rule 102) in the AICPA Code and the GAAP financial statement rule (Rule 203) by following the framework discussed in Chapter 4. Those requirements are summarized here. First, the controller should inform the CFO of any material misstatement in the financial statements. If the CFO does not support correcting the statements, the controller should go to the CEO. If the CEO takes no action to correct the matter, the controller should go to the audit committee of the board of directors. Although one's ethical obligations are satisfied after these steps have been taken, it is also recommended that the controller should prepare an informative memorandum outlining the discussions with respect to correcting the material misstatement of the financial statements just in case the matter winds up in the courts.

As a student, you may think it is unlikely that you will face a similar situation in your career. While this may be true with respect to the GAAP conformity of the financial statements, other situations in which the ethical dilemma is just as difficult could arise. For example, what would you do if you see a co-worker steal a significant amount of money from petty cash and you confront that person, who says it is a "one-time fix" because of personal cash flow problems. Would you remain silent? The issues are similar for the controller in the previous example. No one likes to inform on a co-worker. Recall from Chapter 1 that loyalty is the ethical value that should never take precedence over other values such as honesty and integrity. Otherwise, we can imagine all kinds of cover-ups of information in the interest of loyalty or friendship.

We recommend that the controller should ask whether this is the type of organization that she wants to be associated with on a long-term basis. In the example given, the controller has the technical expertise to decide GAAP matters, yet the CFO and CEO did not respect her skills and knowledge. Once the controller goes along with corporate wrongdoing, she becomes a part of the cover-up, which is the first step down the ethical slippery slope. Moreover, the fraud could be blamed on the controller later on when (and if) the bubble bursts.

Scope Paragraph

The scope paragraph contains four important statements that define the auditor's responsibility in conducting an audit:

1. The auditor conducted the audit in accordance with the standards of the Public Company Accounting Oversight Board (United States).
2. The audit provides "reasonable assurance" that the statements are free of "material" misstatement.
3. The auditor assessed the accounting principles used and the significant estimates made by management and evaluated the overall financial statement presentation.
4. The audit provides a "reasonable" basis for the opinion.

GAAS is to the audit what GAAP is to the financial statements. GAAP represents the rules for recording, reporting, and disclosing financial statement information. The SEC requires an audit opinion for all public companies that states that their accounting is in compliance with GAAP. GAAS establishes the audit standards and procedures that should be followed in conducting an audit. By following these standards, the auditor increases the likelihood of being able to defend against the legal liability issues discussed in Chapter 6. Audit standards will be discussed later in this chapter.

Audit Opinions

Auditors can express an unqualified opinion (clean opinion), an unqualified opinion with an explanatory paragraph, a qualified opinion, an adverse opinion, or a disclaimer. An auditor also can withdraw from the engagement under restricted circumstances.

Opinion Paragraph—Unqualified

An auditor should give an unqualified opinion when the financial statements "present fairly" the company's financial position, results of operations, and cash flows.

Opinion Paragraph—Unqualified with an Explanatory Paragraph

Certain situations call for adding a fourth, explanatory paragraph. For example, a going concern issue could exist when the entity's ability to survive is in doubt. The going concern issue can arise because of continuing operating losses or the excess of cash outflows over cash inflows over an extended period of time and the inability of the company to raise needed funds to continue operations. Start-up companies sometimes have these problems as would a company facing bankruptcy.

Opinion Paragraph—Qualified

The auditor qualifies the report when there is a difference of opinion with management on the application of GAAP that is material in amount or material because of the nature of the difference. One example is an illegal payment that may not have a material effect on the financial statements but is a material event because a law, the Foreign Corrupt Practices Act, has been violated. The users of the financial statements have an ethical right to be informed of such an event regardless of materiality considerations. Other than when a violation of law exists, it remains somewhat unclear when an auditor should disclose a nonmaterial violation of GAAP. Later in this chapter we discuss the concept of materiality and how it may be applied in the context of the audit opinion.

Some managers seek to use accounting techniques that are designed to manipulate earnings regardless of the justifiability of the method under GAAP, thereby creating a conflict. Earnings management, a concept that will be fully discussed in Chapter 7 and is briefly described here, can occur.

Let's assume that the auditor estimates the market value of inventory to be $500,000 below its cost. GAAP requires that inventory should be recorded at year-end at the lower of cost or market. The auditor approaches management and explains that a loss of $500,000 should be recorded. Management responds by saying that amount is not acceptable because it will lower net income below financial analysts' estimates for the year. Management could be concerned that earnings reductions below the targeted amount will lead to a reduction in the share price of stock. Hence, earnings must be "managed" to meet desired goals.

In this case, the auditor has three choices: (1) insist on recording the $500,000 loss, (2) ignore the loss, or (3) negotiate with management for an acceptable amount of loss to record. While in the "real world" the result could be a negotiation process between the auditor and management, the auditor's ethical responsibility is to insist on recording the loss that is justified by GAAP.

Another possibility is that top management pressures the auditor to ignore the entire amount of a write-down. If that occurs, the auditor should seek the support of the audit committee. During the Enron "Dark Ages," practically all boards and audit committees (i.e., Enron, WorldCom, Tyco, and Adelphi) either ignored their fiduciary obligations to shareholders or passively supported management.

In a worst-case scenario for the auditor, management could threaten to change auditors because of a disagreement. If a change occurs, management must file an 8-K form with the SEC explaining the reasons for a change. This filing could trigger an SEC investigation. Nevertheless, the ethics of the accounting profession prohibits auditors from compromising their integrity to satisfy the client or avoid the loss of the client.

If top management threatens an auditor with seeking a different opinion from other auditors or actually seeks it, the company engages in *opinion shopping.* There is nothing (ethically) wrong with a client exercising its right to act with due diligence and discussing a change in auditor with competing auditors if, for example, concerns exist about the quality of work or size of the audit fees. However, when the client seeks other views until finding an auditor who will go along with the client's desired but not necessarily most ethical accounting treatment, we have the classic example of opinion shopping.

Opinion Paragraph—Adverse Opinion

In limited situations, the auditor could conclude that the financial statements taken as a whole do not present fairly the company's financial position or results of operations or cash flows in conformity with GAAP. Adverse opinions should be preceded by a separate paragraph in the audit report that provides all substantive reasons for the auditor's conclusion and the principal effects of the subject matter of the adverse opinion on financial position, results of operations, and cash flows, if practicable.

In reality, an auditor who contemplates giving an adverse opinion should follow the same procedures as one considering a qualified opinion and first attempt to influence management to make the change necessary to avoid that opinion. Management could conclude that it is better to make the change than to risk having either a qualified or, certainly, an adverse opinion. There is no doubt in the latter case that the stock market reaction would be negative. When a qualified opinion is given, it is possible, based on the reasons for the qualification, that investors and creditors accept the auditor's opinion and explanation without a measurable change in stock price. This could occur if the qualification, while reflecting a material event, does not change the fact that the statements "present fairly" with that sole exception.

Opinion Paragraph—Disclaimer

When the auditor is unable to gather sufficient information, the auditor may express a qualified opinion or disclaimer of an opinion. If the auditor is able to express an opinion on the financial statements taken as a whole, even with a lack of sufficient evidence, then opinions should be qualified. The qualification would be explained in a separate paragraph. Another possibility is that the auditor would disclaim an opinion. This occurs when the auditor is unable to obtain sufficient competent evidential matter to express an opinion on the financial statements as a whole. For example, assume that the auditor is unable to observe the client's taking inventory and cannot be satisfied through alternative means. Because the inventory amount affects both the balance sheet and income statement, the auditor could conclude that it is best to disclaim an opinion on the statements taken as a whole.

Withdrawal from an Engagement

From time to time, an auditor could consider withdrawing from an engagement. Withdrawal generally is not appropriate because the auditor is hired by the client to do an audit and render an opinion, not walk away from his obligations when the going gets tough. However, if a significant conflict exists with management or the auditor decides that management cannot be trusted, a withdrawal could be justified. This would trigger the filing of the 8-K form by management.

Generally Accepted Auditing Standards—Overview

GAAP is established by the Financial Accounting Standards Board, a private body with seven members who represent a variety of stakeholder interests. GAAS is established by two organizations. For many years, the AICPA had sole responsibility through its Auditing Standards Board. Following the passage of the Sarbanes-Oxley Act (SOX), however, the SEC established the Public Company Accounting Oversight Board to set auditing standards for public companies that file with the SEC. The AICPA's Auditing Standards Board continues to set auditing standards for privately owned businesses.

This two-tier system can be confusing because the PCAOB has incorporated the GAAS that existed before it was established as its standards as of April 16, 2003. Therefore, GAAS still has widespread applicability to the audits of public companies (incorporated into PCAOB standards) and nonpublic companies and not-for-profit entities (as issued by the AICPA). PCAOB now establishes its own auditing standards for public companies. The standards that this body approves are *required* standards, not "generally accepted." The PCAOB's position is that its standards should be used regardless of what could be "generally accepted" in practice.

The PCAOB also establishes independence rules and quality control standards for registered CPA firms. In addition, it conducts a peer review program by which its representatives review the quality controls in effect at registered firms and issues an opinion to firm management. The PCAOB reports to the SEC in carrying out its responsibilities in regard to this review.

Generally Accepted Auditing Standards—Requirements

An independent auditor plans, conducts, and reports the results of an audit in accordance with GAAS. Auditing standards provide a measure of audit quality and set the objectives to be achieved in an audit. Auditing *standards* differ from auditing *procedures* because the procedures are steps taken by the auditor during the course of the audit to comply with the standards (GAAS).[1]

General Standards

Three general standards relate to the quality of the professionals who perform the audit. These include their (1) adequate technical training and proficiency, (2) independence in mental attitude, and (3) due care in the performance of the audit and preparation of the report.

Standards of Field Work

Standards of field work establish the criteria for judging whether the audit has met quality requirements. These standards should guide the auditor in meeting the expectations for a quality examination. The standards are (1) to adequately plan the audit work and supervise assistants, (2) to obtain a sufficient understanding of internal control to adequately plan the audit and determine the nature, timing, and extent of tests to be performed, and (3) to gather sufficient competent evidential matter through audit procedures including inspection, observation, inquiries, and confirmations to provide a reasonable basis (support) for an opinion regarding the financial statements under audit.

The standards of field work provide the basis for determining whether the audit has been carried out with the level of care expected by the accounting profession. Recall that due care is the basis for Rule 201, General Standards, of the AICPA Code.

Standards of Reporting

Just as the financial statements are the end product of the accountants' work, the audit report is the end product of an auditor's work. The audit report carries particular significance for investors and creditors who rely on financial statements to help make decisions such as buying or selling stock and granting loans. Moreover, the report can be used to identify red flags that create questions about the entity's ability to continue as a going concern and point out any nonconformity with GAAP in a fourth, explanatory paragraph.

Four reporting standards guide auditors: (1) determination of whether the statements have been prepared in conformity with GAAP, (2) identification of situations in which the accounting principles have not been consistently observed in the current period in relation to the preceding period, (3) discussion in the report of any situation identified in the footnotes to the financial statements for informative disclosures that are not adequate, and (4) the expression of an opinion on the financial statements taken as a whole or an indication that an opinion cannot be expressed with adequate support for that conclusion.

Limitations of the Audit Report

Three phrases in the audit report are critical to understanding the limits of the report: (1) *reasonable assurance,* (2) *material,* and (3) *present fairly.* These expressions are used to signal the reader about specific limitations of the audit report.

Reasonable Assurance

The word *reasonable* is often used in law to define a standard of behavior to decide legal issues. In auditing, an auditor should exercise a *reasonable* level of care (due care) to avoid charges of negligence and possible liability to the client. The *reasonable (prudent) person* standard is typically used to judge whether an uninvolved individual looking at the behavior of an auditor internally, perhaps in relation to independence and client relationships, can conclude that the auditor has maintained the appearance of independence.

Reasonable assurance is not an absolute guarantee that the financial statements are free of material misstatement. Auditors do not examine all of a company's transactions. The transactions selected for examination are determined based on materiality considerations and risk assessment. Even then, only a small percentage of transactions are selected, often by statistical sampling techniques.

The auditor makes the reasonable assurance statement in the context of GAAS. The statement means that the auditor has followed GAAS in carrying out audit responsibilities including gathering sufficient competent evidential matter. The auditor uses professional judgment to decide whether available evidence is sufficient to justify an opinion. If the auditor fails to follow GAAS in making that decision, an allegation of negligence is supportable. If the auditor were to purposefully ignore justified audit procedures or evidence that, for example, has negative implications for the client, a charge of constructive fraud or fraud could be sustained in a court of law. These charges can be brought by clients as well as third parties, as will be discussed in Chapter 6.

Materiality

Statement on Auditing Standards (SAS) No. 99, Consideration of Fraud in a Financial Statement Audit, notes, "The auditor has a responsibility to plan and perform the audit to obtain reasonable assurance about whether the financial statements are free of material misstatement, whether caused by error or fraud."[2] The concept of *materiality* is, perhaps, one of the most challenging concepts in accounting. The application of professional judgment to the surrounding circumstances in which materiality is at issue provides the setting to assess whether an item or event is either quantitatively or qualitatively significant enough to warrant financial reporting or disclosure.

Materiality is defined in the glossary of *Statement of Financial Accounting Concepts No. 2,* Qualitative Characteristics of Accounting Information as:

> . . . the magnitude of an omission or misstatement of accounting information that, in the light of surrounding circumstances, makes it probable that the judgment of a reasonable person relying on the information would have been changed or influenced by the omission or misstatement.[3]

Judging Materiality

Materiality in the context of an audit reflects the auditor's judgment of the needs of users in relation to the information in the financial statements and the possible effect of misstatements on user decisions as a group. According to a "Proposed International Standard on Auditing 320 (Revised), Materiality in the Identification and Evaluation of Misstatements:"

> Omissions or misstatements of items are material if they could, individually or collectively, influence the economic decisions of users taken on the basis of financial statements. Materiality depends on the size and nature of the omission or misstatement judged in the surrounding circumstances. The size or nature of the item, or a combination of both, could be the determining factor. [4]

Each Statement of Financial Accounting Standards (SFAS) adopted by FASB states, "The provisions of this Statement need not be applied to immaterial items." The SEC has ruled in *Staff Accounting Bulletin (SAB) No. 99* that this does *not* mean that a public company filing financial statements with the SEC, or its auditor, may rely solely on a quantitative threshold as a "rule of thumb" to determine materiality.[5] For example, an auditor could use a percentage as a numerical threshold such as 5 percent as the materiality test by applying that percentage to the item in question. The result is then compared to some related number such as net income to judge significance.

For example, assume that a company has one item in inventory that cost $400,000. The auditor believes that its current market value is $381,000, or $19,000 (4.75 percent) below cost. Under the 5 percent rule, the item may be judged immaterial and the write-down ignored. However, what if the net income for the year is only $300,000? Then the $19,000 write-down causes cost of goods sold to increase by that amount, and it becomes material because the write-down would be 6.33 percent of net income.

One unintended consequence of the accounting profession's approach to materiality is that a controller who knows that the 5 percent rule is in effect could attempt to decrease expenses or increase revenues by an amount less than 5 percent to increase earnings by an amount that will not be challenged by the auditor. It is somewhat ironic that the auditor can let the difference go by even though it may be wrong because of the materiality standard.

SAB 99 provides that a percentage test may be used to form a preliminary assumption that—without considering all relevant circumstances—a "deviation of less than the specified percentage with respect to a particular item on the registrant's financial statements is unlikely to be material." However, the auditor must go beyond using such a "bright line" test based on the magnitude of misstatement as the sole source of judgment about materiality. According to *SAB 99,* "It cannot be used as a substitute for a full analysis of all relevant considerations."

The U.S. Supreme Court noted in *TSC Industries v. Northway, Inc.,* that judgments of materiality require "delicate assessments of the inferences a 'reasonable shareholder' would draw from a given set of facts and the significance of those inferences to him."[6] In other words, the Court and the accounting profession have similar interpretations that a fact is material if there is a substantial likelihood that it would have been viewed by the reasonable investor as having significantly altered the "total mix" of information made available.

SAS No. 99 greatly advances the accounting profession's assessment of materiality by linking it to obtaining information needed to identify the risks of material misstatement due to fraud. This standard provides guidance to auditors in fulfilling their responsibilities to plan and perform the audit to obtain reasonable assurance about whether the financial statements are free of material misstatement, whether caused by error or fraud.[7]

Errors vs. Fraud

An error can occur due to an innocent mistake in the application of GAAP, omission of information, or a mathematical mistake. Fraud exists when a deliberate decision is made to deceive another party, such as the investors and creditors. An auditor's legal liabilities in connection with fraud will be discussed in Chapter 6.

Let's assume that Risky Software, Inc., records revenue of $1 million on December 28, 2007, as the result of a sale of software to facilitate enterprise resource planning at Shaky Business Co. The sale requires Risky to provide support services including a 24-hour help-desk for one year. Risky records all $1 million of revenue in 2007. However, GAAP requires that the company should separate out the relevant amount that represents support services to which it is committed and record it as deferred revenue. That amount would then be matched with the support services provided over the next 12 months.

Management's intent determines whether the misapplication of GAAP is an error in judgment or a deliberate decision to inflate revenues for 2007. In a court of law, guilt or innocence typically comes down to the credibility of the CFO and CEO who are charged with fraud. Without a "smoking gun," the court could look for parallel actions by these top officers such as selling their own shares of corporate stock after the fraudulent act but before it becomes public knowledge, as occurred at Enron and WorldCom.

Present Fairly

Without an understanding of the term *present fairly,* the users of the financial statements would be unable to assess the reliability of the financial statements. The expression to present fairly is linked to GAAP. *SAS No. 69,* The Meaning of Present Fairly in Conformity with GAAP, points out that the phrase "generally accepted accounting principles" is a technical accounting term that encompasses the conventions, rules, and procedures necessary to define accepted accounting practice at a particular time. GAAP provides a framework to measure financial presentations. The independent auditor's judgment concerning the "fairness" of the overall presentation of financial statements should be applied within the framework of GAAP.[8]

The auditor's assessment of fair presentation depends on whether (1) the accounting principles selected and applied have general acceptance, (2) the accounting principles are appropriate in the circumstances, (3) the financial statements, including the related notes, are informative concerning matters that could affect their use, understanding, and interpretation, (4) the information presented in the statements is classified and summarized in a reasonable manner, that is, neither too detailed nor too condensed, and (5) the financial statements reflect the underlying transactions and events in a manner that is consistent with materiality and reflects their economic substance.

Let's examine lease accounting rules and apply these five criteria. A *lease* is a form of property rental for which the party using the asset (lessee) makes periodic payments to the legal owner of the asset (lessor). Perhaps some of you have leased an apartment or an automobile and are familiar with how the typical lease agreement provides for periodic payments, sometimes with an option to buy the asset for a set price at the end of the lease term.

GAAP for leases comes from a variety of FASB statements, but the one that establishes the lease standards in accounting is *Statement of Financial Accounting Standards (SFAS) No. 17,* Accounting for Leases. *SFAS No. 17* provides that the lessee (user of the property) should determine the present value (PV) of future lease payments and record an asset and liability if any one of four criteria exist.

The capital lease criteria include (1) transfer of ownership to the lessee at the end of the lease term, (2) bargain purchase option for the lessee, (3) lease life of 75 percent or more of the economic life of the leased asset, and (4) the PV equals 90 percent or more of the fair value of the leased asset at the date of the lease. If any one of the four criteria is absent, the lease is treated as an operating lease, and each lease payment is debited to an expense account, offset by a credit to cash, and the asset remains on the books of the lessor, the legal owner of the leased asset.

In a capital lease, the lessor finances the acquisition for the lessee by allowing a period of time in which the lessee makes lease payments. In an operating lease, the lessee makes a payment as the asset is used. Operating leases lead to "off-balance sheet financing" because the amount due to the lessor over the lease contract is not recorded on the lessee's balance sheet as a liability. This creates a potentially troublesome practice from the perspective of the user of the financial statements who could be interested in knowing the company's future cash obligations. GAAP deals with this issue by requiring the lessee to disclose the scheduled lease payments for the next five years.

Capital lease information on the balance sheet of the lessee should reflect the carrying value of the leased asset and a breakdown of the current lease liability and long-term balance. If a company were to combine those numbers and just present the total as a long-term lease, the auditor should question the reasonableness of the presentation. The failure to include the appropriate amount of payments due for the next year in the current liability section misrepresents the current and future liabilities of the lessee, and it implies a higher amount of liquidity than justified. The result is that the financial statements would not "present fairly" the company's financial position. Of course, it is possible that materiality considerations could negate that conclusion if supportable by the facts.

The capital lease treatment of the discounted future lease payments as an asset on the balance sheet of the lessee (and, typically, removal of the asset and liability from the lessor's books) exemplifies putting the economic substance of a transaction over its legal form. Legally, the lessor owns the asset. There has been no sale. However, if one of the four criteria is met, we can conclude, for all intents and purposes, that the lessee effectively owns the asset that is merely being given a fixed period of time for the lessee to pay for it.

Expectations Gap

The independent auditor's responsibility is to audit and report on the financial statements prepared by management. Perceptions of the shortcomings in the effectiveness of independent audits erode public confidence in the integrity of the financial reporting system. Concerns about the quality of financial reporting are nothing new for the accounting profession as you learned in Chapter 4. To address these concerns, the AICPA's Auditing Standards Board in 1988 issued nine new auditing standards to help close the "expectations gap," that is, the difference between what the public and the users of financial statements perceive as the responsibilities of accountants and auditors and what accountants and auditors themselves see as their responsibilities.

The results of a survey of investor views of audit assurance in 1994 by Epstein and Geiger indicate that the investing public holds auditors to a much higher level of accountability for detecting material misstatements due to error and fraud than the profession has assumed. The authors conclude that the profession's perception that an audit should provide only reasonable assurance of financial statement accuracy is held by a minority of investors. The majority of investors expect an audit to provide absolute assurance that the financial statements are free of all types of material misstatements, thereby confirming the existence of the gap. Epstein and Geiger believe that an important factor in closing this expectation gap is to increase auditors' sensitivity to management honesty and integrity (or lack thereof).[9]

One of the nine expectations gap standards issued in 1988 is *SAS No. 55,* Internal Control in a Financial Statement Audit. It attempts to narrow the gap by incorporating the auditor's assessment of the ethics of the organization and top management as an integral part of the internal control system.

One of the five components of internal controls is the control environment. The control environment sets "the tone of the organization, influencing the control consciousness of its people. It is the foundation for all other components of internal control, providing discipline and structure."[10]

The definition of internal control in *SAS No. 55* differs from previous definitions in two important ways: (1) it broadens the definition of internal control and the parties that affect it by linking sound controls to the actions of the board of directors, management, and other personnel, and (2) it identifies five interrelated components of internal control including the control environment, risk assessment, control activities, information and communication systems, and monitoring of controls.[11]

SAS No. 54, Illegal Acts, is another "expectation-gap" standard. It defines illegal acts as violations of laws or governmental regulations. For example, a violation of the Foreign Corrupt Practices Act constitutes an illegal act. It exposes the company to both legal liability and public disgrace. The auditor's responsibility is to determine the proper accounting and financial reporting treatment of a violation once it has been established by the experts that a violation has in fact occurred.

SAS 54 characterizes *illegal acts* as those attributable to the entity whose financial statements are under audit or as acts by management or employees acting on behalf of the entity. Illegal acts by clients do not include personal misconduct by the entity's personnel unrelated to their business activities.[12]

The auditor's responsibility is to detect and report misstatements resulting from illegal acts that have a direct and material effect on the determination of financial statements amounts. For example, tax laws affect accruals and the amount recognized as income tax liability for the period. A company that for tax purposes capitalized an expense and wrote the amount off over a period of years rather than properly expensing the entire amount in the current year violates tax law, triggering an adjustment in the current period financial statements.

The potential violation of laws such as occupational safety and health, environmental protection, and equal employment creates indirect effects on the financial statements. These events are due to operational, not financial matters, and their financial statement effect is indirect, for example, a possible contingent liability that should be disclosed in the notes to the financial statements.

The expectations gap seems to have expanded as evidenced by the frauds at companies such as Enron, WorldCom, and Tyco. The public reaction has been to question the entire system of corporate governance, and Congress reached its limit of patience with the accounting profession. The result was to remove standard setting from the private, accounting arena and turn it over to a public, quasigovernmental entity, the PCAOB.

The AICPA tried once again to close the gap when it issued *SAS No. 99,* the so-called fraud standard. It was one of the last standards set by the AICPA before being replaced by the PCAOB for public company audits.

Auditor's Responsibilities for Fraud Prevention, Detection, and Reporting

The first line of defense against fraud is to have an effective system of internal controls and an independent internal audit function. As described in Chapter 4, internal auditors should have direct and unrestricted access to the audit committee. The head of internal auditing should not have to discuss matters pertaining to the existence of material misstatements in the financial statements with the CFO and CEO, both of whom could be responsible for a fraud.

The example of Cynthia Cooper provides an excellent role model of how the internal audit function should work. The fraud at WorldCom all unraveled in April and May 2002 after Gene Morse, an internal auditor at WorldCom, could not find any documentation to record $500 million in computer expenses. Morse approached his boss, Cynthia Cooper, the company's vice president of internal auditing, who instructed Morse to "keep going."

A series of obscure tips led Morse and Cooper to suspect that WorldCom was cooking the books. Cooper formed an investigation team to determine whether their hunch was right. The team discovered $3.8 billion of misallocated expenses and phony accounting entries.[13]

Cooper approached the CFO, Scott Sullivan, but was dissatisfied with his explanations. Bernie Ebbers, founder and former CEO of WorldCom, had already resigned, so Cooper went to the audit committee. The committee interviewed Sullivan about the accounting issues and did not get a satisfactory answer. Sullivan was asked to resign, refused to do so, and was fired.[14]

Description and Characteristics of Fraud

Fraud comes in a variety of shapes and sizes but has one common element: the intentional underlying action that results in a material misstatement of the financial statements. *SAS 99* identifies two types of misstatements that are relevant to the auditor's consideration of fraud: (1) misstatements arising from fraudulent financial reporting and (2) misstatements arising from the misappropriation of assets.[15]

Fraudulent Financial Reporting

SAS 99 defines fraudulent financial reporting as "intentional misstatements or omissions of amounts or disclosures in financial statements designed to deceive financial statement users where the effect causes the financial statements not to be presented, in all material respects, in conformity with GAAP."[16] The reasons for the deception are many and are identified by *SAS 99* as part of "the fraud triangle," depicted in Exhibit 5.2.

Incentives/Pressures to Commit Fraud

The incentive to commit fraud typically is a self-serving one. It could be caused by internal budget pressures or financial analysts' earnings expectations that are not being met. For example, a CEO could believe that the failure to meet predetermined goals would lead to a loss of performance bonus money or a reduction in stock price, thereby reducing the spread between the current market price and the strike price in the option plan.

Techniques Used to Falsify Financial Information

The techniques used to falsify financial information range from the basic to the exotic. The Waste Management fraud involved the arbitrary lengthening of the useful lives of trash-hauling equipment to reduce annual depreciation charges and increase earnings. The

EXHIBIT 5.2
The Fraud Triangle

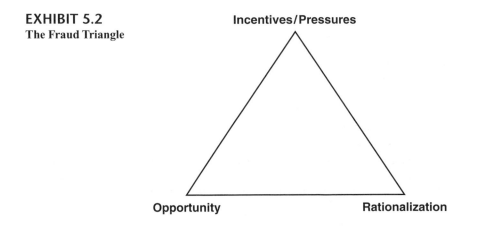

Enron fraud involved financially structured transactions to create "special-purpose entities" (SPEs) whose transactions could then be kept off Enron's books, thereby allowing the company to shift debt to the SPEs. This structure also allowed Enron to engage in transactions with the SPE such as the "sale" of unwanted assets that created paper gains on Enron's books. The effects of these transactions and others inflated earnings, overstated its liquidity, and generally made the company appear to be extraordinarily successful when that was not the case. The Enron saga will be discussed in full in Chapter 7.

Financial results can be manipulated through the use of bogus invoices to record revenue as was the case at ZZZZ Best. In some instances, a company could manipulate its own accounting records to achieve its goal. MicroStrategy is a company that backdated sales agreements to push revenue back into the preceding period. For example, a contract that was legally approved on January 3, 2001, would be dated December 30, 2000.

Another technique is the misapplication of GAAP. At WorldCom, improperly recorded costs referred to as "line costs," represented *annual* payments to other telecommunication providers to gain access to needed Internet capacity for WorldCom customers. These costs were accounted for as capital expenditures rather than being expensed immediately against earnings. The result was to overstate earnings in the first year by the difference between the total amount that should have been expensed and the annual amortization, while earnings in future years were understated by the amortization amount. The line costs were recurring costs that increased each year during the telecommunications boom of the late 1990s, so that the net overstatement of earnings continued to grow over a period of time.

Misappropriation of Assets

The misappropriation of assets involves the theft of company assets; this action leads to financial statements that do not conform to GAAP. For example, an employee could write company checks payable to herself for personal expenses. The diversion of company funds for personal purposes understates cash and overstates expenses. Often the guilty employee tries to "bury" the personal expense in an innocuous account such as office expenses or even miscellaneous expenses.

Some fraudsters seem to have no shame. In the ZZZZ Best fraud, Barry Minkow set up front companies as clients that issued checks from their bank accounts to pay for services never performed. The checks were then deposited into the ZZZZ Best account and revenue was recorded. Minkow would then use some of the money to pay for personal expenses and would bury the expense in ZZZZ Best accounts. The original funds paid by the fictitious company to ZZZZ Best came from funds diverted by Minkow and his cohorts to create the illusion of the front company.

Opportunity to Commit Fraud

The second side of the fraud triangle connects the pressure or incentive to commit fraud with the opportunity to carry out the act. Employees who have access to assets such as cash and inventory should be monitored closely through an effective system of internal controls that helps to safeguard these and other assets. The company should segregate cash-processing responsibilities including the opening of mail that contains remittance advices with checks for the payment of services, the recording of the receipts as cash and a reduction of receivables, the depositing of the money in the bank, and the reconciliation of the balance in cash on the books with the bank statement balance.

The opportunity to commit fraud also occurs when top executives backdate stock options to increase the potential gain for those executives receiving the options. For example, if a company's stock price is rapidly increasing and top management wants to attract new employees to the company, management can agree to set a strike (exercise) price that is dated weeks or months prior to the grant date. The executive gains because of the increased spread between the exercise price and future market price, assuming that the stock price continues to rise. The backdating options problem first become public in the summer of 2006,with UnitedHealth Group, Converse, and Cisco, and it threatens to further erode trust in the financial marketplace.

Rationalization of the Fraud

It is rare when the perpetrators of fraud rationalize their actions after the fraud because most of them are already in denial. However, it is not unusual for someone who is genuinely a good person to get caught up in fraud. For example, there is the case of Betty Vinson, a former WorldCom mid-level accounting manager who pleaded guilty in October 2002 to participating in the financial fraud at the company. Vinson was sentenced to five months in prison and five months of house arrest.

Vinson represents the typical "pawn" in a financial fraud: a lower- or mid-level account-ing person who by all accounts had no interest or desire to commit fraud but got caught up in it when her boss, Scott Sullivan, instructed her to make improper accounting entries. The rationalization Sullivan gave to convince Vinson that the company had to make the numbers appear better than they really were did nothing to ease her guilty conscience. Judge Barbara Jones, who sentenced Vinson, commented, "Ms. Vinson was among the least culpable members of the conspiracy at WorldCom....Still, had Vinson refused to do what she was asked, it's possible this conspiracy could have been nipped in the bud."[17]

Accounting students should reflect on what they would do if they face a situation similar to the one that led Vinson to do something that was out of character. Once she agreed to go along with making improper entries, it was difficult to turn back. The company could have threatened to disclose her role in the original fraud and cover-up if Vinson all of a sudden developed a conscience. The key to maintaining one's integrity and ethical perspective is not to take the first step down the ethical slippery slope.

Vinson became involved in the fraud because she had feared losing her job, her benefits, and the means to provide for her family; on her own initiative, Cynthia Cooper ordered the internal investigation that led to the discovery of the $11 billion fraud at WorldCom. Cooper did all the right things to bring the fraud out in the open. Vinson will have to live with the consequences of her actions for the rest of her life. Cooper, on the other hand, received the Accounting Exemplar Award in 2004 given by the American Accounting Association and was inducted into the AICPA Hall of Fame in 2005.

Tyco: A Case of Corporate Greed

You probably have heard about the Tyco fraud. The actions of former CEO Dennis Kozlowski epitomize the selfishness and greed that overwhelmed some companies in the late 1990s and early 2000s.

Kozlowski spent $2 million for a 40th birthday party for his wife by flying friends and corporate hotshots to the Italian island of Sardinia for fun and games including a Roman toga party complete with entertainment by Jimmy Buffet. There was a board meeting on the last day of the week of fun and frolic, and Kozlowski billed Tyco for only $1 million.

Kozlowski was brazen. Manhattan District Attorney Robert Morgenthau successfully prosecuted him for using Tyco funds to purchase millions of dollars of artwork for his $18 million apartment in New York City, an apartment that was also paid for from Tyco funds. Kozlowski used company "loans" for the purchases, allowing him to avoid paying income tax on the money used. (The loan amounts should have been declared as compensation on Kozlowski's tax return). Of all of the excesses, perhaps his use of corporate funds for his own creature comforts best illustrates Kozlowski's apparent lack of any conscience. For example, he spent $6,000 of Tyco funds on a gold-plated shower curtain!

Kozlowski was also charged with fraudulently transporting $13 million worth of art to Tyco's headquarters in New Hampshire to avoid more than $1 million in New York state and city sales taxes. New York does not tax purchases of merchandise for use outside the state. Kozlowski had the artwork, or, in some cases, empty boxes, sent to New Hampshire, where there is no sales tax. He then had the boxes sent back on the sly to his Manhattan apartment, a place he will not see any time soon. He was convicted on 22 counts of grand larceny, falsifying business records, securities fraud, and conspiracy. Kozlowski was sentenced to a jail term of from 8 and one-third to 25 years and was ordered to pay $97 million in restitution and $70 million in fines.

The corporate governance system at Tyco completely broke down. The company's former CFO, Mark Swartz, a co-conspirator with Kozlowski in the theft of $600 million from Tyco, received the same sentence as Kozlowski. Swartz facilitated the fraud by actions such as hiding unauthorized pay and bonuses and abusing a loan program. He and Kozlowski were responsible for taking actions and making statements that inflated the company's stock price.

Most members of Tyco's board of directors benefited personally as a result of Tyco's practices. For example, one member of the board worked for a law firm that "just happened" to receive as much as $2 million in business from Tyco. This person's pay at the law firm was linked to the amount of work he helped bring in from Tyco. Another director received a $10 million payment for help in engineering an acquisition for Tyco. In all of these transactions and a variety of others in which Tyco board members did business with the company and directors and officers received loaned money from the company, the required related-party disclosures were not made in the financial statements.[18] These situations that present conflicts of interest are dealt with in the Sarbanes-Oxley Act (SOX) through independence requirements for nonexecutive board members and the audit committee.

The news was no better for PricewaterhouseCoopers LLP, the auditors for Tyco. On August 13, 2003, the SEC issued a cease and desist order against Richard P. Scalzo, the PwC engagement partner for the firm's audits of Tyco's financial statements for fiscal years 1997 through 2001. The SEC found that Scalzo recklessly violated the antifraud provisions of the federal securities laws and engaged in improper professional conduct.[19]

Of particular note with respect to the culture at Tyco that enabled the fraud to occur is the finding by the SEC that both PwC and its lead engagement partner failed to follow GAAS and failed in their professional obligations. PwC was aware as early as 1997 that Tyco was not disclosing all required by GAAP on related party transactions and did not adequately plan the audits or conduct the audits with due professional care and objectivity. Accounting and Auditing Enforcement Release (AAER) No. 1839 notes the following:

> Multiple and repeated facts provided notice to Scalzo regarding the integrity of Tyco's senior management and Scalzo was reckless in not taking appropriate audit steps in the face of this information. By the end of the Tyco annual audit for its fiscal year ended September 30, 1998, if not before, those facts were sufficient to obligate Scalzo, pursuant to GAAS, to reevaluate the risk assessment of the Tyco audits and to perform additional audit procedures, including further audit testing of certain items (most notably, certain executive benefits, executive compensation, and related party transactions).[20]

The Tyco fraud is a shocking example of what can happen when all systems involved in the governance of a corporation fail at the same time. In addition to receiving salary and other compensation valued near $30 million, Kozlowski sold $258 million of Tyco stock back to the company. By the time Kozlowski was under indictment for sales tax fraud and quit in 2002, $80 billion of Tyco's shareholder wealth had evaporated.

Kozlowski bought off Tyco's board of directors through favored treatment. The audit committee was irrelevant. The external auditors looked the other way while the company and its top officers violated the duty of care and loyalty to the shareholders that is a required feature of good governance.

Fraud Considerations in the Audit

SAS 99 details 10 areas of fraud considerations that should improve the auditor's ability to detect and report fraud: (1) a description and characteristics of fraud, (2) the importance of exercising professional skepticism, (3) discussion among engagement personnel regarding the risks of material misstatement due to fraud, (4) obtaining the information needed to identify risks of material misstatement due to fraud, (5) identifying risks that could result in a material misstatement due to fraud, (6) assessing the identified risks after taking into account an evaluation of the entity's programs and controls, (7) responding to the results of the assessment, (8) evaluating audit evidence, (9) communicating about fraud with management, the audit committee, and others, and (10) documenting the auditor's consideration of fraud.[21]

Fraud Risk Assessment

Most of the requirements of *SAS 99* call for the auditor to engage in risk assessment during the audit. Actually, the assessment of risk starts with an evaluation of evidence about the potential client before agreeing to accept the audit engagement. One important step is to communicate with the predecessor auditor to find the reason(s) that it is no longer servicing the client. Assessing the integrity of top management and key accounting personnel is of particular importance. The successor auditor also should clarify with the predecessor whether there were any differences of opinion with management over the application of accounting principles and how these were handled, including the role of the audit committee in the matter.[22]

To support risk assessment, the auditor should approach each engagement with a healthy dose of skepticism. This means to be skeptical in gathering information, asking questions, and evaluating the corporate culture. In making the assessment, the auditor should not, of course, approach the audit with an attitude toward management of "You are a crook. Prove me wrong." Instead, a healthy attitude is one that informs management in word and deed that the auditor's responsibility is to ask the tough questions, thoroughly examine relevant documentation, and probe to determine whether the organization's culture promotes ethical decision making and there is support for financial statement amounts and disclosures.

The auditor should obtain information needed to identify the risk of material misstatement due to fraud. According to *SAS 99,* the goal should be to (1) make inquiries of management and others within the organization to obtain their views about the risks of fraud and how they are addressed, (2) consider any unusual or unexpected relationships that have been identified in performing analytical procedures (i.e., financial statement comparisons over time and ratio analysis) in planning the audit, (3) consider whether one or more fraud risk factors exist, and (4) consider other information (i.e., interim financial results and factors associated with the acceptance of the client) that could be helpful in the identification of risks of material misstatement due to fraud.[23]

Fraud Risk Factors

Fraud risk factors are explained in *SAS 99* by linking them to one of the three sides of the fraud triangle. Essentially, they represent "red flags" that should serve as a warning to the auditor that financial stability, operating, and/or corporate culture factors may be a precursor to fraud or indicative that fraud has occurred. The auditor's role is to follow up on these warning signs by asking the tough questions, gathering the necessary information to support or refute the signs, and resist giving in to client pressures to look the other way.

In the audits of both Waste Management and Enron, the auditors, Arthur Andersen, were satisfied with explanations of highly questionable transactions and the related accounting by accepting management's promise to "clean up their act" in the future. Of course, that never happened and, by the time the bubble was ready to burst, the Andersen auditors had fallen to the bottom of the slippery slope by accepting the word of a group of people who had committed fraud.

Revisiting the Expectation Gap

In March 2006, the AICPA's Auditing Standards Board issued eight Statements on Auditing Standards relating to the assessment of risk in the audit of financial statements. These statements establish standards and provide guidance concerning the auditor's assessment of the risks of material misstatement (whether caused by error or fraud) in a financial statement audit and the design and performance of audit procedures whose nature, timing, and extent are responsive to the assessed risks. The statements also establish standards and provide guidance on planning and supervision, determining the nature of audit evidence, and evaluating whether the audit evidence obtained affords a reasonable basis for an opinion regarding the financial statements under audit.[24]

There is no doubt that these standards were motivated by the continuing expectation gap between the public's perception of auditors' responsibilities to ferret out fraud and the accounting profession's traditional role of providing only reasonable assurance that the financial statements are free of material misstatement due to fraud.

The goal of the eight risk assessment standards is to enhance auditors' evaluation of audit risk by requiring, among other things:

1. A more in-depth understanding of the entity and its environment, including its internal control, to identify the risks of material misstatement in the financial statements and what the entity is doing to mitigate them.
2. A more rigorous assessment of the risk of material misstatement of the financial statements based on that understanding.
3. An improved linkage between the assessed risks and the nature, timing, and extent of audit procedures performed in response to those risks.

One important fact to note is that the AICPA set the standards after its responsibilities for setting auditing standards for public companies ended. Still, the AICPA sets auditing standards for nonpublic companies. While the PCAOB has not formally adopted these standards for public companies, on June 17, 2004, it issued *Auditing Standard No. 2, An Audit of Internal Control over Financial Reporting in Conjunction with an Audit of Financial Statements*. It essentially incorporates much of the risk assessment concepts in the AICPA standards and requires a management report on internal control that should be assessed by the external auditors as part of an integrated audit of the financial statements and internal controls.[25] The auditors then issue one opinion on the controls and one on the financial statements.

Internal Control Assessment

The risk that internal controls will not help to prevent or detect a material misstatement in the financial statements is a critical evaluation in providing reasonable assurance. Understanding the system of internal controls and whether it operates as intended enables the auditor to either gain confidence about the internal processing of transactions or creates doubt for the auditor that should be pursued.

SAS No. 55: Internal Control in a Financial Statement Audit

SAS No. 55 is a significant standard on internal control. It identifies five interrelated components of internal control as follows:[26]

1. The *control environment* sets the tone of an organization, influencing the control consciousness of its people. It is the foundation for all aspects of internal control, providing discipline and structure.
2. *Risk assessment* is the entity's identification and evaluation of how risk could affect the achievement of objectives.
3. *Control activities* are the strategic actions established by management to ensure that its directives are carried out.
4. *Information and communication* systems provide the information in a form and at a time that enables people to carry out their responsibilities.
5. *Monitoring* is a process that assesses the efficiency and effectiveness of internal controls over time.

Internal Control—Integrated Framework

SAS No. 78 amends *SAS No. 55* to reflect the changes necessary to recognize the definition and description of internal control contained in *Internal Control—Integrated Framework,* published by the Committee of Sponsoring Organizations (COSO) of the Treadway Commission in 1992. The framework defines internal control as a process effected by an entity's board of directors, management, and other personnel, designed to provide reasonable assurance regarding the achievement of the following objectives: (1) effectiveness and efficiency of operations, (2) reliability of financial reporting, and (3) compliance with applicable laws and regulations.[27]

COSO utilizes the *SAS No. 55* framework and emphasizes the roles and responsibilities of management, the board of directors, internal auditors, and other personnel in creating an environment that supports the objectives of internal control. One important contribution of COSO is in the area of corporate governance. COSO notes that if members of the board and audit committee do not take their responsibilities seriously, the system will likely break down as occurred in the recent scandals.

COSO Findings on Financial Statement Fraud

COSO analyzed the financial reporting by public companies during 1987–1997. It is noteworthy that most of its findings were precursors to what happened during the business frauds and accounting failures of the 1998–2003 period. COSO examined 200 cases of financial statement fraud and found the following:[28]

1. Some companies committing the fraud were experiencing net losses or were in close to break-even positions in periods before the fraud. These pressures may have led some companies to commit fraud to reverse downward spirals while others may have been motivated to preserve upward trends.
2. Top senior executives were frequently involved. In the SEC investigation and subsequent actions as reflected in the AAERs, 72 percent of SEC investigations and actions by the SEC named the CEO and 43 percent the CFO. When considered together, in 83 percent of the cases, the AAERs named one or the other officer or both of them.
3. Most audit committees met infrequently or not at all. Twenty-five percent of the companies did not have an audit committee. Sixty-five percent of the committees did not did not have a member with expertise in accounting or finance.
4. Boards were dominated by insiders and "gray" directors (outsiders with special ties to the company or management) with significant equity ownership and little experience.

Collectively, the directors and officers owned nearly one-third of the companies' stock, with the CEO/president personally owning about 17 percent.

5. In cases of fraud, there were family relationships present between the directors, officers, and/or individuals with significant power. The founder and current CEO were the same person or the original CEO/president in nearly half of the companies.

6. A majority of the audit reports were issued during the fraud period; 55 percent of reports in the last year of the fraud contained unqualified opinions.

7. The remaining 45 percent of the reports issued in the last year contained departures from the unqualified opinion. The reasons were substantial doubt about the entity's ability to continue as a going concern, litigation and other uncertainties, changes in accounting principles, and changes in auditors between fiscal years comparatively reported. Three percent of the audit reports were qualified due to a GAAP departure during the fraud period.

8. Financial statement fraud occasionally implicated the external auditor. Auditors were explicitly named in the AAER for 29 percent of the fraud cases. Auditors were also named for alleged involvement in the fraud (30 of 56 cases) or for negligent auditing (26 of 56 cases).

9. Some of the companies changed auditors during the fraud period. Just over 25 percent changed auditors during the time frame between the beginning of the last clean financial statement period and ending with the last fraudulent financial statement period. A majority of the auditor changes occurred during the fraud period.

COSO describes the nature of the frauds including the types of techniques used, the timing of fraud, and its duration. These matters will be discussed in Chapter 7 on earnings management. One obvious conclusion from these results is the link between the provisions of SOX and the deficiencies noted by COSO.

Enterprise Risk Management—Integrated Framework

In 2001, COSO initiated a project to develop a framework that would be readily usable by managements to evaluate and improve their organizations' enterprise risk management (ERM). The framework incorporates into internal control principles enhanced corporate governance and ERM that is defined as a process, effected by an entity's board of directors, management, and other personnel, applied in strategy setting and across the enterprise, designed to identify potential events that may affect the entity and to manage risk within its risk appetite.[29]

According to COSO, ERM encompasses six elements as follows.[30]

1. *Aligning risk appetite and strategy.* Risk appetite is considered by management in evaluating strategic alternatives, setting related objectives, and developing mechanisms to manage related risks.

2. *Enhancing risk response decisions.* ERM provides the discipline to identify and select among alternative risk responses: risk avoidance, reduction, sharing, and acceptance.

3. *Reducing operational surprises and losses.* ERM provides the capability to identify potential events and establish responses, reducing surprises and associated costs or losses.

4. *Identifying and managing multiple and cross-enterprise risks.* ERM facilitates effective responses to interrelated aspects of risk that affect different parts of the organization and integrated responses to multiple risks.

5. *Seizing opportunities.* ERM allows management to consider a full range of potential events, positioning it to identify and proactively realize opportunities.

6. *Improving deployment of capital.* The risk information provided by ERM enables management to effectively assess overall capital needs and enhance capital allocation.

COSO's ERM is designed to help an entity get where it wants to go and avoid pitfalls and surprises along the way. The components of ERM include the identical ones of *SAS No. 55* and the COSO Integrated Framework, and ERM adds to it strategic issues including objective setting by management, identification of risks and opportunities affecting achievement of an entity's objectives, and risk responses selected by management to align risk tolerance and risk appetite.[31]

The ERM framework represents the accounting profession's response to the increased need to manage risk in the aftermath of the accounting scandals and business failures that caused substantial harm to investors, company personnel, and other stakeholders. The ERM framework adopts the position that management should determine its risk appetite and align it with its strategic objectives. Unfortunately, ERM seems to place emphasis in the wrong areas by focusing on risk appetite. The usefulness of the framework in establishing an ethical culture can be questioned because it is not the ethics of strategic issues that links with corporate goals; instead, the company's "hunger" for risk is made to coincide with strategic objectives.

PCAOB's Integrated Audit Concept

PCAOB recognizes the importance of internal control over financial reporting as the foundation for the financial statement audit. The usefulness of financial statement amounts can be questioned if the underlying system that produced the numbers is not reliable. PCAOB requires auditors to examine the design and effectiveness of internal control sufficient to render an opinion as to that effectiveness.

According to *Auditing Standard No. 2,* "An integrated audit combines an audit of internal control over financial reporting with the audit of the financial statements, such that the objectives of the two audits are achieved simultaneously through a single coordinated process." The auditor's findings in the examination of internal controls are supported by the findings in the audit of the financial statements. Moreover, the integrated audit can help to improve the quality and integrity of both corporate controls over financial reporting and independent financial statement audits.[32]

Public companies are subject to SOX Section 404 requirements to have internal controls reviewed by management and evaluated independently by auditors. The need for an integrated audit of internal control and the financial statements elevates the importance of internal controls to providing accurate and reliable financial statements. Early results seem to support that perspective because 15 percent of public companies that filed financial statements with the SEC in the first full year of implementation of PCAOB *Auditing Standard No. 2* restated their financial statements. This is double the number of 2004, a result that can be explained, at least in part, by the more rigorous requirements of PCAOB *No. 2.* In fact, estimates range from 11 percent–15 percent of public companies that have identified in their filings with the SEC at least one material weakness in the internal controls over financial reporting.[33]

Conclusion

Audit standards have come a long way since the AICPA issued the expectation gap standards in 1988. In particular, the standards today provide a framework for evaluating internal controls and assessing audit risk, and they do a better job of identifying the factors that can help prevent and detect fraud.

The common element in fraud is a knowing attempt by management to make the financial results appear the way management wants them to appear rather than to present them in accordance with GAAP. The underlying problem in these instances is a lack of commitment to ethics above all else. The pursuit of self-interest and greed by members of management test the accountants' and auditors' commitment to follow the profession's ethics standards. Unfortunately, some professionals seem to neglect the foundations of the profession with respect to independence, objectivity, and integrity, and they have taken a trip down the proverbial ethical slippery slope. At the end of the journey lies a loss of reputational capital that is difficult to recover.

The best way to prevent the fraud from happening is to establish an environment within the company that does not tolerate the deviation from ethical standards and in which the company's strategic planning incorporates a commitment to ethical behavior. The tone at the top must be one that helps to create the environment needed to support ethical behavior throughout the organization.

Accounting professionals are subject to legal liability if they fail to follow the profession's standards—GAAP, GAAS, and PCAOB—and to adhere to their ethical responsibilities. In Chapter 6 we will look at a variety of classic cases that have established laws as to when accountants and auditors could be found to have violated their responsibilities to clients and third parties.

Discussion Questions

1. The opening quote in the chapter includes the statement "that the world has changed and that under the new rules you are going to consistently lose if you are using accounting tricks." What do you think Schilit meant by "the world has changed"?

2. Which of the three standard paragraphs of the audit report do you think is the most important? Why?

3. Distinguish between the circumstances when an auditor could give an unqualified opinion with those in which an explanatory paragraph and a qualified opinion would be given.

4. Assume that a local dance company, Texas Two-Step, records revenue from membership fees when cash is received instead of using the accrual basis. What factors should be considered by the auditor in determining whether the incorrect application of GAAP should be reported in the financial statements?

5. Assume that the successor auditor requests permission from a potential client to discuss with the predecessor the reasons and circumstances for the firm's withdrawal from the engagement. What ethical considerations exist for both the predecessor and successor auditors in pursing the contact?

6. Professor Slim Pickens makes the following statement in his Intermediate II accounting class: "The standards of field work provide the foundation to ensure that the financial statements present fairly financial position and results of operations." Discuss what you think Pickens means by the statement. Why do you think he would make that statement in an intermediate class?

7. Briefly discuss in your own words the limitations of the audit report.

8. Some criticize the accounting profession for using expressions in the audit report that seem to build in deniability should the client have committed a fraudulent act. What expressions enable the CPA to build a defense should the audit wind up in the courtroom?

9. Do you think the concept of materiality is incompatible with ethical behavior? Why or why not?

10. *SAS No. 99* points to three conditions that enable fraud to occur. Briefly describe those conditions. Do you think material misstatements in the financial statements of a company can be eliminated if the company were to establish an effective control environment that prevents each of the three factors from influencing the judgment of employees and management?

11. In 2005, the Institute of Management Accountants reported the results of a survey of business, academic, and regulatory leaders conducted by the Center for Corporate Change that found the corporation's culture to be the most important factor influencing the attitudes and behavior of executives. The results also indicate that 88 percent of the representatives who took part in the survey believe that companies devote little management attention to considering the effect of the culture on their executives. What are the elements of the corporate culture? Do you think it is possible for a company to control the culture? Why or why not?

12. Do you think that the "expectation gap" still exists? If so, describe the nature of that gap. If not, provide support for your opinion.

13. What is meant by the expression *risk assessment*? How do the results of risk assessment relate to the company's ability to establish an ethical tone at the top?

14. Hoosiers Basketball Equipment Manufacturing recently reported the results of its operations for the two-year period ending December 31, 2006 and December 31, 2007. Hoosiers' external auditor questions the accounting for the entire manufacturing inventory as a cost of goods sold regardless of the amount left over at the end of the year. Describe the factors to be considered by the auditor in determining how to deal with the situation. Do you think the accounting represents an honest error in judgment? Do you think fraud is present in the accounting? Be sure to support your opinion with reference to discussions in this chapter.

15. In Europe, audit reports use the expression "true and fair view" to characterize the results of the audit. Do you think there is a meaningful difference between that phrase and the "present fairly" statement made in U.S. audit reports? Does one of the statements evoke more of a sense of ethics than the other? Be sure to provide support for your answer.

16. How do ethics and adherence to the provisions of the AICPA Code of Professional Conduct relate to the auditor's obligations to detect and report fraud?

17. In the accounting fraud at the cable company Adelphia, top management had established a "cash management" system that enabled John Rigas, the founder of Adelphia, former CEO and chair of the board of directors, to dip into the fund for personal expenses whenever he wanted. The final approval for such expenditures rested with Timothy Rigas, John's son and Adelphia's CEO during the final years that fraud had occurred. What is wrong with a person who was the founder of a company, its former CEO, and chair of the board utilizing corporate assets for personal reasons?

18. A 2005 poll sponsored by the Wall Street Journal Online and Harris Interactive asked 2,061 U.S. investors whether the regulations and costs of Sarbanes-Oxley were too strict. Overall, 55 percent called the rules too lenient and said that punishment for poor corporate governance should be directed at certain individuals rather than the company as a whole. Are you surprised by these results? Why or why not?

19. The Institute of Internal Auditors states in its November 2005 issue of *The Tone at the Top* that businesses can rely on an industry standard, *Internal Control – Integrated Framework,* to comply with certain provisions in the Sarbanes-Oxley Act by assessing and enhancing companies' internal control systems. How do effective internal controls help an organization to promote efficiency, minimize risks, ensure the reliability of financial statements, and comply with regulations?

20. Betty Vinson got caught up in the fraud at WorldCom out of a concern for her job, health and retirement benefits, and her ability to provide for her family. To what extent should an internal accountant consider these factors in choosing alternative courses of action? Be sure to provide support for your answer.

Endnotes

1. American Institute of CPAs, *AICPA Professional Standards. Volume 1 as of June 1, 2005* (New York: AICPA, 2005); *Statement on Auditing Standards (SAS) No. 95,* Generally Accepted Auditing Standards (includes SAS 98) (New York: AICPA, 2005), AU Section 150.

2. American Institute of CPAs, *AICPA Professional Standards. Volume 1 as of June 1, 2005, Statement on Auditing Standards) No. 99,* Consideration of Fraud in a Financial Statement Audit (includes *SAS 98*) (New York: AICPA, 2002), AU Section 316.

3. Financial Accounting Standards Board, *Statement of Financial Accounting Concepts (SFAC) No. 2,* Qualitative Characteristics of Accounting Information (Stamford, CT: FASB, 1980). A portion of FASB Concepts Statement No. 2, Qualitative Characteristics of Accounting Information, copyright by the Financial Accounting Standards Board, 401 Merritt 7, PO Box 5116, Norwalk, CT 06856-5116, is reproduced with permission. Complete copies of this document are available from the FASB.

4. International Auditing and Assurance Standards Board, *Proposed International Standard on Auditing 320 (Revised),* Materiality in the Identification and Evaluation of Misstatements (ISA 320) (New York: IAASB, September 2005).

5. Securities and Exchange Commission, SEC Staff Accounting Bulletin: No. 99—Materiality, www.sec.gov/interps/account/sab99.htm.

6. *TSC Industries v. Northway, Inc.,* 426 438, 449 (1976).

7. American Institute of CPAs, *AICPA Professional Standards. Volume 1 as of June 1, 2005, Statement on Auditing Standards No. 99,* Consideration of Fraud in a Financial Statement Audit (New York: AICPA, 2002), AU Section 316.

8. American Institute of CPAs, *AICPA Professional Standards. Volume 1 as of June 1, 2005, Statement on Auditing Standards No. 69,* The Meaning of Present Fairly in Conformity With Generally Accepted Accounting Principles and *No. 93,* The Meaning of Present Fairly in Conformity with Generally Accepted Accounting Principles Omnibus Statement on Auditing Standards, 2000 (includes *SAS 91*) (New York: AICPA), AU Section 411.

9. Marc J. Epstein and M. A. Geiger, "Investor Views of Audit Assurance: Recent Evidence of the Expectation Gap," *Journal of Accountancy,* January 1994, pp. 60–66.

10. American Institute of CPAs, *AICPA Professional Standards. Volume 1 as of June 1, 2005, Statement on Auditing Standards) No. 55,* Internal Control in a Financial Statement Audit (New York: AICPA, 1988), AU Section 319.

11. AICPA, *SAS No. 55.*

12. American Institute of CPAs, AICPA *Professional Standards. Volume 1 as of June 1, 2005, Statement on Auditing Standards (SAS) No. 54,* Illegal Acts (New York: AICPA, 1988) , AU Section 317.

13. Susan Pulliam and Deborah Solomon, "Ms. Cooper Says No to Her Boss," *The Wall Street Journal,* October 30, 2002, p. A1.

14. Lynne W. Jeter, *Disconnected: Deceit and Betrayal at WorldCom* (Hoboken, NJ: John Wiley, 2003).

15. American Institute of CPAs, *AICPA Professional Standards. Volume 1 as of June 1, 2005, Statement on Auditing Standards No. 99,* Consideration of Fraud in a Financial Statement Audit (New York: AICPA, 2002), AU Section 316.05-.06. AICPA PROFESSIONAL STANDARDS by AICPA. Copyright 2005 by AMERICAN INSTITUTE OF CERTIFIED PUBLIC ACCOUNTANTS. Reproduced with permission of AMERICAN INSTITUTIONS OF CERTIFIED PUBLIC ACCOUNTANTS in the format Textbook via Copyright Clearance Center.

16. AICPA, *SAS No. 99,* AU Section 316.06-.07.

17. Securities Litigation Watch, "Betty Vinson Gets 5 Months in Prison, slw.issproxy.com/securities_litigation_blo/2005/08/betty_vinson_ge.html.

18. Securities and Exchange Commission, *SEC v. Tyco International Ltd.,* Litigation Release 19657, April 17, 2006.

19. Securities and Exchange Commission, Accounting and Auditing Enforcement Release No. 1839, August 13, 2003.

20. SEC.

21. *SAS No. 99,* AU Section 316.02-.04.

22. American Institute of CPAs, *AICPA Professional Standards. Volume 1 as of June 1, 2005, Statement on Auditing Standards No. 84,* Communications between Predecessor and Successor Auditors (includes SAS 93)(New York: AICPA, 1997), AU Section 315.

23. AICPA, *SAS No. 99,* AU Section 316.19.

24. American Institute of CPAs, *Statement on Auditing Standards No. 104-No.111,* Risk Assessment Standards, March 2006.

25. Public Company Accounting Oversight Board, Auditing Standard No. 2: An Audit of Internal Control over Financial Reporting Performed in Conjunction with an Audit of Financial Statements, June 17, 2004, www.pcaobus.org/Standards/Standards_and_Related_Rules/Auditing_Standard_No.2.aspx.

26. American Institute of CPAs, *AICPA Professional Standards. Volume 1 as of June 1, 2005, Statement on Auditing Standards No. 55,* Consideration of Internal Control in a Financial Statement Audit (includes *SAS Nos. 78 and 94*) (New York: AICPA, 1988), AU Section 319.06-.07.

27. *SAS No. 55* (includes *SAS Nos. 78 and 94*).

28. Committee of Sponsoring Organizations of the Treadway Commission, *Internal Control—Integrated Framework* (New York: AICPA, 1992). Copyright © 1987, 2004 by the Committee of

Sponsoring Organizations of the Treadway Commission. Reproduced with permission from the AICPA acting as authorized copyright administrator for COSO.

29. COSO, *Enterprise Risk Management (ERM)—Integrated Framework: Executive Summary* (New York: AICPA, September 2004).

30. COSO, ERM, p. 1. Copyright © 1987, 2004 by the Committee of Sponsoring Organizations of the Treadway Commission. Reproduced with permission from the AICPA acting as authorized copyright administrator for COSO.

31. COSO, ERM, pp. 3-4.

32. Public Company Accounting Oversight Board, *Auditing Standard No. 2,* An Audit of Internal Control over Financial Reporting Performed in Conjunction with an Audit of Financial Statements (Washington, D. C. .: PCAOB, 2004). www.pcaobus.org/Standards/Standards_and_Related_Rules/Auditing_Standard_No.2.aspx.

33. These results were reported in a "Report on the Effective Application of Section 404 of the Sarbanes-Oxley Act of 2002" prepared by the international CPA firm of Grant Thornton. The results come from two studies: (1) Audit Analytics, Section 404 Internal Control Material Weaknesses Results for the First Three Quarters of Section 404; Disclosures Based on Filings as of November 15, 2005 and (2) Report generated on December 17, 2005, using SEC filings from the Russell 3000.

Chapter 5 Cases

Case 5-1

Arthur Andersen

In her book *Final Accounting*[1] that chronicles the rise and fall of Arthur Andersen, Barbara Ley Toffler, formerly the partner-in-charge of Ethics & Responsible Business Practices consulting services for Arthur Andersen, describes the changes in the firm's culture that contributed to its downfall. She labels employees "Androids" who lived the mantra "keep the client happy." She also points out there was internal fighting between the auditors and consultants, especially after Andersen Consulting had split off from the worldwide firm, Arthur Andersen LLP. As Andersen began to rebuild a consulting practice, conflicts developed between the "new" firm consultants and those who worked for Andersen Consulting. Toffler claims the environment was one that fostered a culture of "billing your brains out" rather than doing quality work.

Questions

1. Assume that you were aware of the culture at Andersen while you were being recruited for a position with a then Big Five accounting firm. Would you accept a position with Andersen if it were the only one of the Big Five that offered you a position? Why or why not?

2. What do you think Toffler may have meant when she said that both accountants and consultants who worked for the firm were "Androids"?

3. Does an attitude of "keeping the client happy" interfere with independence in appearance or in fact? If a firm has a reputation of keeping the client happy, can the firm use a defense of due care in a court case?

4. Why do you think there may be a cultural difference between accountants and consultants who work for a Big Four CPA firm as Toffler indicates in her book with respect to Andersen?

5. Do you think there will come a time when the accounting profession is down to the Big Three? Why or why not? What could cause such an outcome to occur?

[1] Barbara Ley Toffler with Jennifer Reingold, *Final Accounting: Ambition, Greed and the Fall of Arthur Andersen* (New York: Broadway Books, 2003).

Case 5-2

Audit Client Considerations

Lanny Beaudean joined the CPA firm Cardinal & Coyote LLP, the Arizona-based firm with five offices throughout the Phoenix, Scottsdale, and Mesa areas in 2005. He had worked for two years for the Internal Revenue Service in Phoenix, Arizona. Beaudean had passed all four parts of the CPA Exam and decided to work for a CPA firm to gain audit experience that would enable him to sign audit reports in the future. Beaudean has been advancing rapidly and just became a senior at Cardinal & Coyote.

Yancy Corliss, a new audit partner at Cardinal & Coyote, was summoned one day to the office of Sharon Rules, the firm's managing partner. Rules told Corliss that she had been approached by a new client, Jost Furniture Rental, a large southwest chain of home furniture rental catering to young upscale individuals who could live in a city for two years or so and then move on.

Rules asked Corliss to do background checks on Jost and make whatever inquiries are necessary to assess whether Jost is the type of client that the firm would want to accept. Corliss has three days to do the work and report back to Rules. If the decision is to go ahead, Cardinal & Coyote would submit a bid and compete with one other CPA firm for the account. Rules has been told confidentially by Jost's CFO that as long as the bid is within a "competitive range," the firm will get the account.

Corliss assembled his team to review the background and other information about Jost Furniture. Corliss asked Beaudean to head up the assessment and report back to him in two days. During that time, Beaudean would have two other staff members to help with the assignment. Beaudean was excited about his first opportunity to work on new client assessment.

Beaudean met with Vinnie Gabelli, a transplanted Brooklyn native who had graduated from State University of Arizona at Phoenix. Gabelli was like a fish out of water in Arizona even though he had spent 16 months in the master's of accounting program at State University. Gabelli thought a prickly pear was someone who could not make it in Staten Island and moved to Brooklyn for a better life.

Gabelli told Beaudean that he welcomed the opportunity to work with a native of Phoenix and learn about its colorful history. Beaudean also asked Jackie Oloff, a native of Minneapolis, to join the team. Jackie had moved to Phoenix two years ago with her husband who is a professor of accounting at State University.

The team discussed mutual responsibilities, data sources for the information, key areas of risk, and then broke up to start their work. At the end of the day, the team reassembled to share information. Here is a brief list of the findings:

- The predecessor firm, one of the Big Four CPA firms, had helped Jost Furniture with its initial public offering and had audited the financial statements of the company for five years. The firm resigned the account in 2004, following the issuance of a modified opinion on the 2003 financial statements. The firm had issued an unqualified opinion with an explanatory paragraph that raised questions about Jost's ability to continue as a going concern because of persistent operating losses that threatened the company's ability to secure needed financing.

- A large national firm took over from the Big Four firm and audited the financial statements for 2004. That firm also raised going concern questions and was dismissed by Jost's top management.

- Jost's financial statements for 2005 and 2006 were audited by a different regional CPA firm; each was dismissed after one year.

- The financial statements for 2007 had not been audited, and on March 19, 2008, Jost's CEO, Jerry Jost, approached Sharon Rules at a community event and asked her to submit a bid for the Jost audit. Jost asked that the bid be submitted by March 23.

- In a memorandum to the file prepared by Sharon Rules, Gabelli learned that Jerry Jost had admitted to Rules that the company had past problems with various auditors, but he assured her the going concern issues had been resolved. He also told Rules that the company's controller had recently quit, the third time in four years that there had been a turnover at that position. Jost told Rules the company had two final candidates for the position and that he wanted her to help with the final decision because the CPA firm would work closely with staff from the controller's office and the controller.

- Oloff reviewed the financial statements of Jost Furniture for the past three years during which time going concern explanatory paragraphs had been issued. She went through a checklist of risk assessment issues for new clients and stopped when she came to the following: Verify the circumstances of any prior auditor's dismissal or withdrawal by first asking the client for permission to approach the predecessor auditor(s). Oloff felt that Beaudean should do that.

At the meeting at the end of the first day, Gabelli and Oloff told Beaudean about the unusual number of auditor changes in a short period of time apparently due to going concern issues that had been raised in the audit reports for the years 2003 through 2006. Beaudean asked Gabelli to contact the two banks where the company borrows money and check into its payment record. Oloff had a past business relationship with Miles Frazer, the attorney for Jost Furniture. She agreed to contact Frazer to determine whether there were any outstanding litigation issues or other legal matters that the firm should know about. Beaudean will ask Jerry Jost for permission to talk to the predecessor auditor. They all agreed to get these matters done by the end of the second day, and a meeting was set for 5 p.m.

Gabelli found out that a $1 million loan payable to Phoenix Second National Bank had been overdue before payment had been made March 15, 2008. The bank president told Gabelli that Jost had been in violation of a debt covenant agreement that obligated Jost to maintain a current ratio of 1.5:1 at all times during the life of the two-year loan. Jost had gone below the ratio twice. The first time Jost had violated the covenant, the bank accepted the explanation of a temporary cash flow problem. The bank granted the company a three-month extension to meet the requirements of the debt covenant. The bank subsequently found out that the cash flow problem had been due to the fact Jerry Jost had withdrawn $500,000 from the Jost cash account at the bank to help put a down payment on a mortgage loan to buy an upscale house in Scottsdale. The second time it occurred, the bank began foreclosure on the loan on January 31, 2008, but by the time the process had been completed, Jost had paid off the entire $1 million balance that had been due on December 31, 2007.

Oloff had no luck with Miles Frazer, the attorney for Jost. When she called his office, the secretary always told Oloff that Frazer was on another line and she'd take a message. When Oloff asked to leave a voice-mail message, she was told Frazer did not have voice mail. How about leaving an e-mail message, she asked. No e-mail either. Oloff had left five messages for Frazer in the time before the meeting. She had nothing to report except to make an editorial comment about lawyer responsiveness or lack thereof.

Beaudean had met with some resistance from Jerry Jost with respect to receiving permission for Corliss to speak with the predecessor auditor. Jost claimed that there had been a "personality conflict" and Jost was afraid the auditor would speak negatively about the company. Jost did agree

after Beaudean reminded him it was a required part of the procedures auditors follow in making the client acceptance decision.

At 5 p.m. on March 22, the three auditors met in the firm's conference room to discuss their findings. After hearing about Gabelli's concerns and Oloff's charges of stonewalling, Beaudean prepared a memo prior to his meeting with Yancy Corliss to discuss whether to submit a bid for the Jost Furniture Rental audit.

Questions

1. Why is it important to do the type of due diligence testing and risk assessment review conducted by Cardinal & Coyote prior to determining whether to make a bid for the audit of a potential client?

2. Given the facts of the case, what issues should be of concern to Beaudean in making a recommendation to Corliss whether to submit the bid? Explain why the items you mention are issues of concern with respect to the ability of the accounting firm to conduct an effective audit.

3. If you were Lanny Beaudean, what would be your recommendation when you meet with Yancy Corliss? Why?

4. Regardless of your answer to Question 3, assume that Corliss tells Beaudean the firm will make a bid for the Jost Furniture audit. When he asked Corliss what other factors he could have considered in making the decision, Corliss was quite blunt and said, "I'm a new partner in the firm. I have to bring in new business. This client is a slam dunk. If we make a reasonably competitive bid, we will get the account." Now, taking into consideration the answer you gave to Question 3, what would you do if you were Lanny Beaudean with respect to Corliss' explanation?

5. Assume that the firm is awarded the audit of Jost Furniture and starts preliminary audit work on March 24. On March 26, 2008, Jackie Oloff receives the following note in the mail from Miles Frazer:

Dear Jackie:

We go back a long time. I recall when I met you in the Master's of Accounting program at State University. I apologize for not being forthcoming when you asked me if I knew anything about the legal issues facing Jost Furniture. I did not get back to you because I thought it might violate client confidentiality to talk about what I knew. It is all moot now because I was fired by Jerry Jost after complaining about the way his personal actions threaten legal exposure for the company because he uses company funds for personal purposes. Even though Jost always manages to get the board of directors to sign off on the personal loans, he records those loans on Jost's books as a trade account receivable.

I thought you should know this before you decide on submitting a bid for Jost Furniture.

Signed,
Miles Frazer
Attorney at Law

6. What do you think Oloff should do with the information provided in the letter by Miles Frazer? Be specific, and provide support for your answer using ethical reasoning.

Case 5-3

Bubba and Rufus

Background

Tax avoidance is the legal utilization of the tax regulations to one's advantage to reduce the amount of tax that is payable. Examples of tax avoidance include purchasing a home to deduct the interest portion of mortgage payment amounts, property taxes, and other possible expenses such as the costs related to an office in one's home (subject to strict tax requirements). Many people rent apartments without the benefit of any of these write-offs.

Tax evasion occurs when an individual, firm, trust, or other entity uses illegal means to evade taxes. Tax evasion usually entails deliberately misrepresenting or concealing the true state of the individual's tax situation and activities to the tax authorities to reduce taxable income, thereby lowering the tax liability. Simple examples include underreporting income or overstating deductions. More elaborate ones could include setting up offshore accounts to illegally hide income from the government and establishing an abusive tax shelter. You could be interested in knowing that amounts won in a lottery are taxable income, although *losses can be deducted up to the amount of the winnings.*

Tax fraud cases have been on the rise for several years. Criminal tax fraud is very difficult to prove. The government first reviews the evidence to decide whether it has a *prima facie* case and a reasonable probability of conviction. If the government has a *prima facie* case that is minimal evidence supporting a grand jury's finding on each element of the crime, the government survives the taxpayer's motion to dismiss and the case is presented in front of a jury.

Legal Trusts vs. Abusive Tax Trust Evasion Schemes

According to the Internal Revenue Service, trust/estate matters represent the third highest area of growth among top CPA firms.[1] This trend is likely to increase with the aging population in the United States.

A *trust* is a legal entity formed under state law. To create a trust, a person transfers legal title to property to a trustee, who is then charged with the responsibility of using that property for the benefit of another person, called the *beneficiary,* who really has all benefits of ownership except for bare legal title.

Legal trusts are used in estate planning to shelter income, to facilitate the genuine charitable transfer of assets, and to hold assets for minors and those unable to handle their financial affairs. For example, you may want to establish a trust

[1] Abusive Tax Evasion Schemes, www.irs.gov/businesses/small/article/0,,id=106549,00.html

to set aside money for your teenage son or daughter. That money can then be released to your child upon reaching a stated age.

A *trustee* is designated to hold legal title to the trust property, to exercise independent control over it, and to be responsible for its management. Trustees have strict fiduciary obligations under the law.

Trusts established to hide the true ownership of assets and income or to disguise the substance of financial transactions are considered fraudulent trusts. Some examples include wiring income overseas and failing to report it and attempting to protect transactions through bank secrecy laws in tax haven countries.

Trusts must file Form 1120. Trust tax rates are high compared to income tax rates for individual taxpayers who file Form 1040. For 2005, the maximum tax rate on trusts was 39.6 percent, and was applicable to trusts with $8,650 of taxable income. Individuals filing separately are taxed at 10 percent up to $7,300 of income from any source and 15 percent of amounts from more than $7,300 to $29,700. A taxpayer with $8,650 in trust would have paid a tax of $3,422.40 as a trust entity and $932.50 as an individual. Individuals did not reach the 39.6 percent tax rate until their income reached $326,450, and then the rate of taxation, which is the maximum rate on individuals, was 35 percent.

The tax rate differential raises the question of why an individual would set up a trust unless it was for estate purposes or the benefit of a minor child. In the former case, the rate of tax on a trust could be less than the estate tax on property owned at the date of death. Typically, these trusts benefit wealthy people because, as of 2006, the first $2,000,000 of estate assets is not taxed. That amount increases to $3.5 million in 2009. If the estate owned $3.0 million in 2006, only $1.0 million would be subject to tax. The tax rate on the $1 million would be 41 percent. This compares with 39.6 percent, the maximum rates for individuals. The difference in tax on $1 million for an estate and for a trust is $14,000. The estate pays 1.4 percent higher. However, that amount increases with higher estate incomes beyond the $2 million exemption. The maximum rate reached after $2 million of taxable estate is 46 percent in 2006, but that declines to 45 percent in 2007.

Enough of the tax lecture. The point is why an individual would set up a trust to shelter that individual's income when the trust rate is higher than individual tax rates. The answer could be only for a minor child to control the use of certain monies going to that child. Of course, another reason could be that a taxpayer has been duped by an unscrupulous tax accountant who is mainly interested in earning higher fees for setting up the trust. While we would like to think this is a rarity, it has happened before, and the following case describes one instance of a fraud using trusts.

The Case

Bubba Toothless decided, after flunking out of engineering school, to become an accountant. He graduated from Alabama State Polytechnic Institute with a master's degree in taxation. He passed the four parts of the CPA Exam in consecutive attempts during 2005. Bubba worked for a small firm in Birmingham during 2005 until he decided to strike out on his own. He hung out his shingle in downtown Birmingham on January 17, 2006. Bubba struggled with his tax practice during that first busy season. Most people in town were accustomed to going to other tax providers. Bubba quickly realized he had to do something that would "add value" to his tax services for clients.

Bubba started marketing "common law trust" packages to clients throughout the southeast via group seminars, individual client meetings, and an attractive Web site that promised 100 free lottery tickets to the first 100 people who purchased a trust package for $3,995. Bubba netted $3,795 on every purchase of the common law trust package; his only expense was for the one hundred $2 lottery tickets given to each client. By April 16, 2007, Bubba had made more than $450,000 from the sale of the packages.

Bubba marketed common law trusts that alleged legitimate tax deductions for individuals who set up the trust (with Bubba, of course) and then "transferred" ordinary living expenses paid by the taxpayer such as the cost of utilities, food, clothing, vehicles, and education, through the common law trust.

One day Rufus Stoneman came to Bubba's office. They talked about the good old days when a boy could drink six packs of beer while driving his pickup down the highway and, if stopped by the highway patrol, the officer was more likely to ask for a beer than write a ticket for the motor vehicle code violation. Bubba and Rufus hit it off so well that Bubba decided to tell Rufus about his common law trusts. Rufus thought it was the best thing since sliced cheese, so he agreed to let Bubba set up a common law trust. Rufus gave Bubba $2,000 as a down payment on the final product. By April 15, 2008, Rufus had filed his first trust return, gave Bubba the remaining $2,000 and left the office happy as a clam that he had saved more than $10,000 in taxes through the trust.

Fifteen months later, Rufus received the dreaded letter in the mail that he was the target of an IRS investigation into fraudulent common law trusts that had been sold throughout the United States during the period 2005 through 2008. Rufus immediately called Bubba, but reached a phone company recording that the number was no longer in service. No forwarding phone number was available.

Questions

1. What are the ethical responsibilities of a CPA who prepares income tax returns?

2. Assuming that the common law trust set up by Bubba was fraudulent, discuss the ethical and professional obligations that he violated with respect to his professional services and the public interest.

3. Do you think it is ethical to engage in tax avoidance when preparing a tax return for an individual? How about engaging in tax avoidance for a corporation?

4. Do you think Bubba was guilty of setting up devices that encouraged tax fraud? Explain your answer in the context of how a reasonable person could judge whether tax fraud exists.

5. What would you do at this point if you were Rufus? Why?

6. Do you think it is right for the IRS to charge a taxpayer with fraud when that person does not realize that the devices set up by her tax accountant whom she implicitly trusted are fraudulent? Why or why not?

Case 5-4

Health South

The HealthSouth case is unique because the CEO, Richard Scrushy, was acquitted on all accounts while five former HealthSouth employees were sentenced by a federal judge for their admitted roles in a scheme to inflate revenues and reported earnings of the company from 1999 through mid-2002. These amounts are presented in Exhibit 1.

At the time of the fraud, HealthSouth was the nation's largest provider of outpatient surgery, diagnostic imaging, and rehabilitative services. In 2003, the SEC filed a complaint against the company and Scrushy for violating provisions of the Securities Act of 1933 and the Securities and Exchange Act of 1934.[1] The complaint alleges that Health-South, under Scrushy's direction and with the help of key employees, falsified its revenue to inflate earnings and "meet their numbers." Specifically, false accounting entries were made to an account called "contractual adjustment." A contractual adjustment account is a revenue allowance account that estimates the difference between the gross amount billed to the patient and the amount that various healthcare insurers will pay for a specific treatment. HealthSouth deducted this account from gross revenues to derive net revenues that were disclosed on the company's periodic reports filed with the SEC.

The SEC contends that in mid-2002, certain senior officers of HealthSouth discussed with Scrushy the impact of the scheme to inflate earnings because they were concerned about the consequences of the August 14, 2002, financial statement certification required under Section 302 of the Sarbanes-Oxley Act of 2002. Allegedly, "Scrushy agreed that, going forward, he would not insist that earnings be inflated to meet Wall Street analysts' expectations."[2]

The filing also alleges that Scrushy received at least $6.5 million from HealthSouth during 2001 in "Bonus/Annual Incentive Awards." Also, from 1999 through 2002, HealthSouth paid Scrushy $9.2 million in salary. Approximately $5.3 million of this salary was based on the company's achievement of certain budget targets.

On December 10, 2003, U.S. District Judge Inge P. Johnson sentenced Emery Harris, HealthSouth's former vice president of finance who had pleaded guilty in March 2003 to a charge of conspiracy and willfully falsifying books and records to a term of five months in prison on each count to run concurrently, three years of supervised release with five months of unsupervised house detention, and payment of a $3,000 fine and a $200 special assessment. Harris was also ordered to pay $106,500 in forfeiture.[3]

The judge also sentenced each of the following to four years of probation with six months unsupervised home confinement and payment of a $2,000 fine: former Accounting Department Vice Presidents Angela C. Ayers and Cathy C. Edwards, Group Vice President Rebecca Kay Morgan, and Assistant Vice President Virginia B. Valentine. The judge also ordered Ayers and Valentine to pay a $100 special assessment and Edwards and Morgan a $200 special assessment. Morgan was also ordered to pay $235,000 in forfeiture. The four officers all pleaded guilty in April 2003 to conspiracy to commit wire and securities fraud, and Edwards and Morgan also pleaded guilty to wire fraud.

Ayers, Edwards, Morgan, and Valentine all had made false entries into HealthSouth's accounts during the fraud period. Harris admitted falsifying the company's finances to generate false entries, knowing that those entries would be included in the company's filings with the SEC.

On June 28, 2005, Richard Scrushy, then the former CEO of HealthSouth, was acquitted on all charges despite the testimony by more than half a dozen former lieutenants who said he had presided over a $2.7 billion accounting fraud while running the HealthSouth national hospital chain. The jury even heard secretly recorded conversations between Scrushy and a chief financial officer, William T. Owens, in March 2003 discussing balance sheet problems, with Scrushy asking "You're not wired, are you?"

In an ironic twist in the HealthSouth saga, the key prosecution witness in the government's case against Scrushy, William Owens, was sentenced on December 9, 2005, to five years in prison for his role in the accounting fraud at Health-South. Owens had manipulated the company's books and instructed subordinates to make phony accounting entries. He also falsely certified the 2002 financial statements filed with the 10-K Report to the SEC.

---

[1] Securities and Exchange Commission, Civil Action No. CV-03-J-0615-S, U.S. District Court Northern District of Alabama, *Securities and Exchange Commission v. HealthSouth Corporation and Richard M. Scrushy, Defendants.*

[2] Securities and Exchange Commission, Civil Action No. CV-03-J-0615-S.

[3] Department of Justice, "Five Defendants Sentenced in HealthSouth Fraud Case," www.usdoj.gov/opa/pr/2003/December/03_crm_678.htm.

EXHIBIT 1
Misstatement of Net Income by HealthSouth Corporation

Net Income (in millions)	1999 Form 10-K	2000 Form 10-K	2001 Form 10-K	For Six Months Ended June 30, 2002
Actual	$(191)	$194	$ 9	$157
Reported	230	559	434	340
Misstated amount	421	365	425	183
Misstated percentage	220 percent	188 percent	4,722 percent	119 percent

U.S. District Judge Sharon Lovelace Blackburn knocked three years from the prosecutor's sentencing request, stating to Owens, "I believe you told the truth." Blackburn called Scrushy's acquittal a "travesty." Nonetheless, Blackburn said white collar criminals merit stiff sentences if only to send a message of deterrence to other business executives. "Corporate offenders are nothing more than common thieves wearing suits and wielding pens," Blackburn said.[4]

Questions

1. Was it "fair" that the Richard Scrushy was acquitted while the key government witness against him, William Owens, was sentenced to five years in prison for his role in the $2.7 billion accounting fraud at HealthSouth?

2. Scrushy had allegedly certified false financial statements filed with the SEC, a violation of the Sarbanes-Oxley

Act. Because Scrushy was acquitted, does that mean SOX is not working? Explain the reasons for your answer.

3. The main tool used by HealthSouth to overstate net income during a three and one-half-year period was to understate contractual allowances, a contra account to revenue. Because of the scope of the fraud and time period involved, do you think the auditors should have been able to discover the fraud? Briefly explain what techniques the auditors could have used to identify the fraud.

4. Scrushy was paid $14.5 million in salary and bonuses during the period of the fraud. Do you think he is ethically entitled to keep that money? Use ethical reasoning to support your answer.

5. Comment on the statement made by Judge Blackburn: "White collar criminals merit stiff sentences, if only to send a message of deterrence to other business executives." Do you agree with the statement? Why or why not?

[4] Carrie Johnson, "5 Years for HealthSouth Fraud: Former Chief Financial Officer Was Key Witness," *Washington Post,* December 10, 2005, p. D1.

Case 5-5

Imperial Valley Thrift & Loan: A Major Case Study

Bill Stanley of Jacobs, Stanley & Co. started to review the working paper files on his client, Imperial Valley Thrift & Loan, in preparation for the audit of the client's financial statements for the year ended December 31, 2007. The bank was owned by a parent company, Nuevo Financial Group, and it serviced a small western Arizona community near Yuma that reached south to the border of Mexico. The bank's preaudit statements are presented in Exhibit 1.

EXHIBIT 1
IMPERIAL VALLEY THRIFT & LOAN
Balance Sheet (preaudit) December 31, 2007

Assets

Cash and cash equivalents	$1,960,000
Loans receivable	6,300,000
Less: Reserve for loan losses	(25,000)
Unearned discounts & fees	(395,000)
Accrued interest receivable	105,000
Prepayments	12,000
Real property held for sale	514,000
Property, plant, & equipment	390,000
Less: Accumulated depreciation	(110,000)
Contribution to Thrift Guaranty Corp.	15,000
Deferred start-up costs	44,000
Total assets	$8,810,000

Liabilities & Equity

Liabilities

Regular & money market savings	$2,212,000
T-bills & CDs	5,180,000
Accrued interest payable	190,000
Accounts payable & accruals	28,000
Total liabilities	$7,610,000

Equity

Capital stock	$ 700,000
Additional paid-in capital	1,120,000
Retained earnings (deficit)	(620,000)
Total equity	$1,200,000
Total liabilities and equity	$8,810.000

(Exhibit 1 continued on next page)

IMPERIAL VALLEY THRIFT & LOAN
Statement of Operations (preaudit)
For the Year Ended December 31, 2007

Revenues

Interest earned	$ 820,000
Discount earned	210,000
Investment income	82,000
Fees, charges, & commissions	78,000
Total revenues	$1,190,000

Expenses

Interest expense	$ 815,000
Provision for loan losses	180,000
Salary expense	205,000
Occupancy expense including depreciation	100,000
Other administrative expense	160,000
Legal expense	12,000
Thrift Guaranty Corp. payment	48,000
Total expenses	$1,520,000
Net loss for the year	$ 330,000

Bill Stanley knew there were going to be some problems to contend with during the course of the audit, so he decided to review several items in the file to refresh his memory about the client's operations.

Background

The first item Stanley reviewed was the planning memo he had prepared about two months ago. This memo is summarized in Exhibit 2.

The next item Stanley reviewed was an internal office communication on potential audit risks. This communication described three areas of particular concern.

- The client charged off $420,000 in loans in 2006 and had already charged off $535,000 through July 31, 2007. Assume that reserve requirements by law are a minimum of 1.25 percent of loans outstanding. However, given prior history, this statutory amount probably would not be large enough for the loan loss reserve. This, in combination with the prior auditors' concerns about proper loan underwriting procedures and documentation, indicates that we should carefully review loan quality.
- The audit report issued on the 2006 financial statements contained an explanatory paragraph describing the uncertainty about the client's ability to continue as a going concern. The concern was caused by the "capital impairment" declaration by the Arizona Department of Corporations.

- The client had weak internal controls according to the prior auditors. Some of the items to look out for, in addition to proper loan documentation, were whether the preaudit financial statement information provided by the client is supported by the general ledger, whether the accruals were appropriate, and whether all transactions were properly authorized and recorded on a timely basis.

Audit Findings

The audit was conducted during January and February 2008. Based on information gathered during the audit, the following were the areas of greatest concern to Stanley:

1. *Adequacy of Loan Collateral.* A review of 30 loan files representing $2,100,000 of total loans outstanding (33.3 percent of the portfolio) indicated that much of the collateral for the loans was in the form of second or third mortgages on real property. This gave the client a potentially unenforceable position due to the existence of very large senior liens. For example, in the event that foreclosure became necessary to collect Imperial Valley's loan, the client would have to first pay off these large senior liens. Other collateral often consisted of personal items such as jewelry and furniture. In the case of jewelry, often there was no effort made by the client after granting the loan to ascertain whether the collateral was still in the possession of the borrower. The jewelry could have been sold without the client's knowledge.

Exhibit 2
Planning Memo

1. The firm of Jacobs, Stanley & Co. succeeded the firm of Nelson, Thomas & Co. as auditors for Imperial Valley Thrift & Loan. The prior auditors conducted the 2005 and 2006 audits. Jacobs, Stanley & Co. communicated in writing with Nelson, Thomas & Co. prior to accepting the engagement. Additionally, authorization was given by the client for a review of the predecessor auditors' working papers. The findings of these inquiries are summarized in item 6 below and the previously discussed internal office communication.

2. Imperial Valley Thrift & Loan was incorporated in Arizona on June 12, 1988. It is a wholly owned subsidiary of Nuevo Financial Group, S.A., a Mexican corporation. As an industrial loan company, it is restricted to certain types of business, including making real estate and consumer loans and certain types of commercial loans.

3. Imperial Valley accepts deposits in the form of interest-bearing passbook accounts and investment certificates. Most of the depositors are of Spanish descent. The client primarily services the Spanish-speaking community in the Imperial Valley of southern Arizona, which is a rural community located on the Mexican border.

4. The principal officers of Imperial Valley are Jose Ortega and his brother Arturo. They serve as the chief executive officer and the chief financial officer, respectively. Two cousins serve as the chief operating officer and chief compliance officer.

5. Imperial Valley is subject to the regulations of the Arizona Industrial Loan Law and is examined by the Department of Corporations. It was last examined in December 2006 and was put on notice as "capital impaired." Additional capital was being sought from local investors.

6. Based on review of the prior auditors' working papers, the following items were noted:
   a. The client's lack of profitability was due to a high volume of loan losses resulting from poor underwriting procedures and faulty documentation.
   b. Imperial Valley has a narrow net interest margin due to the fact that all deposits are interest bearing and it pays the highest interest rates in the area.
   c. Due to the small size of the client and its focus on handling day-to-day operating problems, the internal controls are marginal at best. There were material weaknesses in their loan underwriting procedures and documentation, as well as in compliance with regulatory requirements.
   d. There are no reports issued by management on the internal controls.

---

2. *Collectibility of Loans.* Many loans were structured in such a way as to require interest payments only for a small number of years (two or three) with a balloon payment for principal due at the end of this time. This structure made it difficult to properly evaluate the payment history of the borrower. Although the annual interest payments may have been made for the first year or two, this was not necessarily a good indication that the borrower would come up with the cash needed to make the large final payment, and the financial statements provided no additional disclosures about this matter.

3. *Weakness in Internal Controls.* Internal control weaknesses were a pervasive concern. The auditors recomputed certain accruals and unearned discounts, confirmed loan and deposit balances, and reconciled the preaudit financial information provided by the client to the general ledger. Some adjustments had to be made as a result of this work. A material weakness in the lending function was identified: Loans were too frequently granted merely because the borrowers were well known to Imperial Valley officials who believed the borrowers could be counted on to repay their outstanding loans. An ability to repay these loans was based too often on "faith" rather than on clear indications that the borrowers would have the necessary cash available to repay their loans when they came due. This was of great concern to the auditors, especially in light of the inadequacy of the loan reserve, as detailed in Item 5.

4. *Status of Additional Capital Infusion.* We are working under the assumption that under Arizona regulatory requirements, a thrift and loan institution must maintain a 6:1 ratio of thrift certificates to net equity capital. Based on the financial information provided by Imperial Valley, the capital deficiency was only $32,000 below capital requirements (preaudit), as follows:

Thrift certificates ratio	$7,392,000
	6
Net equity capital required	$1,232,000
Net equity capital reported	$1,200,000
Deficiency	$ 32,000

However, audit adjustments explained in Exhibit 3 increased the capital deficiency to $622,000, as follows:

Net equity capital required	$1,232,000
Net equity capital (postaudit)	610,000
Deficiency	$ 622,000

Exhibit 3 presents the audit adjusting entries affecting the loans receivable account and related reserve balance. Following AJE #3 is an explanation of this entry excerpted from the working papers.

There was a possibility that the parent company, Nuevo Financial Group, would contribute the additional equity capital. Also, management had been in contact with a potential outside investor about the possibility of investing $600,000. This investor, Manny Gonzalez, has strong ties to in the Imperial Valley community and to the family ownership of Imperial Valley.

5. *Adequacy of General Reserve Requirement.* The general reserve requirement of 1.25 percent had not been met.

Based on the client's reported outstanding loan balance of $6,300,000, a reserve of $78,750 would be necessary. However, audit adjustments for the charge-off of uncollectible loan amounts significantly affected the amount actually required. Additionally, the auditors felt that a larger percentage would be necessary because of the client's history of problems with loan collections; initially, a 5 percent rate was proposed. Management felt this was much too high, arguing that the company had improved its lending procedures in the last few months and that it expected to have a smaller percentage of charge-offs in the future. A current delinquent report received in February 2008 showed only two loans from 2007 were still on the past due list. The auditors agreed to a 2 percent reserve, and an adjusting entry (AJE #3) was made.

Regulatory Environment

Imperial Valley Thrift & Loan was approaching certain regulatory filing deadlines during the course of the audit. Stanley had a meeting with the regulators at which representatives of

---

EXHIBIT 3
Audit Adjustments

AJE #1	Reserve for loan losses	$ 200,000	
	Loans receivable		$ 200,000
	To write down loans to net realizable value		
AJE #2	Reserve for loan losses	300,000	
	Unearned discounts & fees	80,000	
	Loans receivable		380,000
	To write off loans more than 180 days past due in compliance with statutes		
AJE #3	Provision for loan losses	590,000	
	Reserve for loan losses		590,000
	To increase the reserve balance to 2 percent of outstanding loans as follows:		
	Reserve balance (preaudit)		$ (25,000)
Less: Adjusting entry			
#1		$ 200,000	
#2		300,000	
			500,000
Subtotal			$ 475,000
Add: Desired balance			
Loan balance (preaudit)		$6,300,000	
Less: AJE #1		(200,000)	
#2		(380,000)	
Loan balance (postaudit)		$5,720,000	
Reserve requirement		2% percent	
Desired balance (approx.)			115,000
Adjustment required			$ 590,000

management were present. Gonzalez also attended the meeting because he had expressed some interest in making a capital contribution. There was much discussion about Imperial Valley's ability to keep its doors open if the loan losses were recorded as proposed by the auditors. This was a concern because the proposed adjustments would place the client in a position of having net equity capital significantly below minimum requirements.

The regulators were concerned about the adequacy of the 2 percent general reserve because of the prior collection problems experienced by Imperial Valley. The institution's solvency was a primary concern. At the time of the meeting, the regulators were quite busy trying to straighten out problems caused by the failure of two other savings and loan (S&L) institutions in Arizona. Many depositors had lost money as a result of the failure of these S&Ls. The regulators were concerned that a domino effect could occur as had happened in the early 1990s and that Imperial Valley would get caught up in the mess. Also, the regulators were unable to make a thorough audit of the company on their own, so they relied quite heavily on the work of Jacobs, Stanley & Co. In this sense, the audit was used as leverage on the institution to get more money in as a cushion to protect depositors. The regulators viewed this as essential in light of the other S&L failures and the fact that the insurance protection mechanism for thrift and loan depositors was less substantial than depository insurance available through FDIC in commercial banks and in savings and loan institutions.

Summary of Client and Auditor Position

The management of Imperial Valley Thrift & Loan placed a great deal of pressure on the auditors to reduce the amount of the loan write-offs. It maintained that the customers were "good for the money." Managers pointed out those payments to date on most of the loans had been made on a timely basis. However, it was the auditors' contention that the payments to date, which were mostly annual interest amounts, were not necessarily a good indication that timely balloon principal payments would be made. They believed that it was very difficult to adequately evaluate collectibility of the balloon payments, primarily because the borrowers' source of cash for loan repayment had not been identified. They could not objectively audit or support borrowers' good intentions to pay or undocumented resources as represented by client management.

The client believed that the auditors did not fully understand the nature of its business. Managers pointed out that a certain amount of risk had to be accepted in their business because they primarily made loans that commercial banks and savings and loan institutions did not want to make. "We are the bank of last resort for many of our customers," commented bank President Eddie Salazar. Salazar then commented that the auditors' inability to understand and appreciate this element of the thrift and loan business was the main reason the auditors were having trouble evaluating collectibility on the outstanding loans.

To ensure that they were not being naïve about the thrift and loan industry, the auditors checked with colleagues in another office of the firm who know more about this type of business. One professional in this office explained that the real secret to this business is to follow up ruthlessly with any nonpayer. The auditors certainly did not feel this was being done by the management of Imperial Valley.

The auditors knew that Manny Gonzalez was a potential source of investment capital for Imperial Valley. They believed it was very important to give Gonzalez an accurate picture because the audit firm would be a potential target for a lawsuit if it painted a rosier picture than actually existed and Gonzalez made an investment.

Board of Trustees

The auditors approached the nine-member board of trustees who oversaw the operations of Imperial Valley and that serve as the audit committee. The auditors had hoped to solicit the support of the board in dealing with management over the audit opinion issue as detailed in the next section. Of the nine board members, four were officers of the bank and five were outsiders. The five outsiders all had major loans with the bank that were due in the next two years. They supported management on the validity of collateral and loan collectibility issues.

Audit Opinion

The management of Imperial Valley Thrift & Loan was pressuring the auditors to give an unqualified opinion. If the auditors decided to give a qualified or an adverse opinion or to disclaim an opinion, in the client's view, this would present a picture to its customers and the regulators that its financial statements were not accurate. The client maintained that such an opinion would be a blow to its integrity and would shake depositors' confidence in the institution. The five outside members of the board of trustees argued that their situation was typical. All five had a current cash flow problem but guaranteed the auditors that future flows would come in on time to meet required loan payments. The auditors pointed out that the bank's procedures "flew in the face" of the Sarbanes-Oxley Act. The five outside members had blank looks on their faces.

On one hand, the auditors were very cognizant of their responsibility to the regulatory authority, and they were also concerned about providing an accurate picture of Imperial Valley's financial health to Manny Gonzalez or other potential investors. On the other hand, they wondered whether they were holding the client to standards that were too strict. After all, the audit report issued in the prior year by the previous auditors contained only an explanatory paragraph on the capital impairment issue. The auditors also wondered whether the doors of the institution would be closed by the regulators if they gave an adverse opinion or disclaimed an opinion. What impact could this action have on the depositors and the economic health of the community? Bill Stanley wondered. "Whose interests are we really representing—

depositors, shareholders, management, the local community, or regulators, or all of these?

Stanley knew that he would soon have to make a recommendation about the type of audit opinion to be issued on the 2007 financial statements of Imperial Valley Thrift & Loan. Before approaching the advisory partner on the engagement, Stanley drafted the following memo to file:

Memo: Going-Concern Question

The question of the going-concern status of Imperial Valley Thrift & Loan is being raised because of the client's continuing operating losses and high level of loan losses. The client lost $920,000 after audit adjustments in 2007. This is in addition to a loss of $780,000 in 2006. Imperial Valley has also reported a loss of $45,000 for the first two months of 2008.

Imperial Valley is also out of compliance with regulatory capital requirements. After audit adjustments, the client has net equity capital of $610,000 as of December 31, 2007. The Arizona Department of Corporations requires a 6:1 ratio of thrift certificates to capital. As of December 31, 2007, these regulations would require net equity capital of $1,232,000. Imperial Valley was therefore undercapitalized by $622,000 at that date, and no additional capital contributions have been made subsequent to December 31. It is possible, however, that either the parent company, Nuevo Financial Group, or a private investor, Manny Gonzalez, will contribute additional equity capital.

We have concluded that there is a substantial doubt as to the bank's ability to continue in business. The reasons for this conclusion include the following:

- The magnitude of losses, particularly loan losses, indicated a possibility that Imperial Valley is not well managed.
- The losses are continuing in 2008. Annualized losses to date, without any provision for loan losses, are $270,000.
- Additional equity capital has not been contributed to date, although Gonzalez has $600,000 available.
- Our review of client loan files and lending policies raises an additional concern that loan losses may continue. If this happens, it would only exacerbate the conditions mentioned herein.

It would not be possible to test the liquidation value of the assets at this time should Imperial Valley not continue in business. The majority of client assets are loans receivable. These would presumably have to be discounted in order to be sold. In addition, there is some risk that the borrowers will simply stop making payments.

In conclusion, it is our opinion that a going-concern question exists for Imperial Valley Thrift & Loan at December 31, 2007. Pending the resolution of the question of capital adequacy, at a minimum, our audit report will include an explanatory paragraph describing the substantial doubt we have about Imperial Valley's ability to continue as a going concern. We should also consider the possibility of issuing a qualified opinion.

Questions

1. Assume that Imperial Valley Thrift & Loan was a publicly owned entity and subject to the requirements of the Sarbanes-Oxley Act. Using the facts of the case and other assumptions you may want to make, discuss whether the bank would be in compliance with the provisions for boards of directors, audit committees, and internal controls. Comment on corporate governance in general at Imperial Valley.

2. The auditors were quite concerned about the possibility that the amount of the adjustment to the reserve balance would not be sufficient to handle possible uncollectible loan amounts and write-offs due to inadequate collateral. Why should this be a matter of concern to the auditors with respect to their audit of the December 31, 2007, financial statements of Imperial Valley Thrift & Loan? Consider in forming your answer the position of Eddie Salazar, bank president, when he asked, "Why should we be concerned about an understatement of the reserve this year since any such understatement could be taken care of with an adjustment in 2008?"

3. Using the decision-making model presented in Chapter 3, analyze the case from the perspective of the advisory partner and determine with a decision on what type of opinion to recommend to management.

Case 5-6

Kazweski & Dooktaviski

Kazweski and Dooktaviski (KD) were general partners in a limited partnership located in Cincinnati, Ohio, that was created in 2000 to generate profits for its limited partners from trading in real estate. The partnership had its financial statements audited by Rench & Bose LLP, a Cincinnati-based accounting firm with offices throughout Ohio. The firm had given unqualified opinions on its audits of KD for the years 2004 to 2006 and stated that the audits were conducted in accordance with generally accepted auditing standards.

Moe Jorgan was the audit manager for these audits and Pony Terez was the partner in charge of the engagement. On August 20, 2007, Jorgan and Terez called a meeting of the KD audit engagement team to review the findings of a peer review of Rench & Bose that had been conducted by another CPA firm and included the KD audits. The peer reviewers issued a modified opinion on Rench & Bose's quality controls and its adherence to professional standards.

In addition to Jorgan and Terez, the other members of the KD audit engagement team included four staff members who had been hired after graduating from The State University of Ohio at Cincinnati. The staff members began working for Rench & Bose on July 1, 2007. The audit senior was Tod Kazweski, the son of one of KD's general partners.

The peer review pointed out several deficiencies that had to be addressed in a report to be filed with the Ohio State Board of Accountancy. The following summarizes the findings of the peer review:

- KD assets that were supposedly being held by the brokerage firm Pennant Co. had not been confirmed in writing. Instead, Tod Kazweski obtained verbal confirmation from Pennant for the $25 million balance.
- The auditors failed to consider obtaining audit evidence from other sources to verify the brokerage account balance.
- The auditors did not discover that KD had been audited prior to Rench & Bose's engagement, even though the

firm's permanent file contained a document that referred to KD's prior CPA.

- The auditors had not discussed audit matters with the prior auditors and had not discovered that the prior auditors were fired from the KD audit over a difference of opinion concerning the application of an accounting principle.
- Tod Kazweski failed to inform either Jorgan or Terez about the verbal confirmation from Pennant of the $25 million balance.
- There were no memos in Rench & Bose's KD audit working papers or anywhere else that discussed the fact that Tod Kazweski is the son of one of the general partners of KD.

Questions

1. Discuss the apparent departures from generally accepted auditing standards by the Rench & Bose auditors in their audit of KD.

2. Explain how independence had been compromised in the KD audit. What steps could have been taken by the firm to avoid the independence problem?

3. What is the level of care required by an auditor in the conduct of an audit in accordance with GAAS? Given the limited facts in the case, do you think Rench & Bose met that standard in the KD audit?

4. Assume that it is eventually discovered that the oral confirmation of KD's brokerage account balance had been confirmed through the examination of audit evidence. Does that mean the confirmation issue is no longer relevant because everything turned out all right? Why or why not? What could occur in the future if this matter is not properly dealt with by the firm?

5. Do you think the limited liability partners have a right to be concerned about the performance of the general partners? Why or why not?

Case 5-7

Marcus Yamabuto

Marcus Yamabuto graduated from State University in June 2007. He began working for a large regional firm, Huang & Garcia, in September 2007. The first major audit to which Yamabuto was assigned was Dunco, a secondary manufacturer of plasma monitors. Dunco is the original equipment manufacturer of 42-inch and 50-inch plasma screens. Dunco sells its monitors to major manufacturers including Jujitsu and Dontuchi.

Yamabuto was assigned to review sale documents and freight bills to determine the amount of freight, the terms of the sale, and the proper cutoff treatment. During the course of his examination, Yamabuto discovered $2.4 million of revenue that had been prematurely recognized for the year ended December 31, 2007. He determined the problem by matching the invoices with corresponding freight bills. He noticed that the shipping date of one transaction was January 2, 2008. There was a note signed by the freight forwarder, "Picked up for shipment at Dunco warehouse on January 3, 2008."

Yamabuto is not sure how to proceed. He contacts you, his best friend and co-worker, for advice.

Questions

1. What advice would you give to Yamabuto? Include in your answer the reasons for providing that advice from both accounting and ethical perspectives.

   Ignoring your answer to Question 1, assume that Yamabuto approaches his supervisor on the audit, Eileen Moldey, and tells her about his findings. Moldey contacts the partner in charge of the audit, Dusty Mite, and they meet the next morning.

   Mite: I've discussed the matter with the CFO, Goal Tendz, and he provided an explanation for the discrepancy. According to Tendz, the goods were loaded on the freight forwarder's trucks at Dunco's warehouse on December 31 and left there because the company did not start the trip to Dontuchi's headquarters to deliver the product until January, after the New Year's holiday. Therefore, the revenue as recorded for 2007 will remain on the books.

   Moldey: That sounds fine to me. How about you, Marcus. Are you on board?

2. As Marcus's best friend, assume that you are able to give Marcus advice after finding out about this new information and before he has to respond to Moldey. What would you advise and why?

   Ignoring your answer to Question 2, answer Questions 3–5, assuming that Marcus did "get on board."

3. If Huang & Garcia were to issue an unqualified opinion on the audit of Dunco, will the firm have violated its professional and ethical standards? Explain which ones would be violated or why you think no standards would have been violated.

4. Do you think Dunco has committed fraud? Why or why not?

5. Professor Maximilian B. Torres said the following in a commentary published by the Acton Institute (www.acton.org):

   > Fraud, that in every conscience leaves a sting,
   >
   > May be by man employ'd on one, whose trust
   >
   > He wins, or on another, who withholds
   >
   > Strict confidence.

   Comment on Torres' statement in general and with respect to the facts of this case.

Case 5-8

Peachtree Enviro-Management Systems

Peachtree Enviro-Management Systems is a large provider of trash-hauling services primarily in the Atlanta area. The company grew in its early years from $1 million in assets, $700,000 in revenue, and $100,000 in net income in 2001 to $20 million in assets, $15 million in revenues, and $4 million in net income in 2004. During 2005 through 2007, the company was audited by Spahn and Burdette LLP. In 2008, Peachtree changed its auditors to Aaron and Matthews LLP whose audit engagement team developed the following information during its audit of the financial statements of Peachtree.

Year	Assets	Revenues	Net Income
2004	$20 million	$15 million	$4 million
2005	30 million	21 million	6 million
2006	35 million	25 million	7 million
2007	40 million	30 million	16 million

Peachtree Enviro-Management had expanded during the time period by acquiring very profitable, smaller trash-hauling companies. Peachtree took control of the selling companies' stock and consolidated the net assets into its year-end financial statements, but the trash-hauling companies continued to operate as separate legal entities.

In 2008, Peachtree decided to paint all trash-hauling equipment of the acquired companies at Peachtree's cost to have a common logo on the side of all trucks. The total cost was $10 million; the accountant for Peachtree recorded these costs as capitalized fixed asset amounts and included them in the property, plant, and equipment account on Peachtree's books. Peachtree had set an estimated 10-year life with no salvage value. The straight-line method of depreciation was used.

The audit engagement team of Aaron and Matthews scheduled a meeting the next day to discuss the accounting for the painting costs.

Questions

1. Do you think the painting costs should have been capitalized? Why or why not?

2. If you answered yes to Question 1, discuss whether the painting costs should be depreciated over the same time period as the trash-hauling equipment. If you answered no to Question 1, explain how the painting costs should have been handled and the accounting support for that treatment.

3. Prepare an annual analysis of the following amounts for the time period 2004 to 2007:

   a. Revenue as a percentage of assets.

   b. Net income as a percentage of revenue.

   c. Net income as a percentage of assets.

   Do any of these relationships provide red flags that could cause you to further examine the relationship(s)? What would you look for? Why?

4. Given the information in this case, do you believe errors in the application of accounting principles have occurred? Why or why not? Do you believe fraud has occurred? How would you know the difference?

5. Do you think the percentage relationships calculated in this case represent a material misstatement in the financial statements? Why or why not?

6. What could have motivated the management of Peachtree to account for the painting costs as capital items? Evaluate management's action in light of the ethical principles discussed in the text.

Case 5-9

The Audit Report

Zoe Foster is the manager in charge of the audit of Sky Hook Inc., publicly owned professional sports consulting organization located in Springfield, Massachusetts. Foster reviewed the draft audit report on Sky Hook in Exhibit 1 that was prepared by the senior in charge of the audit, Frank D'Amato, and then had the following conversation with D'Amato:

Foster: Listen, Frank, you need to go back and redo the audit report for Sky Hook.

D'Amato: Why? What's wrong?

Foster: I think you need to figure that out for yourself. I realize this is the first time you've been asked to do an audit report, and there were a few complications in this audit, but some of the mistakes are Audit 101 issues.

D'Amato: Can you give some guidance here?

Foster: Let's just say we can't issue an unqualified opinion because of the difference of opinion with the client on the potential marketability of the inventory held at its warehouse in Boston.

D'Amato: When do you want the revised draft?

Foster: Yesterday!

D'Amato went back to his office and reviewed the hardcopy file of the current audit to look for working papers that could provide support for the audit opinion. The problem was that there was no other information about the opinion because it was unqualified. That meant D'Amato would have to look at the computer files to see whether back-up inventory information exists.

Exhibit 1
Audit Report for Sky Hook, Inc.

Independent Auditor's Report

We have audited the accompanying balance sheet of Sky Hook, Inc. as of December 31, 2007, and the related statements of income and retained earnings for the year then ended. These statements are the responsibility of the Company's management. Our responsibility is to express an opinion on these financial statements based on our audit.

We conducted our audit in accordance with generally accepted auditing standards prepared by the American Institute of CPAs. Those standards require that we plan and perform the audit to obtain reasonable assurance about whether the financial statements are free of material misstatement. An audit includes examining evidence supporting the amounts and disclosures in the financial statements. An audit also includes assessing the accounting principles used and significant estimates that we made as well as evaluating the overall financial statement presentation. We believe that our audit provides a reasonable basis for any opinion.

In our opinion, the financial statements referred to above present fairly the financial position of Sky Hook as of December 31, 2007, and the results of its operations for the year then ended in conformity with generally accepted accounting principles established by the Financial Accounting Standards Board.

Johnson and Garson LLP
Boston, Massachusetts

December 31, 2007

Instead, D'Amato decided to telephone Dana Hawkins, the sole staff member on the Sky Hook audit. Hawkins had been assigned to another audit, so she told D'Amato she could talk for only a few minutes. D'Amato asked whether she recalled any issues with the Sky Hook inventory held in Boston. Hawkins told D'Amato that the physical inventory in Boston was never observed so she couldn't recall very much. D'Amato asked Hawkins to review the inventory files to see whether there was other information about the Boston inventory. Hawkins asked D'Amato when he would need a response from her. D'Amato replied, "Two days ago!"

Questions

1. Describe all deficiencies in the audit report other than the inventory matter.

2. Do you think it was right for D'Amato to ask Hawkins for her help? Why or why not? Be sure to provide ethical support for your answer.

3. Discuss the accounting issues that Foster should have considered before making the statement, "We can't issue an unqualified opinion because of the difference of opinion with the client on the potential marketability of the inventory held at its warehouse in Boston."

4. What additional audit steps could have been taken to overcome the fact that the physical inventory in Boston was never observed? Given the limited facts of the case, do you think a qualified opinion would be appropriate? Why or why not?

5. Assume that no adjustments/corrections to the original audit report are made. What ethics rules in the AICPA Code would have been violated by the firm of Johnson & Garson (Zoe's firm) and its auditors?

Case 5-10

The Hollinger Chronicles: A Major Case Study

Introduction

The case of Hollinger International resembles Enron, Adelphia, and Tyco all wrapped up in one. Its chief executive officer (CEO) improperly removed documents from the company during an investigation of its activities. Conflicts of interest existed because the CEO acted on behalf of two or more related-party entities. The CEO engaged in uncontrolled self-dealing by treating company funds as his own personal piggy bank. And, although there was no $2 million birthday party for the CEO's wife on the island of Sardinia, there was a birthday dinner party at New York's La Grenoulie Restaurant at a cost of $42,870 to the company.

The Hollinger case has it all: a member of the British House of Lords, a former U.S. secretary of state, and a former governor of one of the nation's largest states. The Special Committee that was formed in June 2003 to investigate the fraud made its report public on August 30, 2004, calling it the "Hollinger Chronicles." The Committee characterized what went on at Hollinger as a "corporate kleptocracy." As the report points out," this is a story about how Hollinger was systematically manipulated and used by its controlling shareholders for their sole benefit, and in a manner that violated every concept of fiduciary duty." [1]

The corporate governance systems at Hollinger completely broke down. Top management represented their own interests, not those of the shareholders, thereby violating the duty of care in making business judgments and the duty of loyalty in dealing fairly by managing the corporation with unselfish loyalty.

The board of directors and audit committee, especially the CEO, Lord Conrad Black, did not act independently of management. Black wore two hats by also serving as the chair of the board of directors.

The actions of the external auditors failed to measure up to the fraud standards in *Statement of Auditing Standards (SAS) No. 99,* Consideration of Fraud in a Financial Statement Audit. The internal controls either were nonexistent or were overridden by top management.

The timeline of the case occurs both before and after enactment of the Sarbanes-Oxley Act (SOX) in August 2002. Prior to 2002, Black signed off on financial statements filed with the Securities and Exchange Commission (SEC). Black violated Section 302 when he did the same with the 2002 10-K Report filed with the Commission. That section prohibits the CEO and top accounting officials from certifying the accuracy of the financial statements filed with the SEC that contain materially false information or omit information that is necessary to make the statements not misleading.

The SEC issued its first complaint against Hollinger on January 19, 2004, in Accounting and Auditing Enforcement Release (AAER) No. 1946.[2] The filing occurred less than two weeks after the company had removed Black as its chairman and he had resigned as CEO. This followed the announcement of a $200 million lawsuit against Black and David Radler, the deputy chair, president and chief operating officer, charging that they had diverted corporate assets for personal purposes.

The SEC followed up by filing a lawsuit in U.S. District Court for the Northern District of Illinois on November 15, 2004. The suit charges Black, Radler, and Hollinger Inc. with multiple violations of the securities acts through the commission of fraud in relation to improper payments and related-party transactions.[3]

The Hollinger case can serve as an example of the need for SOX, and the facts of the case help to analyze whether SOX provisions could have served as a deterrent had they been in effect throughout the Hollinger Chronicles.

Background

Organization Structure

Imagine that you and your brother set up a company primarily to own the controlling interest in another public company. Just for good measure, you set up a third, private company to own a controlling interest in the first company. Now, the third company controls the first company that controls the second company, so the third company also controls the second company. Confused yet?

Of course, you and your brother really are all three companies because you are the chair of each board of directors and the chief executive officer of two of them, and your brother is the president or chief operating officer of all three and a deputy chair in two. It sounds like you can do pretty much whatever you want to do. That is what happened with Black and Radler through their ownership and management of all three companies. Figure 1 depicts the organization structure at Hollinger.

Hollinger, Inc. is a publicly held Canadian mutual fund company whose primary holding is its shares of stock in Hollinger, International. From about 1998 to 2004, Hollinger, Inc. (referred to as "the Company") had no operations.

---

[1] Special Committee of the Board of Directors to Investigate Hollinger International, http://everything2.com/index.pl?node_id=1673609.

[2] Securities and Exchange Commission, Accounting and Auditing Enforcement Release (AAER) No. 1946, www.sec.gov/litigation/litreleases/lr18550.htm.

[3] *United States Securities and Exchange Commission v. Conrad M. Black, F. David Radler, and Hollinger, Inc.*

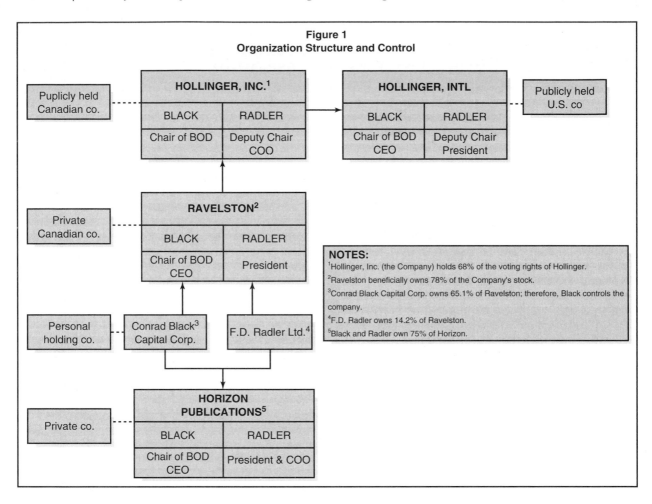

Figure 1
Organization Structure and Control

During that time, it was the controlling shareholder of Hollinger, International (referred to as "Hollinger") through direct and indirect ownership of all shares of Class B common. This stock had a 10-to-1 voting preference over shares of Hollinger's Class A common. The Company owned approximately 18.2 percent of the combined equity but 68 percent of combined voting power in Hollinger.

Hollinger is a Delaware corporation with its principal place of business in Chicago. The company is listed on the New York Stock Exchange. Hollinger owns and operates newspaper publishing businesses in the United States and abroad. From 1998 through 2004, it owned, through its wholly owned subsidiaries, the *Chicago Sun-Times, The Daily Telegraph,* a London newspaper, and the *Jerusalem Post,* as well as almost 400 hundred smaller newspapers and other entities.

Ravelston is a privately owned Canadian company that beneficially owns approximately 78 percent of the company's stock and Ravelston, in turn, is owned by Conrad Black through Conrad Black Capital Corporation (65.1 percent), a personal holding company, and F.D. Radler Ltd. (14.2 percent). Ravelston, therefore, effectively owns Hollinger, and Black and Radler control Ravelston.

The top management at Hollinger, including Black and Radler, were employed through a contract with an affiliate

of Ravelston that received payments from Hollinger for its management of that entity. These arrangements led to the top executives at Hollinger working for Black as the CEO; they also were subordinate to and drew benefits from Black in their roles at Ravelston. The overlapping ownership and management structure is analyzed in the Special Committee Report. It appears in Table 1.

Cast of Characters

Conrad Black was born in Canada but renounced his Canadian citizenship in 2001 after unsuccessfully attempting to gain dual British-Canadian citizenship. The Canadian government would not approve, so Black gave up his Canadian citizenship to become a British citizen and accept a peerage in the British House of Lords. Ironically, Black now seeks to restore his Canadian citizenship so he can request U.S. trials to be moved to Canada.

Between 1999 and 2003, Black signed Hollinger's annual 10-K reports as its chair and CEO. He certified Hollinger's annual and quarterly reports between August 2002 and August 2003 that were filed with the SEC pursuant to SOX.

David Radler signed Hollinger's 10-K reports between 1999 and 2003 as the deputy chair and president of Hollinger.

Table 1
Hollinger International—Overlaps in Management, Board of Directors, and Ownership[*]

| | Ravelston Shareholder | Hollinger, Inc. (Company) | | Hollinger International (Hollinger) | |
		Officer	Director	Officer	Director
Conrad M. Black	Yes 65.1%	Chairman CEO	Yes	Chairman[3] CEO[4]	Yes
F. David Radler	Yes 14.2%	Deputy chair President & CEO	Yes	Deputy chair[5] President & COO[5]	Yes
	Yes	Executive VP	Yes	Executive VP[6]	Yes
Peter Atkinson	0.98%	President General counsel	1		5
	Yes	Executive VP	Yes	Executive VP[7]	No
J.A.Boultbee	0.98%	President Former CFO		Former CFO	
	Yes	Vice chairman	Yes	Vice chairman[8]	Yes
Daniel W. Colson	2.9%		2	Deputy Chair & CEO of Telegraph	

[1]Resigned effective January 13, 2004.
[2]Resigned effective December 22, 2003.
[3]Removed on January 17, 2004.
[4]Resigned effective November 19, 2003.
[5]Resigned effective November 17, 2003.
[6]Resigned effective April 27, 2004.
[7]Terminated effective November 17, 2003.
[8]Resigned effective March 24, 2004.
[*]Taken from The Special Committee Report.

Radler served as Black's right-hand man and supervised newspaper sales through which he and other managers siphoned off millions of dollars in fees that should have gone to Hollinger. On September 21, 2005, Radler pled guilty to a lesser charge (originally five counts of mail fraud and two counts of wire fraud; Radler pled guilty to one count of mail fraud), apparently as part of a deal for a shorter sentence in exchange for testimony against Black.

Peter Atkinson served as the executive vice president and was a director of Hollinger from 1996 until April 27, 2004. In January 2004, he resigned as executive vice president. John Boultbee served as a director from 1990 until 1995 and became executive vice president in 1998. He also served as the chief financial officer from 1995 through 2002. During the period 1999 through 2002, Boultbee signed many of Hollinger's quarterly 10-Q reports. Both Atkinson and Boultbee owned, directly or indirectly, 0.98 percent of Ravelston. They shared to some extent in the diverted amounts.

Hollinger's Board of Directors

Hollinger had 10 members of the board immediately before the events that led to the collapse of management and the board; five were inside directors and five were outsiders.

The five inside directors included Black, his wife, Radler, Atkinson, and Daniel Colson, who was the deputy chair of Hollinger's board and CEO of the *London Telegraph*. He also owned stock in Ravelston.

Black and Radler were majority shareholders in Ravelston, and Ravelston received management fee payments for their services to Hollinger from Hollinger funds. Now, add to the equation the fact that the Company owned the majority voting power in Hollinger while Black was the chair and CEO of the Company and Radler served as its deputy chair, president, and chief operating officer, and it is easy to see how the organization's framework and overlapping ownership interests enabled the frauds to occur. Of course, Black and Radler were the ones who established a culture of deceit and selfishness.

With the exception of Shmuel Meitar, a communications and media business specialist, the outside board members reads like a list from "Who's Who" and included:

- Richard Burt, the former chief negotiator of the Strategic Arms Reduction Talks and an ambassador to Germany.

- Henry Kissinger, the former Secretary of State and National Security Advisor under Presidents Nixon and Ford.

- Richard Perle, the former Assistant Secretary for the Department of Defense for International Security Policy during the Reagan Administration.
- James Thompson, the former four-term governor of Illinois.

The Fraudulent Noncompetition Payments

The SEC civil fraud lawsuit (Litigation Release No. 18969) filed on November 15, 2004, in the U.S. District Court, Northern District of Illinois against Black, Radler, and the Company alleges that from approximately 1999 through 2003, the defendants engaged in a fraudulent and deceptive scheme to divert cash and assets from Hollinger and concealed their self-dealing from Hollinger's public shareholders. The SEC complaint asked the court to do the following:

- Enjoin the defendants from further violations of the securities laws.
- Order the defendants to disgorge their ill-gotten gains and pay prejudgment interest.
- Order the defendants to pay civil penalties.
- Bar Black and Radler from serving as an officer or director of another public company.
- Impose a voting trust on the shares of Hollinger held directly or indirectly by Black and the Company.[4]

On March 23, 2005, federal prosecutors asked the district court to grant a motion to stay all discovery in the SEC's civil lawsuit to prevent the release of SEC documents to the defendants in its lawsuit. A stay was granted pending the outcome of a criminal investigation by the U.S. Attorney's Office that began on November 17, 2005.

The SEC complaint (11-35) details several fraudulent noncompetition payments from approximately 1999 through

[4] Securities and Exchange Commission, www.sec.gov/litigation/litreleases/lr18969.htm.

2001. These payments had been made in connection with a series of Hollinger sales of its U.S. and Canadian newspaper properties. As a result of these payments, portions of the sales proceeds, which should have gone to Hollinger for the benefit of all of its shareholders, were diverted in the amount of $85 million to Black and Radler, the Company, Ravelston, and other corporate insiders. A summary of the payments appears in Table 2.

During the period 1999–2001, the Company received $16.55 million, Black and Radler received $19 million each, Atkinson and Boultbee received $1.9 million each, and Ravelston, the company controlled by Black, received $26.3 million. These amounts represent 3.7 percent and 6.2 percent of Hollinger's gross and net income, respectively, for 1999 and increased to 11.6 percent and 54.2 percent in 2000. In 2001, Hollinger experienced a large loss, so the percentages are not computed.

The buyer of the properties did not request Hollinger's officers to execute the noncompetition agreements, and none of the Hollinger officers was asked to sign such agreements. All that was needed was for Hollinger, as a separate legal entity, to sign a noncompete agreement, which would have covered Black and Radler without the need for separate payments to these or other officers of Hollinger. On one occasion, Black and Radler engineered purported noncompetition payments to themselves for their agreements not to compete with a wholly owned subsidiary of Hollinger in the absence of any purchase or sale of newspapers.

The amounts received by the Company from the noncompete payments in 1999 were used by it to repay debt due to Hollinger. This created a double benefit for the Company because not only was $15.2 million diverted from the sales proceeds that should have gone to Hollinger, but also the Company then turned around and used that money to repay a loan due to Hollinger.

The CanWest Transaction

Perhaps the CanWest transaction best illustrates the extent to which Black schemed to defraud Hollinger. On July 30,

Table 2
Fraudulent Noncompetition Payments

Year	Amount	Recipient	Payment as a % of Hollinger	
			Gross Income	Net income
1999	$15.2M	Company	3.7%	6.2% ('99)
2000	1.35M	Company	—	—
2000 – 2001	19.0M	Black		
	19.0M	Radler	11.6%	54.2% ('00)
	1.9M	Atkinson		
	1.9M	Boultbee		
	26.3M	Ravelston	$361.5M loss	$337.5M loss ('01)

2000, Hollinger and its subsidiaries executed a transaction agreement to sell several of its Canadian newspapers to CanWest for approximately $2.6 billion, of which $51.6 million was allocated as consideration for noncompetition agreements. The transaction was strictly between Hollinger and CanWest, yet the Company, Ravelston, Black, Radler, Atkinson, and Boultbee were identified in the transaction agreement as parties to the noncompetition agreement along with Hollinger.

Black negotiated the transaction on behalf of Hollinger. Black and Radler determined the allocation of the noncompete payment. Atkinson asked Black if he and Boultbee could be given "noncompetition" payments to serve as bonuses for their work on the CanWest transaction. Black agreed to add their names to the list of the chosen.

On July 25, 2000, the Hollinger board received a summary of the proposed CanWest transaction. The summary stated, "The purchase price was increased as a result of a reduction of Management Service Fees charged by Ravelston with respect to the ongoing management of the Newspaper Assets. Prior to closing, Ravelston and the Audit Committee will negotiate an appropriate sharing of such purchase price increase." Apparently, the purchase price was increased

because the future operating results of CanWest would be higher because it would not have to pay the management service fee to Ravelston.

In preparation for an audit committee meeting on September 11, 2000, a memorandum was sent explaining that Black, Radler, Hollinger, Ravelston, Atkinson, and Boultbee had been requested to execute noncompetition agreements. At the same time, Ravelston proposed that the Ravelston company, controlled by Black, receive approximately 0.9 percent of the purchase price, "in consideration for Ravelston reducing its management fee and consenting to CanWest having an early termination of its management arrangements." The audit committee approved CanWest's desire for the noncompete agreements and Ravelston's termination fee request without knowing that CanWest had not requested the noncompete payments. Thompson, the audit committee chair, presented it to the board and it, too, approved based on the "fairness" of the allocations.

Hollinger did not disclose the CanWest noncompete transactions in its 2000 Form 10-K filed on April 2, 2001. It first disclosed the payments in its Form 10-Q for the quarter ended March 31, 2001, and then later in its Forms 10-K for 2001 and 2002. These disclosures appear in Exhibit 1.

Exhibit 1
Examples of Disclosures about the CanWest Transaction

Form 10-Q for the Quarter Ended March 31, 2001
Also, as required by CanWest as a condition to the transaction, Ravelston, [the Company], and Messrs. Black, Radler, Boultbee, and Atkinson, entered into noncompetition agreements with CanWest pursuant to which each agreed not to compete directly or indirectly in Canada with the Canadian businesses sold to CanWest for a five-year period, subject to certain limited exceptions, for aggregate consideration received by Ravelston and the executives of $53 million paid by CanWest in addition to the purchase price referred to above, consisting of $38 million paid to Ravelston, $19 million paid to Mr. Black, $19 million paid to Mr. Radler, $2 million paid to Mr. Boultbee, and $2 million paid to Mr. Atkinson.

2001 Form 10-K
Also, as required by CanWest as a condition to the transaction [Hollinger], Ravelston, the Company, Lord Black, and three senior executives entered into noncompetition agreements with CanWest pursuant to which each agreed not to compete directly or indirectly in Canada with the Canadian businesses sold to CanWest for a five-year period, subject to certain limited exceptions, for aggregate consideration of $53 million received by Ravelston and the executives paid by CanWest in addition to the purchase price referred to above of which $25.2 million was paid to Ravelston and $27.8 million was paid to Lord Black and the three senior executives. [Hollinger's] independent directors have approved the terms of these payments.

2002 Form 10-K
Further, CanWest required as a condition to the transaction that [Hollinger], Ravelston, the Company, Lord Black, and three senior executives entered into noncompetition agreements with CanWest pursuant to which each agreed not to compete directly or indirectly in Canada with the Canadian businesses sold to CanWest for a five-year period, subject to certain limited exceptions, for aggregate consideration of $53 million received by Ravelston and the executives paid by CanWest in addition to the purchase price referred to above of which $25.2 million was paid to Ravelston and $27.8 million was paid to Lord Black and the three senior executives. [Hollinger's] independent directors have approved the terms of these payments.

The disclosures identify CanWest as the originator of the request for noncompete payments, and the annual reports indicate the payments were approved by Hollinger's independent directors. The SEC charged Black and Radler with recklessness in not knowing that Hollinger's 2001 and 2002 Forms 10-K and Form 10-Q for the quarter ended March 31, 2001, were materially false and misleading because they contained misstatements and omissions of material facts. Black and Radler signed Hollinger's 2001 and 2002 Forms 10-K with the omissions and misstatements. Black also certified Hollinger's 2002 Form 10-K pursuant to Section 302 of SOX as the CEO of Hollinger. An example of Hollinger's disclosures on Form 10-K for 2001 and 2002 appears in Exhibit 2.

By policy and practice, Hollinger should have had all related-party transactions reviewed and approved by the audit committee of the board of directors. According to the charges filed by the SEC, to perpetrate their scheme, Black and Radler made misstatements and omissions of material fact regarding the purported noncompetition payments to the audit committee and board. On November 17, 2003, Hollinger filed a Form 8-K with the SEC along with a press release disclosing some of the payments. Perhaps the filing was motivated by the more stringent requirements for filing that form in the aftermath of SOX.

The Report of the Special Committee

Abusive Practices

On June 17, 2003, after its shareholders raised allegations of unauthorized transfers of corporate assets, Hollinger's board established a Special Committee of independent directors to investigate possible misconduct, initiate and prosecute litigation based on its investigation, recover misappropriated assets, and protect the interests of all Hollinger shareholders.

The Report of the Special Committee of the Board identified a variety of abusive practices, in addition to the noncompetition payments, that include the Company's taking approximately $80 million in Hollinger cash as "loans" without paying market levels of interest and, as previously mentioned, using Hollinger's own cash to repay debt (http://everything2.com/index.pl?node_id=1673609). The Committee concluded that Black and Radler freely used Hollinger's cash and credit to benefit the Company without adequately compensating Hollinger, in part to maintain the Company's "stranglehold" control over Hollinger.

The Report labels the noncompetition payments as a form of unauthorized compensation and identifies another form of "compensation" in the use of Hollinger cash to pay personal expenses of Black and his wife and of Radler and his family. Although the total amount taken from the personal piggy bank set up by Black from Hollinger cash for these purposes was nowhere near the amount of the account of Dennis Kozlowski, the former CEO of Tyco, the two officers managed to travel in style. Hollinger bought a Challenger aircraft for $11.6 million that was given to Radler and leased a Gulfstream IV at a cost of $3 to $4 million each year for the Blacks. Operating costs for both of these aircraft totaled more than $23 million from 2000 to 2003.

Perhaps the most abusive practice was the substantial amounts that were taken out of Hollinger and paid to Ravelston on behalf of Black and Radler as their management fees. The Committee Report describes a camouflaged system that was designed to make it more difficult for the audit committee and

---

Exhibit 2
Examples of Disclosures about the Noncompete Agreements

2001

In connection with the sales of U.S. newspaper properties in 2000 to satisfy a closing condition, the Company, Lord Black, and three senior executives entered into noncompetition agreements with purchasers to which each agreed not to compete directly or indirectly in the United States with the U.S. businesses sold to purchasers for a fixed period, subject to certain limited exceptions, for aggregate consideration of $0.6 million paid in 2001. These amounts were in addition to the aggregate consideration paid in 2001 in respect to these noncompetition agreements of $15 million in 2000. Such amounts were paid to Lord Black and the three senior executives. The Company's independent directors have approved the terms of these payments.

2002

During 2000, we sold most of our remaining U.S. community newspaper properties for total proceeds of approximately $215 million. In connection with those sales to satisfy a closing condition, the Company, Lord Black, and three senior executives entered into noncompetition agreements with purchasers to which each agreed not to compete directly or indirectly in the United States with the U.S. businesses sold to purchasers for a fixed period, subject to certain limited exceptions, for aggregate consideration of $0.6 million paid in 2001. These amounts were in addition to the aggregate consideration paid in 2001 in respect of these noncompetition agreements of $15 million in 2000. Such amounts were paid to Lord Black and the three senior executives. The Company's independent directors have approved the terms of these payments.

external auditors to know exactly how much was transferred from Hollinger to Ravelston for this purpose.

The Management Fees

The Special Committee's compensation experts concluded that "from 1997–2003, Black and Radler received 'management fees' of $218.4 million through [the Company] and Ravelston." The experts analyzed the fees and identified $196.9 million of the total amount that represented compensation to the five senior officers.

One issue that permeates the Hollinger case from a corporate governance perspective is the fairness of Black and Radler's practices to all of Hollinger's shareholders. The Report notes that Hollinger did not benefit from the Ravelston structure. Moreover, shareholders could not learn what compensation Black and the others were receiving by reading Hollinger's proxy statement that was prepared before each annual meeting. The aggregate management fees to Ravelston were disclosed, but investors had no way to know that almost all of this amount represented compensation to the individuals. An analysis by compensation experts of total fees paid to Black, Radler, and their associates at Ravelston during the 1997 to 2003 period indicates that more than $400 million had been paid from all sources including the noncompete payments, personal expenses, and other transfers from Hollinger. This represents 95.2 percent of Hollinger's adjusted net income over the relevant period.

Black's public defense of the Ravelston management system was that the amount of the management fee each year had been approved by the audit committee, yet the Hollinger board was never given truthful and accurate information to enable it to understand how much Black or Radler made directly and indirectly in annual compensation from Hollinger. When the audit committee approved the Ravelston management fees, it did so without knowing the level of compensation for each officer and how this would compare to officers at other publishing companies. Also, the audit committee did not know how much more the Ravelston fee had cost Hollinger compared with what it would have cost Hollinger to follow normal compensation and hiring practices for senior executives.

Where Were the Auditors?

Where were the KPMG auditors whose job it was to protect the interests of the shareholders? While Black failed to fully disclose to the auditors the information they needed to investigate the noncompete payments and management fees over a five-year period ending in 2003, the auditors knew of the payments, at least in general, but it does not seem from the Special Committee report that they were actively engaged in trying to find out just what was going on at Hollinger. Ultimately, they gave up when on December 24, 2003, the firm announced that it was resigning from the engagement after the embattled holding company refused the firm's demands to make a number of management changes.

Hollinger's 2003 Form 10-K was filed with the SEC on January 18, 2005. Since then, it has worked diligently with a reconstituted board to file financial statements with the SEC on a timely basis.

The Lawsuits Just Keep on Coming

In March 2005, Black learned that U.S. authorities had opened a criminal investigation into his activities. Also, the Ontario Securities Commission (OSC) had filed notice that it would launch proceedings against Black, three former associates, and the Company for alleged violations of securities laws. The OSC set June 2005 as the date for the hearing on the allegations.

On March 30, 2005, the Company filed a $636 million lawsuit in Canada against Black and other former executives, charging that they had blocked corporate opportunities, breached their fiduciary responsibilities, and misappropriated management fees and noncompetition payments.

On May 3, 2005, a group of Hollinger directors settled a shareholder lawsuit and agreed to pay Hollinger $50 million that would come from their liability insurance policies. Earlier, on May 11, 2004, Hollinger had reached agreement with former director Atkinson, who paid $2.8 million, which represents 100 percent of the amount he received plus interest from noncompete payments and management fees. David Radler pleaded guilty on September 21, 2005, and agreed to a 29-month jail term and a fine of $250,000. The lone holdout other than Black was John Boultbee, the former CFO of Hollinger, who on December 7, 2005, pleaded not guilty to fraud charges. He was ordered released after posting bail of $1.5 million.

In a scene reminiscent of the Enron debacle, on May 20, 2005, Black was caught on tape removing dozens of boxes out the back door of the Company offices in Toronto. He agreed to return the boxes after the security tape was played in court.

The scope of the legal proceedings against Black expanded on November 17, 2005, when Patrick Fitzgerald, U.S. Attorney for the Northern District of Illinois, charged Black and other former top executives with 11 counts of fraud relating to the alleged diversion of millions from Hollinger. The charges included the fraud scheme involving Hollinger's sale of Canadian newspapers to CanWest. Black pleaded not guilty and was released after posting a $20 million U.S. bond.

An expanded 15-count indictment was returned on December 15, 2005; it added four new charges against Black: one count each of racketeering, obstruction of justice, money laundering, and wire fraud. The obstruction charge refers to the removal of boxes from the Company headquarters. The racketeering count alleges that Black masterminded the activities of a group of individuals and entities that comprised the "Hollinger Enterprise." The indictment identified racketeering in the form of noncompete payments that improperly diverted funds away from Hollinger, the abuse of perquisites, and the making of false and fraudulent statements to Hollinger's shareholders and other outsiders including filings with the SEC that contained material falsehoods and omissions. Lord Black faces a maximum of 95 years in prison if convicted on all charges.

Questions

1. Certain sections of the Sarbanes-Oxley Act could have helped to deter the transactions and relationships that occurred at Hollinger had the company implemented the procedures required by SOX. Because most of the case occurs prior to enactment of SOX in August 2002, Hollinger's actions were not subject to it. The one area in which the SEC charged Hollinger with a violation was the certification of financial statements in Form 10-K for 2002. Review the following provisions of SOX and assess whether they provide for measures that could have mitigated the wrongful actions at Hollinger had the company incorporated them into its control environment. You can download the act (H. R. 3763) from the AICPA's Center for Public Company Audit Firms (www.aicpa.org/sarbanes/index.asp).

   a. Title III—Corporate Responsibility

   b. Title IV—Enhanced Financial Disclosures

   c. Title VIII—Corporate and Criminal Fraud Accountability

2. Independence is a critical requirement for external auditors. According to the AICPA Code of Professional Conduct, "A member should maintain objectivity and be free of conflicts of interest in discharging professional responsibilities. A member in public practice should be independent in fact and appearance when providing auditing and other attestation services." Evaluate this standard against the role and relationship between KPMG and the individuals and entities included in the case.

3. Sound corporate governance principles include a standard of "entire fairness" for judging transactions between controlling shareholders and the controlled company. To protect the noncontrolling shareholders from the acts of the controlling shareholders, any transactions between a controlling shareholder and the controlled company must result from a process used to negotiate terms that are "entirely fair," and the substantive economic terms themselves must be "entirely fair." Consider this standard and discuss whether the transactions described in this case were "entirely fair" economically or procedurally.

4. Review the footnote disclosures in Exhibits 1 and 2. Evaluate the accuracy of the statements given the facts of the case. What was the role of the auditors, KPMG, with respect to the accuracy of these statements?

5. *SAS 99* describes two types of misstatements that are relevant to the auditor's consideration of fraud. Describe the two types of misstatements and characteristics of fraud. Was either of them present at Hollinger? Provide examples of the type(s) you identify from the facts of the case.

6. *SAS 99* identifies three conditions that are generally present when fraud occurs: incentives or pressures, opportunities, and rationalizations. Use the facts of the case to determine whether one or more of the conditions could have motivated the actions of Conrad Black given the environment at Hollinger and the Company's relationships with related entities. Provide support for your answers.

Chapter

6

Legal and Regulatory Obligations in an Ethical Framework

It's not that we are trying to avoid our legitimate responsibilities. We are trying to put reasonable limitations on our exposure. Excessive liability creates an incentive for accountants to restrict the free flow of commercial information which is so important to our free enterprise system. When someone wishes to rely on an accountant's report for a significant business decision, it is only fair that the accountant have knowledge of the intended reliance.

Robert Mednick

The preceding statement was made by Robert Mednick, the former chair of Arthur Andersen's Worldwide Committee on Professional Standards and Worldwide Managing Partner—Professional and Regulatory Matters in response to a question posed by an interviewer for *The CPA Journal* with respect to the effort led by the AICPA in the mid-1980s to reform accountants' legal liability.[1] Mednick served at that time as chair of the AICPA Task Force on Accountants Liability.

Mednick points out in the interview that the number of lawsuits against accountants in the years 1975 to 1985 increased from 117,000 to 273,600. In many of the cases, the courts and juries found someone to compensate the injured parties for their losses. Under the joint and several liability principle, each negligent party could be held liable for the total of damages suffered, even though it was deemed responsible for only a small portion of the loss. In other words, a $10 million class action lawsuit bought by the shareholders of a public company that named the investment bankers, accountants, and lawyers could recover 100 percent of the amount from the accountants. During the 1970s and 1980s, accountants and auditors were deemed to have "deep pockets," and sometimes the firms preferred to settle out of court rather than become involved in protracted litigation.

In the mid-1990s, the accounting profession lobbied Congress for securities litigation reform and in 1995, Congress passed the Private Securities Litigation Reform Act.[2] The act established a proportionate liability standard making each defendant liable solely for that defendant's portion of the damages that correspond to the percentage of responsibility of that defendant. John Coffee, a noted professor of securities law at Columbia University, believes that the act decreased the threat of private enforcement against accountants while the SEC had turned its attention to CPA firms that were cross-selling services to clients and otherwise loosening audit independence standards.[3]

One implication of proportionate liability is that accountants and auditors may have unconsciously veered away from the due care standard that is an essential part of carrying out professional responsibilities in an ethical manner. This action results from changes in the ethics standards forced on the accounting profession as a result of the FTC challenges described in Chapter 4.

Legal Liability: An Overview

University of Southern California Professor Zoe-Vonna Palmrose identifies the four general stages in an audit-related dispute: (1) the occurrence of events that result in losses for users of the financial statements, (2) the investigation by plaintiff attorneys before filing the suit to link the user losses with allegations of material omissions or misstatements of financial statements, (3) the legal process that commences with the filing of the lawsuit, and (4) the final resolution of the dispute.[4] The first stage comes about as a result of some loss-generating event including client bankruptcy, fraudulent financial reporting, and the misappropriation of assets. The latter two events will be discussed later.

Auditors can be sued by clients, investors, creditors, and the government for failure to perform services adequately and in accordance with the profession's ethics standards. Auditors can be held liable under common law and statutory law. *Common law* liability evolves from legal opinions issued by judges in deciding cases. These opinions become legal principles that set a precedent and guide judges in deciding similar cases in the future. *Statutory law* reflects legislation passed at the state or federal level that establishes certain courses of conduct that must be adhered to by covered parties.[5]

Exhibit 6.1 summarizes the types of liability and auditors' actions that result in liability.

Common Law Liability

Common law liability requires the auditor to perform professional services with due care. Recall that *due care* is a basic principle and rule of conduct in the AICPA Code. Evidence of having exercised due care exists if the auditor can demonstrate having performed services

EXHIBIT 6.1
Summary of Types of Liability and Auditors' Actions Resulting in Liability

Source: William F. Messier, Jr., Steven M. Glover, and Douglas F. Prawitt, *Auditing and Assurance Services: A Systematic Approach* (New York, NY: McGraw-Hill/Irwin, 2006).

Types of Liability	Auditors' Actions Resulting in Liability
Common law—clients	Breach of contract (privity relationship)
	Negligence
	Gross negligence/constructive fraud
	Fraud
Common law—third parties	Negligence
	Gross negligence/constructive fraud
	Fraud
Federal statutory law—civil liability	Negligence
	Gross negligence/constructive fraud
	Fraud
Federal statutory law —criminal liability	Willful violation of federal statutes

with the same degree of skill and judgment possessed by others in the profession. Typically, an auditor would cite adherence to generally accepted auditing standards (GAAS) as evidence of having exercised due care in the audit.

Liability to Clients

An accountant has a contractual obligation to the client that creates a *privity relationship*. A client can bring a lawsuit against an accountant for failing to live up to the terms of the contract.

Ultramares v. Touche   In the 1933 landmark case, *Ultramares v. Touche,* the New York State Court of Appeals held that a cause of action based on negligence could not be maintained by a third party who was not in contractual privity. The court did leave open the possibility that a third party could successfully sue for gross negligence that constitutes constructive fraud and fraud.[6]

The *Ultramares* decision was the first of three different judicial approaches in deciding the extent of an accountant's liability to third parties. The other two are the Restatement of Torts approach and the Foreseeable Third Party approach. See the following sections.

Liability to Third Parties

Rusch Factors, Inc. v. Levin   The courts have deviated from the *Ultramares* principle through a variety of decisions. For example, in 1968, a federal district court in Rhode Island decided *Rusch Factors, Inc. v. Levin,*[7] which held an accountant liable for negligence to a third party not in privity of contract. In that case, Rusch Factors had requested financial statements prior to granting a loan. Levin audited the statements, which showed the company to be solvent when it was actually insolvent. After the company went into receivership, Rusch Factors sued, and the court ruled that the *Ultramares* doctrine was inappropriate. In its decision, the court relied heavily on the *Restatement (Second) of the Law of Torts.*[8]

The Restatement (Second) of Torts approach, sometimes known as *Restatement 552,*[9] expands an accountants' legal liability exposure for negligence to any third parties to whom the accountant supplies the work and any third parties or groups (even though specific identities are unknown) identified by the client as intended recipients of the work. This is known as the *foreseen third-party concept* because even though there is no privity relationship, the accountant knew that party or those parties would rely on the financial statements for a specified transaction. Assume, for instance, that a client asks an accountant to prepare financial statements and the accountant knows those statements will be used to request a loan from a financial institution(s). The accountant may not know the specific bank to be approached but does know the purpose for which the statements will be used. The third parties as a class of potential users can be foreseen.

A majority of states now use the modified privity requirement imposed by Section 552 of the Restatement (Second) of Torts. The Restatement modifies the traditional rule of privity by allowing nonclients to sue accountants for negligent misrepresentation provided that they belong to a "limited group" and provided that the accountant had actual knowledge that the professional opinion would be supplied to that group. In some state court decisions, a less restrictive interpretation of Section 552 has been made. For example, a 1986 decision by the Texas Court of Appeals in *Blue Bell, Inc. v. Peat, Marwick, Mitchell & Co.,* held that if an accountant preparing audited statements knows or should know that such statements will be relied upon, the accountant may be held liable for negligent misrepresentation.[10]

H. Rosenblum v. Adler   A third judicial approach to third-party liability expands the legal liability of accountants well beyond *Ultramares.* The *Foreseeable Third Party* approach results from a 1983 decision by the New Jersey Supreme Court in *H. Rosenblum, Inc v. Adler.*[11] In that case, the Rosenblum family agreed to sell its retail catalog showroom business to Giant Stores, a corporation operating discount department stores, in exchange for Giant common stock. The Rosenblums relied on Giant's 1971 and 1972 financial statements, which had been audited by Touche Ross & Co. When the statements were found to be fraudulent and the stock was determined worthless, the investors sued Touche. The lower courts did not allow the Rosenblums' claims against Touche on the grounds the plaintiffs did not meet either the *Ultramares* privity test or the Restatement. The case was taken to the New Jersey Supreme Court, which overturned the lower courts' decision ruling that auditors should be liable to all reasonably foreseeable third parties who rely on the financial statements.

The *Rosenblum* decision caused great consternation in the accounting profession. The fear was that somehow the courts expected accountants to anticipate the third parties that could use the financial statements, which was like looking into a crystal ball and predicting the future. Fortunately for the profession, very few states followed the *Rosenblum* ruling. In fact, in 1994, the New Jersey Legislature passed the accountants' liability statute (N.J.S.A. 2A:53A-25), which limits accountants' liability for negligence and effectively overruled *Rosenblum.*

Credit Alliance v. Arthur Andersen & Co.   The pendulum appears to have shifted in favor of returning to an *Ultramares*-like standard. In 1985, the New York Court of Appeals expanded the privity standard in the case of *Credit Alliance v. Arthur Andersen & Co.*[12] to include a near privity relationship between third parties and the accountant. In the case, Credit Alliance was the principal lender to the client and demonstrated that Andersen had known Credit Alliance was relying on the client's financial statements prior to extending credit. The court also ruled that there had been direct communication between the lender and the auditor regarding the client.

The *Credit Alliance* case established the following tests that must be satisfied for holding auditors liable for negligence to third parties: (1) the accountant's knowledge that the financial statements are to be used for a particular purpose, (2) the intention of the third party to rely on those statements, and (3) some action by the accountant linking him or her to the third party who provides evidence of the accountant's understanding of intended reliance. The 1992 New York Court of Appeals decision in *Security Pacific Business Credit, Inc. v. Peat Marwick Main & Co.* [13] sharpened the last criteria in its determination that the third party must be known to the auditor who directly conveys the audited report to the third party or acts to induce reliance on the report.

Bily v. Arthur Young   In 1992, the California Supreme Court reversed a previous decision of the California Court of Appeals in favor of the auditors in *Bily v. Arthur Young.* The litigation was brought by investors of Osborne Computer Corporation, a computer manufacturing company.[14] Following a promising start from 1980–1982, the company began to plan for an initial public offering. Osborne retained Arthur Young to prepare audit reports, and the firm issued an unqualified opinion on February 11, 1983. However, the offering was postponed as being premature at the suggestion of the underwriters. To obtain needed cash, the company issued warrants to investors in exchange for direct loans. The warrants entitled the holders to purchase blocks of the company stock at favorable prices. As the warrant transactions closed on April 8, 1983, the company's performance began to deteriorate sharply. The company declared bankruptcy on September 13, 1983. Plaintiffs claimed they relied heavily on Arthur Young's unqualified audit opinion in making their investments. It was discovered that the firm had been aware of material weaknesses in the company's controls yet failed to disclose them as a qualification to its audit report or report to management.

In reversing the lower court decision, the California Supreme Court concluded that "an auditor owes no general duty of care regarding the conduct of an audit to persons other than the client. An auditor may, however, be liable for negligent misrepresentation in an audit report to those persons who act in reliance upon those misrepresentations in a transaction which the auditor intended to influence, in accordance with *Restatement 552.*" Thus, the court limited auditors' responsibility to the third party by reversing from "reasonable foreseeable" to "actually foreseen" groups.[15] A summary of legal issues and guiding principles in deciding the auditor's liability to third parties appears in Exhibit 6.2.

Liability for fraud is not restricted to cases in which the auditor knew of the deceit. Some courts have interpreted gross negligence as an instance of fraud. Gross negligence, or constructive fraud, occurs when the auditor acts so carelessly in the application of professional standards that it implies a reckless disregard for the standards of due care.

The auditors' defense against third-party lawsuits requires proof that (1) the auditor did not have a duty to the third party, (2) the third party was negligent, (3) the auditor's work was performed in accordance with professional standards, (4) the third party did not suffer a loss, (5) any loss to the third party was caused by other events, or (6) the claim is invalid because the statute of limitations has expired.

The legal liability of accountants is not limited to audited statements. In the *1136 Tenants Corp. v. Max Rothenberg & Co.*[16] case in 1967, the accounting firm was sued for negligent failure to discover an embezzlement by the managing agent who had hired the firm to "write up" the books. (This expression now is called a "compilation." In 1967, it meant the accountant wrote up the client's accounts into GAAP financial statements, but they were unaudited.) The firm was held liable for failure to inquire or communicate concerning missing invoices despite a disclaiming notation on the financial statements informing users that "No independent verifications were undertaken thereon." The firm moved to dismiss the case, but the court denied the motion and held that even if a CPA "acted as a robot, merely doing copy work," there was an issue as to whether there were suspicious circumstances relating to missing invoices that imposed a duty on the firm to warn the client. When the case went to trial, the court found that there had been an engagement to audit and entered a judgment for more than $237,000 despite the firm's oral evidence that it was employed for $600 annually to write up the books.

The *1136* case affected auditing standards in two notable areas. First, the engagement letter was developed to clarify the responsibilities of accountants and auditors in performing professional services. The engagement letter formalizes the relationship between the auditor and the client. It serves as a contract detailing the responsibilities of the accountant or auditor and expectations for management. While engagement letters are not required by accounting or auditing standards, they do help to clarify the obligations of professionals and any legal matters.

As a result of the *1136* case, the Accounting and Review Services Committee of the AICPA, a senior technical committee, was created to formulate standards to be followed by

EXHIBIT 6.2 **Auditor Legal Liability to Third Parties**

Legal Approach	Case	Legal Principle	Legal Liability to Third Parties
Ultramares	*Ultramares v. Touche*	Privity (only clients can sue)	Possibly gross negligence that constitutes (constructive) fraud
Restatement (2nd) Law of Torts	*Rusch Factors*	Foreseen third-party users	Nonclients can sue for negligent misrepresentation
Foreseeable third party	*H. Rosenblum*	Reasonably foreseeable third-party users	Must rely on the financial statements
Near privity relationship	*Credit Alliance*	3-pronged approach: knowledge of accountant, intention of third party, link between accountant & third party	Liable for negligence to third parties
Actually foreseen third party	*Bily v. Arthur Young*	Third party must act in reliance on auditor's misrepresentation	Negligent misrepresentation

accountants who perform two levels of service, a compilation and a review. These services were briefly discussed in Chapter 4.

Statutory Liability

The most relevant sources of liability for auditors are the Securities Act of 1933, the Securities Exchange Act of 1934, and the Sarbanes-Oxley Act (SOX) of 2002. These laws create potential civil liabilities for auditors for failing to adhere to the requirements of the laws in carrying out professional obligations. Criminal liability exists when an auditor defrauds a third party by knowingly being involved with falsifications in financial statements. SOX makes it a felony to destroy or create documents to impede or obstruct a federal investigation. Obstruction of justice charges were brought against Arthur Andersen in its audit of Enron, and the charge itself led to a parade of clients abandoning the firm and ultimately to its demise.

Securities Act of 1933

The Securities Act of 1933[17] regulates the initial offering of securities through the mails or interstate commerce. Companies must file registration statements (S-1, S-2, and S-3 forms) and prospectuses that contain financial statements that have been audited by an independent CPA.

Section 11 of the Securities Act of 1933 makes it unlawful for the *initial* registration statement to contain any untrue material fact or to omit a material fact. Any purchaser of securities may sue; the purchaser generally must prove that (1) the specific security had been offered through the registration statements, (2) damages had been incurred, and (3) there had been a material misstatement or omission in the financial statements included in the registration statement. The plaintiff need not prove reliance on the financial statements unless the purchase took place after one year of the offering.

If items (2) and (3) are proven, it is a *prima facie* case (sufficient to win against the CPA unless rebutted) and shifts the burden of proof to the accountant, who may escape liability by proving that (1) after a reasonable investigation, the CPA concluded that there was a reasonable basis to believe that the financial statements were true and there was no material misstatement (due diligence defense), (2) the plaintiff knew the financial statements were incorrect when the investment was made (knowledge of falsehood defense), or (3) the loss was due to factors other than the misstatement or omission (lack of causation defense).

Key Court Decisions of the 1933 Act

McKesson & Robbins

The *McKesson & Robbins* case[18] in 1939 was the first instance in which auditing practices were subject to significant public scrutiny. The case involved a conspiracy to defraud the company by its former president, Donald Coster. Joseph Wells, the founder and former CEO of the Association of Certified Fraud Examiners (ACFE), points out in his book *Frankensteins of Fraud* that behind Coster's mask as the much admired CEO of McKesson & Robbins Pharmaceuticals lurked Philip Musica, bootlegger, government snitch, and swindler. While the kindly Dr. Coster was courted for the U.S. presidency, he was living a secret life bleeding McKesson & Robbins for millions of dollars.[19]

Coster and his brothers undertook an elaborate scheme that included dummy trading companies, fictitious warehouses, and the creation of forged documents. A cynic could contend that Coster's actions served as a (negative) role model for Barry Minkow in ZZZZ Best some 40-plus years later.

A 1939 investigation by the SEC revealed that Coster and his confidants had stolen around $2.9 million of McKesson & Robbins cash in the previous 12 years. However, due to the lack of two "then-not-required" audit procedures, physical observation of inventory and direct confirmation of accounts receivable, Price Waterhouse & Co. had failed to detect $19 million nonexistent assets (of total assets of more than $87 million) and $1.8 million gross profit on fictitious sales of $18 million that were included in McKesson's 1937 certified financial statements.

The due diligence defense available to the auditor under Section 11 requires that the auditor must have made a reasonable investigation of the facts supporting or contradicting the information included in the registration statement. The test is whether a "prudent person" would have made a decision similar to the auditor's decision under similar circumstances. There is a link to be made between the legal notion of a prudent person test and *rights theory.* Recall that the universality principle in rights theory provides that an ethical action is one that others would take in similar circumstances for similar reasons.

Escott v. Bar Chris Construction Corp.

A leading case under Section 11 is *Escott v. BarChris Construction Corp.* in which the court held that the auditor's actions in reviewing events subsequent to the balance sheet date (subsequent events) was not conducted with due diligence because the senior auditor in charge of reviewing these events had not spent sufficient time and accepted unconvincing answers to key questions. The court determined that there had been sufficient warning signs that further investigation was necessary.[20]

Securities Exchange Act of 1934

The Securities Exchange Act of 1934[21] regulates subsequent trading of securities sold on national stock exchanges such as the New York Stock Exchange and NASDAQ. It requires ongoing filing of quarterly (10-Q) and annual (10-K) reports and other information to keep the registration statement current. Certain information including annual financial statements must be audited. The quarterly statements must be reviewed. The basic difference as discussed in Chapter 4 is that an audit provides "reasonable assurance" that the financial statements are free of material misstatement and the omission of material information while a review provides only limited assurance.

The liability of auditors under the Securities Exchange Act often centers on Section 10 and Rule 10b-5. Section 10 makes it unlawful for a CPA to (1) employ any device, scheme, or artifice to defraud, (2) make an untrue statement of material fact or omit a material fact, or (3) engage in any act, practice, or course of business to commit fraud or deceit in connection with the purchase or sale of the security. Section 18 makes it unlawful to make a false or misleading statement with respect to a material statement unless done in "good faith."

Once a plaintiff has established the ability to sue under Rule 10b-5, the following elements must be proved: (1) a material, factual misrepresentation or omission, (2) reliance on the financial statements, (3) damages suffered as a result of reliance on the financial statements, and (4) the intent to deceive, manipulate, or defraud *(scienter—the legal term the courts apply to Rule 10b-5, the intent to deceive, manipulate, or defraud).*

Key Court Decisions of the 1934 Act

Ernst & Ernst v. Hochfelder

An important case that strengthens the scienter requirement is the 1976 U.S. Supreme Court reversal in *Ernst & Ernst v. Hochfelder*[22] The U.S. Court of Appeals had ruled in favor of Hochfelder and reversed the lower court opinion. The court decision includes this statement:

> One who breaches a duty of inquiry and disclosure owed another is liable in damages for
> aiding and abetting a third party's violation of Rule 10b-5 if the fraud would have been

discovered or prevented but for the breach, and that there were genuine issues of fact as to whether [Ernst] committed such a breach and whether inquiry and disclosure would have led to discovery or prevention of the. . .fraud.

The case involved the president of a brokerage firm who had induced Hochfelder to invest in "escrow" accounts that the president represented would yield a high rate of return. The president converted those funds to personal use. The fraud came to light after the president committed suicide, leaving a note that described the brokerage as bankrupt and the escrow accounts as "spurious." Hochfelder's cause of action rested on a theory of negligent nonfeasance. The premise was that Ernst had failed to utilize "appropriate auditing procedures" in its audits of the brokerage, thereby failing to discover internal practices of the firm said to prevent an effective audit. The practice principally relied on the president's rule that only he could open mail addressed to him or to his attention at the brokerage even if it arrived in his absence. Hochfelder argued that had Ernst conducted a proper audit, it would have discovered this "mail rule."

The U.S. Supreme Court reversed the decision, ruling that a private cause of action for damages does not come under Rule 10b-5 in the absence of any allegation of scienter. The Court cited the language in Section 10 that it is unlawful for any person to use or employ any manipulative or deceptive device or contrivance in contravention of SEC rules. The Court ruled that the use of those words clearly shows that it was intended to prohibit a type of conduct quite different from negligence. It said that the word *manipulative* connotes intentional or willful conduct designed to deceive or defraud investors, a type of conduct that did not exist in the case.

Auditor defenses under the Securities Exchange Act of 1934 include, in addition to a lack of scienter, non-negligent performance of services, a lack of duty to the third party, and the absence of any causal connection demonstrating that the third party relied on audit work and suffered damages as a result. The best defense for an auditor is to view professional responsibilities as going beyond mere adherence to the technical requirements of GAAS. The standards cannot cover every situation. When the rules are unclear or provide only vague guidance on an audit matter, the auditor should act in accordance with the ethical principles described in Chapters 1 and 2.

Equity Funding

The *Equity Funding* case changed the way that CPA firms audited clients and brought attention to the red flags that could indicate that fraud is present. Equity Funding's principal line of business was to create "funding programs," which included the sale of life insurance combined with mutual fund investment. Equity Funding derived its income from commissions on the sales. The fraud started just before the company went public; it was motivated by an attempt to increase the company's earnings. Equity Funding inflated its earnings by recording fictitious commissions from the sale of its product that the company called "reciprocals." The company also borrowed funds but did not record them as liabilities; instead, it recorded the cash as payments on the loan receivable by participants in the program. By reducing the loans receivable, Equity Funding could record more fictitious commissions. The last part of the fraud involved creating fictitious insurance policies, which were then reinsured with other insurance companies. This enabled the company to obtain additional cash to pay premiums on policies, which in turn required that more fictitious policies be created on its books.[23]

Equity Funding collapsed in 1973 when a former employee disclosed the existence of the massive fraud. During the period of the fraud, Equity Funding was audited first by Wolfson, Weiner and ultimately by Seidman & Seidman. A lengthy audit by Touche Ross during the bankruptcy proceedings disclosed that the company had generated more than $2 billion of fictitious insurance policies.

On November 1, 1973, a federal grand jury in California indicted 22 executives and employees of Equity Funding including Stanley Goldblum, the chair and CEO of the company. According to the indictment, Goldblum wanted to achieve a level of growth that was not attainable through legitimate business operations. He arranged for various officers and employees to make fictitious bookkeeping entries to inflate the company's income and assets. He also directed employees to create fictitious insurance policies. On November 2, 1970, an employee was instructed to write a computer program creating fictitious polices with a face value of $430 million and a total yearly premium of $5.5 million. In 1971, some phony policies were reinsured, and some employees were instructed to create death claims on some of the policies.

Creating phony accounting entries is relatively easy, but creating the documentation for 64,000 phony policies was a big challenge, even at Equity Funding. Management wanted to be able to satisfy the auditors, who would ask to see a sample of polices for review. The auditors would examine the policies' documentation on file and then cross-check for premium receipts and reserve policy information. However, in all but a handful of cases, no policy files were available. To solve this problem, management created an in-house institution: the forgery party!

At Equity Funding, policy files that the auditors requested would often be "temporarily unavailable." Employees would work at night to forge the missing files to have them ready for auditor review the next day. The fact that the auditors were duped was the least of their embarrassment. One night when the auditor left his brief case unlocked, an Equity Funding executive, in full sight of others, opened the case and took the audit plan and was able to anticipate the next steps. Another time, an auditor wanted to send out policy confirmations to a sample of policyholders. Equity Funding officials, eager to help, did some clerical chores for the auditor. The result was letters addressed to branch sales managers and agents, who dutifully filled out the forms for the fictitious policyholders.[24]

Joe Wells characterized Equity Funding in *Frankensteins of Fraud* by stating that Victor Frankenstein made the dead live just as Stanley Goldblum gave life to 64,000 phony policy holders in his Equity Funding insurance scam. The lawsuit led to a verdict in California against three auditors who did not report evidence of the large scale fraud. The court sentenced them to serve two-year prison terms, spend four years on probation, and do 2,000 hours of charity work.

Crazy Eddie

Some New Yorkers remember television commercials of an electronics company called Crazy Eddie, Inc., that aired during the mid- and late 1980s. The former chair and CEO, Eddie Antar, advertised that his prices were lower than the competition. An actor would come on the screen, act like a madman, and scream: "Our prices are insane." In the aftermath of the fraud at Crazy Eddie, cynics could claim that Eddie Antar was insane.

On July 16, 1990, the SEC obtained a judgment for $73,496,432 plus interest against Antar in the U.S. District Court for the District of New Jersey. Antar became a fugitive and fled to Israel that year. He lived under an alias until June 1992 when he was arrested. He was sent back to the U.S. in January 1993. The SEC initiated lawsuits in Britain, Liechtenstein, and Israel to recover misappropriated assets. With interest, the final judgment against Antar now exceeds $84 million.[25]

On February 10, 1997, the SEC announced that District Court Judge Harold A. Ackerman had sentenced Antar to a federal prison term of 82 months followed by two years of supervised release. Subsequent to his release, Antar joined the ex-cons speakers' circuit, following in the footsteps of Barry Minkow, and he now talks about how accountants can prevent frauds like Crazy Eddie from occurring. His central message seems to be that accountants cannot afford to trust anyone. "A skilled fraudster will either charm you or try to intimidate you into not asking the questions that could result in exposure of illegal financial activity."[26]

According to SEC Litigation Release No. 14251 issued on February 10, 1997, Antar pleaded guilty to the following:

1. In 1985, he caused the value of inventory that Crazy Eddie reported to its auditors to be falsely overstated by approximately $2 million.
2. He caused the inventory counts to be artificially inflated by the falsification of count sheets or inventory tickets when Crazy Eddie took a physical inventory at the end of its fiscal year on March 2, 1986, and at the end of fiscal year 1987, thereby overstating the inventory by millions of dollars.
3. Just before the year-end 1986, he caused approximately $2 million from outside sources to be deposited into Crazy Eddie's bank accounts in such a way that the money would be booked as proceeds of retail sales.
4. His primary purpose in perpetrating these fraudulent schemes was to increase the price of Crazy Eddie stock to public investors.[27]

Four different accounting firms audited Crazy Eddie's financial statements. Perhaps for the fourth firm—if not the third—the proverbial "red flag" should have gone up with the large number of auditor changes. Nevertheless, in the mid-1980s, Peat Marwick became Crazy Eddie's audit firm when it merged with Main Hurdman. Following poor operating results and dropping stock prices, a takeover group gained control of the company, and the new owners replaced Peat Marwick with Touche Ross.

One of the criticisms against Peat Marwick was that it had charged a relatively modest audit fee and, allegedly, the firm "lowballed" the engagement to obtain Crazy Eddie as an audit client, realizing that it could make up for lost audit revenue by selling the company consulting services.[28] If this were true, Peat Marwick may have compromised its independence and objectivity because the firm could have been reluctant to go against top management when a difference of opinion on an accounting issue existed because the client could hold back on the consulting services pending the firm's acquiescence to the demands of top management.

Whether or not the firm cut corners in the audit and staffing because of the low fee, the court ruled against the accountants in a lawsuit brought by purchasers of the company's stock prior to the disclosure of fraudulent financial statements, alleging that the registration statements and prospectuses had been false and misleading in violation of Sections 11 and 13 of the Securities Act of 1933. The plaintiffs charged that the accountants had violated GAAP and GAAS by failing to uncover the fraud and fictitious activities. The court held that the plaintiffs did not have to prove fraud or negligence but only that any material misstatements in the registration statement were misleading.

On April 27, 2000, Judge Ackerman issued an order setting the amounts of disgorgement and prejudgment interest for the defendants in the case who were ordered to pay the following amounts for their insider trading in connection with the sales of common stock in Crazy Eddie: disgorgement total, $19.38 million; interest, $54.21 million; total amount, $73.59 million. *Disgorgement* is paid by defendants who have gained falsely obtained monies to plaintiffs to make those who have suffered financial loss at least partially whole once again. In rejecting the defendant's contention that the amount of their disgorgement should be $0, Judge Ackerman stated the following:

> As innovative as it was, the core of Crazy Eddie was rotten, and the investing public, once it became aware of that fact, would not have dawdled in ridding itself of the stock. The extensive fraud would certainly have driven off the investors, and the defendants' contention that the stock retained some value despite the frauds at the company simply lacks persuasiveness.[29]

Implications of Legal Decisions for Auditors' Responsibilities

Several case rulings contributed to advancements in procedures now used by auditors in conducting an examination of the financial statements of client entities. These are summarized in Exhibit 6.3.

Financial Fraud Detection and Disclosure

The Private Securities Litigation Reform Act includes a provision that requires auditors to report illegal acts including financial statement fraud to management and ensure that the issuer's audit committee or the issuer's board of directors in the absence of such a committee is adequately informed with respect to illegal acts that have been detected or otherwise come to the accountant's attention during the course of the audit unless the illegal act is clearly inconsequential. If the auditor concludes that an illegal act with a material effect on the financial statements has not been dealt with by senior management in a timely manner and with appropriate remedial actions, the auditor should directly report its conclusions to the board of directors.

If a board of directors receives such a report from the auditors, management has one business day from the receipt of such report to inform the SEC, copying the auditors on the notice to the SEC. If the auditor fails to receive a copy of such notice within the required one-business-day period, the independent public accountant should either (1) resign from the engagement or (2) furnish the SEC a copy of its report within the next business day following the failure to receive timely notice. Auditors are not liable in a private action for any finding, conclusion, or statement expressed in a report made pursuant to these rules.

Sarbanes-Oxley Act

The Sarbanes-Oxley Act (SOX) of 2002 (H. R. 3763)[30] created additional obligations and restrictions for management and auditors that change the landscape of legal liability. The relevant provisions of SOX are discussed next.

Section 302. Corporate Responsibility for Financial Reports

This section requires the certification of periodic reports filed by the CEO and CFO of public companies with the SEC. The certification states that "based on the officer's knowledge, the report does not contain any untrue statement of a material fact or omit to state a material fact necessary in order to make the statements, in light of the circumstances under which such statements were made, not misleading." The HealthSouth fraud was the first case that the SEC brought against company officers for a false certification.

Section 308. Fair Funds for Investors

In a securities action brought by the SEC against a public company, the court order may grant disgorgement against a member of top management, such as the CEO and CFO, for

EXHIBIT 6.3
Legal Cases and Auditor Responsibilities

Case	Audit Procedures
Bily v. Arthur Young	Review of internal controls
Crazy Eddie	Procedures for taking inventory
1136 Tenants Corp.	Engagement letters; compilations and reviews
Equity Funding	Responsibilities for fraud detection
Escott v. Bar Chris	Due care; professional skepticism; subsequent event review
Hochfelder	"Appropriate" auditing procedures
McKesson & Robbins	Physical inventory observation; accounts receivable confirmation

violating the law or SEC regulations. These funds are typically returned to the parties that were harmed (i.e., investors) because the statements made or actions taken by the CEO or CFO caused them harm.

Following the acquittal of HealthSouth CEO Richard Scrushy for conspiracy and securities fraud on June 28, 2005, the SEC filed a civil lawsuit against Scrushy, seeking $786 million in penalties and disgorgement because of his role in the $2.7 billion fraud at HealthSouth. On February 22, 2006, attorneys for Scrushy asked a federal judge to dismiss all charges against him because the SEC had failed to support its claims that he knew about the company's accounting fraud. The judge scheduled a trial for April 2, 2007, to hear all evidence and witnesses in the matter.[31]

Section 401. Disclosures in Periodic Reports

Section 401 amends the Securities Exchange Act of 1934 to include the requirement that each financial statement filed with the SEC should reflect all material correcting adjustments that have been identified by the audit firm in accordance with GAAP and the SEC's rules and regulations. The rule extends the disclosure requirements in securities laws to include all material off-balance-sheet transactions and any other transaction with a material current or future effect on financial condition or changes thereto, operating results, liquidity, capital expenditures, capital resources, or significant components of revenues or expenses.

Enron established thousands of off-balance-sheet entities to hide debt, improve liquidity, enhance financial position, and mask operating results. The technique used to establish off-balance-sheet entities will be discussed in Chapter 7. Section 401 was motivated by the fraud at Enron and the company's failure to fully disclose all information about these entities that investors and creditors had a legal (and ethical) right to know.

Section 801. Corporate Criminal Fraud Accountability

Section 801 makes it clear that anyone who "knowingly alters, destroys, mutilates, conceals, covers up, falsifies, or makes a false entry in any record, document, or tangible object with the intent to impede, obstruct, or influence the investigation" of fraud is subject to fine, imprisonment for not more than 20 years, or both. Auditors are required to retain working papers for a minimum of five years from the end of the fiscal period in which the audit or review was concluded.

Section 806. Protection for Employees of Publicly Traded Companies Who Provide Evidence in Fraud Cases

This so-called whistle-blower provision of SOX protects employees who provide information about a fraud by prohibiting the discharge, demotion, discrimination, suspension, or threatening or harassing action against an employee who provides information in a federal or regulatory investigation or to Congress or to the employee's supervisor. A person who alleges discharge or discrimination under this section can file a complaint with the Secretary of Labor. An employee who brings a successful action will be entitled to "reinstatement with the same seniority status that the employee would have had, but for the discrimination; the amount of back pay with interest; and compensation for any special damages sustained as a result of the discrimination, including litigation costs, expert witness fees, and reasonable attorney fees."[32]

The Department of Labor delegated to the Occupational Safety and Health Administration (OSHA) the enforcement authority of the whistle-blower provisions of Sarbanes-Oxley. OSHA's regulations require that an employee must first establish a *prima facie* case of retaliation. This is generally interpreted as meaning that the employee must be engaged in a protected activity or conduct; that the employer knew "actually or constructively" that the conduct had occurred; and that the employee suffered an unfavorable personnel action; and that the circumstances "were sufficient to raise the inference that the protected activity was a contributing factor to the unfavorable action."[33]

Section 807. Criminal Penalties for Defrauding Shareholders of Publicly Traded Companies

Section 807 provides that anyone who knowingly commits fraud with respect to securities registered under the Securities Exchange Act of 1934 will be subject to fine or imprisonment of not more than 25 years, or both. Bernard Ebbers, the former CEO of WorldCom, was sentenced to 25 years in prison on July 13, 2005, for his role in the $11 billion fraud. Even with possible time off for good behavior, Ebbers, who was 63 years old at the time of sentencing, would remain locked up until 2027, when he would be 85.

Section 906. Corporate Responsibility for Financial Reports

Section 906 establishes penalties for the false certification of financial statements under Section 302. The maximum fine is $1 million and maximum imprisonment is 10 years, or both. If the false certification was made willfully, the penalties go up to $5 million and 20 years, or both.

Other Relevant Provisions of SOX

1. The maximum penalty under Section 801 for tampering with records or otherwise impeding investigations under Sarbanes-Oxley is a 20-year prison sentence, a fine, or both.
2. The SEC can prohibit persons such as CEOs and CFOs from serving as officers or directors of public companies as part of a cease-and-desist order.
3. Anyone who retaliates against an informant providing information under Section 806 is subject to a fine, imprisonment of not more than 10 years, or both.

Whistle-Blowing: A Clash of Loyalty, Confidentiality, and Doing the Right Thing

We break away from the discussion of legal liability to point out some of the most difficult ethics situations faced by accountants and auditors. The cases deal with when can (should) you blow the whistle on financial wrongdoing? There are two kinds of whistle-blowing: internal and external. Internal whistle-blowing means that the auditor brings the matter to the supervisor and that person goes to the partner in charge who discusses the matter with top management of the client and the audit committee of the board of directors. The audit committee has the responsibility to oversee the financial reporting process in the company and to ensure that the statements are accurate and reliable. In this sense, the audit committee should support the external auditors when they demonstrate that there is a departure from GAAP that creates a material misstatement in the financial statements.

The Private Securities Litigation Reform Act of 1995 contains a specific provision for auditor disclosure of corporate fraud or external whistle-blowing, that is, when a material misstatement is made purposefully with the intent to deceive and with the knowledge of top management. According to the act, the auditors should report possible illegal acts to management and the audit committee, and fraud is an illegal act. If neither takes appropriate remedial action by informing the SEC within one business day and by sending a copy of the report to the auditors, the auditors must notify the board of directors in writing and forward this to the SEC within one business day. Therefore, the reporting of illegal acts, such as the deliberate overstatement of net income, internally and to the SEC is the expected ethical standard. Management's failure to report can affect the audit opinion as discussed in Chapter 5.

Returning to the receivables example in Chapter 1, if the auditor follows the provisions in Section 806 and blows the whistle on overstated receivables by going outside the firm and the client entity, that auditor violates the confidentiality obligation to the client in the AICPA Code. A client has a right to expect that the auditors will not divulge certain information about the client's financial activities without the express permission of the client or if other exceptions to confidentiality exist, as was discussed in Chapter 4.

Let's assume, for example, that the auditor knows a reporter at *The Wall Street Journal.* The auditor calls the reporter and blows the whistle on the company. The auditor knows that she has violated the code of conduct for CPAs. She is willing to pay the price for the action of following her ethical standards, which could include losing her job and license to practice as a CPA. How could she justify such an action? She could reason that the virtue of honesty always takes precedence over loyalty to one's employer or client. If it does not, important information could be hidden from the public in the name of confidentiality. She could wonder what she would do if the issue was illegally dumping toxic waste instead of fraudulent financial statements. Would she feel comfortable ignoring that information, assuming that her audit firm and the client told her to do just that? Would she want others to do the same? In other words, she could reason out a course of action using the universality perspective of rights theory and divulge the confidential information. Remember, however, that there is no ethical obligation to engage in external whistle-blowing and the CPA who does so must carefully consider the professional and legal consequences of that act.

Perspective on Sarbanes-Oxley

The stringent penalties under Sarbanes-Oxley may, over time, help to reduce instances of financial statement fraud. However, the SEC has had an arsenal of laws at its disposal for many years, but that does not seem to have made much of a difference. As described in Chapter 4, the history of accounting frauds is as old as the SEC's tenure.

The "bottom line" may be that the government will not be successful in its effort to legislate ethics. Still, a set of civil and criminal deterrents is an important part of a healthy securities regulatory system.

Other Laws Affecting Accountants and Auditors

In addition to the Private Securities Litigation Reform Act, two laws have influenced audit procedures, legal liability, and ethics requirements under the due care principle. These include (1) the Foreign Corrupt Practices Act and (2) the U.S. Federal Sentencing Guidelines.

Foreign Corrupt Practices Act (FCPA)

The FCPA establishes standards for the acceptability of payments made by U.S. multinational entities or their agent to foreign government officials. FCPA was motivated when, during the period 1960 to 1977, the SEC cited 527 companies for offering bribes and making other dubious payments to win foreign contracts. Lockheed Corporation was one of the companies caught in the scandal. It was determined that Lockheed had made about $55 million in illegal payments to foreign governments and officials. One such payment of $1.7 million to Japanese Premier Tanaka led to his resignation in disgrace in 1974.[34]

FCPA makes it a crime to offer or provide payments to officials of foreign governments, political candidates, or political parties for the purpose of obtaining or retaining business. It applies to all U.S. corporations, whether they are publicly or privately held, and to foreign companies filing with the SEC.[35] The Department of Justice is responsible for all criminal enforcement and for civil enforcement of the antibribery provisions with respect to domestic entities and foreign companies and nationals. The SEC is responsible for civil enforcement of the antibribery provisions with respect to registrants.

Under the FCPA, a corporation that violates the law can be fined up to $1million while its officers who directly participated in violations of the act or had "reason to know" of such violations can be fined up to $10,000, imprisoned for up to five years, or both. FCPA also prohibits corporations from indemnifying fines imposed on directors, officers, employees, or agents. FCPA does not prohibit "grease payments" to foreign government employees whose duties are primarily ministerial or clerical because such payments are sometimes required to persuade recipients to perform their normal duties.[36]

As a result of the criticisms of the antibribery provisions of the 1977 FCPA, Congress amended it as part of the Omnibus Trade and Competitiveness Act of 1988 to clarify when a payment is prohibited,[37] as follows:

- A payment is defined as illegal if it is intended to influence a foreign official to act in a way that is incompatible with the official's legal duty.
- The reason to know standard is replaced by a "knowing" standard, so that criminal liability for illegal payments to third parties applies to individuals who "knowingly" engage in or tolerate illegal payments under the act.
- The definition of permissible facilitating, or "grease" payments, is expanded to include payments to any foreign official who facilitates or expedites payments for the purpose of expediting or securing the performance of a routine governmental action.
- Examples of acceptable payments under the previous item include (a) obtaining permits, licensees, or other official documents to qualify a person to do business in a foreign country, (b) processing governmental papers, such as visas or work orders, (c) providing police protection and mail pickup and delivery or scheduling inspections associated with contract performance or inspections related to the transit of goods across country, (d) providing telephone service, power, and water; unloading and loading cargo; or protecting perishable product or commodities from deterioration, and (e) actions of a similar nature.

Two affirmative defenses for those accused of violating the act include (1) the payment is lawful "under the written laws" of the foreign country and (2) the payment can be made for "reasonable and bona fide expenditures." These include lodging expenses incurred by or for a foreign official to promote products or services or execute the performance of a contract.

Individuals can be prosecuted under the 1988 amendment even if the company for which they work is not guilty. Penalties for violations were raised to $2 million for entities and $100,000 for individuals. The maximum term of imprisonment is kept at five years. A new $10,000 civil penalty was enacted.

Internal Accounting Control Requirements

The law requires all SEC registrants to maintain internal accounting controls to ensure that all transactions are authorized by management and recorded properly. As discussed in Chapter 5, Section 404 of the Sarbanes-Oxley Act requires management to prepare a report on its internal controls, and auditors must evaluate that report and issue their own opinion on the controls.

The SEC made it clear that an effective internal audit program to deal with violations of the Foreign Corrupt Practices Act can help to deter any penalty. In October 2001, the SEC settled a nonbribery action against Gisela de-Leon Meredith, the controller of the Chestnut Hill Farms subsidiary of Seabord Corp. She was charged with causing inaccuracies in Seabord's books and covering up her actions. However, de-Leon Meredith had to agree only to a cease-and-desist order, and the SEC took no action against the company. In providing reasons for its lenient treatment, the SEC credited Seabord's cooperation, specifically by coming forward with details of its internal investigation, not invoking attorney-client privilege, and promptly notifying the SEC of the company's restatement plans.

The SEC set forth in its proceeding against de-Leon Meredith (AAER No. 1470)some of the criteria it will consider in determining whether, and how much, to credit self-policing, self-reporting, remediation, and cooperation. These have implications for the "due diligence" requirement under the Federal Sentencing Guidelines discussed next. It may also provide insight into the nature of the corporate culture that, at least in the SEC's view, strengthens the internal control environment that is so critical to establishing a strong system of internal controls. As discussed in Chapter 5, the due diligence requirement has important implications for auditors who must evaluate the control environment under GAAS. These criteria follow:

1. What is the nature of the misconduct involved? Did it result from inadvertence, honest mistake, simple negligence, reckless or deliberate indifference to indicia of wrongful conduct, willful misconduct or unadorned venality? Were the company's auditors misled?

2. How did the misconduct arise? Is it the result of pressure placed on employees to achieve specific results, or a tone of lawlessness set by those in control of the company? What compliance procedures were in place to prevent the misconduct now uncovered? Why did those procedures fail to stop or inhibit the wrongful conduct?

3. Where in the organization did the misconduct occur? How high up in the chain of command was knowledge of, or participation in, the misconduct? Did senior personnel participate in, or turn a blind eye toward, obvious indicia of misconduct? How systemic was the behavior? Is it symptomatic of the way the entity does business, or was it isolated?

4. How long did the misconduct last? Was it a one-quarter, or one-time, event, or did it last several years? In the case of a public company, did the misconduct occur before the company went public? Did it facilitate the company's ability to go public?

5. How much harm has the misconduct inflicted upon investors and other corporate constituencies? Did the share price of the company's stock drop significantly upon its discovery and disclosure?

6. How was the misconduct detected and who uncovered it?

7. How long after discovery of the misconduct did it take to implement an effective response?

8. What steps did the company take upon learning of the misconduct? Did the company immediately stop the misconduct? Are persons responsible for any misconduct still with the company? If so, are they still in the same positions? Did the company promptly, completely and effectively disclose the existence of the misconduct to the public, to regulators and to self-regulators? Did the company cooperate completely with appropriate regulatory and law enforcement bodies? Did the company identify what additional related misconduct is likely to have occurred? Did the company take steps to identify the extent of damage to investors and other corporate constituencies? Did the company appropriately recompense those adversely affected by the conduct?

9. What processes did the company follow to resolve many of these issues and ferret out necessary information? Were the Audit Committee and the Board of Directors fully informed? If so, when?

10. Did the company commit to learn the truth, fully and expeditiously? Did it do a thorough review of the nature, extent, origins and consequences of the conduct and related behavior? Did management, the Board or committees consisting solely of outside directors oversee the review? Did company employees or outside persons perform the review? If outside persons, had they done other work for the company? Where the review was conducted by outside counsel, had management previously engaged such counsel? Were scope limitations placed on the review? If so, what were they?

11. Did the company promptly make available to SEC staff the results of its review and provide sufficient documentation reflecting its response to the situation? Did the company identify possible violative conduct and evidence with sufficient precision to facilitate prompt enforcement actions against those who violated the law? Did the company produce a thorough and probing written report detailing the findings of its review? Did the company voluntarily disclose information not directly requested by the SEC; information that could not have been otherwise uncovered? Did the company ask its employees to cooperate with [the investigation] and make all reasonable efforts to secure such cooperation?

12. What assurances are there that the conduct is unlikely to recur? Did the company adopt and ensure enforcement of new and more effective internal controls and procedures designed to prevent a recurrence of the misconduct? Did the company provide [the investigators] with sufficient information for [them] to evaluate the company's measures to correct the situation and ensure that the conduct does not recur?

13. Is the company the same company in which the misconduct occurred, or has it changed through a merger or bankruptcy reorganization?[38]

In September 2004, Lockheed Martin, the world's largest defense contractor, announced an agreement to purchase Titan, a defense technology company, for an estimated $1.8 billion. The merger fell apart after both companies jointly disclosed to the Department of Justice and SEC potential FCPA concerns uncovered during due diligence. They related to payments made by Titan to foreign consultants involved in the sale of the company's radio systems to foreign military and security services. These payments were made in Africa, Asia, and the Middle East—areas of the world with historical corruption problems.[39]

Federal Sentencing Guidelines—Duty of Care

In 1991, state and federal authorities began to investigate Caremark International for alleged violations of Medicare's antireferral law. The investigations led to indictments, substantial fines, and a shareholder's derivative suit alleging that the company directors had breached their fiduciary duty of care.

When the proposed settlement of the derivative action reached the Delaware Court of Chancery,[40] it ruled in *Caremark International Derivative Legislation* that directors have an affirmative fiduciary obligation to ensure that adequate information and reporting systems exist in a corporation to provide timely and accurate information to the board and management about compliance with legal requirements. In that sense, it provides a framework for corporate governance standards. The *Caremark* view of this duty of care goes beyond the more passive standard that allows a board to rely on the integrity of employees to comply with legal and regulatory requirements.[41]

Of special interest is the court's discussion of the increasing tendency to employ criminal law to ensure corporate compliance. On November 1, 1991, the U.S. Sentencing Commission's *Amendments to the Sentencing Guidelines* for U.S. courts became effective. The guidelines provide scheduled fines and a complex formula for determining how a company will be sentenced after being charged with committing federal crimes.

The guidelines allow federal judges to mitigate any sentence imposed on a company according to a mathematical formula tied to conduct that the government seeks to encourage. Important factors in reducing a fine or sentence follow:

- The presence of an effective compliance program.
- Voluntary disclosure of an offense or noncompliance.
- Cooperation with regulatory investigations.
- Assumption of responsibility for the misconduct.
- After an offense has been detected, the company must take all "reasonable steps" to respond "appropriately" to the offense and to prevent further similar offenses.

Considering the impact of the sentencing guidelines on corporate compliance, the *Caremark* court opined that "any rational person attempting in good faith to meet an organization's governance responsibility would be bound to take [the sentencing guidelines] into account." We would hope this would be the case in the business world today, but evidence suggests that the corporate governance systems envisioned in the sentencing guidelines either did not exist or broke down during the scandals of the late 1990s and early 2000s. In Chapter 7, we discuss the causes of breakdowns in those systems in selected companies such as Xerox and Enron.

Application of the sentencing guidelines in securities fraud cases can be tricky business. Under the guidelines, a recommended sentence range is determined based mainly on how much money investors lost as a result of the conduct for which the defendant was found guilty. In the case of Bernard Ebbers, former CEO of WorldCom, the stock price declined from $64.50 on June 21, 1999 to $.83 on June 25, 2002, before the accounting restatements were announced. Because it was common knowledge that there were financial statement credibility problems well before the announced restatement, the 25-year sentence given to Ebbers in all likelihood reflects the 99 percent decline in value.

Conclusion

We end this chapter the same way we began by linking the Private Securities Litigation Reform Act to a successful effort by the accounting industry to limit legal liability. Some blame the passage of the act at least partly for accountants and auditors to feel freer to play loose with GAAP rules because the likelihood of having to settle lawsuits out of court to avoid deep pocket claims was lessened by changing the legal standard from joint and several liability to proportionate liability. In this regard, Congress could have unwittingly contributed to the environment in the accounting profession between 1995 and 2003, just subsequent to the enactment of Sarbanes-Oxley, by legislation indicating that the firms no longer had to fear being blamed for all of the damages in a fraud lawsuit even when other professionals played a prominent role.

The statement by Robert Mednick that set the tone for the chapter seems to imply that if auditor legal liability remains unchecked, auditors could restrict the dissemination of financial information that investors and creditors have a need, and an ethical right, to receive. This does not speak well for the CPA profession that has a public interest obligation above all else. Mednick's comment seems to reflect the tenor of the debate in the early and mid-1990s that the deep-pockets-motivated lawsuits had to stop or the profession would not effectively carry out its professional responsibilities. Only time will tell whether the Sarbanes-Oxley Act will be successful in changing the culture in the profession that is reflected by Mednick's comments.

Discussion Questions

1. Refer to the opening quote by Robert Mednick. What points can be made to support his position? What points can be raised in opposition?

2. Distinguish between common law liability and statutory liability for auditors. What is the basis for the difference in liability?

3. In a lawsuit brought by a plaintiff against a defendant in West Virginia, the court stated its interpretation of the relevant legal principle as follows: "In order to establish a prima facie case of negligence. . . , it must be shown that the defendant has been guilty of some act or omission in violation of a duty owed to the plaintiff. No action for negligence will lie without a duty broken." Using the AICPA Code of Conduct as your guide, interpret this statement in the context of auditor (CPA) ethical obligations to clients.

4. What is meant by the auditors' privity relationship? To which party(ies) does the auditor have a privity relationship? Provide legal support for your answer.

5. Distinguish between the legal concepts of actually foreseen third-party users, foreseeable third-party users, and reasonably foreseeable third-party users. How does each concept affect the auditor's legal liability?

6. Why was the *Rosenblum* ruling of such great concern to the accounting profession? Do you think the New Jersey Supreme Court ruling was "correct"? Why or why not?

7. Describe what the law requires with respect to the three-pronged approach of the near-privity relationship. Explain how these requirements create a legal liability for auditors.

8. In the *1136 Tenants Corp.* case, the court decided that a CPA has a legal liability to the client even though the level of service being performed is not an audit of the client's financial statements. Explain why the court reached this decision and how it has affected professional standards since the ruling.

9. Statutory liability is predicated on the auditor defrauding a third party by knowingly being involved with falsifications in the financial statements. From an ethical perspective, how does such an action by the auditor potentially harm the third party?

10. Explain what is meant by the "prudent person" perspective that could be used by an auditor. How does this relate to the ethical obligations of CPAs under the AICPA Code of Conduct? How does it relate to virtue ethics?

11. A great concern in society these days is the area of operational risk for banks with ATM machines. Use your own personal experience to describe the operational risks that could cause a loss to a bank as a result of fraudulent activities of a user of the ATM. Can you suggest any steps a bank can take to prevent it from happening in the future?

12. A *subsequent event* is one that occurs after the date of the financial statements (i.e., December 31, 2007) but prior to the auditor having dated (or possibly issued) the audit report (i.e., March 15, 2008). Why is it important from a legal perspective that an auditor be held responsible for certain material subsequent events?

13. What are the legal requirements for a third party to sue an auditor under Section 10 and Rule 10b-5 of the Securities Exchange Act of 1934? How do these requirements relate to the *Hochfelder* decision?

14. Draw a parallel between the *Equity Funding* ruling and the *ZZZZ Best* case discussed in Chapter 4. What are the common elements in both cases?

15. Subsequent to "Crazy" Eddie Antar's release from prison, he joined the speaker's circuit to present his point of view about the fraud at his former company and provide suggestions of how to avoid such frauds in the future to accountants. Comment on the ethicality of the following:

    a. An ex-con goes on the speaker's circuit but does not accept money or any other form of gift or payment in return.

    b. An ex-con like Minkow or Antar is paid money that he forfeits through "disgorgement" to be given to the former victims of his crime.

    c. An ex-con is compensated for his or her services as a speaker just like any other person who is asked to speak to a professional group.

16. Section 401 of the Sarbanes-Oxley Act requires that each financial statement to be filed with the SEC reflect all material correcting adjustments that have been identified by the audit firm in accordance with GAAP and the SEC's rules and regulations. Why do you think Congress wanted this provision in SOX? Which group within the corporate governance framework of a public company is responsible for ensuring that management reflects all noted adjustments? Why do you think the particular group that you identify should have that responsibility?

17. How does SOX Section 806 promote whistle-blowing? Do you think it is ethically proper for a law to encourage whistle-blowing on the part of corporate employees? Why or why not? How do legal considerations relate to a CPA's ethical responsibilities for whistle-blowing?

18. How did the passage of the Foreign Corrupt Practices Act influence the accounting profession and its accounting and auditing requirements? Do you think it is ethically (and culturally) appropriate for a U.S. law such as the FCPA to establish standards for U.S. multinationals when those companies operate outside the country?

19. The U.S. Federal Sentencing guidelines establish a duty of care requirement for corporations and its employees. Some have labeled this law the "good parenting" statute. Explain what you think could be meant by this statement.

20. The Private Securities Litigation Reform Act of 1995 changed the legal landscape for auditors in many ways. Explain the implications of the act for auditor legal liability.

Endnotes

1. James L. Craig, Jr., "The War on Accountants' Legal Liability," *The CPA Journal,* March 1990. Reprinted from *The CPA Jounral,* March 1990, copyright 1990, with permission from the New York State Society of Certified Public Accountants.

2. H. R. 1058, The Private Securities Litigation Reform Act, www.lectlaw.com/files/stf04.htm.

3. John C. Coffee, Jr., *What Caused Enron? A Capsule Social and Economic History of the 1990s,* Columbia Law School Working Paper Series. www.law.columbia.edu/center_program/law_economics/wp_listing_1/wp_listing/211-220?#rtregion:main.

4. Zoe-Vonna Palmrose, *Empirical Research in Auditor Litigation: Considerations and Data, Studies in Accounting Research No. 33* (Sarasota, FL: American Accounting Association, 1999).

5. William F. Messier, Jr., Steven M. Glover, and Douglas F. Prawitt, *Auditing and Assurance Services: A Systematic Approach* (New York: McGraw-Hill/Irwin, 2006).

6. *Ultramares v. Touche,* 174 N.E. 441 (N.Y. 1931).

7. *Rusch Factors, Inc. v. Levin,* 284. F.Supp. 85, 91.

8. A *tort* is a wrongful act other than a breach of contract that may lead to a civil action by one party (the plaintiff) against another party (the defendant) in a court of law.

9. Restatement (Second) of Torts, Section 652-A-E (1997), www.tomwbell.com/NetLaw/Ch05/R2ndTorts.html.

10. *Blue Bell, Inc. v. Peat, Marwick, Mitchell & Co.,* 715 S.W. 2d 408 (Dallas 1986).

11. *H. Rosenblum, Inc. v. Adler,* 93 N.J. 324 (1983).

12. *Credit Alliance v. Arthur Andersen & Co.,* 483 N.E. 2d 100 (N.Y. 1985).

13. *Security Pacific Business Credit, Inc. v. Peat Marwick Main & Co.,* 597 N.E. 1080 (N.Y. 1997).

14. Osborne Computer was founded in 1980 based on a product of portable computers. The Osborne 1 portable featured a 5-inch 52-column display, two floppy-disk drives, a Z80 microprocessor, and 64k of RAM, and it could fit under an airplane seat. Osborne 1 sold for $1,795 in 1981. The price tag set market expectations for bundled hardware and software packages for several years to come. Despite early success, Osborne struggled under heavy competition from Apple and IBM. The short-lived success of Osborne began to come apart in 1983 when the company boasted of an upcoming product that it failed to deliver. Demand for existing products declined as a result, and unsold inventory started to pile up. The company tried cutting prices—to $1,295 in July 1983 and $995 by August—but sales did not recover. Osborne abruptly declared bankruptcy. Employees who showed up for work were met by security guards who instructed them to leave. No entitlements were paid, and the guards tried to stop employees from stealing company property.

15. *Bily v. Arthur Young,* 834 P. 2d 745 (Cal. 1992).

16. *1136 Tenants Corp. v. Max Rothenberg & Co.,* 27 App. Div. 2d 830, 277 NYS 2d 996 (1967).

17. Securities Act of 1933, Title 18 of the U.S. Code.

18. *United States of America before the Securities and Exchange Commission in the Matter of McKesson and Robbins, Inc. (Accountancy in Transition)* (New York: Garland Publishing, 1982).

19. Joseph T. Wells, *Frankensteins of Fraud: The 20th Century's Top Ten White-Collar Crimes* (Austin, TX: ACFE, 2000).

20. Messier et al., p. 795.

21. Securities Exchange Act of 1934, Title 15 of the U.S. Code.

22. *Ernst & Ernst v. Hochfelder,* 425 U.S. 185 (1976).

23. Raymond L. Dirks and Leonard Gross, *The Great Wall Street Scandal* (New York: McGraw-Hill, 1974).

24. "A Scandal Unfolds," *The Wall Street Journal,* April 2, 1973, p. 14.

25. "A Fraudster Speaks Out about White Collar Fraud," www.whitecollarfraud.com.

26. Ibid.

27. *Securities and Exchange Commission v. Sam M. Antar, et al.* Civil Action No. 93-3988, Litigation Release No. 15814, July 16, 1998.

28. M. I. Weiss, "Auditors: Be Watchdogs, Not Just Bean Counters," *Accounting Today,* November 15, 1993, p. 41.

29. Securities and Exchange Commission, Litigation Release No. 16544, May 9, 2000.

30. U. S. House of Representatives, H. R. 3763, Sarbanes-Oxley Act of 2002, www.sarbanes-oxley.com/section.php?level=1&pub_id=Sarbanes-Oxley.

31. Michael Tomberlin, "Scrushy Lawyers Seek Dismissal of SEC Suit," *The Birmingham News,* February 22, 2006.

32. U.S. House of Representatives, H.R. 3763, Sarbanes-Oxley Act of 2002, http://www.sarbanes-oxley.com/section.php?level=1&pub_id=Sarbanes-Oxley.

33. 69 Fed. Reg. 52114.

34. Richard D. Ramsey and A. F. Alkhafaji, "The 1977 Foreign Corrupt Practices Act and the 1988 Omnibus Trade Bill," *Management Decision* 29, no. 6.

35. Foreign companies that list stock on U.S. exchanges have the option to convert their statements from home-country GAAP to U.S. GAAP or provide a reconciliation of their financial information that is based on local GAAP to U.S. GAAP. In January 2005, the European Union (EU) countries adopted International Financial Reporting Standards (IFRS) that must be used by all companies doing business in the EU. EU countries have been pressuring the SEC to accept these standards in lieu of conversion to U.S. GAAP or reconciliation.

36. United States Code (U.S.C.) Section 78 dd (1982).

37. Omnibus Trade and Competitiveness Act of 1988. Public Law 100-148, August 23, 1988.

38. Securities and Exchange Commission, Accounting and Auditing Enforcement (AAER) No. 1470, October 23, 2001.

39. "Does Your Target Have Clean Hands Overseas?" *Mergers & Acquisitions: The Dealmakers Journal,* April 1, 2005, www.foley.com/publications/pub_detail.aspx?pubid=2625.

40. The Delaware Court of Chancery is widely recognized as the preeminent forum in the United States for the determination of disputes involving the internal affairs of thousands of Delaware corporations and other business entities. The court has jurisdiction to hear all matters related to equity. Its decisions can be appealed to the Delaware Supreme Court.

41. *Caremark International Derivative Legislation,* 1996 De. Ch LEXIS 125 (Del. 1996).

Chapter 6 Cases

Case 6-1

Busyboto Scooter Sales, Inc.

Busyboto Scooter Sales, Inc. is the largest manufacturer of scooter bikes in the world. In 2003, the company announced a revolutionary scooter, Wassup X-777, a 250cc bike with sporty styling and advanced electronic features, including the Busyboto B-matic transmission and the Busyboto smart card key system. In its first full year of sales, 195,000 units of the Wassup X-777 were sold in Asia alone. Scooter sales began in the United States in 2004, and the company sold 375,000, 450,000, and 600,000 units, respectively, in calendar years 2004 through 2006.

Customers seem to gravitate to the sleek design of the Busyboto B-Matic including a reduced cowl profile. The shapes of the inner stop lamps and turn signals have been changed from a strange triangular shape to the more appealing round shapes equipped with 10 LEDs per side for increased visibility and sharp rear view. The scooters are the first in the world to be outfitted with an auto shift mode and kick-down gear shifter to create a unique driving experience finely tuned to driving conditions.

On January, 25, 2008, during the audit of the company's calendar year 2007 financial statements, Stu Forstman identified certain financial irregularities with respect to activities of the U.S. subsidiary of Busyboto Scooter Sales. The irregularities concerned material payments to influential people in the Central American country of Zootsuitia to gain a contract to supply the country with 100,000 scooters by 2009. Forstman convinced his superiors to accept the explanation of Hank Koosner, the officer in charge of the Zootsuitia operation, despite evidence that contradicts his explanation and indicates that the irregularities may be illegal.

Questions

1. Is it ethical for a U.S. company to make questionable payments to influential people and decision makers in a country in which it does business? Describe the possible legal implications of the facts of the case for the U.S. subsidiary of Busyboto Scooter sales under the Foreign Corrupt Practices Act.

2. Do you think it is "right" for Congress to establish a law that controls the actions of U.S. multinational entities while operating in foreign countries? Why or why not?

3. What level of care is required of the auditors in this case? Based on the limited facts of the case, do you think the audit firm has met its burden of care? Why or why not?

4. Distinguish between constructive fraud and actual fraud. What evidence, if any, exists in this case that could indicate that one or the other legal liability exists for the auditors? Be specific and state any assumptions you made in interpreting the facts of the case.

5. Assume that Forstman went to his superiors with a recommendation that a complete investigation should be opened on how the company operates in Zootsuitia including additional information that is independently obtained on the questionable payments. After a brief meeting with his superiors, Forstman is told in no uncertain terms to "let sleeping dogs lie." Assume that Forstman is a CPA and member of the AICPA. What are his ethical responsibilities under these circumstances?

6. Assume that Forstman knows that the audit firm will not tolerate dissent on the Zootsuitia issue. He is concerned that he will lose his job if he starts to rock the boat. What would you do if you were in Forstman's place? Why?

Case 6-2

Foreign Corrupt Practices Act

Allison Yancy and Ginger Boggs just finished playing four hours of board games following a contentious meeting with top management over the responsibility of Monosystems International for instituting a program of due diligence to prevent any further violation of the Foreign Corrupt Practices Act (FCPA). Both had worked for Monosystems from 1996 to the present. The CEO of the company was recently fired following the disclosure of a $10 million bribe paid to the president of Jumungy, a small country in east Africa, for the exclusive rights to market board game products in that country. The company was fined $2 million, and the CEO was sent to jail for five years and fined $100,000.

Valerie Uno is the current CEO of Jumungy. Uno told Yancy and Boggs in no uncertain terms that, in response to their suggestion, the company would not appoint a director of business ethics or establish an office of business ethics in the company. Uno contends it is not required under the FCPA. Yancy and Boggs believe that although the act may not specifically require it, the company should, in the spirit of compliance, elevate the business ethics function to the vice presidential level. The meeting ended after Uno told Yancy and Boggs to prepare a memorandum that would outline why they believe the creation of the position they advocate is necessary.

Questions

1. Describe the *Caremark* standard of due diligence discussed in the chapter. Do you think the statement in the case by Yancy and Boggs that "the company should, in the spirit of compliance, elevate the business ethics function to the vice presidential level" is consistent with the requirements stated in the *Caremark* case? Why or why not?

2. Do you believe Jumungy can comply with the expectations of the SEC for self-policing, self-reporting, remediation, and cooperation that were outlined by the SEC in its proceeding against de-Leon Meredith without establishing a companywide ethics program and/or ethics officer? Why or why not? Can a company show its commitment to business ethics in some way other than by implementing Yancy and Boggs' proposal? If so, how can it show its commitment?

3. Chapter 3 has a discussion of the provisions of an effective system of corporate governance. How should a company that is serious about fostering ethical behavior build ethics into its corporate governance system?

4. Assume that Yancy and Boggs approach you as a trusted adviser, CPA, and overall good person, and they ask you to identify the five most important points they should include in their memo to Uno. What would you say? Why?

5. Assume that Yancy and Boggs do exactly as you advised and are quite confident that the steps they have outlined in their memo meets both the technical requirements and spirit of the FCPA. Uno, however, decides not to adopt any of these suggestions, claiming that they would cost too much and provide too little benefit in combating wrongful acts. Is a cost-benefit analysis a proper way to evaluate the advisability of implementing an ethics program? Explain the reasons for your answer.

6. What would you do at this point if you were in the position of Yancy and Boggs? Why?

Case 6-3

KnowledgeWare

On September 28, 1999, the SEC filed a civil injunctive action in federal court in Atlanta, Georgia, charging seven former executives of the computer software company KnowledgeWare, Inc. with carrying out a multimillion dollar financial fraud scheme that materially inflated KnowledgeWare's reported earnings during the fiscal year ended June 30, 1994, and charging two of those defendants with committing illegal insider trading.[1]

The KnowledgeWare fraud would not be a large or interesting enough study if it were not for the fact that the CEO and chair of the board of directors was former professional football star Francis A. Tarkenton. Tarkenton played quarterback for the Minnesota Vikings for 13 years in the 1960s and 1970s. He is in the football Hall of Fame, although he had the dubious distinction back then of having led his team into three Super Bowl games, all ending in losses. Tarkenton was named the NFL's Most Valuable Player in 1975.

Since retirement, Tarkenton has taken his trademark freewheeling quarterbacking style into the business world. He has started as many as 30 separate companies, including a short-lived fast-food franchise called Scramblers. Today, Tarkenton runs several business Web sites and a sports memorabilia Web site.

The SEC charged Tarkenton and six others with engaging in a fraudulent scheme to inflate KnowledgeWare's financial results and to meet sales and earnings projections. In all, KnowledgeWare reported at least $8 million in revenue from sham software sales. The company "parked" inventory with software resellers and other supposed customers that were given the right not to pay for the software either orally or in "side letters" that were kept separate from other sales documents. As a result of this scheme, KnowledgeWare falsely reported record sales revenue and dramatic increases in earnings in press releases and in quarterly reports filed with the SEC and disseminated to the public in 1993 and 1994.

Even after restating those quarterly results, the company continued to mislead investors by claiming in its 1994 annual report and other public documents that the restatement resulted from a problem with the "collectibility" of reseller receivables—without disclosing that KnowledgeWare had

created the problem by "selling" software and simultaneously granting the "purchaser" the right not to pay for it.

Tarkenton and two others directed the fraudulent scheme and made materially false statements to purchasers of KnowledgeWare stock. Materially false and misleading statements also were made to KnowledgeWare's auditors.

Tarkenton settled with the SEC by agreeing to pay a civil money penalty of $100,000 and disgorge $54,187, the amount of the incentive compensation he received in 1994 on the basis of KnowledgeWare's materially overstated quarterly earnings plus prejudgment interest thereon. The president and chief operating officer agreed to the same penalties. The CFO paid a $25,000 civil penalty and $2,812 in disgorgement. Overall, the total amount of penalties, disgorgement, and interest paid by the seven defendants in the case was about $514,000.

Questions

1. Based on the limited facts of the case, cite the violations of securities laws committed by the officers of KnowledgeWare. How do these laws protect the investing public? What is meant by the term *disgorgement?*

2. The auditors in the KnowledgeWare case were not charged. Based on the facts of the case, does it seem that there were any violations of the AICPA Code of Professional Conduct? If so, cite the specific rules violated and why. If not, justify your answer.

3. What accounting issues are raised by the facts that the software resellers had agreed to accept inventory subject to being able to return it to KnowledgeWare with no questions asked? Do you think there were any ethical obligations on the part of the software resellers in the case? Be specific in answering this question.

4. When the KnowledgeWare story of fraud broke in the press, many Vikings fans and lifelong football fans of Tarkenton were in disbelief. They thought that there had to have been a mistake. After all, Tarkenton had been their football hero for many years. Should we hold athletes to the same ethical standards as other people? Does it matter whether they violate ethics while playing professionally as opposed to doing it after retirement? How would you characterize the ethical obligation of a sports person who is admired by the general public?

[1] Securities and Exchange Commission, Litigation Release No. 16306, SEC v. Francis A. Tarkenton, Donald P. Addington, Rick W. Gossett, Lee R. Fontaine, William E. Hammersla, III, Eladio Alvarez and Edward Welch, Civil Action File No. 1:99-CV 2497 (N.D. Ga September 28, 1999), http://sec.gov/litigation/litreleases/lr16306.htm.

Case 6-4

Reznor v. J. Artist Management (JAM), Inc.

The *Entertainment Law Reporter* reported in September 2005 that the claim by Nine Inch Nails lead singer Trent Reznor that his former management contract was unconscionable had been dismissed by the court because the contract terms were not unusual for the music industry, but the court ruled that a jury must decide whether the manager breached a fiduciary duty by committing fraud and conversion.[1]

Michael Trent Reznor met John Malm, Jr., a part-time promoter of local rock bands, in Cleveland, Ohio, in 1985. Malm became Reznor's manager and formed J. Artist Management, Inc (JAM). Reznor became the lead singer in the band Nine Inch Nails, which performed its first show in 1988. Reznor and Malm signed a management agreement under which JAM was to receive 20 percent of Reznor's gross compensation.

In 1986, Malm hired accountant Richard Szekelyi and his firm, Navigent Group, to provide financial consulting services to Reznor personally and to examine Reznor's financial records. Szekelyi discovered flawed accounting between the two parties to the detriment of Reznor by about $4 million. The primary cause was that Malm had received tax benefits that should have gone to Reznor.[2]

Reznor filed a separate lawsuit against codefendants Szekelyi and Navigent Group, charging them with negligence, breach of fiduciary duty, and aiding and abetting fraud. The codefendants sought summary judgment to dismiss Reznor's claims, stating they had not breached any standard of care in preparing or presenting reports of Reznor's financial status, nor did Szekelyi fail to counsel Reznor adequately concerning other transactions. The court granted the summary judgment dismissing the charges against Szekelyi and Navigent.[3]

Questions

1. Did a privity relationship exist between Szekelyi and Reznor? Why or why not?

2. What is the duty of care that should be imposed on Szekelyi with respect to his work for Reznor? Provide legal support for your answer.

3. What legal principles could Szekelyi use to defend himself against the charges in the case?

4. Assume that Szekelyi is a CPA. Identify the provisions of the AICPA Code of Professional Conduct (principles, rules, and interpretations) that should be of concern to Szekelyi in performing professional services. To whom does Szekelyi owe an ethical obligation? Is it to Reznor? Is it to JAM? Explain the basis for your answer.

5. Based on the facts of the case, do you think that Malm breached his fiduciary duty to Reznor? Why or why not?

---

[1] *Entertainment Law Reporter,* September 2005, Recent Cases Section or Column, Volume 27, Number 4.

[2] Roger LeRoy Miller and Gaylord A. Jentz, *Business Law Today,* 7th ed. (Mason, Oh: South-Western, 2007), pp. 1087–1088.

[3] *Reznor v. J. Artist Mgmt,* 365 F.Supp.2d 565, S.D.N.Y. 2005.

Case 6-5

Second National Bank v. First National Bank

The Background

This case[1] involves three parties:

1. A customer, Paul Gerry, who went to a bank and established a relationship after which (about one year later) he was allowed to open a revolving credit line with the bank,

2. The bank, First National Bank, which granted the revolving line of credit to Gerry.

3. A secondary, participating bank, Second National Bank, that signed a participation contract with First National to pick up $2 million of a $20 million loan.

The case involves the following facts:

- On October 6, 2007, Gerry approached the bank and negotiated a $20 million revolving line of credit. Shortly thereafter, First National became concerned about the loan because it learned (after the fact, according to the bank) that Gerry was being investigated in Massachusetts for Medicaid fraud at one of the nursing homes he owned. The investigation may actually have been underway at the time of the loan's closing.

- Second National Bank claims to have had no knowledge of the investigation and stated that First National did not disclose the facts before the closing. First National disputes that claim. Based on the difference of interpretation, Second National attempted to terminate its participation contract with First National, sued that bank, and asked for a return of the $2 million. Second National states in its pleadings that even if First National did not know about the investigation when Second National agreed to participate in the loan, Second National justifiably relied on First National's assessments of Gerry's creditworthiness and suffered pecuniary loss as a result.

Legal Issues

Second National's complaint has four counts.

1. Second National claimed that First National had breached its "duty of disclosure" by failing to disclose material information. First National counterclaims that Second National was able to do an independent assessment of Gerry's creditworthiness before agreeing to participate. The court dismissed this count immediately after discovering that Second National had signed a document acknowledging its right to do an independent assessment of Gerry's creditworthiness.

[1] This case is based on the facts of *Banco Totta e Acores v. Fleet National Bank*, 768 F. Supp. 943, July 3, 1991.

2. Second National charged First National with intentional misrepresentation. In its ruling, the court cited *Rusch Factors, Inc. v. Levin.* In that case, the judge allowed an action to go forward against an accountant for negligent preparation of financial statements. In the *Rusch* decision, the court stated, "One who, in the course of his business, profession or employment, or in a transaction in which he has a pecuniary interest, supplies false information for the guidance of others in their business transactions, is subject to liability for pecuniary loss caused to them by their justifiable reliance upon the information, if he fails to exercise reasonable care or competence in obtaining or communicating the information." The court in the Gerry matter elaborated by stating that the tort of intentional misrepresentation, or, in common law parlance, deceit, is well established in the law. The court went on to cite the requirements that a plaintiff must prove to sustain such a charge.

3. Second National charged that First National willfully and wantonly breached its duty of care and good faith by making material misrepresentations and omissions. The fraud claim was treated the same as Count 2, intentional misrepresentation.

4. Second National claimed that First National had been unjustly enriched as a result of its refusal to refund to Second National the money the latter contributed to the Gerry loan. The court withheld judgment on this matter pending the outcome of its deliberations on Counts 1–3.

Questions

1. Discuss the requirements that a plaintiff must prove to sustain a charge of intentional misrepresentation or fraud. Use as your guide the chapter discussion about liability to third parties.

2. Draw appropriate parallels between the facts of this case and an auditor's legal liability to third parties. How do you interpret the facts and legal issues in this case with respect to the cases discussed in the chapter?

3. Given the limited facts of the case, do you think the court should have found for Second National in any one or more of the counts? Why or why not?

4. Would your answer to Question 3 be any different if there was no clear-cut indication that Second National had a right to do an independent assessment of the financial condition of Gerry prior to becoming a participating lender? Why or why not?

5. In the court ruling, the judge cited another case in Massachusetts as guiding the Second National decision. In the other case, plaintiffs/sellers sued defendants/buyers

for failing to make the final payment on a note for the purchase of a delicatessen. The buyers asserted a counterclaim, alleging that they had been induced to buy the operation by false and material misrepresentations made to them by the sellers concerning the delicatessen's past revenues. Before the sale, the buyers had examined the tax returns of the business and expressed concern over the low profits, but they had been reassured by the sellers' verbal representations that in reality the business was much more profitable than indicated by the records. Consequently, the buyers agreed to the sale. Given the facts of this second case, discuss how you think the judge in that case could apply the facts in deciding the *Second National v. First National* case? That is, what could the judge have looked for in deciding the buyers' counterclaim that could be the determining factor in the ruling?

Case 6-6

The Enron 401-k Retirement Plan

The Enron failure was not just about a company that had gone from being one of the largest, seemingly most successful companies in the United States during the 1990s to the most striking example of corporate greed run amok. It is also about being the first company in which 18,000 to 20,000 employees lost money because their retirement accounts were invested in Enron stock in large part because of consistently favorable results that were reported internally to employees even when the stock price was going down.

Many observers were shocked to learn after the fact that corporate insiders (allegedly) knew the whole, truthful story, and some even sold their own shares for millions of dollars while the fraud unraveled. On May 25, 2006, Ken Lay and Jeff Skilling, the chief executives at the helm of Enron during the fraud, were convicted of fraud and conspiracy, and Skilling of insider trading.[1] (Note: Lay died before he appealed his conviction. Since his conviction could be appealed, it was vacated. This means that Ken Lay was convicted but will be considered not guilty.)

The Blackout Period

Enron limited employees' investment freedom from the beginning by matching employee contributions only with company stock and by preventing employees from selling that stock until age 50. During the time period that the company's problems were becoming public knowledge, Enron chose to change administrators of its 401-k plan, and the company locked employees into the decisions they had already made for a period of about three to four weeks.[2] The timing was bad for employees as they watched Enron's stock price decline further and further from its peak price of $90 in September 2000 to below $9 per share in mid-November 2001. After the company restated its earnings by almost $600 million in 2000 and took an additional charge of $1.2 billion to its stockholders' equity, the stock price dropped below $1.

The Tittle Class Action Lawsuit . . . and Others

Prior to Enron's filing for bankruptcy in December 2001, a consolidated class action lawsuit that was motivated by an individual suit filed by Enron employee Pamela Tittle, who had lost $140,000 on Enron stock in her retirement account, was brought on behalf of Enron employees who had lost almost $1 billion on Enron stock held in their 401-k retirement accounts. The suit alleged that the company breached its fiduciary duty to employees by encouraging them to invest in Enron stock at artificially inflated prices.

On September 12, 2005, a partial settlement was reached in the lawsuit that allowed a claim in Enron's bankruptcy proceedings in the amount of $356.25 million (less attorney's fees and expenses). Another partial settlement for $1.25 million was reached to pay claims to all persons who were participants or beneficiaries in the 401-k plans during the period from January 1, 1995 through December 28, 2005, the effective date of the settlement. This settlement resolved claims against Arthur Andersen LLP and David B. Duncan, the lead auditor for the firm, for the alleged breach of fiduciary duties by violating the Employee Retirement Income Security Act of 1974 (ERISA) and for negligence.[3]

On March 31, 2006, Northern Trust Company, a Chicago financial services company, settled for $37.5 million a retirement plan participant lawsuit filed against it in connection with the collapse of Enron. Northern Trust had served as the administrator for Enron's 401-k and employee stock ownership plans.

ERISA Requirements

The federal Employee Retirement Income Security Act of 1974 (ERISA) protects the interests of plan participants and their beneficiaries. The law is enforced by several federal agencies including the Department of Labor (enforces fiduciary rules, reporting and disclosure requirements), the Internal Revenue Service (oversees the provisions of the law regarding tax treatment of plans and contributions), and

---

[1] Alexei Barrionuevo and Vikas Bajaj, "Enron Chiefs Guilty of Fraud and Conspiracy," *New York Times,* May 25, 2006.

[2] Section 306 of the Sarbanes-Oxley Act of 2002 deals with the blackout period loss of employees in 401-k plans by requiring the plan administrator to notify plan participants and affected beneficiaries 30 days in advance of the expected beginning date and length of the blackout period. Insider trading is prohibited during the blackout period, and any profit realized by a director or executive officer from the purchase, sale, or other acquisition or transfer in violation of the law is recoverable by the issuing company regardless of the intent for the sale.

[3] Andersen still has about 200 employees, a far cry from its 28,000 when the firm was on top of the profession. The staff is mainly consumed with fighting and settling litigation. The remaining asset of the firm is its Q Center comprehensive conference and training facilities outside Chicago in St. Charles, Illinois. The center has been rated highly for its state-of-the-art facilities including LAN setup, videoconferencing, interactive audience response, full audio, Web casting, and event production. *Meeting News* rated it as one of the 25 top conference centers for service, expertise, quality of overall environment, amenities, food, and recreation. From Web site at www.qcenter.com/home.asp.

the Pension Benefit Guaranty Corporation (PBGC), which administers a government insurance program for terminated underfunded pension plans.

In recent years, corporate America has witnessed an increase in the number of claims alleging ERISA violations and the costs associated with these claims. From 1996 to 2002, the average indemnity payment increased more than 22 percent, from $715,000 to $875,000, and the average cost of mounting a defense went up 471 percent, from $70,000 to $400,000.

ERISA imposes certain obligations on the individuals or entities that are responsible for the administration and management of employee benefit plans such as 401-k plans. The fiduciaries of a 401-k plan are required to observe two rules, the exclusive benefit rule and the prudent man rule. A 401-k plan fiduciary also must administer the plan in accordance with its terms and is subject to ERISA's cofiduciary liability and prohibited transaction rules.

The Exclusive Benefit Rule

ERISA section 404(a)(1)(A) requires a fiduciary to discharge duties with respect to a retirement plan for the exclusive benefit of plan participants and their beneficiaries and for the purpose of defraying the expenses of administering the plan. Section 403(c) provides that "the assets of a plan shall never inure to the benefit of any employer and shall be held for the exclusive purposes of providing benefits to participants in the plan and their beneficiaries and defraying reasonable expenses of administering the plan."

The Prudent Man Rule

Under the prudent man rule of ERISA section 404(a)(1)(B), the duties of a 401-k plan fiduciary must be discharged with the care, skill, and diligence that would be exercised by a reasonably prudent person who is familiar with such matters. This is a restatement of the prudent person standard developed as part of other areas of common law.

Fiduciary Liabilities

Examples of allegations of breaches of fiduciary duty include the failure to adequately diversify plan assets; the failure to discharge duties in accordance with the plan documents; self-dealing transactions, such as using plan assets for personal gain or acting on behalf of parties whose interests are adverse to the plan; and allowing transactions between the plan and parties in interest, such as permitting the use of plan assets by a person who provides services to the plan.

A variety of parties can sue fiduciaries including the plan participants (employees) and their beneficiaries, who are likely to sue for recovery of benefits or enforcement of their rights under ERISA. The Department of Labor can sue to stop acts that violate ERISA and to collect civil penalties for prohibited transactions. Third-party administrators also can sue, as can the PBGC.

The most common fiduciary liability claims involve the improper denial of benefits, failure to adequately fund a plan, conflict of interest, improper advice or counsel, improper change in benefits, imprudent investment, misleading representation, lack of investment diversity, improper termination of a plan, incorrect benefit calculation, and the unacceptable choice of insurance company, mutual fund, or third-party service provider including the investment manager and actuary.

The Debate in Class

One day two students engaged in a class debate as to whether Enron was responsible for the 401-k mess or it was a case of employees failing to exercise prudence in making their own investment choices. Here is a selected part of the debate.

Student 1:   They should hang Ken Lay, Jeff Skilling, and Andy Fastow and then parade their bodies in the public square.

Student 2:   Get real. The Enron employees made their own investment choices. They failed to conduct their own due diligence before allowing their 401-k funds to be invested in Enron stock. After all, the company didn't require them to put funds into company stock.

Student 1:   That's unrealistic. Don't you recall the class discussion the other day? Overall, about 19 percent of 401-k assets are in company stock. I mean, you're going to trust the managers who hired you and are running the company on behalf of the shareholders, of which you are one.

Student 2:   So what you are saying is so long as the stock was a good buy from the beginning and there was no misleading information or arm twisting—I mean it wasn't a shoddy investment—then if the stock goes south, you can't argue after the fact that there was too much company stock in the plan. Do you really believe what you're saying?

Questions

1. Compare the fiduciary responsibilities of 401-k plan trustees to the due care standard of ethical behavior required of CPAs under the AICPA Code, especially auditors of public companies.

2. Evaluate the ethics of top management of Enron regarding their sale of their stock holdings while the bubble was bursting at Enron. In particular, what is wrong with encouraging employees to invest their 401-k monies in company stock?

3. Of what importance is the fact that the company contributed its share to the 401-k plans by matching employee contributions with Enron stock?

4. Whom do you blame for the employee loss of $1 billion in Enron's 401-k retirement plan? Use ethical reasoning including stakeholder analysis to support your answer.

5. Consider the two points of view expressed by the two students in the class debate. Assume that your professor asked you to craft a response to the two students. What would you say? Why?

Case 6-7

The Ethics of the Private Securities Litigation Reform Act (PSLRA)

The PSLRA became effective on December 22, 1995, following a long and hard battle won by the accounting profession to limit the legal liabilities of accountants and auditors in response to a massive increase in the number of lawsuits and charges that many raised frivolous issues. The PSLRA changes the legal standards for liability from joint and several to proportionate liability. It also establishes a fraud detection and reporting requirement to the SEC that reduces the time for management to report fraud to the commission or for the auditor to act when the one-day-business-reporting requirement is not met.

The PSLRA contains two additional provisions of note:

1. Section 21(D)(b)(1) of the Reform Act provides that the complaint must specify each statement alleged to have been misleading, the reason or reasons why the statement is misleading, and, if an allegation regarding the statement or omission is made on "information and belief," the complaint *should state with particularity all facts* on which that belief is formed. This is to include "facts giving rise to a strong inference that the defendant acted with the required state of mind."

2. Under a "forward-looking safe harbor provision" included in 15 U.S.C., a company may not be held liable under the federal securities laws for projections and other forward-looking statements, such as estimates and future judgments, either written or oral, that later prove to be inaccurate if:

    a. The forward-looking statement is identified as a forward-looking statement and is accompanied by meaningful cautionary statements identifying important factors that could cause actual results to differ materially from those in the forward-looking statement or the statement is immaterial; or

    b. The plaintiff fails to prove that the forward-looking statement was made with actual knowledge that the statement was false or misleading.

Questions

1. Evaluate the ethics of passing the PSLRA. That is, was it a good law to pass? Why or why not?

2. In filing a lawsuit under the PSLRA, do you think it is right for plaintiffs to have to meet the strict pleading standards established under the act including to demonstrate "facts giving rise to a strong inference that the defendant acted with the required state of mind"? Why or why not?

3. Do you think it is possible for an accountant to accurately describe "meaningful cautionary statements" when making a forward-looking projection? Do you think the knowledge of the falsehood approach (scienter) should be used by the courts in making that determination in a lawsuit against the accountant? Why or why not? Remember, scienter is a legal term for intent to deceive, manipulate, or defraud.

4. The AICPA Code of Conduct contains a confidentiality obligation for CPAs. How does that obligation relate to the requirements of the Financial Fraud Detection and Disclosure Provision in the PSLRA? Do you think a CPA who informs the SEC of a financial fraud situation at the client entity would be in violation of the Code? Under what circumstances could this occur?

5. The Financial Fraud Detection and Disclosure provision contains a reporting requirement for the auditor unless an illegal act is "clearly inconsequential." Do you think an illegal act can ever be inconsequential? On what basis do you make that decision?

Case 6-8

The Lecturer

The *Los Angeles Times* reported on March 25, 2006 (page B7) that a business school lecturer at the University of Southern California (USC) had been arrested by FBI agents for allegedly bilking students out of more than $1.5 million and spending much of the money on show horses (that apparently were not to be used in the classroom). Authorities said that the lecturer lured students and their gullible parents into investing in a real estate scheme.

The lecturer told students the investments would be put in Nevada and Illinois commercial properties and would yield a 190 percent return. The lecturer deposited $718,000 of their money into a personal bank account and used much of the remaining funds for personal expenses including $500,000 to buy and care for show horses, a $73,000 Cadillac Escalade, and $52,000 for personal brokerage accounts.

Authorities stated that suspicions grew when monthly statements failed to arrive and the investors did not receive their returns. Two students confronted the lecturer one dark and dreary night asking for a return of their money. The lecturer put them off for a while and then proceeded to draw up fake sales agreements showing that the lecturer had bought or owned the projects. The students were having none of it, thinking, "Fool me once, shame on you; fool me a second time, shame on me."

Questions

1. Should college lecturers and professors be held to the same legal standards of conduct as accountants and auditors? Why or why not? What if the lecturer or professor is a CPA? Would that change your answer?

2. What are the responsibilities of students and their parents in becoming involved with a college professor in an investment outside of class? That is, putting aside the question of the rightness or wrongness of such an activity, how do you assess blame in the case? Is it 100 percent the professor's fault? Is it 100 percent the students' and their parents' fault? Provide logical reasoning in support of your answer.

3. Identify the primary stakeholders in this case and their interests in the resolution of the matter.

4. The lecturer in this case is the founder, president, and chief executive officer of a realty investor company. That could be why USC asked the lecturer to teach the course in which the investment opportunities were offered to the students and their parents. What do you think should be the ethical responsibilities of a lecturer or professor with respect to discussing possible outside business and financial activities with students?

5. What are the ethical responsibilities of a university that hires a faculty member to teach a course to its students?

Case 6-9

Whistle-Blowing under Sarbanes-Oxley

The case of George Hernondez is a unique one under the whistle-blower protection provision of the Sarbanes-Oxley Act because it is the first documented case in which someone who sued under Section 806 of the act was given the right to return to his job after bringing a successful action. George has to make up his mind whether he wants to return to work in light of the expected animosity for him by fellow employees.

George worked in the controller's office of Scarborough Faire Industries (SFI). The company was close to terminating George's employment because of well-documented performance problems and difficulties getting along with his co-workers; he had been with SFI for just over two years. The company had generated numerous memoranda indicating that it would likely fire him in January 2008 after the holiday season.

In December 2007, George was given an assignment to assess the company's inflated levels of inventory over the preceding two years. He provided his preliminary analysis on January 3, 2008, asserting that the company's methods would lead to erroneous inventory management reporting. The following business day, George was discharged.

George filed a lawsuit under Section 806 of the Sarbanes-Oxley Act claiming to have been fired as a direct result of his report that identified specific members of management as responsible for erroneous inventory management. OSHA ruled in favor of George and awarded him approximately $100,000 in back wages and legal expenses as well as $10,000 for counseling charges incurred during the ordeal. It also ordered SFI to reinstate George and to post the ruling

in a conspicuous spot in the company's office for no less than 60 days. SFI is appealing the decision.

George was given notice by the company that he had to return to his reinstated position in two weeks or forfeit that right. George then asked for 30 days to complete the counseling program he had started almost one year earlier.

Questions

1. Assume that the company's statements about George's impending firing in January 2008 were correct and his performance evaluations were unacceptable. Under the circumstances, should SFI have been able to fire George? Why or why not?

2. Assume that George had worked extra hard and very long hours to dig up dirt on the company's inventory management procedures, Do you think he should be able to sue under Section 806? Why or why not? Would your opinion change if George had spent twice the time and exerted double the effort to find the irregularity as compared with his work habits in general for SFI?

3. Would it surprise you to know that the vast majority of cases brought under Section 806 since the passage of Sarbanes-Oxley have gone in favor of the employer? Why or why not? What do you think could explain this finding?

4. If you were in George's position, what factors would be of greatest concern to you in deciding whether to return to work? Would you go back to SFI in two weeks? In 30 days?

Case 6-10

Who Is Responsible?

On August 21, 2007, Comfi Beds and Furniture, Inc. planned to purchase Sleep Ezy Corporation and hired the accounting firm of Loosy and Goosy LLP to review the audit that had been prepared by Billy Bob and Brothers, CPAs (the accounting firm for Sleep Ezy) as of the fiscal year-end July 31, 2007. Loosy and Goosy advised Comfi Beds that Billy Bob had performed a high-quality audit and that Sleep Ezy's inventory was stated fairly on the general ledger and balance sheet as of the audit date. As a result of these representations, Comfi Beds went forward with the purchase of Sleep Ezy.

Several months after the purchase, Comfi Beds discovered that the audit by Billy Bob had been materially inaccurate and misleading, primarily because the inventory had been grossly overstated on the balance sheet. Subsequent to the discovery, a former Sleep Ezy employee who had begun working for Comfi Beds exposed an e-mail exchange between Billy Bob and the former CEO of Sleep Ezy. The exchange revealed that Billy Bob had cooperated in overstating the inventory on the books of Sleep Ezy.

Questions

1. If Loosy and Goosy's review was conducted in good faith and conformed to GAAP, could Comfi Beds hold Loosy and Goosy liable for negligently failing to detect the inventory overstatement in Billy Bob's audit? Why or why not?

2. Review the various principles discussed in the chapter that have been adopted by the courts concerning accountants' legal liability. Based on your review and analysis, could Billy Bob have been liable to Comfi Beds?

3. What is scienter? To what extent does scienter exist with respect to any potential legal liability of Billy Bob? How about Loosy and Goosy?

4. Generally, what requirements must be met before Comfi Beds can recover damages under Section 10(b) of the Securities Exchange Act of 1934 and SEC Rule 10b-5? Could Comfi Beds meet these requirements?

Earnings Management and the Quality of Financial Reporting

Increasingly, I have become concerned that the motivation to meet Wall Street earnings expectations may be overriding common sense business practices. Too many corporate managers, auditors, and analysts are participants in a game of nods and winks. In the zeal to satisfy consensus earnings estimates and project a smooth earnings path, wishful thinking may be winning the day over faithful representation.

Arthur Levitt

This statement by former SEC Chairman Arthur Levitt was made in a speech to the New York University Center for Law and Business on September 28, 1998. Levitt linked the practice of "earnings management" to an excessive zeal to project smoother earnings from year to year that casts a pall over the quality of the underlying numbers. Levitt identifies the cause as a "culture of gamesmanship" in business rooted in the emphasis on achieving short-term results such as meeting or exceeding financial analysts' earnings expectations.[1]

The accounting scandals at companies such as Enron, WorldCom, and Tyco allegedly involved the use of inside information by top management to sell shares owned at a relatively favorable current price as compared to future prices. Presumably, the executives knew that the earnings had been manipulated and that either the manipulation could no longer be sustained or the bubble was about to burst. While the executives sold their shares and typically enhanced their wealth, thousands of employees lost millions of dollars of accumulated wealth in stock ownership and 401-k plans. The trigger for the sale was inside information about the future viability of the company.

Motivation to Manage Earnings

Earnings can be as pliable as putty when a charlatan heads the company reporting them.

Warren Buffet (1930–)

This statement by the American investment entrepreneur Warren Buffet emphasizes the importance of having an ethical person at the head of a company because a CEO who practices fraud can twist earnings to make them look better than they really are, thereby deceiving the users of the financial statements. Recall that the public relies on the integrity of accountants and auditors to ensure that the financial statements are accurate and reliable and include all information needed by investors and creditors to make informed decisions. The quality of financial information suffers when such information is omitted or materially misstated, and the public is at a distinct disadvantage in the market place. We no longer have a level playing field in terms of investors acting on incorrect information while managers have inside information about the correct results.

Levitt attributes the practice of earnings management to the pressure on Wall Street to "make the numbers." He identifies a pattern created by earnings management whereby "companies try to meet or beat Wall Street earnings projections in order to grow market capitalization and increase the value of stock options." He notes that auditors, on the one hand, are under pressure to retain the firm's clients and on the other are under pressure by management "not to stand in the way."[2]

Levitt talks about another motivation to manage earnings: to smooth net income over time. The ideal pattern of earnings for a manager is a steady increase each year over a period of time. The results make it appear that the company is doing better than it really is and that the manager should be given credit for the positive results. The market reacts by bidding up the price of the stock, and the manager is rewarded for the results with a performance bonus and stock options with a prospective value that increases over time because of the smoothing of net income.

Levitt concludes that "these practices lead to erosion in the quality of earnings and therefore, the quality of financial reporting." The notion that accounting information should represent what it purports to represent, or representational faithfulness[3] is distorted by the use of devices such as accelerating the recognition of revenue, delaying the recognition of an expense, and creating "cookie jar reserves" to smooth net income. These techniques used to manage earnings will be discussed later.

Definition of Earnings Management

There is no generally accepted definition of *earnings management* in accounting. General agreement does exist that the end result of earnings management is to distort the application of GAAP, thereby bringing into question the ethics of the practice. The question to be answered is whether the distortion is the result of appropriate decision making given that choices exist in the application of GAAP or is motivated by a conscious effort to manipulate earnings for one's advantage, which is fraud.

There is a variety of definitions of earnings management. Schipper defines it as a "purposeful intervention in the external reporting process, with the intent of obtaining some private gain (as opposed to, say, merely facilitating the neutral operation of the process)."[4]

Healy and Wahlen define it as "when managers use judgment in financial reporting and in structuring transactions to alter financial reports to either mislead some stakeholders about the underlying economic performance of the company, or to influence contractual outcomes that depend on reported accounting numbers."[5]

Dechow and Skinner note the difficulty of operationalizing earnings management based on the reported accounting numbers because they center on managerial intent, which is unobservable. Dechow and Skinner offer their own view that a distinction should be made between making choices in determining earnings that can include aggressive, but acceptable, accounting estimates and judgments as compared to fraudulent accounting practices that are clearly intended to deceive others.[6]

Schipper's definition emphasizes a *purposeful act* by management in pursuit of its own self-interests as could be the case when earnings are manipulated to get the stock price up in advance of the exercise of stock options. Healy and Wahlen focus on *management's intent* to deceive the stakeholders by using accounting devices to positively influence reported earnings. Both definitions raise issues about the ethics of earnings management under virtue theory, which links the appropriateness of one's actions to the intent or motivation for action.

Dechow and Skinner take a different approach to earnings management because they contend the practice can be acceptable if linked to the choice of alternative accounting principles and estimates that report higher earnings than other methods could report given the circumstances. Only outright fraud is an unacceptable earnings management action.

Thomas E. McKee wrote a book on earnings management from the executive perspective. He defines earnings management as "reasonable and legal management decision making and reporting intended to achieve stable and predictable financial results." McKee believes that earnings management reflects a conscious choice by management to smooth earnings over time but does not include devices designed to "cook the books." He criticizes Schipper, Healy and Wahlen, and Dechow and Skinner for taking "unnecessarily negative view[s] of earnings management." McKee contends that a more positive definition is needed that portrays managers' motives in a positive light rather than the negative view adopted by others.[7]

Ethics of Earnings Management

The authors of this book believe that the acceptability of earnings management techniques should be judged using the ethics framework established earlier in the book. Virtue ethics examines the reasons for actions taken by the decision maker as well as the action itself. In all cases mentioned previously (Enron, WorldCom, and Tyco), the intent is to alter earnings, and the actions are motivated by self-interest and the perceived interests of the company. The stakeholders are either left out of consideration or purposefully deceived by the earnings management action.

McKee's explanation that earnings management is good because it creates a more stable and predictable earnings stream by smoothing net income cannot overcome the fact that a smooth net income by choice does not reflect what investors and creditors need or want to know because it masks true performance. Therefore, McKee's explanation for the "goodness" of earnings management is nothing more than a rationalization for an unethical act. From a virtue perspective, earnings management is unethical.

From a rights perspective, earnings management either ignores or does not consider the rights of the investors and creditors to receive accurate, reliable, and transparent financial statements. Because the ethics of the accounting profession places the public interest (investors and creditors) ahead of all other interests, earnings management is unethical from a rights perspective.

Using McKee's view of earnings management again, the right of top management to project a smooth and stable earnings flow trumps all other rights. Recall that the moral point of view in accounting emphasizes the view that the rights of others need to stressed over one's own rights in making ethical decisions.

One could be able to rationalize the ethics of earnings management from a utilitarian perspective. The decision would be made by weighing the benefits to management as individuals and the perceived benefits to the company and its shareholders with respect to increases in share price against the costs of the action with respect to the long-term negative effects on investors and creditors because of the false and misleading financial information. However, from an ethical perspective, a decision maker who rationalizes an (unethical) action that is designed to smooth earnings by claiming that it benefits the company and its stakeholders falls victim to the fraud triangle described in *SAS No. 99* and illustrated in this text in Exhibit 5.2.

Recall that according to *SAS No. 99,* the first side of the triangle develops as pressures grow to falsify earnings.[8] McKee's perspective assumes the pressure is all right because it helps to move closer to the goal of smooth earnings over time. Then, the opportunity to manipulate earnings must exist, such as top management can override internal controls. The triangle is complete when the decision maker who commits fraud attempts to rationalize it as a temporary fix to a problem.

The Acceptability of Earnings Management from a Materiality Perspective

In 1999, the SEC reacted to what it deemed to be the rationalization for not reporting on misstatements in the financial statements-based materiality considerations. The SEC *issued Staff Accounting Bulletin No.99*—Materiality.[9] In it, the SEC clearly indicated that the use of materiality criteria to dismiss material misstatements in the financial statements has no basis in law and is not acceptable. The SEC did state that the use of a percentage as a numerical threshold, such as 5 percent, could provide the basis for a preliminary assumption—without considering all relevant circumstances—a deviation of less than the specified percentage with respect to a particular item on the registrant's financial statements is unlikely to be material. However, the SEC ruled that both qualitative and quantitative factors must be considered when assessing materiality.

GemstarTV Guide International

The danger of relying only on a quantitative analysis can be seen in SEC Accounting and Auditing Enforcement Release (AAER) No. 2125 with respect to KPMG's audit of Gemstar-TV Guide International. The SEC stated that $364 million of revenue had been improperly reported and certain disclosure policies were inconsistent with Gemstar's accounting for revenue and/or did not comply with GAAP disclosure requirements. These deficiencies bear directly on the quality of financial report information.[10]

AAER No. 2125 found that the KPMG auditors concurred in Gemstar's accounting for overstated revenue from licensing and advertising transactions in March 2000, December 2000, December 2001, and March 2002. Also, KPMG did not object to Gemstar's disclosure and issued audit reports stating that KPMG had conducted its audits in conformity with GAAS and that the financial statements fairly presented its results in conformity with GAAP. In reaching these conclusions, the KPMG auditors unreasonably relied on representations by Gemstar management and/or unreasonably determined that the revenues were immaterial to Gemstar's financial statements. The KPMG auditors' materiality determinations were unreasonable in that they considered only quantitative materiality factors (i.e., that the amount of revenue was not a large percentage of Gemstar's consolidated financial results) and failed to consider qualitative materiality (i.e., that the revenue related to business lines closely watched by securities analysts and had a material effect on the valuation of Gemstar stock).

The SEC complaint reads like a "what's what" in earnings management, and it provides insight into the techniques that some companies use to manage earnings. The complaint alleges that Gemstar materially overstated its revenues by nearly $250 in the following ways:

- Recording revenue under expired, disputed, or nonexistent agreements and improperly reporting this as licensing and advertising revenue.
- Recording revenue from a long-term agreement on an accelerated basis in violation of GAAP and Gemstar's own policies that required recording and reporting such revenue ratably over the terms of the agreement (consistent with the matching theory).
- Inflating advertising revenue by improperly recording and reporting revenue amounts from multiple-element transactions.
- Engaging in "round-trip" transactions whereby Gemstar paid money to a third party to advertise its services and capitalized that cost while the third party used the funds received from Gemstar to buy advertising that was 100 percent recorded as revenue by Gemstar in the period of transaction.
- Failing to disclose that it had structured certain settlements for the purpose of creating "cookie jar reserves" of advertising revenue to smooth net income.
- Improperly recording advertising revenue from nonmonetary and barter transactions even though Gemstar could not properly establish the advertising fair value.

Gemstar's misstatements were reported in Forms 10-K, 10-Q, and the 8-K filed with the SEC. These public statements misrepresented Gemstar's true financial position and failed to disclose material information about that performance.

Professional Judgment

The auditor's consideration of materiality is a matter of professional judgment and is influenced by the perceived needs of a reasonable person. Qualitative considerations also influence the auditor in reaching a conclusion as to whether misstatements are material. Some of the relevant qualitative factors to consider follow:

- The potential effect of the misstatement on trends, especially trends in profitability.
- A misstatement that changes a loss into income or vice versa.
- The potential effect of the misstatement on the entity's compliance with loan covenants or other contractual agreements and regulatory provisions.
- The existence of statutory or regulatory reporting requirements that affect materiality thresholds.
- The sensitivity of the circumstances surrounding the misstatement, for example, increased bonuses or other forms of executive compensation, the implications of the misstatements involving fraud and possible illegal acts, and the ability to meet financial analysts' earnings expectations.[11]

Restatements of Financial Statements

A financial statement restatement occurs when a company, either voluntarily or under prompting by its auditors or regulators, revises its public financial information that had been previously reported. The number and varied restatements of financial statements by publicly owned companies have increased significantly in recent years as a result of increased scrutiny following the widely publicized accounting scandals at Enron and WorldCom.

The Huron Consulting Group reports that the number of public companies filing amended financial statements with the SEC because of restated financial statements increased from 2000 through 2005. The dramatic increase in the size of amended financial statements may reflect a heightened awareness of the need to present earnings in accordance with GAAP and closer scrutiny of a company's financial results in the post Sarbanes-Oxley years. Exhibit 7.1 presents the comparative data.[12]

EXHIBIT 7.1
Comparison
of Financial
Restatements: 2000
through 2005

	Financial Restatements	
Year	Number of U.S. Companies	Percentage Change
2000	233	—
2001	270	16%
2002	330	22
2003	511	55
2004	613	20
2005	1,195	95

Earnings Management Techniques

Schilit identifies seven common financial shenanigans. We use his framework later to discuss earnings manipulations at four companies charged by the SEC with accounting fraud. The basic techniques are explained here.[13] The number of examples is limited to three to focus only on the most common techniques within each category.

1. Recording Revenue Too Soon or That Is of Questionable Quality

This could be the most common technique because many opportunities arise to accomplish the goal including recording revenue before the earnings process has been completed or before an unconditional exchange has occurred. Schilit describes six transactions that can lead to early recognition of revenue, three of which will be discussed in this chapter:

• Recording revenue when future services remain to be provided.

• Recording revenue before shipment or before the customer's unconditional acceptance.

• Recording revenue even though the customer is not obligated to pay.[14]

2. Recording Bogus Revenue

Typically, revenue transactions "made up" to improve the numbers will lead to fictitious revenue. Schilit provided three examples:

• Recording sales that lack economic substance.

• Recording as revenue supplier rebates tied to future required purchases.

• Releasing revenue that was improperly held back before a merger.[15]

3. Boosting Income with One-Time Gains

The gains (and losses) from the sale of operating and investment assets that should be recorded in an income account can be classified in other ways if the intent is to boost operating income. These include:

• Boosting profits by selling undervalued assets.

• Including investment income or gains as part of revenue.

• Including investment income or gains as a reduction in operating expenses.[16]

4. Shifting Current Expenses to a Later or Earlier Period

A common approach used to shift expenses to a later period is by capitalizing a cost in the current period and expensing it over a period of time rather than expensing the item completely in the current period. This was the technique used by WorldCom to inflate earnings by about $11 billion. Additional examples include these:

• Changing accounting policies and shifting current expenses to an earlier period.

- Failing to write down or write off impaired assets.
- Reducing asset reserves.[17]

5. Failing to Record or Improperly Reducing Liabilities

The liability account is often used to manipulate earnings because when liability amounts that should be recorded are not, expenses are understated. When liabilities are improperly reduced, the same effect on expenses occurs. The result is to overstate earnings. Some examples follow:

- Failing to record expenses and related liabilities when future obligations remain.
- Releasing questionable reserves ("cookie jar reserves") into income.
- Recording revenue when cash is received even though future obligations remain.[18]

6. Shifting Current Revenue to a Later Period

Some companies delay recording revenue when it is relatively high in a given year. One way to accomplish this is to create a reserve with the excess revenues and release them back into the income stream at a later date when it can do more good. The technique is known as "cookie jar reserves." Here are some common examples:

- Deliberately overstating the allowance for uncollectibles and adjusting it downward in future years.
- Deliberately overstating the estimated sales returns account and adjusting it downward in future years.[19]

7. Shifting Future Expenses to the Current Period as a Special Charge

A company could choose to accelerate discretionary expenses such as repairs and maintenance into the current period if the current years' revenue is relatively high in relation to expected future revenue or future expenses are expected to be relatively high. The motivation to shift future expenses to the current period could be to smooth net income over time. Some examples include:

- Inflating a special charge amount
- Writing off R & D costs from an acquisition
- Accelerating discretionary expenses

On the other hand, delaying repairs and expense, a technique that McKee undoubtedly would label as appropriate given the goal of providing smooth and predictable earnings, raises several ethical issues because it creates a risk that machines could break down prematurely with the following possible effects: (1) the quality of product suffers, (2) production slows and fails to meet deadlines, (3) costs to repair the machines are actually higher than they would have been had maintenance been completed on a timely basis, and (4) customer goodwill is lost.

These possible results of a decision to delay repair and maintenance clearly have ethical implications for a variety of stakeholders including investors (lack of full disclosure about the condition of machines and new policy), employees (efficiency could suffer through no fault of their own and could affect bonus payments received), and customers (upset because of a possible delay in receiving final product and possible quality issues).

Descriptions of Financial Shenanigans

In this section, we describe financial shenanigans that occurred at four companies: Waste Management, Xerox, Lucent, and Sunbeam during the mid-1990s to early 2000s. These companies were chosen because they illustrate many of the techniques identified by Schilit.

The Case of Waste Management

On June 19, 2001, the SEC brought an action against Arthur Andersen for its audit of Waste Management, charging that Andersen had issued materially false and misleading audit reports on Waste Management, Inc.'s financial statements for the period 1993 through 1996. For each year 1993 through 1996, Andersen had issued an audit report on Waste Management's financial statements stating that the company's financial statements were presented fairly, in all material respects, in conformity with GAAP and that Andersen had conducted its audit of those statements in accordance with GAAS. The SEC found that Andersen's representations were materially false and misleading.

In February 1998, Waste Management announced that it was restating its financial statements for the five-year period 1992 through 1996 and the first three quarters of 1997.[20] The company's pretax earnings were overstated by $1.43 billion through 1996, the largest restatement until WorldCom's announcement on June 26, 2002, that it had inflated income by approximately $3.8 billion, which was eventually increased to about $11 billion.

Aggressive Accounting Practices

In its consent agreement with Andersen, the SEC points out that, "As early as 1988, members of Andersen's audit engagement team recognized that Waste Management employed 'aggressive' accounting practices to enhance its earnings, some of which violated GAAP." These practices understated operating expenses or delayed their recognition to another accounting period, thereby increasing current period income. They included, among other things, the following aggressive practices:

- The increase of useful life of depreciable assets.
- Non-GAAP method of capitalizing interest on landfill development costs.
- Failure to properly accrue tax and self-insurance expense.
- Improper charges of operating expenses to the environmental remediation reserves (liabilities).
- Refusal to write off permitting and/or project costs on impaired or abandoned landfills.

The Role of Arthur Andersen

The Andersen partners applied an analytical procedure for evaluating the materiality of audit findings referred to as the "roll forward" method.[21] Utilizing the method, these partners determined that because the majority of postaudit journal entries (PAJEs) concerned prior period misstatements, the impact of the PAJEs to current period misstatements on the company's 1993 financial statements was not material. The partners instructed the lead engagement partner to inform the company that Andersen would issue an unqualified audit report.

The partners also instructed the lead partner to emphasize that Andersen expected the company to change its accounting practices and to reduce the cumulative amount of the PAJEs in the future. In fact, a proposed plan called a Summary of Action Steps was developed to reduce the cumulative amount of the PAJEs and to change, among other things, the accounting practices that give rise to the PAJEs and to other known and likely misstatements. The proposed plan outlined action steps to be taken that were characterized as "must do" to write off the cumulative amount of the PAJEs to correct for aggressive accounting over five to seven years. The action steps were agreed to and signed off by Waste Management's CEO, CFO, and CAO.

Waste Management did not follow the agreed-to plans, however, and new items surfaced that further tested Andersen's willingness to bend the rules of GAAP. On December 31,

1995, Waste Management exchanged investment interests in two companies that created a $160 million gain. In its 1995 financial statements, the company used the gain to offset $160 million in unrelated operating expenses and misstatements identified in prior years PAJEs. The offset of the gain against the expenses was shown in the Sundry Income, Net account. The amount netted represented 10 percent of the 1995 pretax income before special charges. The company made no disclosure of the netting in the notes to its financial statements or in management's discussion and analysis (MD&A), thereby bringing into question the quality of financial reporting.

The Andersen partners knew that Waste Management's proposed treatment netting the gain against operating expenses was not in conformity with GAAP and instead should be reported separately in the consolidated income statement with a discussion in the MD&A and footnotes. In fact, a discussion was held about its appropriateness with the firm's practice director, who concluded that "although the netting did not conform to GAAP and the netted items would not be disclosed, Andersen did not need to qualify or withhold its audit report." The reason given was that these amounts were not material to the company's 1995 financial statements taken as a whole. The SEC concluded that the amount was material; the misstatements represented 10 percent of pretax income.

On June 19, 2001, the SEC issued a civil injunction against Andersen in the Waste Management case whereby the firm consented to (1) the entry of a permanent injunction enjoining it from violating sections 10(b) and 10b-5 of the Securities Exchange Act of 1934, (2) pay a civil money penalty in the amount of $7 million, and (3) a censure based on the SEC's finding that Andersen had engaged in improper professional conduct and the issuance of the permanent injunction. The ink on the agreement barely had time to dry when, on December 2, 2001, Enron, Andersen's most infamous client, filed for Chapter 11 protection in the United States.

The Case of Xerox

Motivation for Fraudulent Scheme of Top Management

On June 3, 2003, the SEC filed a civil fraud injunctive action in the U.S. District Court for the Southern District of New York charging six former senior executives of Xerox Corporation, including its former CEOs Paul Allaire and G. Richard Thoman and former CFO Barry D. Romeril with securities fraud and aiding and abetting Xerox's violations of the reporting, books and records, and internal control provisions of the federal securities laws. The complaint charged the former executives with engaging in a fraudulent scheme that lasted from 1997 to 2000 that misled investors about Xerox's earnings to "polish its reputation on Wall Street and to boost the company's stock price."[22]

The quality of the financial reports came into question because Xerox failed to disclose GAAP violations that led to acceleration in the recognition of approximately $3 billion in equipment revenues and an increase in pretax earnings by approximately $1.4 billion in Xerox's 1997–2000 financial results. The executives agreed to pay more than $22 million in penalties, disgorgement, and interest without admitting or denying the SEC's allegations.

The Litigation Release notes the ethical tone at the top set by CEOs Allaire and Thomas and CFO Romeril, which equated business success with meeting short-term earnings targets. Romeril directed or allowed lower ranking defendants in Xerox's financial department to make accounting adjustments to results reported from operating divisions to accelerate revenues and increase earnings. These individuals utilized accounting methods to meet earnings goals and predictions of outside securities analysts. Allaire and Thomas then announced these results to the public through meetings with analysts and in communications to shareholders, celebrating that Xerox was enjoying substantially higher earnings growth than the true operating results warranted.

Fraudulent Accounting Devices

A description of two selected fraudulent accounting devices follows.

1. Fraudulent Lease Accounting   Xerox sold copiers and other office equipment to its customers for cash, but more frequently entered into long-term lease agreements in which customers paid a single negotiated monthly fee in return for the equipment, service, supplies, and financing. Xerox referred to these arrangements as "bundled leases."

The leases met the criteria under *Statement of Financial Accounting Standards (SFAS) No. 13* to be accounted for as "sales-type" lease whereby the fair value of the equipment leased would be recognized as income in the period the lease is delivered less any residual value the equipment is expected to retain when the lease expires. GAAP permits the financing revenue portion of the lease to be recognized only as it is earned over the life of the lease. *SFAS No. 13* also specifies that the portion of the lease payments that represents the fee for repair services and copier supplies should be prorated over the term of the lease, matching it against the financing income.

Until the mid-1990s, Xerox followed satisfactory procedures for revenue recognition. However, it encountered more copier sales competition around the world and perceived a need to continue reporting record earnings. Management told KPMG that it was no longer able to reasonably assign a fair value to the equipment as it had in the past. The company abandoned the value determinations made at the lease inception for public financial reporting purposes but not for internal operating purposes and substituted a formula that management could manipulate at will. Xerox did not test the value determinations to assess the reliability of the original method or whether the new method did a better job of accurately reflecting the fair value of copier equipment.[23]

Xerox's "topside" lease accounting devices consistently increased the amount of lease revenues that Xerox recognized at the inception of the lease and reduced the amount it recognized over the life of the lease. One method called ROE (for return on equity) pulled forward a portion of finance income and recognized it immediately as equipment revenue. The second method, margin normalization, pulled forward a portion of service income and recognized it immediately as equipment revenue. These income acceleration methods did not comply with GAAP because there was no matching of revenue with the period during which (1) financing was provided, (2) copier supplies were provided, and (3) repairs were made to the leased equipment.

2. "Cushion" Reserves   From 1997 through 2000, Xerox violated GAAP through the use of approximately $496 million of reserves to close the gap between actual results and earnings targets. Xerox had created reserves through charges to income prior to 1997. These cookie jar reserves were released into income to make the numbers look better than they really were. The result was a smoothing of net income over time. This practice violated *SFAS No. 5,* Accounting for Contingencies, which allows a company to establish reserves only for identifiable, probable, and estimable risks and precludes the use of reserves, including excess reserves, for general or unknown business risks because they do not meet the accrual requirements of *SFAS No. 5.*

KPMG's Sanctions by the SEC

The SEC issued a cease-and-desist order against KPMG LLP on April 19, 2005, for its role in auditing the financial statements of Xerox during the 1997 through 2000 period. AAER No. 2234 details KPMG's consent to institute a variety of quality control measures including the provision of oversight of engagement partner changes of audit personnel and related independence issues.[24]

On February 22, 2006, the SEC announced that all four remaining KPMG staff in the action in connection with the $1.2 billion fraudulent earnings manipulation scheme by Xerox from 1997 through 2000 had agreed to settle the charges against them. Three of the current or former KPMG partners agreed to permanent injunctions, payment of $400,000 in penalties, and suspensions from practice before the SEC. All four partners were charged with filing materially false and misleading financial statements with the SEC and aiding and abetting Xerox's filing of false financial reports. The SEC charged that the partners knew or should have known about improper "topside adjustments" that resulted in $3 billion of the restated revenues and $1.2 billion of the restated earnings.[25]

The concurring review partner on the audit engagement team was cited because the adjustments enabled Xerox to change the allocations of revenues it received from leasing photocopiers and other types of office equipment. The partner agreed to a censure by the SEC for failing to exercise due care and professional skepticism and to adhere to GAAS.[26]

Xerox paid a record fine of $10 million. On April 20, 2005, KPMG settled with the SEC over the financial fraud at Xerox, agreeing to pay $10 million in penalties in addition to disgorging nearly $10 million in audit fees and another $2.7 million in interest.

The Case of Lucent Technologies

On May 20, 2004, the SEC charged Lucent Technologies, Inc., with securities fraud and violations of the reporting, books and records, and internal control provisions of the federal securities laws. It also charged nine current and former Lucent officers, executives, and employees with securities fraud and aiding and abetting the violations of federal securities laws. The SEC complaint alleges that Lucent fraudulently and improperly recognized approximately $1.148 billion of revenue and $470 million in pretax income during the fiscal year 2000. As part of the settlement, Lucent agreed to pay a $25 million penalty for its lack of cooperation.

The Lucent case is typical of the frauds that occurred in the late 1990s and early 2000s. The company's accounting techniques violated GAAP and were motivated by its drive to realize revenue, meet internal sales targets, and obtain sales bonuses for management. Top management either violated or circumvented internal controls. The board of directors and audit committee were either not involved or turned away from their obligations.

According to AAER No. 2016,[27] Lucent officers improperly granted and/or failed to disclose various side agreements, credits, and other incentives (extracontractual commitments) made to induce its customers to purchase the company's products. The premature recognition of revenue occurred by "selling" $135 million in software to a customer that could choose from a software pool by September 29, 2001, and Lucent recognized $135 million in revenue in its fiscal year ending September 30, 2000. The parties reached an agreement to separately document additional elements of the software pool transaction that would give the customer additional value in the form of side agreements. Top management postdated three letters documenting the side agreements with fictitious dates in October 2000. The effect of the postdated letters was to create the appearance that the side agreements were reached after September 30, 2000, and were not connected to the software pool agreement.

This and other transactions engaged in by Lucent enabled the company to manage earnings in a way that smoothed net income over time. Lucent's story as a separate entity began in April 1996 when AT&T spun off the company. Schilit points out that Lucent's stock price increased from a low of about $14 per share on January 1, 1997, to a high of about $78 by September 1999. The stock price began to decline after that to a low of about $7 per share on January 1, 2002.[28]

By 1999, operating income had reached $5.4 billion, tripling in two years. Moreover, net income had grown more than tenfold during that time period. The auditors either did not notice or ignored these red flags. These amounts and percentage changes in net income are presented in Exhibits 7.2 and 7.3.[29]

The earnings trend continued through 2000. The earnings manipulations can be matched with the following shenanigans presented in Exhibit 7.4 to smooth net income.[30]

EXHIBIT 7.2
Lucent Technologies, Inc.

Source: Howard Schilit, *Financial Shenanigans*, 2nd Edition (New York, NY: McGraw-Hill/Irwin, 2002).

Sales and Income Amounts			
Item	September 1999	September 1998	September 1997
Sales	$48.3 billion	$31.8 billion	$27.6 billion
Operating income	5.4 billion	2.6 billion	1.6 billion
Net income	4.8 billion	1.0 billion	0.4 billion

EXHIBIT 7.3
Lucent Technologies, Inc.

Source: Howard Schilit, *Financial Shenanigans*, 2nd Edition (New York, NY: McGraw-Hill/Irwin, 2002).

Percentage Changes in Income Accounts		
	September 1998 to September 1999	September 1997 to September 1998
Sales	52%	15%
Operating income	104	63
Net income	380	150

EXHIBIT 7.4   Lucent Technologies, Inc.: Financial Shenanigans

Source: Howard Schilit, *Financial Shenanigans*, 2nd Edition (New York, NY: McGraw-Hill/Irwin, 2002).

Technique	Description	Shenanigan Number
Recorded revenue too soon	Restated year 2000 earnings, removing $679 improperly included revenue	No. 1
Boosted income with one-time gains	During fiscal 1998, recorded $558 of pension income—over 50% of earnings for the year	No. 3
Failed to write down impaired assets	Reduced the allowance for doubtful accounts and released the previous reserves despite an increase in receivables of 32%	No. 4
Shifted current expenses to a later period	Reduced the allowance for inventory obsolescence although the inventory balance increased	No. 4
Reduced liabilities by changing accounting assumptions	Modified its accounting approach and assumptions for pensions	No. 5
Released reserves into income	Released $100 million of a previously recorded restructuring reserve, boosting operating income	No. 5
Created new reserves from 10 acquisitions	Wrote off $2.4 billion (58% of the cumulative purchase price) as in-process R&D. This new reserve could later be released into earnings	No. 7

The Case of Sunbeam Corporation

One of the earliest frauds was at Sunbeam. The SEC alleged in its charges against Sunbeam that top management engaged in a scheme to fraudulently misrepresent Sunbeam's operating results in connection with a purported "turnaround" of the company. When Sunbeam's turnaround was exposed as a sham, its stock price plummeted, causing investors to lose billions of dollars. The defendants in the action included Sunbeam's former CEO and chairman Albert J. Dunlap, former principal financial officer Russell A. Kersh, former controller Robert J. Gluck, and former vice-presidents Donald R. Uzzi and Lee B. Griffith, as well as Arthur Andersen LLP partner Phillip Harlow.[31]

The SEC complaint describes several questionable management decisions and fraudulent actions that led to the manipulation of financial statement amounts in the company's 1996 year-end results, quarterly and year-end 1997 results, and first quarter 1998 results. The fraud was enabled by weak or nonexistent internal controls, inadequate or nonexistent board of directors and audit committee oversight, and the failure of the Andersen auditor to follow GAAS. A brief summary of the case follows.

Chainsaw Al

Al Dunlap, a turnaround specialist who had gained the nickname "Chainsaw Al" for his reputation of cutting companies to the bone, was hired by Sunbeam's board in July 1996 to restructure the financially ailing company. He promised a rapid turnaround, thereby raising expectations in the market place. The fraudulent actions he took helped to raise the market price of its stock to a high of $52 per share in 1997. After the disclosure of the fraud in the first quarter of 1998, Sunbeam's share price dropped by 25 percent to $34.63. The price continued to decline as the board of directors investigated the fraud and fired Dunlap and the CFO. An extensive restatement of earnings from the fourth quarter of 1996 through the first quarter of 1998 eliminated one-half of the reported 1997 profits. On February 6, 2001, Sunbeam filed for Chapter 11 bankruptcy protection under U.S. Bankruptcy Court.

Cookie Jar Reserves

The illegal conduct began in late 1996 with the creation of cookie jar reserves that were then used to inflate income in 1997. Sunbeam then engaged in fraudulent revenue transactions that inflated the company's record-setting earnings of $189 million by at least $60 million in 1997. The transactions were designed to create the impression that Sunbeam was experiencing significant revenue growth, thereby further misleading the investors and financial markets.

Channel Stuffing

Anxious to extend the selling season for its gas grills and to boost sales in 1996, CEO Dunlap's "turnaround year," the company tried to convince retailers to buy grills nearly six months before they were needed in exchange for major discounts. Retailers agreed to purchase merchandise that they would not physically receive until six months after billing. In the meantime, the goods were shipped to a third-party warehouse and held there until the customers requested them. These "bill-and-hold" transactions led to recording $35 million in revenue too soon. However, the auditors (Andersen) reviewed the documents and reversed $29 million.[32]

In 1997, the company failed to disclose that Sunbeam's 1997 revenue growth was, in part, achieved again at the expense of future results. The company had offered discounts and other inducements to customers to sell merchandise immediately that otherwise would have been sold in later periods, a practice referred to as *channel stuffing*. The resulting revenue shift threatened to suppress Sunbeam's future results of operations.

Sunbeam either did not realize or totally ignored the fact that by stuffing the channels with product to make one year look better, the company had to continue to find outlets for its product in advance of when customers desired it. In other words, the practice created a balloon effect in that the same amount or a higher amount of accelerated revenue was needed year after year. Ultimately, Sunbeam (and its customers) just could not keep up, and there was no way for Sunbeam to fix the numbers.[33]

Sunbeam's Shenanigans

Exhibit 7.5 presents Schilit's analysis of Sunbeam's accounting that identifies three forms of aggressive accounting that fit into three of the seven shenanigans.[34]

Schilit also points to red flags that should have helped the auditors to identify the fraud at Sunbeam including these:

1. *Excessive charges shortly after Dunlap arrived.* The theory here is that an in-coming CEO will create cookie jar reserves by overstating expenses even though it reduces earnings for the first year based on the belief that increases in future earnings through the release of the reserves or other techniques makes it appear that the CEO has turned

EXHIBIT 7.5
Sunbeam
Corporation:
Aggressive
Accounting
Techniques

Source: Howard Schilit,
Financial Shenanigans, 2nd
Edition (New York, NY:
McGraw-Hill/Irwin, 2002).

Technique	Example	Shenanigan number
Recorded bogus revenue	Bill and hold sales	No. 2
Released questionable reserves into income	Cookie jar reserves	No. 5
Inflated special charges	Created a litigation reserve	No. 7

the company around as evidenced by turning losses into profits. Some companies could take it to an extreme and pile on losses by creating reserves in a loss year, believing that it did not matter whether it showed a $1.2 million loss or a $1.8 million loss ($.6 million reserve) for the year. This is known as the *big bath theory.*

2. *Watch for a decline in those reserves.* Fluctuations in the reserve amount should raise a red flag because it evidences earnings management. The use of the word *reserves* in accounting is restricted. While students could be more familiar with the terminology *allowance for uncollectibles,* banks typically refer to their allowance as a *reserve for loan loss.*

3. *Watch for receivables growing much faster than sales.* A simple ratio of the increase in receivables to the increase in revenues provides another warning signal. Schilit provides the following for Sunbeam's operational performance in Exhibit 7.6.[35]

4. *Compare accrual earnings with cash from operating activities.* While Sunbeam made $189 million in 1997, its cash flow from operating activities was (60.8 million). This is a $250 million difference that should have raised a red flag even under a cursory analytical review. Accrual earnings and cash flow from operating activity amounts are not expected to be equal. Financial analysts tend to rely on the cash figure because of the inherent unreliability of the estimates and judgments that go into determining accrual earnings.

The Story of Enron

The uniqueness of the decisions and manipulations at Enron and its link to the passage of the Sarbanes-Oxley Act (SOX) warrants a detailed discussion. The "story of Enron" is one of structuring financial transactions to keep debt off the books and report higher earnings.

In the Beginning . . .

Enron was created in 1985 through Omaha-based InterNorth Inc.'s takeover of Houston Natural Gas Corp. InterNorth paid a huge premium for Houston Natural Gas, creating $5 million in debt. The company's debt payments of $50 million a month quickly led to the sell-off of billions of dollars' worth of assets. Its debt load was so high that it forced the company into financing projects with borrowings that were kept off the balance sheet.

Jeff Skilling, who worked for the company, suggested that Enron's problems were due to a fluid market for natural gas; the industry needed long-term supply contracts. Prices were

EXHIBIT 7.6
Sunbeam
Corporation

Source: Howard Schilit,
Financial Shenanigans, 2nd
Edition (New York, NY:
McGraw-Hill/Irwin, 2002).

	Operational Performance ($ millions)		
	9 months 9/97	9 months 9/96	Change %
Revenue	830.1	715.4	16%
Gross profit	231.1	123.1	86
Operating revenue	132.6	4.0	3215
Receivables	309.1	194.6	59
Inventory	290.9	330.2	12
Cash flow from operations	(60.8)	(18.8)	N/A

volatile, however, and contracts were available only for 30-day spot deals. Producers were unwilling to commit to the long term, always believing the price could go up.

Skilling's "Gas Bank" Idea

Enron needed to find a way to bridge the gap between what the producers and big gas users wanted. Skilling discussed ways to pool the investments in gas-supply contracts and then sell long-term deals to utilities through a "gas bank." The gas bank called for Enron to write long-term contracts enabling it to start accounting for those contracts differently. Traditionally, accounting books revenue from a long-term contract when it comes in, but Skilling wanted Enron to book all *anticipated* revenue immediately as if it was writing up a marketable security. The technique lends itself to earnings management because of the subjectivity involved in estimating future market value.

Counting all expected profits immediately meant a huge earnings kick for a company that was getting deeply into debt, but it also put Enron on a treadmill: To keep growing, it would have to book bigger and bigger deals every quarter. The result was to shift focus from developing economically sound partnerships to doing deals at all costs.

The marketplace did not seem to like the Enron deals. The initial gas bank plan had not persuaded gas producers to sell Enron their reserves. To entice the producers, the company needed to offer them money up front for gas that would be delivered later. The problem was where to get the cash.

Fastow's Special-Purpose Entities

In 1991, to revitalize the gas bank, Enron's CFO Andy Fastow began creating a number of partnerships. The first series was called Cactus. The Cactus ventures eventually took in money from banks and gave it to energy producers in return for a portion of their existing gas reserves. That gave the producers money up front and Enron gas over time.

Fastow worked to structure ventures that met the conditions under GAAP to keep the partnership activities off Enron's books and on the separate books of the partnership. To do so, the equity financing of the partnership venture had to include a minimum of 3 percent ownership. Control was not established through traditional means, which was the ownership of a majority of voting equity and combining of the partnership entity into the sponsoring organization (Enron), as is done with parent and subsidiary entities in a consolidation. Instead, the independent third parties were required to have a controlling and substantial interest in the entity. Control was established by the third-party investors exercising management rights over the entity's operations. There were a lot of "Monday morning quarterbacks" in the accounting profession who questioned the economic logic of attributing even the possibility of control to those who owned only 3 percent of the capital.

Bethany McLean and Peter Elkind are two *Fortune* magazine reporters credited with prompting the inquiries and investigations that brought down the Enron house of cards. McLean had written a story posing the simple question, "How, exactly, does Enron make its money?"[36] Well, in the go-go years of the 1990s, all too often no one asked this kind of question or, perhaps, did not care about what the answer could be.

According to McLean and Elkind, a small group of investors was pulled together known internally as the Friends of Enron. When Enron needed the 3 percent, it turned to the friends. These business associates and friends of Fastow and others were independent only in a technical sense. Although they made money on their investment, they did not control the entities or the assets within in them. "This, of course, was precisely the point."[37]

The 3 percent investments triggered a *special purpose vehicle or special purpose entity* (SPE). The advantage of the independent partnership relationship was that the SPE *borrowed* money from banks and other financial institutions that were willing to loan money to it with an obligation to repay the debt. The money borrowed by the SPE was often "transferred" to Enron in a sale of an operating asset that Enron no longer needed. The sale transaction typically led to a recorded gain because the cash proceeds exceeded the book value of the asset sold. Exhibit 7.7 depicts the typical relationship.

The SPE enabled Enron to keep debt off its books while benefiting from the transfer and use of the cash borrowed by the SPE. To enhance the attractiveness of the structured transaction, Enron would add to its managed earnings by "selling" an underperforming operating asset to the SPE at a gain. The result was increased cash flow and liquidity and inflated earnings. The uniqueness of the transactions engaged in by Enron was that they initially did not violate GAAP. Instead, Enron took advantage of the rules to structure transactions that enabled it to achieve its goals for enhanced liquidity and profitability.

The Growth of SPEs

Eventually, Enron would grow addicted to these arrangements because they hid debt. Not only did the company turn to its "friends" but also increasingly had to borrow from banks and financial institutions it did business with. After all, these entities did not want to turn down a company like Enron that was, at its peak, the seventh largest in the United States. Enron let the risk-shifting feature of the partnerships lapse, however, negating their conformity with GAAP. Over time, the financial institutions that were involved in providing the 3 percent for the SPEs became concerned of the SPEs' ability to repay the interest when due. These institutions asked Enron to relieve the risk of the SPEs' failure to repay the investments. Later, partnership deals were backed by promises of Enron stock. This meant that, if something went wrong, Enron would be left holding the bag. The result was that there was no transfer of risk to the SPE, a condition of the GAAP rules to treat the entity as separate, not consolidate it with Enron.

EXHIBIT 7.7
Enron Corporation:
How a Special-
Purpose Entity Works

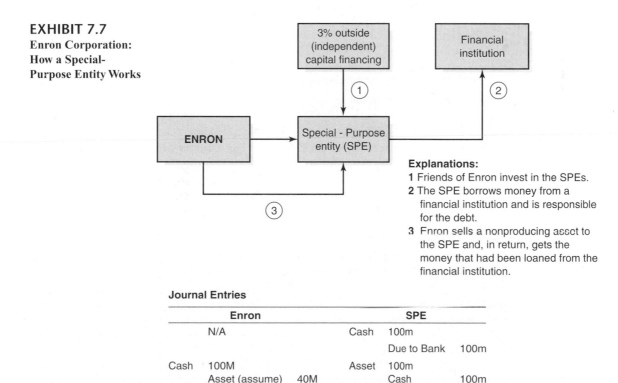

Explanations:
1 Friends of Enron invest in the SPEs.
2 The SPE borrows money from a financial institution and is responsible for the debt.
3 Enron sells a nonproducing asset to the SPE and, in return, gets the money that had been loaned from the financial institution.

Journal Entries

Enron			SPE		
N/A			Cash	100m	
			Due to Bank		100m
Cash	100M		Asset	100m	
	Asset (assume)	40M	Cash		100m
	Gain on sale	60M			

The Culture at Enron

The tension in the workplace grew with employees working later and later, first until 6 p.m., then 11 p.m., and finally into the next morning. Part of the pressure resulted from Skilling's new employee evaluation policy. Workers called it "rank and yank." Employees were evaluated in groups, with each rated on a scale of 1 to 5. The goal was to remove the bottom 20 percent of each group every year.

Ultimately, the system was seen as a tool for managers to reward loyalists and punish dissenters. It was seen as a cutthroat system and encouraged a "yes" culture in which employees were reluctant to question their bosses—a fear that many would later come to regret.

Let the Force Be with You

In late 1997, Enron entered a number of partnerships to improperly inflate earnings and hide debt. Enron created Chewco, named after the *Star Wars* character Chewbacca, to buy out its partner JEDI in another venture, which was legally kept off the books. For JEDI to remain off the balance sheet, however, Chewco had to meet certain accounting requirements (a minimum 3 percent ownership). Enron skirted the already weak rules required to keep Chewco off its books, however, and JEDI helped to overstate Enron's profits by $405 million and understate debt of $2.6 billion.

Because Enron needed to close the deal by year-end, Chewco was a rush job. Enron's executive committee presented the Chewco proposal to the board of directors, including Kenneth Lay, on November 5. Fastow left out a few key details, however: He failed to mention that there was virtually no outside ownership in Chewco, which he maintained was not affiliated with Enron. Nor did he reveal that one of his protégés, Michael Kopper, would manage the partnership. Indirectly if not directly, Fastow would control the partnership through Kopper. Enron had a code of ethics that prohibited an officer from becoming involved with another entity that did business with Enron. Involvement by Fastow in these related-party entities was forbidden by the code. Nevertheless, the board of directors waived that requirement so Fastow could become involved with Chewco.

The board approved the deal even though Enron's law firm, Vinson & Elkins, prepared the requisite documents so quickly that very few people actually read it before approving it. Arthur Andersen, the firm that both audited Enron and did significant internal audit work for the company (pre-Sarbanes Oxley), claimed that Enron withheld critical information. The firm billed the company only $80,000 for its review of the transaction, indicating a cursory review at best. Chewco, Fastow's involvement, the board approval, and a rapid approval process all came together because of a lack of internal controls. The Star Wars' transactions were the beginning of the end for Enron because Chewco was inappropriately treated as a separate entity even though Fastow was involved in the SPE's management and the investment was inappropriately kept off the books of Enron. When Enron finally collapsed, its off-balance-sheet financing stood at an estimated $17 billion.

Enron Just Keeps on Going

The greatest pressures were in Fastow's finance group. In 1999, he constructed two partnerships, LJM Cayman and LJM2 that readily passed through the board, the lawyers, and the accountants. They were followed by four more, known as the *Raptors.* Fastow and Enron used SPEs once; it worked, so they did it again. It did not take long to blur the lines between what is legal and what is not. When one employee in the finance group was asked by a student what he did at Enron, he answered by saying, "I remove numbers from our balance sheet and inflate earnings."

As Enron pushed into new directions—wind power, water, high-speed Internet, paper, metals, data storage, advertising—it became a different company almost every quarter. Entrepreneurship was encouraged; innovation was the mantra. The quarter-by-quarter scramble to post ever better numbers became all-consuming. Enron traders were encouraged to use *prudence reserves,* to essentially put aside some revenue until another quarter when it could be needed. Long-term energy contracts were evaluated using an adjustable curve to forecast energy prices. When a quarter looked tight, analysts were told to simply adjust the curve in Enron's favor.

Executive Compensation

Enron's goal of setting its executive pay in the 75th percentile of its peer group, including companies like Duke Energy, Dynegy, and PG&E to which it compared itself to assess overall corporate performance, was easily exceeded. In 2000 base salary, Enron exceeded the peer group average by 51 percent. In bonus payments, it outdistanced its peers by 383 percent. The stock options granted in 2000—valued at the time of grant at $86.5 million—exceeded the number granted by peers by 484 percent. Top management became accustomed to the large payouts and the desire for more became of part of the culture of greed at Enron.

While Enron was the first player into the new energy market enabling it to score huge gains, over time competitors caught on, and profit margins shrank. Skilling began looking for new pastures and in 1996, he set his sights on electricity. Enron would do for power what it had done for natural gas. The push into electricity only added to the pressures boiling inside Enron. Earlier in 1996, Ken Lay, Enron's CEO, had predicted that the company's profits would double by 2000. This was a statement that would come back to haunt Lay in his civil trial in 2006, alleging that he knowingly hyped Enron's stock to keep funds flowing even though he knew the company was coming apart at the seams.

Lay pushed on as if nothing was wrong. Enron instituted a stock option plan that promised to double employee salaries after eight years. Fresh off a $2.1 billion takeover of Portland General Corp., an electric utility, Lay said his goal was nothing less than to make Enron the world's greatest energy company.

Enron found another way to get the executives going. It gave out stock options that would provide cash over time and added the sweetener that if profits and the stock price went up enough, the schedule for those options would be sharply accelerated. It provided the incentive to find ways to increase profits and improve stock price, all in the name of greed. Essentially, Enron had created a culture of the pursuit of self-interest.

Because the stock did well—until its slide and Enron's ultimate bankruptcy in December 2001— Enron executives did extremely well. But while the stock market could have favored Enron executives on the way out, their gilded path was laid out well in advance by the Enron board's inattentiveness and oblivious largesse.

Congressional Investigation

In 2000, Skilling was granted 867,880 options to buy shares in addition to his salary and bonus totaling $6.45 million. In that year, he exercised and sold more than 1.1 million shares from options he had received in prior years and pocketed $62.48 million.

Skilling testified before Congress that he did not dump Enron shares as he told others to buy because he knew or suspected that the company was in financial trouble. Skilling's increase in shares of Enron was due to more and more options. Even under Enron's option plan, in which options vested fully in three years, an unusually quick rate, Skilling wound up holding many Enron shares he could not legally sell.

The board granted the then Chairman and CEO Ken Lay 782,380 options on top of his salary and bonus of $8.3 million, plus perks valued at $381,155. He sold about 2.3 million shares for $123.4 million.

The House of Cards Comes Tumbling Down

Lay and Skilling used as their defense in their 2006 civil trial that Enron was a successful company brought down by a crisis of confidence in the market. The government contended that Enron appeared successful but actually hid its failures through dubious, even criminal, accounting tricks. In fact, Enron by most measures was not particularly profitable, a fact obscured by its share price until later. There was one area, however, in which it succeeded like few others: executive compensation.

As the stock market began to decline in the late 1990s, Enron's stock followed the downward trend. The never-ending number of deals even as business slowed gave pause to Wall Street. By April 2001, concerns as to whether the company was adequately disclosing financial information from its off-balance-sheet financing transactions mounted.

The pressure continued both internally and externally from a slowing economy, competition from other entities that had caught on to Enron's gimmicks, and stock market declines. Differences of opinion exist as to why Skilling made the decision, but on August 14, 2001, he, who just six months prior had been named the CEO of Enron, resigned. He gave as his public reason the ever popular, "I need to spend more time with my family." However, Enron executive Sherron Watkins was dubious and sent an anonymous letter to Ken Lay, who now served as CEO and chair of the board of directors, warning Lay of an impending scandal.

Sherron Watkins' Role   "Has Enron become a risky place to work? For those of us who did not get rich over the last few years, can we afford to stay?" Sherron Watkins' words were in an unsigned letter sent to Ken Lay after he had encouraged employees to write about their concerns anonymously. She described in detail problems with Enron's partnerships, problems that the letter claimed would cause huge financial upheavals at the company in as little as a year. "I am incredibly nervous that we will implode in a wave of accounting scandals," the letter's author wrote. "Skilling is resigning for 'personal reasons,' but I think he wasn't having fun, looked down the road and knew this stuff was unfixable and would rather abandon ship now than resign in shame in two years."[38]

Lay took a copy of the letter to James V. Derrick, Jr., Enron's general counsel, who agreed it needed to be investigated. They decided to assign the task to Vinson & Elkins, which had helped prepare some of the legal documents for some of the partnerships. Enron wanted answers fast, seemingly regardless of the due diligence, and the company instructed the outside lawyers not to spend time examining the accounting treatment recommended by Arthur Andersen, although that was at the heart of the letter's warnings.

Powers Committee Report

Vinson & Elkins began its investigation. Even while they investigated Fastow's role, the conflicts mounted. Kopper, who had sold his Chewco assets to Enron to deflect criticisms of Fastow's role, made a profit on the sale and then insisted that Enron cover the $2.6 million tax liability from the sale. The Powers Committee, formed by the audit committee to investigate the failure of Enron, concluded on this matter: "There is credible evidence that Fastow authorized Enron's payment to Chewco," adding that the payment, made against the explicit instructions of Enron's general counsel, was "one of the most serious issues we identified in connection with the Chewco buyout."[39]

Three days after beginning their investigation, the Vinson & Elkins lawyers investigating Watkins' warnings reported their findings to Lay and Derrick that there was no reason for concern. Everything in Fastow's operation seemed to be on the level. They promised a written report in a matter of weeks. By then, it would be too late.

The Final Days

In November 2001, Enron announced that it had overstated earnings by $586 million since 1997. In December 2001, Enron made the largest bankruptcy filing ever. By January 2002, the Justice Department confirmed an investigation of Enron. The very next day, Andersen admitted to shredding documents related to its audit of Enron, an act of obstructing justice that would doom the firm following a Department of Justice lawsuit. It hardly mattered what the outcome of the lawsuit would be; Enron's clients started to abandon the firm in droves after the announcement of the lawsuit. Ultimately, the jury decided that the firm had obstructed justice, a decision that would be overturned later due to a technicality.

The Lay-Skilling Criminal Trial

Following the unanimous jury verdict on May 26, 2006, that found both Ken Lay and Jeff Skilling guilty of fraud and conspiracy, Lay was quoted as saying "Certainly we're surprised." Skilling commented, "I think it's more appropriate to say we're shocked. This is not the outcome we expected."[40] Nothing more supports our statements throughout this book about the link between one's personal and professional ethics than these decisions against Lay and Skilling.

Skilling was convicted of 19 counts of fraud, conspiracy, and insider trading. Lay was convicted on six counts in the joint trial and four charges of bank fraud and making false statements to banks in a separate nonjury trial before U.S. District Judge Sam Lake related to Lay's personal finances. The sentencing for Lay and Skilling, somewhat ironically, was set for September 11, 2006. If convicted on all counts, Skilling would serve 185 years in prison. For Lay, the fraud and conspiracy convictions carried a combined maximum punishment of 45 years. The bank fraud case adds 120 years, 30 years for each of the four counts. Ken Lay passed away just weeks after the verdict. Since Lay died before he could appeal his case, his conviction was vacated or abated (i.e., the law considered Lay as never indicted, tried, or convicted). Also, in October 2006, Skilling was sentenced to 24 years and 4 months and ordered to pay $46 million for Enron employees and more than $18 million in fines.

Enron: A Review of Important Accounting Issues

The fraud at Enron was caused by a variety of factors including these:

- Improperly failing to consolidate the results of an SPE (Chewco) with Enron because it lacked the necessary independence from Enron's management due to the fact that Andrew Fastow had direct or indirect control over the SPE. Fastow was the CFO of Enron and apparently directed the sale of Chewco to the company, a transaction that further clouded the legitimacy of the accounting for the SPE as a separate entity.
- Failing to adequately disclose the related-party relationship between Enron and those SPEs that were independent of the company under GAAP.
- Overstating earnings by using mark-to-market accounting for investments in long-term gas contracts.

The quality of its financial reports was poor:

- Failure to adequately disclose the related-party transactions made it impossible for investors and creditors to know the full extent of these transactions and loans that were made to Enron based on vastly understated debt.
- Sale of assets to SPEs in return for the transfer of borrowed funds from the SPE with the subsequent recording of a gain masked the true earnings and made it appear the company was doing better than it really was.
- Use of reserves, and failure to explain the basis for creation of such reserves, made it impossible to judge the acceptability of these transactions.
- Failure to disclose Fastow's dual role with the SPEs and as CFO of Enron made it impossible for investors and creditors to have the information they had an ethical right to receive to evaluate the nature, scope, and substance of off-balance-sheet transactions.

Enron managed earnings through the following techniques:

- Used reserves to increase earnings when reported amounts were too low.
- Used mark-to-market estimates to inflate earnings in violation of GAAP.
- Selected which operating assets to "sell" to the SPEs, thereby affecting the amount of the gain on transfer and earnings effect.

The lack of strong controls contributed to the fraud as evidenced by the following:

- Top management overrode or ignored internal controls in the approval process for Chewco, the LJMs, and the Raptors.
- Oversight by the board of directors was either negligent, as was the case with waiving the ethics code for Fastow, or nonexistent.
- A culture was established to make the deals at any cost, thereby diluting the due diligence process that should have raised red flags on some of the transactions.
- A culture of fear was created within Enron with its "rank-or-yank" policy and cutthroat competition.

FASB Rules on SPEs

While it could seem that the GAAP rules on SPEs are naïve, there are legitimate reasons for establishing the concept that an entity could isolate a business operation or some corporate assets. The idea was to control risk in a project such as investing in a new oil refinery. By following the rules to set up an SPE, an oil company could keep the large amount of debt off the books while using the funds from the SPE to construct the refinery. The off-balance-sheet effect helps to control risk if the project fails. The original motivation by the FASB in allowing SPEs was to establish a mechanism to encourage companies to invest in needed assets while keeping the related debt off its books.

Fastow's "creativity" was in using a not so well-known technique under GAAP to satisfy Enron's unique needs. These transactions have come to be known as *structured finance* or *financial engineering*. After Enron's success, other companies turned to the same techniques. The primary criticism of the technique by the public and regulators was that the rules required a relatively low percentage of outside ownership to keep the SPE off Enron's books.

FASB Interpretation No. 46(R)

After much debate about how to fix the original SPE ownership percentage and consolidation rules, the FASB issued on December 24, 2003, a revision of its proposed Interpretation: *FASB Interpretation 46(R), Consolidation of Variable Interest Entities.*[41] Basically, *Interpretation 46 (R)* requires unconsolidated variable interest entities to be consolidated by their primary beneficiaries if the entities do not effectively disperse risk among parties involved. Variable interest entities that effectively disperse risks would not be consolidated unless a single party holds an interest or combination of interests that effectively recombines risks that were previously dispersed.

The new rules apply an economic reality test to the consolidation of a variable interest entity. No longer is there a percentage ownership test. Instead, the dispersion of risk determines the consolidation status. By effectively dispersing risk, the primary beneficiary controls its own risk with respect to activities of the unconsolidated variable interest entity.

Sarbanes-Oxley Act of 2002

The passage of the Sarbanes-Oxley Act and establishment of the Public Company Accounting Oversight Board (PCAOB) directly results from the frauds at Enron, World Com, and others described in this book. We have discussed the act in various chapters of the text, but it is important to reiterate that the PCAOB has relieved the accounting profession (AICPA) of its authority over establishing independence, ethics, quality control, and auditing standards for public companies that are registered with the SEC. PCAOB also assumes the peer review function over registered CPA firms.

The act dealt directly with several aspects of the Enron fraud, further connecting Enron to reform in the accounting profession. These include the following:

- Prohibiting the provision of internal audit services for audit clients. Andersen provided the major part of internal audit services for Enron. Overall, Andersen earned from Enron in its last full year as accountants $27 million from nonaudit services and $25 million from audit services.
- Off-balance-sheet financing activities must be disclosed in the notes to the financial statements. Enron's SPEs were never referred to as providing off-balance-sheet financing.
- Related-party transactions require disclosure in the notes. The activities with the SPEs qualify as related-party transactions. By some accounts, Enron had more than 3,000 SPEs, yet the footnote disclosure in its last year before filing for bankruptcy was limited to one page.

Enron also suffered from the same lack of controls and inadequate corporate governance that infected so many other companies during the accounting scandals. For example, the board of directors did not act independently, and the audit committee members were not independent of management. The internal environment at Enron, especially the tone at the top, promoted a culture of making deals regardless of the risks.

The internal controls at Enron were either ignored or overridden by management (i.e., the board waived its ethics policy so that Fastow could [indirectly] control Chewco while serving as Enron's CFO). This created a conflict of interest that enabled Fastow to enrich himself through control of Chewco at the expense of Enron. The result is a serious breach of fiduciary responsibilities and failure to serve as true agents for the interests of the shareholders.

Lessons to Be Learned from Enron

What is the moral of the Enron story? Certainly, we could say that weak internal controls equates with possible fraud. Also, we could point to the need for an ethical tone at the top to help prevent fraud. Once Enron developed an appetite for establishing SPEs and keeping these transactions off the books, the company became more and more addicted to the cash provided through the SPEs. Even if it wanted to stop the transactions, Enron and its top management were already sliding down the ethical slippery slope faster and faster. It had made the mistake of taking the first step, and turning back was not an option. Moreover, some of the cash was used for personal purposes such as to buy Enron stock, which could then be used as collateral for larger loans from banks that routinely did business with Enron.

The bottom line factor that kept the Enron fraud going well passed the point of no return was greed. Skilling saw Fastow getting rich, Lay saw Skilling getting rich, all Enron employees thought they saw Lay getting rich, and then Lay hyped Enron stock to the employees for their 401Ks as a way for them, eventually, to get rich.

Conclusion: Back to the Future	We end our journey at the same place we started. Without a strong ethical base built on core values that are embedded in the Principles of the AICPA Code of Professional Conduct, CPAs could be tempted to give in to the pressures that sometimes exist to compromise their values in light of the demands of a superior or client entity.
	Your authors have wondered through this journey whether there is anything new under the sun in public accounting. The scandals of the 1980s repeated themselves in the 1990s and in the 2000s. Calls for stronger internal controls and an internal control report by management have gone unheeded for more than 30 years, but finally Section 404 of the Sarbanes-Oxley Act dictates that requirement. Generally accepted auditing standards that have called for more meaningful communication between

auditors and audit committees have been ignored over the years, but now SOX requires specific communications to help prevent or detect material misstatements in the financial statements.

What will it take in the future to avoid history repeating itself again? One thing we know is that it will take more than the SOX. What is needed is a strong internal control environment backed by adherence to ethical values and effective corporate governance systems. What is needed is a true commitment to ethics in one's personal as well as professional life. At the end of the day, all we have is our personal integrity and reputation for honest, hard work.

We do believe that SOX is an important step in moving down the road of ensuring accurate, reliable, and transparent financial reports. The act establishes important *requirements* to ensure audit and audit committee independence including internal control reporting and monitoring. It enhances *disclosure and transparency*, a big problem in the Enron fraud. It creates an *independent* oversight board to establish needed ethics rules, audit standards, and quality reviews. It legalizes the requirement of financial statement *certification* by the CEO and CFO to enable the SEC to go after those who violate this provision, the HealthSouth case notwithstanding. SOX creates a whistle-blowing process and enhances fraud responsibilities and penalties. What is needed now is strict enforcement of the act, legal liabilities for violations, and the sight of more and more CEOs and CFOs doing the "perp walk," assuming that it is justified

You have learned in this book that earnings management was widely practiced during the accounting scandals of the late 1990s and early 2000s. The motivation often publicly stated was to respond to internal pressures brought about by financial analysts' earnings estimates. These pressures were driven by hungry investors that became accustomed to substantial growth and stock price returns in traditionally short periods of time. A corrosive factor that enabled the fraud was stock option grants that increased in value as the current market price went up in comparison to a fixed exercise price. Recently, the public has become aware that some companies could have backdated stock options to increase the financial benefits to executives.

We leave you with one final quote that focuses on the role of the investing public in instigating the frauds. This quote comes from Joseph E. Abbott, the vice president and controller of West Pharmaceuticals Services, Inc. in Lionville, Pennsylvania:

> Investors should remember that if we do see companies start hitting estimates and not beating them, that would not be such a bad thing. It could mean there is less earnings management going on.[42]

Discussion Questions

1. Explain what you think Arthur Levitt meant in the opening quote, "Too many corporate managers, auditors, and analysts are participants in a game of nods and winks."

2. Can earnings management be an ethical practice? Discuss why or why not.

3. Comment on the statement that materiality is in the eye of the beholder.

4. Can immaterial misstatements of the financial statements violate securities laws and require the auditor to take certain actions? What actions should the auditor take? How do these kinds of misstatements relate to the auditor's ethical obligations to protect the public interest?

5. On January 4, 2005, Krispy Kreme Doughnuts Inc. announced it would restate its financial statements for the 2004 fiscal year. The restatement, the company said, was due to errors in how it accounted for the repurchase of franchises. It explained that such a restatement could reduce its earnings by seven to eight cents a share and cause the company to default on its credit agreement. The company's stock price fell $1.83 that day, or about 15 percent. Explain what you believe to be the factors that cause a company's stock price to decline by a significant amount on the day of the announcement of a restatement of earnings.

6. What steps could a company take to restore the confidence of investors after an earnings restatement announcement?

7. Comment on the statement that what a company's income statement reveals is interesting but what it conceals is vital.

8. Explain why accrual earnings and cash flow from operating activities are different amounts. Which of the two numbers do you think is more reliable. Why?

9. With respect to Schilit's financial shenanigans, how would you characterize a company practice in which the books are held open after the end of each quarter to determine the amount of revenue from contracts not yet finalized or executed that should be recorded in that quarter?

10. A variety of sales transactions can occur with multiple elements to them that need to be evaluated with respect to how to properly recognize revenues and match related costs. Based on the information in this chapter, choose a company and explain the way in which that company made the decision to recognize revenue with multiple-element contracts. Do you think that company was engaged in earnings management? Why or why not?

11. Tinseltown Construction just received a $2 billion contract to construct a modern football stadium in Orange, California, for the new National Football League team, the Los Angeles Devils of Orange. The company estimates it will cost $1.5 billion to construct the stadium. Explain how Tinseltown can make revenue recognition decisions that enable it to manage earnings over the three-year duration of the contract.

12. Explain why companies use off-balance-sheet financing techniques instead of borrowing of funds. What are the implications of off-balance-sheet financing for the quality of financial reporting?

13. In the Enron case, the company eventually turned to "back-door" guaranteeing of the SPEs' debt to satisfy equity investors. Explain why such an action negated the transfer of economic risk requirement to keep the SPEs off Enron's books.

14. Assume that the guarantee referred to in Question 13 was for a $16 million loan. The loan agreement required that Enron stock not fall below $40 per share. If the share price did decline below that trigger amount, for example, to $32 per share, the bank could either call the loan or increase the guaranteed number of Enron shares based on the new $32 price. If the bank decides to increase the number of shares guaranteed, what would be (a) the original number of shares in the guarantee and (b) the new number of shares? Why would it be important for Enron to disclose information about the guarantee in its financial statements?

15. DaimlerChrysler decides to pool its vehicle loans and sell them on the open market as an "asset-backed security" (ABS). The idea is to receive cash immediately for the loans by establishing a special-purpose entity to receive the loans and, in turn, issue a collateralized ABS to investors in the open market. Explain the implications of the transaction for the financial statements of DaimlerChrysler.

16. In the speech "A QT Report Card for High Quality Financial Reporting," at the Critical Issues in Accounting Forum program sponsored by Wake Forest University, Lynn Turner, former chief accountant of the SEC, made the following analogy to describe representational faithfulness:

   A map's representational faithfulness may be determined by how well the map describes the coastline. In the same way, a financial statement's representational faithfulness may be evaluated by how well it represents the economic resources and obligations of the company, and by how well the transactions and events that change those resources and obligations are described.

   If a company purposefully understates an estimated allowance for sales returns to inflate revenue in the current year, how does this accounting influence the representational faithfulness and quality of financial information?

17. Andersen was the auditor for Sunbeam, Waste Management, WorldCom, and Enron. No other accounting firm audited as many failed companies as did Andersen. Is it possible that Andersen's involvement with these four business frauds and accounting failures was a coincidence? Explain why you think it could have been a coincidence or why you do not think that is the case.

18. *Statement on Auditing Standards No. 90, Audit Committee Communications,* requires the auditor to discuss with an entity's audit committee the quality, not just the acceptability, of the accounting principles that entity uses. Describe what should be included in a discussion about the quality of accounting principles.

19. In a Duke University survey of 400 corporate financial executives, two of five said they would use legal ways to book revenues early if that would help them meet earnings targets. More than one in five would adjust certain estimates or sell investments to book higher income.[43] Comment on the ethics of both of these statements by the financial executives in the Duke survey.

20. Who is responsible for earnings management: top management, internal accountants, internal auditors, external auditors, audit committee, board of directors, or other? Which of those might instigate the practice? Who might just go along with something that has already been done? Which might just look the other way and ignore the effects on the financial statement? Be sure to discuss the ethical obligations of each group in the practice of earnings management.

Additional References

- John A. Byrne, *Chainsaw: The Notorious Career of Al Dunlap in the Era of Profit-At-Any-Price* (New York: Harper Business, 1999), pp. 153–70.

- Lynne W. Jeter, *Disconnected: Deceit and Betrayal at WorldCom* (Hoboken, NJ: John Wiley, 2003).

- Thomas E. McKee, *Earnings Management: An Executive Perspective* (Mason, OH: South-Western, 2005).

- Bethany and P. Elkind McLean, *The Smartest Guys in the Room: The Amazing Rise and Scandalous Fall of Enron* (New York: Penguin Books, 2003).

- Howard Schilit, *Financial Shenanigans: How to Detect Accounting Gimmicks and Fraud in Financial Reports,* 2nd ed. (New York: McGraw-Hill, 2002).

- Mimi Swartz and S. Watkins, *Power Failure: The Inside Story of the Collapse of Enron* (New York: Doubleday, 2003), pp. 275–76.

- Barbara Ley Toffler, *Final Accounting: Ambition, Greed, and the Fall of Arthur Andersen* (New York: Broadway Books, 2003).

Endnotes

1. Arthur Levitt, "The 'Numbers Game,'" Remarks by Chairman Arthur Levitt, Securities and Exchange Commission, before the NYU Center for Law and Business, September 28, 1998, www.sec.gov/news/speech/speecharchive/1998/spch220.txt.

2. Levitt.

3. Financial Accounting Standards Board, *Statement of Financial Accounting Concepts (SFAC) No. 5,* Recognition and Measurement in Financial Statements of Business Enterprises (Stamford, CT: FASB, 1986).

4. K. Schipper, "Commentary on Earnings Management," *Accounting Horizons*, December 1989, pp. 91–102.

5. P.M. Healy and J.M. Wahlen, "A Review of Earnings Management Literature and Its Implications for Standard Setting," *Accounting Horizons,* December 1999, pp. 365–83.

6. P.M. Dechow and P.J. Skinner, "Earnings Management: Reconciling the Views of Accounting Academics, Practitioners, and Regulation," *Accounting Horizons,* June 2000, pp. 235–50.

7. Thomas E. McKee, *Earnings Management: An Executive Perspective* (Mason, OH: South-Western, 2005).

8. American Institute of CPAs, *AICPA Professional Standards. Volume 1 as of June 1, 2005, Statement on Auditing Standards (SAS) No. 99,* Consideration of Fraud in a Financial Statement Audit New York: AICPA, 2002), AU Section 316.05–.06.

9. Securities and Exchange Commission, *SEC Staff Accounting Bulletin (SAB): No. 99,* Materiality. www.sec.gov/interps/account/sab99.htm.

10. Securities and Exchange Commission, Accounting and Auditing Enforcement Release No. 2125, *In the Matter of KPMG [v. Gemstar],* www.sec.gov/litigation/admin/34-50564.htm.

11. SEC, SAB No. 99.

12. L.E. Turner and T.R. Weirich, "A Closer Look at Financial Statement Restatements," *The CPA Journal,* December 2006, pp. 13–23.

13. Howard M. Schilit, *Financial Shenanigans: How to Detect Accounting Gimmicks and Fraud in Financial Reports,* 2nd ed. (New York: McGraw-Hill, 2002).

14. Schilit, pp. 63–82.

15. Schilit, pp. 83–96.

16. Schilit, pp. 97–112.

17. Schilit, pp. pp. 113–36.

18. Schilit, pp. 137–51.

19. Schilit, pp. 152–64.

20. Securities and Exchange Commission, Accounting and Auditing Enforcement Release No. 1405, *In the Matter of Arthur Andersen. LLP,* June 19, 2001, www.sec.gov/litigation/admin/34-44444.htm.

21. SEC, AAER 1405.

22. Securities and Exchange Commission, Litigation Release No. 18174, *Securities and Exchange Commission v. Paul A. Allaire, G. Richard Thoman, Barry D. Romeril, Philip D. Fishbach, Daniel S. Marchibroda and Gregory B. Tayler*, Accounting and Auditing Enforcement Release No. 1796, June 5, 2003, www.sec.gov/litigation/litreleases/lr18174.htm.

23. Securities and Exchange Commission, Litigation Release No. 17645, Accounting and Enforcement Release No. 1542, *Securities and Exchange Commission v. Xerox Corporation,* Civil Action No. 02-CV-2780 (DLC) (S.D.N.Y.), April 11, 2002.

24. Securities and Exchange Commission, Litigation Release No. 19573, Accounting and Enforcement Release No. 2379, *SEC v. KPMG LLP, et al.,* Civil Action No. 03-CV 0671 (DLC) (S.D.N.Y.), February 22, 2006.

25. Securities and Exchange Commission, Accounting and Auditing Enforcement Release No. 2234, *In the Matter of KPMG LLP,* April 19, 2005, www.sec.gov/litigation/admin/34-51574.pdf.

26. Securities and Exchange Commission, Accounting and Enforcement Release No. 2380, *In the Matter of Thomas J. Yoho, CPA. Responden,* Administrative Proceeding File No. 3-12215, February 22, 2006.

27. Securities and Exchange Commission, Accounting and Enforcement Release Litigation Release No. 2016, *Securities and Exchange Commission v. Lucent Technologies, Inc., Nina Aversano, Jay Carter, A. Leslie Dorn, William Plunkett, John Bratten, Deborah Harris, Charles Elliott, Vanessa Petrini, Michelle Hayes-Bullock, and David Ackerman,* Civil Action No. 04-2315 (WHW) (D.N.J.), filed May 17, 2004, www.sec.gov/litigation/complaints/comp18715.pdf.

28. Schilit, pp. 18–19.

29. Schilit, p. 19.

30. Schilit, p. 21.

31. Securities and Exchange Commission Litigation Release No. 17001, *Securities and Exchange Commission v. Albert J. Dunlap, Russell A. Kersh, Robert J. Gluck, Donald R. Uzzi, Lee B. Griffith, and Phillip E. Harlow,* 01-8437-CIV-Dimitrouleas (S.D. Fla., May 15, 2001).

32. SEC, Litigation Release No. 17001.

33. John A. Byrne, *Chainsaw: The Notorious Career of Al Dunlap in the Era of Profit-At-Any-Price* (New York: Harper Business, 1999), pp. 153–70.

34. Schilit, pp. 164–66.

35. Schilit, pp. 71–72.

36. Bethany McLean and Peter Elkind, *The Smartest Guys in the Room: The Amazing Rise and Scandalous Fall of Enron* (New York: Penguin Books, 2003).

37. McLean and Elkind, p. 166.

38. Mimi Swartz and Sherron Watkins, *Power Failure: The Inside Story of the Collapse of Enron* (New York: Doubleday, 2003), pp. 275–76.

39. Report of Investigation by the Special Investigative Committee of the Board of Directors of Enron Corp, February 1, 2002, http://fl1.findlaw.com/news.findlaw.com/wp/docs/enron/specinv020102rpt1.pdf.

40. Michael Graczyk, "Lay Say's He's 'Shocked' at Enron Verdict," www.cbsnews.com/stories/2006/05/26/ap/business/mainD8HRJ2C80.shtml.

41. Financial Accounting Standards Board, *FASB Interpretation 46(R),* Consolidation of Variable Interest Entities (Norwalk, CT: FASB, 2003).

42. Johnson, Tom, "Rosy Outlook for 3Q Profits," *CNN Money*, September 30, 1999. http://money. cnn.com/1999/09/30/companies/earnings_outlook/.

43. John Graham, Campbell Harvey, and Shivaram Rajgopal, "The Economic Implications of Corporate Financial Reporting," Social Science Research Network, http://papers.ssrn.com/ sol3/papers.cfm?abstract_id=491627

Chapter 7 Cases

Case 7-1

Cubbies Cable

Ernie Binks is a big baseball fan, so it is quite natural for him, at a time like this, to recall a phrase attributed to Yogi Berra: "It was déjà vu all over again."

Binks is the partner in charge of the Cubbies Cable audit for the accounting firm of Santos & Williams LLP. Cubbies is a family-owned regional cable company headquartered in Chicago. Binks is involved in a second dispute in three years with client management. The first dispute concerned the disclosure of a contingent liability related to a class action lawsuit against Cubbies for age discrimination in hiring. Cubbies did not disclose the possibility of loss even though all signs pointed to a verdict against the company. Cubbies argued that there was nothing to confirm the CPA firm's position in that regard and would disclose it only if the company lost the lawsuit.

The current dispute involves the capitalization of cable construction costs that the client wants to expense. Binks reviewed a memorandum in the working papers prepared by John Kessinger, the audit manager. The document summarizes the facts on the second dispute. This memo is presented in Exhibits 1 and 2.[1]

Cubbies recently completed a major cable installation project at a condominium complex across the street from Wrigley Field in Chicago. The revenue earned from that job enabled the company to complete the third quarter of 2007 with record earnings. Revenues at September 30, 2007, exceeded revenues at September 30, 2006, by 22 percent. Net income for the nine months ended September 30, 2007, was 24 percent above the amount for the same period in the prior year.

Binks is now preparing for a meeting with Rod Hondley, the advisory partner on the Cubbies Cable audit. Hondley has already made it known that he supports the client's position. Binks knows that Santos & Williams operates by this simple philosophy: You have to let the client win one somewhere along the line or you could lose that client.

Binks contemplates his options: either to go along with the client's position (the option supported by Hondley) or to maintain his own position. It is at this point that he thinks about another "Yogi-ism": "When you come to a fork in the road, take it."

[1] Financial Accounting Standards Board, "Financial Accounting by Cable Television Companies," *Statement of Financial Accounting Standards, No. 51* (Stamford, CT: FASB, November 1981), paragraph 17.

Exhibit 1
Memo on Capitalization of Cable Equipment

November 30, 2006

1. Cubbies Cable is a locally owned cable television company that services the neighborhoods in Chicago that surround Wrigley Field, the home of the Chicago Cubs. Cubbies Cable was incorporated as a closely held company in 2004. We have audited the company's financial statements since September 30, 2005. The audited statements are used by Chicago First National Bank in granting short-term loans to Cubbies Cable. In particular, the company has a debt covenant agreement with the bank that obligates Cubbies to maintain a specified level of liquidity as indicated by the working capital and "quick" ratios.

2. During the 12-month period ending March 30, 2007, Cubbies constructed a new cable system in parts of Chicago that enabled it to increase its presence in that market. The revenue from the system through September 30, 2007, exceeded projections by more than 20%. The sharp increase over expected revenue was the cause of the conflict with the client.

3. A difference of opinion arose over the proper accounting for cable construction costs. The client wanted to expense all of the costs in the year ended September 30, 2007. We suspect that the client wanted to decrease net income for the year. Two different types of costs were involved:

   a. **Cable television plant:** Costs associated with constructing the *cable television plant* and providing cable service include *head-end costs, cable,* and *drop costs.* The client wanted to expense all of these costs. However, Statement of Financial Accounting Standards No. 51, "Financial Reporting by Cable Television Companies," requires that cable television plant costs incurred during the prematurity periods be capitalized in full. We had protracted discussions with Cubbies Cable regarding this issue, and we were told there was no way the company would agree to capitalize any of the costs. Given that Cubbies was not publicly owned, our only recourse is to take the matter to the board of directors. Another concern is that 9 of the 11 members of the board are family members of the CEO or past officers of Cubbies Cable. We expect this situation to work against us in convincing the client that its proposed accounting procedure is not in accordance with generally accepted accounting principles.

   b. **Interest cost:** The client initially expensed all costs during the *prematurity period.* We convinced the client to change its accounting to capitalize costs during the construction period. We used for support our reference to SFAS No. 51. This statement requires application of SFAS No. 34, "Capitalization of Interest Cost," to interest costs incurred during the construction of an asset. The application of paragraphs 13 and 14 of SFAS No. 34 to the client's situation requires that interest costs incurred during the prematurity period be capitalized in full by applying the interest capitalization rate to the average amount of accumulated expenditures for the asset during the period. The purpose of this procedure is to capitalize the amount of interest costs incurred during the prematurity period that theoretically could have been avoided if expenditures for construction of the cable television plant had not been made.

   See definitions in Exhibit 2 for all italicized words.

Exhibit 2
Definitions of Terms from SFAS Nos. 28, 29, and 51

SFAS No. 51, "Financial Reporting by Cable Television Companies" (Paragraph 17)

Cable Television Plant. This refers to the cable television system required to render services to subscribers and includes the following equipment:

Head-End. The equipment used to receive television signals, including the studio facilities required to transmit the programs to subscribers.

Cable. This consists of cable and amplifiers placed on utility poles or underground that maintain the quality of the signal to subscribers.

Drops. This consists of the hardware that provides access to the main cable in order to bring the signal from the main cable to the subscriber's television set and devices to block channels.

Converters and Descramblers. These are devices attached to the subscriber's television sets when more than 12 channels are provided, such as Pay-per-View programming or two-way communication.

Prematurity Period. This refers to the period of time during which the cable television system is partially under construction and partially in service. It begins with the first earned subscriber revenue and ends with the completion of the first major construction period or achievement of a specified, predetermined subscriber level at which no additional investment will be required other than that for the cable television plant.

Questions

1. Given the limited facts in this case, do you agree with the client on its position in the first dispute with respect to the treatment of the contingency? Why or why not? Use accounting reasoning and your knowledge of contingency rules to help in answering the question.

2. What effect would the client's position have on your answer to Question 1? What effect could the firm's position on relations with clients have when disputes on the proper accounting treatment exist?

3. What do you think was the motivation for Cubbies Cable in taking the position to expense all cable costs during the nine months ended September 20, 2007?

4. Would you question the audit firm's integrity in this situation because Cubbies agreed with the firm on the issue of capitalizing interest during the prematurity period? In other words, should CPAs be prepared to "horse trade" when dealing with clients and determining the proper GAAP to apply in a particular situation?

5. Who are the stakeholders in this situation? Identify the major ethical issues that should be of concern to Binks in deciding whether to just go along with the firm in its support of the client or to take some other action.

6. What would you do at this point if you were in Binks' position? Why?

Case 7-2

Edvid, Inc.

Charles Hutton is the partner in charge of the Edvid, Inc., audit for the year ended December 31, 2007. His firm was hired on September 30, 2007, to replace the predecessor auditor who had audited the company's financial statements since it was formed in 2003.

Edvid is a privately owned company that produces training programs on DVDs for sale to business and government agencies. The company has built up a library of DVDs that it offers to business customers on two-year rental contracts. After that, the training programs typically become outdated, so the customers turn them in for replacement products. Customers do not receive any refunds, there are no residual or replacement costs, and all videos must be returned to Edvid. The old DVDs are sold at a discount to the Federal Emergency Management Administration (FEMA).

Edvid's business model is unique in that business customers must pay a $1,000 fee to join the program and then are eligible to rent up to 10 DVDs over a two-year period. The tapes are developed by Edvid based on the needs of the members of its program. Edvid mails questionnaires frequently to determine customer interest in training topics. It has its own professional instructors who develop the material and then it is produced on DVDs for distribution.

A typical contract with a customer who rents 10 tapes for two years appears in Exhibit 1.

EXHIBIT 1
EDVID, INC.
Terms of Rental Contract

Total contract price/DVD	$1,000	
Contract life	2 years	
Payment terms		
Initial payment	$ 300	
Quarterly payments (7 quarters@$100)	700	$1,000
Costs associated with each DVD		
Royalties paid to instructors	10	
Advertising and promotion	10	
Commissions	20	
Telephone, postage, and printing	10	50

Edvid recognizes revenue on each contract as shown in Exhibit 2.

EXHIBIT 2
EDVID, INC.
Revenue Recognition on Rental Contract

Payment Designation	Portion Recognized	Year
Initial payment ($300)	100%	Year 1
Balance due ($700)	0	Year 1
Balance due ($700)	100	Year 2

During the Edvid audit, Hutton questions the delay in recognizing 70 percent of revenue. He discusses the matter with George Mutton, Edvid's chief financial officer, who points out that by recognizing 70 percent of the revenue on all DVD contracts in the second year of the two-year period, the company is likely to show an increasing trend in profits over time as long as the number of contracts increases each year. Mutton emphasizes that such results have enabled Edvid to secure needed funding from venture capitalists each year since 2003.

Hutton is surprised that Mutton chose to delay recognition of 70 percent of the revenue. Typically, most of his clients would want to recognize as much revenue as possible in the first year of a two-year contract. His suspicions and desire to exercise due care prompt him to review the financial statements of Edvid for the past three years. Hutton then prepares the schedule shown in Exhibit 3.

EXHIBIT 3
EDVID, INC.
**Contract Revenue Compared with Net Income
For the Years Ended December 31, 2004–2006**

Years	Total Revenue (all contracts)	Net Income
2004	$108 million	$ 8.6 million
2005	129 million	11.0 million
2006	156 million	14.0 million

Questions

1. Explain why you think Hutton was concerned with Mutton's delay of the recognition of 70 percent of the revenue? What do you think Hutton meant by his "desire to exercise due care"?

2. Compute the following:

   a. The amount of profit on each contract to sell 10 DVDs over a two-year period.

   b. The percentage increase in revenue from 2004 to 2005 and 2005 to 2006.

   c. The percentage increase in net income from 2004 to 2005 and 2005 to 2006.

3. Describe the rules for recognizing revenue in accounting. Do you think Edvid violated those rules? Why or why not?

4. Is there anything wrong with what Edvid is doing in recording contract revenue? Be sure to use specific ethical values, virtues, and standards of behavior in supporting your answer.

5. Who are the stakeholders affected by Edvid's action, and how are they affected?

6. If you were in Charles Hutton's position, what would you do? Why?

7. Hutton approaches Mutton and states emphatically that the numbers must be changed for the past three years. Mutton refuses to do so and informs Hutton that the accounting is justified based on the long-term interests of Edvid.

a. Do any accounting issues exist that Hutton could use to try to influence Mutton's decision? Be specific.

b. What ethical values could drive Hutton in formulating an argument to use in his discussions with Mutton?

c. Are there any provisions of the AICPA Code of Professional Conduct that apply to the situation discussed by Hutton and Mutton? Be specific in answering this question.

Case 7-3

Excello Telecommunications

Excello Telecommunications sells equipment to buyers in "bill and hold" transactions in which the company sells the equipment to the buyer, bills the customer, and then holds the merchandise for later delivery. On December 20, 2007, Excello sold $1.2 million of equipment to Data Equipment Systems. During the next week, Excello's CEO learned that the company was $1.0 million short of revenue targets. In an effort to meet those goals, which would mean higher bonuses and possibly higher stock prices, Excello's CFO approached Data Equipment Systems with three offers to modify the December 20 agreement. The first would give Data Systems control over the product by the end of the year but allow it to exchange the product for any other it desired after the year-end. The second would transfer ownership to Data Systems by the end of the year in return for the purchase by Excello of similar equipment with a 10-year useful life for the same amount as the sale. The third would give Data Systems control of the merchandise by year-end but allow it to return the merchandise for a full credit anytime after year-end.

Questions

1. Evaluate the ethics of each of the three alternatives.
2. Evaluate each alternative from a revenue recognition perspective. Given your answers to Question 1 and this one, which alternative would you recommend to Data Equipment Systems if you were the company's chief financial officer? Why?
3. Assume that the amount of net income from the first and third transactions was not material to the overall net income, but the second one was material. Would that change your recommendation? Why or why not?
4. Assume that Data Systems selected the second alternative. Excello's CFO decided to record all of the revenue from the sale immediately and in the current year while capitalizing and writing off the cost of the similar equipment acquired next year over 10 years. Do you agree with the accounting for these transactions? Why or why not? Be sure to back up your answer with reference to GAAP.

Case 7-4

Fannie Mae: The Government's Enron

The SEC is suing Fannie Mae, a government-sponsored provider of home mortgages. What is going on?

Background

The Federal National Mortgage Association (Fannie Mae) and the Federal Home Loan Mortgage Corporation (Freddie Mac) are government-sponsored entities that operate under Congressional charters to "help lower- and middle-income Americans buy homes."[1] Both entities receive special treatment aimed at increasing home ownership by decreasing the cost for home owners to borrow money. They do this by purchasing home mortgages from banks, guaranteeing them, and then reselling them to investors. This helps the banks eliminate the credit and interest rate risk and lengthen the mortgage period. Fannie Mae and Freddie Mac receive advantages over commercial banks including these: (1) The U.S. Treasury can buy $2.25 billion of each company's debt, (2) Fannie Mae and Freddie Mac receive exemption from state and local taxes, and (3) the implied government backing gives them the ability to take on large amounts of home loans without increasing their low cost of capital.

Fannie Mae makes money either by buying, guaranteeing, and then reselling home mortgages for a fee or by buying mortgages, holding them, and then taking on the risk. By selling the mortgages, Fannie Mae eliminates the interest rate risk. There is less profit from this conservative approach than by holding the mortgages they buy. By holding the mortgages, Fannie Mae can make money on the spread because it has such a low cost of capital. In 1998, Fannie Mae's holdings hit a peak of $375 billion of mortgages and mortgage-backed securities on its own books, not to mention the more than $1 trillion of mortgages it guaranteed. This process of holding mortgages on its books helped Fannie Mae to expand rapidly. It also stimulated unprecedented profit growth because there was more profit to be made by keeping the mortgages than by guaranteeing and then reselling them to other investors.

One reason for growth in the telecommunications sector in the 1990s was the building of overcapacity in telecommunications equipment inventory based on the belief the economic growth bubble of the early 1990s would never end. Fannie Mae was similarly affected by the bubble in making and holding home mortgage loans. Just as telecommunication companies such as Global Crossing and Qwest were motivated to keep revenue and net income increasing quarter after quarter, the pressure also was on the top management of Fannie Mae to keep up the pace of growth.

Fannie Mae's CEO, Franklin Raines, was so optimistic that at an investor conference in May 1999, he claimed, "The future is so bright that I am willing to set as a goal that our EPS [earnings per share] will double over the next five years."[2] This sounds remarkably similar to alleged statements made by Ken Lay to Enron's employees about the bright future for that company.

As growth pressures continued, Fannie Mae began to use more derivatives to hedge interest rate risk. Critics looked at Fannie Mae's portfolio and expressed concern that with the risk involved in using derivatives, Fannie Mae could be at risk of defaulting. They pointed out that unlike federally guaranteed commercial bank deposits and the partial government guarantee of pension obligations through the Pension Benefit Guarantee Corporation, there was no federal guarantee of Fannie Mae. Behind the scenes, Fannie Mae encouraged the concept that if it did default, the government would back it.

Fannie Mae was growing, and the market loved it. Top executives were receiving large bonuses for the growing profits. The growth was due to increased risk, but people believed that, at the end of the day, the government would come to the rescue of Fannie Mae if that became necessary.

The Accounting Scandal

The discovery of Fannie Mae's accounting scandal began in 2001 when Freddie Mac fired Arthur Andersen, Enron's accountant, right after the Enron scandal exploded. Freddie Mac then hired PricewaterhouseCoopers. When PwC came in, the firm looked very closely at Freddie Mac's books and found that it had understated its profits in an attempt to smooth earnings. Freddie Mac agreed to a $5 billion restatement and fired many of its top executives. Meanwhile, Fannie Mae continued on its course and accused Freddie Mac of causing "collateral damage." The Fannie Mae Web site even included the statement, "Fannie Mae's reported financial results follow [GAAP] to the letter. There should be no question about our accounting."

To a cynic, that statement could have had the unintended consequence of raising suspicion about Fannie Mae's accounting. After all, the markets had already been through it with Enron.

The government agency that regulates Fannie Mae and Freddie Mac, the Office of Federal Housing Enterprise Oversight (OFHEO), had stated days before Freddie Mac's restatement that Freddie's internal controls were "accurate and reliable." Once the restatement was made public, OFHEO had no choice but to look more deeply into Fannie Mae's accounting to make sure such a serious misjudgment did not happen again.[3]

[1] Bethany McLean, "Fannie Mae: The Fall of Fannie Mae," *Fortune,* January 10, 2005.

[2] McLean.

[3] McLean.

OFHEO is much weaker than most regulatory agencies such as the SEC and Justice Department that went after Enron in the obstruction of justice case. Fannie Mae essentially established OFHEO in 1992 as the regulatory agency that oversaw its operations and accounting. Fannie Mae was able to control its own regulator because it had enough influence in Congress to have OFHEO's budget cut. Fannie Mae had political influence because of its connections with realtors, homebuilders, and trade groups. Fannie Mae also made large contributions to various organizations and gained political clout.

After the Enron debacle, the White House wanted to make sure to avoid another scandal. The government provided the funding needed to bring in an independent investigator, Deloitte & Touche to reaudit the fraud periods and then to be the independent auditor. The firm uncovered massive accounting irregularities at Fannie Mae. In September 2004, OFHEO released results of its investigation and "accused Fannie Mae of both willfully breaking accounting rules and fostering an environment of 'weak or nonexistent' internal controls."[4]

The investigation focused on the use of derivatives and Fannie Mae's deferring derivative losses on the balance sheet, thus inflating profits. OFHEO and Deloitte believed that the derivative losses should be recorded on the income statement. The dispute involved the application of *Statement of Financial Accounting Standards No. 133,* Accounting for Derivative Instruments and Hedging Activities. The SEC's chief accountant determined that Fannie Mae had failed to comply with the requirements for hedge accounting, including *SFAS No. 133*'s rigorous documentation requirements.[5]

Fannie Mae was required by law to document its derivative use and file with the SEC. But, "Fannie Mae's application of *SFAS 133* (and its predecessor standard, *SFAS 91*) did not comply in material respects with the accounting requirements of GAAP."[6] In particular, Fannie Mae's practice of putting losses on the balance sheet rather than on the income statement resulted in overstated earnings and excess executive compensation.

OFHEO issued a report[7] charging that in 1998 Fannie Mae had recognized only $200 million in expenses when it should have recognized $400 million. The underreporting of expenses led to earnings of $3.23 per share and a total of $27 million in executive bonuses. These charges prompted investigations by the SEC and Justice Department.

Two weeks after the OFHEO report and charges against Fannie Mae, the House of Representatives Subcommittee on Capital Markets had a hearing. Raines initially deflected criticisms by saying, "These accounting standards are highly complex and require determinations on which experts often disagree."[8] Raines was quite convincing in defense of OFHEO charges that Fannie Mae executives had not manipulated earnings in an attempt to increase bonuses. In the end, Raines won because the tone of the OFHEO reports made it seem as though the regulator was out to get Fannie Mae.

Perhaps feeling his oats after the victory in the House, Raines demanded that the SEC review OFHEO's findings. On December 15, 2004, the SEC announced that "Fannie did not comply 'in material respects' with accounting rules, and that as a result, Fannie Mae would have to restate its results over $9 billion."[9] Other than the WorldCom fraud that appears to have been as large as $13 billion or more, the Fannie Mae fraud has the "dubious" honor of being the next largest fraud to date.

The OHFEO had been vindicated. The Fannie Mae board was told that both Raines and CFO Tim Howard had to be fired. Soon after, both resigned, and Fannie Mae fired KPMG and appointed Deloitte & Touche as the new auditor. Deloitte was asked to audit the 2004 statements of Fannie Mae and reaudit previous statements from 2001.

OFHEO Report May 23, 2006

On May 23, 2006, OFHEO issued a more extensive report[10] of a comprehensive three-year investigation that officially charged senior executives at Fannie Mae with manipulating accounting to collect millions of dollars in undeserved bonuses and to deceive investors. The fraud led to a $400 million civil penalty against Fannie Mae, more than three times the $125 million penalty imposed on Freddie Mac for understating its earnings by about $5 billion from 2000 to 2002 to minimize large profit swings. The $400 million is one of the largest penalties ever in an accounting fraud case. Of this amount, $350 million will be returned to investors damaged by the alleged violations.

The OFHEO review, involving nearly 8 million pages of documents, details what the agency called an arrogant and unethical corporate culture. The report, which concluded an 18-month investigation led by former Senator Warren Rudman, was commissioned by Fannie Mae's board of directors. The final 2,600 page report charged Fannie Mae executives with perpetrating an $11 billion accounting fraud in order to meet earnings targets that would trigger $25 million in bonuses for top executives. The report charges former CFO Howard and former controller Leanne G. Spencer as the chief culprits. Along with former chairman and CEO Raines, who had earned $20 million (including $3 million

---

[4] McLean.

[5] Jonathan Weil and James R. Hagert, "Fannie Faces Billions in New Losses: Fresh Accounting Concerns for the Mortgage Company May Further Dent Capital," *The Wall Street Journal,* March 3, 2005.

[6] Securities and Exchange Commission, SEC Form 8-K for Federal National Mortgage Association (Fannie Mae), December 28, 2004.

[7] Office of Federal Housing Enterprise Oversight, *Report of the Findings to Date: Special Examination of Fannie Mae,* September 17, 2004, www.ofheo.gov/media/pdf/FNMfindingstodate17sept04.pdf

[8] McLean.

[9] McLean.

[10] Office of Federal Housing Enterprise Oversight, *Report of the Special Examination of Fannie Mae,* May 2006, www.ofheo.gov/media/pdf/FNMSPECIALEXAM.PDF.

in stock options) in 2003 and $17.7 million in 2002, these executives created a "culture that improperly stressed stable earnings growth."[11] Rudman told reporters that the management team Raines had hired was "inadequate and in some respects not competent."[12]

Criticisms of Internal Environment

From 1998 to mid-2004, the smooth growths in profits and precisely hit earnings targets each quarter reported by Fannie Mae were illusions deliberately created by senior management using faulty accounting. The report "shows that Fannie Mae's faults were not limited to violating accounting standards but included inadequate corporate governance systems that failed to identify excessive risk-taking and poor risk management," Randal Quarles, U. S. Treasury undersecretary for domestic finance, said in a statement. "OFHEO's findings are a clear warning about the very real risk the improperly managed investment portfolios of [Fannie Mae and Freddie Mac] pose to the greater financial system."[13]

Fannie Mae agreed to make changes in its operations including these:

- Limit the growth of its multibillion-dollar mortgage holdings, capping them at $727 billion.

- Make top to bottom changes in its corporate culture, accounting procedures, and ways of managing risk.

- Replacing the chairman of the board's audit committee. The board named accounting professor Dennis Beresford to replace audit committee chairman Thomas Gerrity.

The report also faulted Fannie Mae's board of directors for failing to discover "a wide variety of unsafe and unsound practices" at the largest buyer and guarantor of home mortgages in the country. It signaled out senior management for failing to make investments in accounting systems, computer systems, other infrastructure, and staffing needed to support a sound internal control system, proper accounting, and GAAP–consistent financial reporting.

KPMG's Audits

As for the role of KPMG as Fannie Mae's auditors, the report alleges that external audits performed by the firm failed to include an adequate review of Fannie Mae's significant accounting policies for GAAP compliance. KPMG also improperly provided unqualified opinions on financial statements even though they contained significant departures from GAAP. The failure of KPMG to detect and disclose the serious weaknesses in policies, procedures, systems, and controls

in Fannie Mae's financial accounting and reporting, coupled with the failure of the board of directors to oversee KPMG properly, contributed to the unsafe and unsound conditions at Fannie Mae.

SEC Civil Action

The SEC filed a civil action against Fannie Mae on May 23, 2006, charging that it had engaged in a financial fraud involving multiple violations of GAAP in connection with the preparation of its annual and quarterly financial statements. These violations enabled Fannie Mae to show a stable earnings growth and reduced income statement volatility, and, for the year ended 1998, Fannie Mae was able to maximize bonuses and meet forecasted earnings.[14] The SEC action thoroughly details a variety of deficiencies in accounting and financial reporting. Four of the more serious situations are described next.

Improper Accounting for Loan Fees, Premiums and Discounts

Statement of Financial Accounting Standards (SFAS) No. 91 requires companies to recognize loan fees, premiums, and discounts as an adjustment over the life of the applicable loans, to generate a "constant effective yield" on the loans.[15] Because of the possibility of loan prepayments, the estimated life of the loans could change with changing market conditions. *SFAS No. 91* requires that any changes to the amortization of fees, premiums, and discounts caused by changes in estimated prepayments be recognized as a gain or loss in its entirety in the current period income statement. Fannie Mae referred to this amount as the "catch-up adjustment." In the fourth quarter of 1998, Fannie Mae's accounting models calculated an approximate $439 million catch-up adjustment in the form of a decrease to net interest income. Rather than book this amount consistent with *SFAS No. 91,* senior management of Fannie Mae directed employees to record only $240 million of the catch-up amount in that year's income statement. By not recording the full catch-up adjustment, Fannie Mae understated its expenses and overstated its income by a pretax amount of $199 million. The unrecorded catch-up amount represents 4.3 percent of the 1998 earnings before taxes and 4.9 percent of 1998 net interest income for the fiscal year 1998.

Improper Hedge Accounting

Fannie Mae used debt to finance the acquisition of mortgages and mortgage securities, and it turned to derivative instruments

---

[11] Stephen Labaton and Eric Dash, "Report on Fannie Me Cites Manipulation to Secure Bonus," *New York Times,* February 23, 2006. http://www.nytimes.com/2006/02/23/business/23cnd-fannie.html?ex=1298350800&en=07329f61e35cf709&ei=5089&partner=rssyahoo&emc=rss.

[12] Labaton and Dash.

[13] Under Secretary Randal K. Quarles Statement On Treasury Reaction to OFHEO Report, May 23, 2006, http://www.ustreas.gov/press/releases/js4278.htm.

[14] Securities and Exchange Commission, Case Number 1:06CV00959, *Securities and Exchange Commission v. Federal National Mortgage Association,* May 23, 2006.

[15] Financial Accounting Standards Board, *Statement of Financial Accounting Standards No. 91,* Accounting for Nonrefundable Fees and Costs Associated with Origination or Acquiring Loans and Initial Direct Costs of Leases (Norwalk, CT: FASB, 1982).

to hedge against the effect of fluctuations in interest rates on its debt costs. Application of *SFAS No. 133* required that Fannie Mae adjust the value of its derivatives to changing market values.[16] Critics contended that this standard opened the door to earnings volatility, and it would appear that Fannie Mae's desires to create earnings stability was used as the motivation for the application of the standards in *FAS No. 133*.

Financial instruments react differently to interest rate movements, making it difficult to perfectly hedge a debt issuance with an offsetting derivative. To the extent that instruments do not perfectly offset each other, *SFAS No. 133* generally requires companies to measure and record this "ineffectiveness" in their income statement. It represents the differential between the change in the value of the derivative and the change in the value of the hedged item. This process is commonly referred to as the *long-haul* method. Thus, consistent with the standard, earnings volatility associated with the use of derivatives is minimized to the extent hedge relationships are "effective."

SFAS No. 133 allows for an exception whereby qualifying companies can avoid the burdensome requirement of measuring and recording hedge ineffectiveness and income statement volatility that can otherwise result from *SFAS No. 133*. These exceptions, known as the *short-cut* or *matched terms* methods, were not applicable in Fannie Mae's case but were chosen by management based on erroneous interpretations and unjustified reliance on materiality apparently to avoid income statement volatility. By failing to comply with the requirements of *SFAS No. 133*, Fannie Mae failed to qualify for hedge accounting. This failure led to its publicly issuing materially false and misleading financial statements for the periods covering the first quarter 2001 to the second quarter 2004. The vast majority of the $11 billion restatement is the result of Fannie Mae's improper hedge accounting.

Accounting for Loan Loss Reserve

During the period 1997 through 2003, management failed to provide any quantitative estimate of losses in their loan portfolio instead relying on a qualitative judgment. The failure to establish and implement an appropriate model for determining the size of the loan loss reserve was a violation of the GAAP rules in *SFAS No. 5*. [17]

Fannie Mae maintained an unjustifiably high level of loan loss reserve in case it was needed to compensate for possible future changes in the economic environment. This violates the GAAP requirement that the estimate of loss reserves should be based on losses currently inherent in the loan portfolio. At year-end 2002, Fannie Mae's reserve was overstated

by at least $100 million. This overstatement resulted in a $100 million understatement of earnings before tax, which represented 1.6 percent of the earnings before tax and 8 cents of additional earnings per share on the year-end 2002 figure of $4.52.

Classifications of Securities Held in Portfolio

SFAS No. 115[18] requires the classification of securities acquired as either held-to-maturity or trading at the time of acquisition. Once a security is classified, it can be reclassified only in narrow circumstances. Rather than adhere to the guidance in *SFAS No. 115*, Fannie Mae initially classified the securities it acquired as held-to-maturity and then at the end of the month of acquisition, decided on the ultimate classification. GAAP requires that the accounting classification be made at the time of acquisition.

Questions

1. Review the facts of the Fannie Mae case and describe analogous situations with respect to the Enron fraud as described in this chapter.

2. If you were asked to assess blame in the Fannie Mae fraud, how would you do it? In particular, what would be the degree of responsibility that you would assign to the government? How about the auditors? What about Fannie Mae as an entity? How about the management of Fannie Mae? Are there any others who hold some responsibility for the fraud at Fannie Mae? Be sure to justify your answers using accounting rules and/or ethical standards.

3. The following statement appears in the case: "As for the role of KPMG as Fannie Mae's auditors, the report alleges that external audits performed by the firm failed to include an adequate review of Fannie Mae's significant accounting policies for GAAP compliance." Explain what you think is meant by (a) an adequate review and (b) significant accounting policies for GAAP compliance.

4. Identify where you believe there were deficiencies in Fannie Mae's internal controls and why you consider them to be deficiencies. Be sure to include in your discussion how the items you identify affected the accuracy and reliability of Fannie Mae's financial reports.

5. In some instances in the case, it appears that Fannie Mae tried to manage earnings. In other cases, it appears that the opposite affect occurred. How can you explain these differences? Why do you think the company would record two or more transactions in ways that have opposite affects on earnings both in the current and future years?

---

[16] Financial Accounting Standards Board, *Statement of Financial Accounting Standards No. 133,* Accounting for Derivative Instruments and Hedging Activities (Norwalk, CT: FASB, 1998).

[17] Financial Accounting Standards Board, *Statement of Financial Accounting Standards No. 5,* Accounting for Contingencies (Norwalk, CT: FASB, 1975).

[18] Financial Accounting Standards Board, *Statement of Financial Accounting Standards No. 115,* Accounting for Certain Investments in Debt and Equity Securities (Norwalk, CT: FASB, 1993).

Case 7-5

Florida Transportation

Florida Transportation, a privately held company headquartered in Orlando, Florida, buys transportation equipment, sells it to leasing companies, and then leases back the transportation equipment for its own use. The company recently purchased four high-speed trains from a German manufacturer for its use in the Orlando–Miami corridor. The high-speed train form of transportation has become popular for families visiting Disneyworld. The cost of a one-way ticket between the two destinations is $30 for coach class and $40 for business class. A round-trip ticket costs $55 and $75, respectively. Children under 12 ride for $15 each way and $25 round-trip. Children under 5 years old ride for free. By comparison, it would cost at least $100 to drive the 400 plus miles round-trip between the two cities.

Sale and Leaseback Agreements

Under these agreements, Florida Transportation sells the high-speed trains to Leasing Associates in an all cash transaction and then leases it back. Part of the purpose of the sale and leaseback transaction is to provide needed financing for Florida Transportation. The terms of the sale and leaseback agreement are summarized in Exhibit 1 and Exhibit 2 contain selected definitions from the relevant accounting standards to help determine how Florida Transportation should account for the lease.

Mickey Duck is a CPA and the CFO of Florida Transportation. Duck has been asked by Donald Mouse, the CEO, to determine the proper accounting for the sale and leaseback transaction. Duck went on line and accessed the provisions of *SFAS No. 28,* Accounting for Sales with Leasebacks from the Web site of the Financial Accounting Standards Board. *SFAS No. 28* amends *SFAS No. 13,* Accounting for Leases, and calls for the seller-lessee to defer the profit on a sale and leaseback transaction if the seller retains substantially all of the use of the property through the leaseback. Duck downloads the two exhibits (see Exhibits 1 and 2) that he developed and takes them to his meeting with Mouse. His position is to treat the transaction as a sale (with deferred profit) and then the leaseback of the high-speed trains as a capital lease. Duck believes this is the proper accounting for the transaction with Leasing Associates.

Questions

1. From an accounting point of view, do you agree with Duck's position? Why or why not? Be sure to cite references to the SFASs in this case and any relevant revenue recognition rules.

2. Assume that Mouse takes the position that the sale part of the transaction should be recorded as immediate revenue and the leaseback should be treated as an operating lease.

Exhibit 1
Sale-Leaseback Agreement

Cost of the high-speed train	$2,000,000
Estimated useful life	40 years
Estimated residual value	n/a
Sale price to Leasing Associates	$3,000,000

Terms of the leaseback

Leaseback Period

- Ten-year periods, renewable four times, for a total of 40 years
- Renewal subject to approval of the buyer-lessor
- Seller-lessee can sell its rights to the high-speed trains at any time, but purchaser company assumes all obligations under this lease agreement, including payments to Leasing Associates.

Leaseback Rentals

- Annual payments each January 1 to Leasing Associates based on a 10% interest rate and 40-year lease is $278,889.

Exhibit 2
Definitions of Terms from SFAS Nos. 28, 29, and 51

SFAS No. 28, "Accounting for Sales with Leasebacks" (Paragraph 3)

If the seller-lessee relinquishes the right to substantially all of the remaining use of the property sold (retaining only a minor portion of such use), the sale and leaseback should be accounted for as separate transactions, based on their respective terms.

If the seller-lessee retains the right to substantially all of the remaining use of the property sold, the sale and leaseback should be accounted for as a continuous transaction, based on capital and operating lease criteria.

SFAS No. 28, "Accounting for Sales with Leasebacks" (Paragraph 3a)

Substantially All and Minor. The phrase *substantially all and minor* is used in the context of the concepts underlying the classification criteria of SFAS No. 13. In that context, a test based on the 90% recovery criterion of Statement No. 13 could be used as a guideline. That is, if the present value of a reasonable amount of rental for the leaseback represents 10% or less of the fair value of the asset sold, the seller-lessee could be presumed to have transferred to the purchaser-lessor the right to substantially all of the remaining use of the property sold, and the seller-lessee could be presumed to have retained only a minor portion of such use.

Do you believe Mouse can justify that position from an ethical perspective by reference to the relevant pronouncements mentioned in Question 1? Why or why not?

3. Is there an earnings management element to Mouse's position? Why or why not? Is it possible to classify Mouse's position as one of the financial shenanigans identified by Schilit? If so, which one? If not, what element(s) is missing?

4. What are the ethical obligations for Mickey Duck? How do these obligations provide support for his position as stated in the case?

5. Assume that Mouse tells Duck to quack off if he doesn't like the "Big Cheese's" position. What would you do if you were Mickey Duck? Why?

Case 7-6

Gelt and Moola

Gelt Systems is a Delaware corporation based in Portland, Oregon. It designs and develops network communication hardware and software products and provides related support services. Gelt is audited by Ducks and Beavers LLP, a regional firm located in Portland.

Daisy Love has worked for Ducks and Beavers for six months since graduating from the accounting program at Portland State University. This is Love's first audit assignment after having worked on small business write-up clients that receive compilation reports. This is also Love's first ethical dilemma since graduating from PSU.

On March 21, 2008, at 4:59 p.m., Love discovered a transaction by Gelt that just does not pass the smell test. Unfortunately, there is no one at the firm to call for advice because the senior on the audit has been in the hospital for the past five days since suffering a herniated disk. The manager is out of town until April 4. Daisy is the only staff member still on the Gelt audit. All other staff returned to the main office after lunch. Love is quite nervous that Donny Donero, the partner in charge of the audit, is scheduled to meet with Franc Marx, the chief financial officer of Gelt Systems, on March 23 at 7:59 a.m. to discuss the results of the audit and the firm's audit opinion. Assume that Donero is a CPA.

The transaction that concerns Love took place with Moola Yearning, a closely held computer products company in Portland, on December 30, 2007, one day before the close of calendar year 2007. Gelt invested cash in and/or gave credits for several of its products to Moola in return for equity or debt in that company and Moola's agreement to purchase Gelt products either directly or indirectly through a third party reseller.

Questions

1. From an accounting perspective, why do you think Love could be concerned with the Moolah transaction? Be specific in your answer.

2. Given that Ducks and Beavers is a licensed CPA firm in Oregon and a member of the Oregon Society of CPAs, what are Love's ethical responsibilities with respect to the Moola transaction?

3. At 8:59 p.m. on March 21, Love decides to walk to the PSU library to think things through. In the library, she encounters Hubert Josephs, her favorite accounting professor. Josephs says hello to Love and asks how she has been. Love replies somewhat sheepishly, "All right." She then goes back to work. Josephs walks away with a concerned look on his face because he had always found Love to be a gregarious person. She now seemed to be a different person. While thinking about what to do, Love comes up with an idea that puts a smile on her face: Why not ask Dr. Josephs for his advice? Would you recommend that she ask Josephs for his advice because he has always been approachable in the past? Why or why not? What ethical considerations should exist for Love before deciding?

4. Regardless of your answer to Question 3, what would you do with respect to Donny Donero's meeting with the CFO of Gelt Systems on March 23? Would you try to talk to Donero before the meeting? Provide support for your answer with reference to ethics and accounting reasoning.

5. Assume that you fully disclosed to Donero the details of the December 30, 2007, transaction. What would you do if you were Donero with respect to the meeting with Marx? Assume that that you know Marx has been pressured by the CEO of Gelt Systems to record all of the cash that Gelt invested in Moola as revenue in the current year based on Moola's agreement to buy future product.

6. What should be the ethics and accounting concerns for Franc Marx, the CFO of Gelt Systems? Be specific in your answer.

7. Based on your responses to Questions 5 and 6 and assuming that Donero followed through with your suggestion, would your concerns about the ethical issues change once Donero has explained the position of Ducks and Beavers? Why or why not?

Case 7-7

Parmalat: Europe's Enron

After the news broke about the frauds at Enron and WorldCom in the United States, there were those in Europe who used the occasion to beat the drum: "Our principles-based approach to accounting standard setting is better than your rules-based approach." Many in the United States started to take a closer look at the principles-based approach in the European Community, especially in the United Kingdom, that relies less on bright-line rules to establish standards that typically have loopholes or are subject to CPA/financial engineers who seem to be able to find the loopholes. A principles-based approach relies more on objective standards that guide decision making in the application of accounting standards supported by ethical judgment.

The Parmalat scandal broke in late 2003 when it became known that company funds totaling almost 2.7 billion pounds (4 billion euros) that were meant to be held in an account at the Bank of America did not exist. The Parmalat situation described here makes it clear that Europe is not isolated from financial fraud. It also proves that the quality of financial reporting and financial transparency are issues of global concern. At the end of the day, these issues could be more important than whether a principles-based or rules-based approach is used.

The Italians Act

On March 19, 2004, Milan prosecutors brought charges against Parmalat founder Calisto Tanzi, other members of his family, and an inner circle of company executives for their part in one of Europe's biggest corporate fraud scandals. After three months of investigation, the prosecutors charged 29 individuals, the Italian branches of the Bank of America, and the accounting firm of Deloitte & Touche and Grant Thornton with market rigging, false auditing and regulatory obstruction, following the disclosure that 10 billion pounds (15 billion euros) were found to be missing from the bank accounts of the multinational dairy group in December 2003. The company has since declared bankruptcy and 16 suspects, including Carlos Tanzi, are in jail. Clearly, there is a family element to the scandal much like the Rigas family at Adelphia. Other suspects include Tanzi's son Stafano, his brother Giovanni, former Parmalat finance chief Fausto Tonna, and lawyer Liampaolo Zini. Former internal auditors and three former Bank of America employees also have been jailed for their roles in the fraud.[1] The judge also gave the go-ahead for Parmalat to proceed with lawsuits against the auditors. Parmalat's administrator, Enrico Bondi, is also

pursuing another lawsuit against Citigroup in New Jersey state courts.

Parmalat Diverted Company Cash to Tanzi Family Members

In transactions that could engender pride in Dennis Kozlowski, the former CEO of Tyco, Parmalat transferred approximately 350 million euros ($406 million) to various businesses owned and operated by Tanzi family members between 1997 and 2003. These family members did not perform any equivalent services for Parmalat that would warrant these payments. Furthermore, Parmalat failed to disclose that the transfers were to related-party interests.

U.S. Banks Caught in the Spotlight

Italian magistrates and officials from the U.S. Securities and Exchange Commission are examining the role of lenders to Parmalat (known for its long-life milk products), which collapsed into bankruptcy in late December 2003, following the disclosure of major holes in its financing. The SEC's inquiries focused on up to 836 million pounds ($1.5 billion) of notes and bonds issued in private placements with U.S. investors. The banks investigated include Bank of America, JP Morgan Chase, Merrill Lynch, and Morgan Stanley Dean Witter.

Bondi is working with the authorities to identify all financing transactions undertaken by Parmalat from 1994 through 2003. During the investigation, it was noted that Parmalat's auditor from 1990 to 1999, Grant Thornton, did not have copies of crucial audit documents relating to the company's Cayman Islands subsidiary Bonlat, which is at the center of the scandal. The emergence of a 6 billion pound hole at Bonlat triggered the Parmalat collapse. The accounting firm has since handed over important audit documents to investigators.[2]

The SEC Charges

The SEC filed an amended complaint on July 28, 2004, in its lawsuit against Parmalat Finanziaria S.p.A. in U.S. District Court in the Southern District of New York. The amended complaint alleges that Parmalat engaged in one of the largest financial frauds in history and defrauded U.S. institutional investors when it sold them more than $1 billion in debt securities in a series of private placements between 1997 and

[1] Sophie Arie, "29 Named in Parmalat Case," *The Guardian,* March 19, 2004, www.guardian.co.uk/parmalat/story/0,,1172990,00.html.

[2] Oliver Morgan, "Parmalat: US Banks Caught in the Spotlight," *Guardian Unlimited,* January 4, 2004, www.guardian.co.uk/parmalat/story/0,,1115482,00.html.

2002. Parmalat consented to the entry of a final judgment against it in the fraud.[3]

The complaint includes the following amended charges:

1. Parmalat consistently overstated its level of cash and marketable securities by at least $4.9 billion at December 31, 2002.

2. As of September 30, 2003, Parmalat had understated its reported debt by almost $10 billion through a variety of tactics including:

    a. Eliminating about $6 billion of debt held by one of its nominee entities.

    b. Recording approximately $1.6 billion debt as equity through fictitious loan participation agreements.

    c. Removing approximately $500 million of liabilities by falsely describing the sale of certain receivables as nonrecourse when in fact the company retained an obligation to ensure that the receivables were ultimately paid.

    d. Improperly eliminating approximately $1.6 billion of debt through a variety of techniques including mischaracterization of bank debt as intercompany debt.

3. Between 1997 and 2003, Parmalat transferred approximately $500 million to various businesses owned and operated by Tanzi family members.

4. Parmalat used nominee entities to fabricate nonexistent financial operations intended to offset losses of operating subsidiaries, to disguise intercompany loans from one subsidiary to another that was experiencing operating losses, to record fictitious revenue through sales by its subsidiaries to controlled nominee entities at inflated or entirely fictitious amounts, and to avoid unwanted scrutiny due to the aging of the receivables related to these sales, which were either sold or transferred to nominee entities.

In the consent agreement without admitting or denying the allegations, Parmalat agreed to adopt changes to its corporate governance to promote future compliance with the federal securities laws, including:

- Adopting bylaws providing for governance by a shareholder-elected board of directors, the majority of whom will be independent and serve finite terms, and specifically delineating in the bylaws the duties of the board of directors.

- Adopting a code of conduct governing the duties and activities of the board of directors.

- Adopting an insider dealing code of conduct.

- Adopting a code of ethics.

[3] U.S. Securities and Exchange Commission, Litigation Release No. 18803/ July 28, 2004. Accounting and Auditing Enforcement Release No. 2065/ July 28, 2004, *Securities and Exchange Commission v. Parmalat Finanziaria, S.p.A.,* Case No. 03 CV 10266 (PKC) (S.D.N.Y.), www.sec.gov/litigation/litreleases/lr18803.htm.

The bylaws will also require that the positions of the chairman of the board of directors and managing director be held by two separate individuals, and Parmalat must consent to having continuing jurisdiction of the U.S. District Court to enforce its provisions.

Parmalat Sues Bank of America

On February 2, 2006, a U.S. federal judge allowed Parmalat to proceed with much of its $10 billion lawsuit against Bank of America Corporation including claims that the bank had violated U.S. racketeering laws. Enrico Bondi was appointed as the equivalent of a U.S. bankruptcy trustee to pursue claims that financial institutions including Bank of America abetted the company in disguising its true financial condition. Bondi has accused the bank of helping to structure mostly off-balance-sheet transactions intended to "conceal Parmalat's insolvency" and of collecting fees it did not deserve. The judge also gave the go-ahead for Parmalat to proceed with lawsuits against two auditors. Bondi is also pursuing another lawsuit against Citigroup in New Jersey state courts.[4]

Questions

1. Parmalat is an Italian company with operations primarily throughout Europe, yet the U.S. Securities and Exchange Commission filed charges against it in U.S. courts. What justification is there for the SEC to file charges against the Italian company?

2. Comment on the quality of financial reporting at Parmalat during the period of time covered by the SEC lawsuit against the company. Be sure to cite specific problems and explain why each one deviates from what would be considered transparent financial reporting.

3. Identify the types of fraud engaged in by Parmalat. Be sure to include your justification for classifying the transaction as a fraud.

4. Based on the limited information in the case, classify the improper transactions engaged in by Parmalat into one of the seven "financial shenanigan" groups identified by Schilit. Provide a brief explanation why you selected that group.

5. In his suit against the Bank of America, Enrico Bondi, the trustee representing Parmalat in its reorganization, accused the bank of helping to structure mostly off-balance-sheet transactions intended to "conceal Parmalat's insolvency" and collecting fees that it did not deserve. Assuming that the bank actually did the work related to structuring these transactions and other work for Parmalat, why should the bank not collect its regular fee? Discuss the ethics of prohibiting the bank from collecting these amounts, even though it did work for Parmalat, and provide reasons for your answer.

[4] Parmalat Suit against Bank of America Can Proceed, *The New Zealand Herald,* February 2, 2006, www.nzherald.co.nz/section/print.cfm?c_id=3&objectid=10366504.

Case 7-8

Solutions Network, Inc.

"We can't recognize revenue immediately, Paul, since we agreed to buy similar software from Data Systems Solutions (DSS)," said Sarah Young. "That's ridiculous," replied Paul Henley. "Get your head out of the sand, Sarah, before it's too late."

Sarah Young is a certified public accountant (CPA) and the controller for Solutions Network, Inc. She is meeting with Paul Henley, the company's chief financial officer on January 7, 2008, to discuss the accounting for a software systems transaction with DSS prior to the company's audit for the year ended December 31, 2007. Henley is not a CPA.

Young has excluded the amount in contention from revenue and net income for 2007. Henley wants the amount to be included in the 2007 results. Henley told Young that the order came from the top to record the revenue on December 28, 2007, the day the transaction with DSS was finalized. Young pointed out that Solutions Network had ordered essentially the same software from DSS to be shipped and delivered early in 2008. Therefore, Solutions Network should delay revenue recognition on this "swap" transaction until that time. Henley argued against Young's position, stating

that title had passed from the company to DSS on December 31, 2007, when the software product was shipped with F.O.B. shipping point.

Background

Solutions Network, Inc., became a publicly owned company on March 15, 2007, following a successful initial public offering (IPO). It built up a loyal clientele in the five years prior to the IPO by establishing close working relationships with technology leaders including IBM, Apple, and Dell Computer. The company designs and engineers systems software to function seamlessly with minimal user interface. Several companies provide similar products and consulting services; one is DSS. However, DSS operates in a larger market providing IT services management products that coordinate the entire business infrastructure into a single system.

Solutions Networks grew very rapidly in the five years prior to its IPO. The revenue and earnings streams during those years are as follows.

	(in millions)	
Year	Revenues	Net Income
2002	$148.0	$11.9
2003	175.8	13.2
2004	202.2	15.0
2005	229.8	16.1
2006	267.5	17.3

Young has prepared the following estimates for 2007:

	(in millions)	
Year	Revenues	Net Income
2006 (projected 12/31)	$287.5	$17.9

The Transaction

On December 28, 2007, Solutions Network offered to sell its Internet infrastructure software to DSS for its internal use. In return, DSS agreed to ship similar software 30 days later to Solutions Network for that company's internal use. The companies had conducted several transactions during the previous

five years, and while DSS had initially balked at the transaction because it provided no value added to the company, it did not want to upset one of the fastest growing software companies in the industry. Moreover, Solutions Network could be able to help identify future customers for DSS's IT services management products.

The $30 million of revenue would increase Solutions Network's net income $1.9 million over the projected amount for

2007. For Solutions Network, the revenue from the transaction was enough to enable the company to meet targeted goals, and the higher level of income would provide extra bonus money at year end for Sarah Young, Paul Henley, and Ed Fralen, the chief executive officer.

Accounting Considerations

Normally, Sarah would not object to Paul's proposed accounting for the transaction with DSS. However, she knows that regardless of the passage of title to DSS on December 31, 2007, the transaction is linked to Solutions Networks' agreement to take the DSS product 30 days later. While she does not anticipate any problems in that regard, she is uncomfortable with recording the revenue on December 31 because DSS did not complete its portion of the agreement by that date.

Sarah is also concerned about the fact that another transaction occurred during the previous year that she had questioned but, in the end, she went along with Paul's accounting for this transaction. On December 28, 2006, Solutions Network sold a major system for $20 million to Laramie Systems but executed a side agreement with Laramie on December 29, 2006, that gave the customer the right to return the product for any reason for 27 days after January 1, 2007. Even though Solutions Network recorded the revenue on December 29, 2006, and Sarah felt uneasy about it, she had not objected because Laramie did not return the product. Sarah never brought it up again. Now, she is concerned that a pattern could be developing.

Questions

1. Comment on the corporate culture at Solutions Network. If you were in Sarah Young's position, would this transaction raise any red flags? If so, be specific in identifying potentially troublesome situations. Evaluate Sarah Young's decision not to contest the December 28, 2006, transaction from an ethics perspective. Do you think the decision was "right" or "wrong"?

2. Describe the rules in accounting for revenue recognition in general and relate them to the two transactions mentioned in the case. Be sure to include proper citations from the pronouncements of the Financial Accounting Standards Board and other relevant material. Do you believe the transactions have been accounted for properly?

3. Prepare the following:

   a. A schedule of the percentage of net income to revenues from 2002 through the projected amounts for 2007 Use the *original amounts reported,* including that for 2006, and show the percentage changes in revenue and net income each year.

   b. A schedule using the same requirements as in part (*a*) to calculate the relevant amounts, assuming that (a) the company restates the results for 2006 and (b) Solutions Network records the $30 million transaction with DSS in 2007 but does not correct the 2006 results.

4. Redo the comparative analysis required by Question 3 using 2005 as the base year and show the effects on comparative revenues and net income from 2005 through 2007, assuming that (1) Solutions Network was allowed to record revenue for 2006 and 2007 the way it wants and (2) the company follows GAAP rules for recording revenue in both years. Comment on the results of your percentage analyses including the underlying motivation that could exist for Paul Henley and Ed Fralen in their desire to record revenue their way.

5. Assume that Sarah is to meet with Paul on January 14, 2008, to finalize the accounting for the DSS revenue. Sarah asks Beth, her best friend, for advice. Beth is not a CPA but has been the CFO for a large international firm for many years. Therefore, you can assume that Beth is knowledgeable about revenue recognition rules and other relevant principles. Prepare a draft of the recommendation Beth could make to Sarah that outlines the ethical issues, alternatives, and a recommended course of action. Be sure to support the recommended course of action with ethical reasoning.

6. Regardless of your answer to Question 5, assume that Sarah asks for more time to consider the matter when she meets with Paul on January 14. She points out that the auditors will not arrive until February 1, 2008; therefore, the company should be certain of the appropriateness of its accounting before that time. Paul reacts angrily, and tells Sarah that she can pack her bags and go if she does not support the company in its revenue recognition of the DSS transaction. Assume that you are in Sarah's position. What ethics considerations exist that could help you to decide on a course of action? What would you do and why?

Case 7-9

Sweat Hog Construction Company

Ever since the economy of southwest Texas began to decline in 2006, Sweat Hog Construction Company has been more aggressive in seeking new business opportunities. One such opportunity is the Computer Assistance Vocational Training School, which has contracted for a new 1-million-square-foot facility in San Marcos, Texas. Computer Assistance trains computer programmers for jobs in business and government. It is the largest computer training school in the southwestern part of the United States.

Gabe Kotter is the passive owner of Sweat Hog Construction. The company began operating in 1995 when Kotter hired Michael Woodman to be the president of the company. Sweat Hog Construction is a family-owned business that has been very successful as a mechanical contractor of heating, ventilation, and air conditioning systems (HVAC). However, the economic downturn of 2006 put pressure on the company to diversify its operations. Although it made a profit in 2006, the company's net income was 50 percent lower than in previous years. As a result of these factors, the company decided to expand into plumbing and electrical contract work.

In March 2007, Sweat Hog successfully bid for the Computer Assistance job with a low bid to secure the $3 million contract that is expected to be completed by June 30, 2008. Woodman knows that the company has little margin for error on the contract. The estimated gross margin of 11.5 percent is on the low side of historical margins, which have been between 10 to 15 percent on HVAC contracts. Because it is a fixed-price contract, the company will have to absorb any cost overruns.

The Computer Assistance contract is an important one for Sweat Hog Construction. It represents about 20 percent of the average annual revenues for the past five years. Moreover, First National Bank of Texas has been pressuring the company to speed up its interest payments on a $2 million term loan payable to the bank that is renewable on March 15, 2008. The company has been late in five of its last six monthly payments. The main reason is that some of the company's customers have been paying their bills later than usual because of tight economic conditions. However, the company expects to get back on the right tract very soon after the Computer Assistance job begins.

Everything started well on the contract. For the quarter ended June 30, 2007, Sweat Hog had an estimated cumulative gross profit of $75,000 on the contract under the percentage-of-completion method. This represents a 20 percent gross margin. Costs started to increase during the September quarter and, even though cumulative gross margin decreased to 10 percent, it was still within projected amounts. Unfortunately, the $54,000 estimated gross profit for the nine months ended December 31, 2007, represents only a 3 percent gross margin for the first year of the contract. Exhibit 1 contains cost data, billings, and collections for the year.

Vinny Barbarino is a CPA and Sweat Hog's controller. He knows that cash collections on the Computer Assistance project have been slowing down, in part because the company is behind schedule, and tension has developed between the company and Computer Assistance. He decides to contact Juan Epstein, general manager for the project. Epstein informs Barbarino that the tension between the company and Computer Assistance escalated recently when Epstein informed top management of Computer Assistance that the electrical work could not be completed by the June 30, 2008, deadline. If the facility does not open as scheduled for the summer months, Computer Assistance could be required to return deposits from students. Consequently, it could lose the revenue that is projected for the July and August summer term.

Woodman calls for a meeting with Epstein and Barbarino on February 6, 2008, to discuss the Computer Assistance contract. Woodman knows that Sweat Hog's external auditors will begin their audit of the December 31, 2007, year-end financial statements in two weeks. Woodman wants to make

---

EXHIBIT 1
SWEAT HOG CONSTRUCTION
Company Computer Assistance Contract
Year Ended December 31, 2007

	Quarter Ending		
	June 30	**September 30**	**December 31**
Costs to date	$ 300,000	$ 900,000	$1,740,000
Estimated costs to complete	2,100.000	1,800,000	1,170,000
Progress billings each quarter	250,000	600,000	950,000
Cash collections each quarter	150,000	350,000	400,000

sure the problems with the contract have been corrected. He asks Barbarino to bring him up to date on the recent cost increases on the contract.

Barbarino informs Woodman that the internal job cost data indicate that $420,000 was incurred for the month of January 2008. About 10 percent of the work was completed during that month. Barbarino emphasizes that this is consistent with recent trend data that indicate the estimated costs to complete the contract have been significantly understated. In fact, for the quarter ended December 31, 2007, the company lost approximately $40,000 on the contract, although there is a cumulative gross margin of about $60,000 for 2007. However, this cumulative margin represents only 2 percent of revenue, and the gross margin percentage is declining. Barbarino had analyzed the cost data in preparation for the meeting. He estimates that total costs on the contract could be as high as $4.2 million. He recommends that the $1.17 million estimate to complete the contract at December 31, 2008, should be increased by at least $1 million.

Woodman is stunned by this information. He cannot understand how the company got into this predicament; it has consistently made profits on its contracts, and there has never before been any tension with clients. The timing is particularly troublesome because First National Bank is expecting audited financial statements by March 1, 2008. Woodman asks Epstein whether he agrees with Barbarino's assessment about the anticipated higher level of future costs. Epstein hesitates at first, but he eventually admits to the likelihood of the cost overruns. He points out that the workers are not as skilled with electrical work as they are with HVAC work. Consequently, some degree of learning is taking place on the job.

Woodman dismisses Epstein at this point and asks Barbarino what would happen if the company reports the estimated costs at December 31, 2007, without any adjustments. Woodman emphasizes that the company would make the necessary adjustments in the first quarter of 2008, and gross profit on the

contract with Computer Assistance ultimately will be correct. This approach will enable the company to renew its loan and will give it some time to rethink its business strategy.

Barbarino immediately tells Woodman that he is not comfortable with this approach because the profit on the contract for the nine months ended December 31, 2007, would be significantly overstated. He points out that the auditors are likely to question the low cost estimates. Woodman becomes a bit irritated with Barbarino at this point. He tells Barbarino that the bank is not likely to renew the company's $2 million loan if the statements reflect what Barbarino suggests. He concludes by stating, "The auditors have never been a problem before. I do not expect any problems from them on this issue either, given that the firm has gone along with whatever we've asked of them in the past."

Questions

1. Do you think that Woodman believes his position reflects an attempt to manage earnings? Put yourself in Woodman's place. Assume that the auditors question the accounting for contract costs. How would you justify to the auditors the recording of contracts without any cost adjustments?

2. Now put yourself in the place of the auditor just listening to Woodman's explanation. Use your own explanation to Question 1 and prepare a response for Woodman.

3. What should be the ethical issues of concern for Barbarino? Be sure to address virtue-based reasoning, philosophical ethics, and the AICPA Code of Professional Conduct.

4. Assume that Woodman gets his way and there are no adjustments to the estimated contract costs in recording revenue. Using the decision-making model presented in Chapter 3, analyze the alternatives available to Barbarino. Given the limited facts in this case, what would you do if you were in Barbarino's position? Why?

Case 7-10

United Thermostatic Controls

United Thermostatic Controls, headquartered in San Jose, California, is a publicly owned company that manufactures and markets residential and commercial thermostats used to regulate temperature in furnaces and refrigerators. United primarily sells its product to retailers in the domestic market. Its operations are decentralized according to geographic region. United is a publicly owned company, and its common stock is listed and traded on the New York Stock Exchange. The organization chart for United is presented in Figure 1.

Frank Campbell is the director of the Southern sales division. Worsening regional economic conditions and a reduced rate of demand for United's products have created pressures to achieve sales revenue targets set by United management. Also, significant pressures exist within the organization for sales divisions to maximize their revenues and earnings for

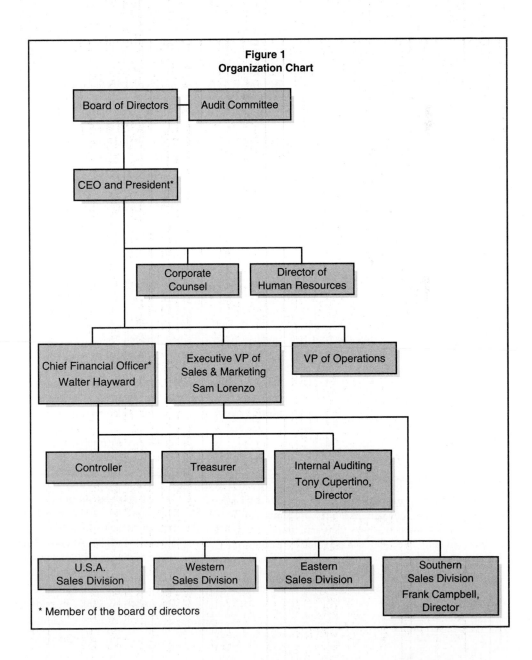

Figure 1
Organization Chart

Board of Directors

Audit Committee

CEO and President*

Corporate Counsel

Director of Human Resources

Chief Financial Officer*
Walter Hayward

Executive VP of Sales & Marketing
Sam Lorenzo

VP of Operations

Controller

Treasurer

Internal Auditing
Tony Cupertino, Director

U.S.A. Sales Division

Western Sales Division

Eastern Sales Division

Southern Sales Division
Frank Campbell, Director

* Member of the board of directors

Exhibit 1
United Thermostatic Controls

Budgeted and Actual Sales Revenue
First Three Quarters in 2007

Quarter Ended	U.S.A. Sales Division			Western Sales Division		
	Budget	Actual	% Var.	Budget	Actual	% Var.
March 31	$ 632,000	$ 638,000	.009	$ 886,000	$ 898,000	.014
June 30	640,000	642,000	.003	908,000	918,000	.011
September 30	648,000	656,000	.012	930,000	936,000	.006
Through September 30	$1,920,000	$1,936,000	.008	$2,724,000	$2,752,000	.010

Quarter Ended	Eastern Sales Division			Southern Sales Division		
	Budget	Actual	% Var.	Budget	Actual	% Var.
March 31	$ 743,000	$ 750,000	.009	$ 688,000	$ 680,000	(.012)
June 30	752,000	760,000	.011	696,000	674,000	(.032)
September 30	761,000	769,000	.011	704,000	668,000	(.051)
Through September 30	$2,256,000	$2,279,000	.010	$2,088,000	$2,022,000	(.032)

2007 in anticipation of a public offering of stock early in 2008. Budgeted and actual sales revenue amounts by division for the first three quarters in 2007 are presented in Exhibit 1.

Campbell knows that actual sales lagged even further behind budgeted sales during the first two months of the fourth quarter. He also knows that each of the other three sales divisions exceeded their budgeted sales amounts during the first three quarters in 2007. He is very concerned that the Southern division has been unable to meet or exceed budgeted sales amounts. He is particularly worried about the effect this could have on his and the division managers' bonuses and share of corporate profits.

In an attempt to improve Southern's sales revenue for the fourth quarter and for the year ended December 31, 2007, Campbell reviewed purchase orders received during the latter half of November and early December to determine whether shipments could be made to customers prior to December 31. Campbell knows that sometimes orders that are received before year-end can be filled by December 31, thereby enabling the division to record the sales revenue during the current fiscal year. It could simply be a matter of accelerating production and shipping to increase sales revenue for the year.

Reported sales revenue of the Southern division for the fourth quarter of 2007 was $792,000. This represented an 18.6 percent increase over the actual sales revenue for the third quarter of the year. As a result of this increase, reported sales revenue for the fourth quarter exceeded the budgeted amount by $80,000, or 11.2 percent. Actual sales revenue for the year exceeded the budgeted amount for the Southern division by $14,000, or .5 percent. Budgeted and actual sales revenue amounts, by division, for the year ended December 31, 2007, are presented in Exhibit 2.

During the course of their test of controls, the internal audit staff questioned the appropriateness of recording revenue of $150,000 on two shipments made by Southern in the fourth quarter of the year. These shipment descriptions follow.

1. United shipped thermostats to Allen Corporation on December 31, 2007, and billed Allen $85,000, even though Allen had specified an earliest delivery date of February 1, 2008. Allen intended to use the thermostats in the heating system of a new building that would not be ready for occupancy until March 1, 2008.

2. United shipped thermostats to Bilco Corporation on December 30, 2007, in partial fulfillment of an order.

Exhibit 2
United Thermostatic Controls

Budgeted and Actual Sales Revenue
For the Year Ended December 31, 2007

| Quarter Ended | U.S.A. Sales Division | | | Western Sales Division | | |
	Budget	Actual	% Var.	Budget	Actual	% Var.
March 31	$ 632,000	$ 638,000	.009	$ 886,000	$ 898,000	.014
June 30	640,000	642,000	.003	908,000	918,000	.011
September 30	648,000	656,000	.012	930,000	936,000	.006
December 31	656,000	662,000	.009	952,000	958,000	.006
2007 Totals	$2,576,000	$2,598,000	.009	$3,676,000	$3,710,000	.009

| Quarter Ended | Eastern Sales Division | | | Southern Sales Division | | |
	Budget	Actual	% Var.	Budget	Actual	% Var.
March 31	$ 743,000	$ 750,000	.009	$ 688,000	$ 680,000	(.012)
June 30	752,000	760,000	.011	696,000	674,000	(.032)
September 30	761,000	769,000	.011	704,000	668,000	(.051)
December 31	770,000	778,000	.010	712,000	792,000	.112
2007 Totals	$3,026,000	$3,057,000	.010	$2,800,000	$2,814,000	.005

United recorded $65,000 revenue on that date. Bilco had previously specified that partial shipments would not be accepted. Delivery of the full shipment had been scheduled for February 1, 2008.

During their investigation, the internal auditors learned that Campbell had placed pressure on the accountants to record these two shipments early to enable the Southern division to achieve its goals with respect to the company's revenue targets. The auditors were concerned about the appropriateness of recording the $150,000 revenue in 2007 in the absence of an expressed or implied agreement with the customers to accept and pay for the prematurely shipped merchandise. The auditors noted that, had the revenue from these two shipments not been recorded, the Southern division's actual sales for the fourth quarter would have been below the budgeted amount by $70,000, or 9.8 percent. Actual sales revenue for the year ended December 31, 2007, would have been below the budgeted amount by $136,000, or 4.9 percent. The revenue effect of the two shipments in question created a 5.4 percent shift in the variance between actual and budgeted sales for the year. The auditors believed that this effect was significant with respect to the division's revenue and earnings for the fourth

quarter and for the year ended December 31, 2007. The auditors decided to take their concerns to Tony Cupertino, the director of the internal auditing department. Cupertino is a licensed CPA in the State of California.

Cupertino discussed the situation with Campbell, who informed Cupertino that he had received assurances from Sam Lorenzo, executive vice president of sales and marketing, that top management would support the recording of the $150,000 revenue because of its strong desire to meet or exceed budgeted revenue and earnings amounts. Moreover, top management is very sensitive to the need to meet financial analysts' consensus earnings estimates. The company, according to Campbell, is concerned that earnings must be high enough to meet analysts' expectations because any other effect could cause the stock price to go down. In fact, Sam Lorenzo has already told Campbell that he did not see anything wrong with recording the revenue in 2007 because the merchandise had been shipped to the customers before year-end and the terms of shipment were FOB shipping point.

At this point, Cupertino is uncertain whether he should take his concerns to Walter Hayward, the chief financial officer, who is also a member of the board of directors, or take them directly to the audit committee. Cupertino is not even certain that he should pursue the matter any further because of the financial performance pressures that exist within the organization. However, he is very concerned about his responsibility to coordinate the work of the internal auditing department with that of the external auditors.

Questions

1. Describe Tony Cupertino's ethical responsibilities.

2. Briefly discuss the revenue recognition rules in accounting under *SFAC No. 5* and *SAB No. 101*. Has United Thermostatic violated any of these rules with respect to its accounting for the Allen and Bilco shipments? Explain why or why not.

3. Assume that Tony Cupertino decides to delay contacting Walter Hayward and, instead, contacts the CFO of Bilco Corporation and offers a 10 percent discount on the total $130,000 cost of merchandise if Bilco agrees to allow the partial shipment on December 30, 2007. Cupertino adds that the $13,000 would be deducted from the remaining $65,000 to be shipped during January 2008. Evaluate Cupertino's actions with respect to the following:

   a. Is the offer ethical or unethical? Why?

   b. Is Cupertino engaging in earnings management? Why or why not?

   c. Assume that the CFO of Bilco agrees but insists the $13,000 come off the price of the partial shipment on December 30, 2007. Because Bilco will not pay for it until January 6, 2008, would the $13,000 affect the recorded revenue of the $65,000. If so, how will it affect that amount, and where would it be presented in the financial statements. If not, explain why.

4. Without regard to the facts or your answers to Question 3, assume you are in Cupertino's position. Use the decision-making model in Chapter 3 to determine what action Cupertino should take in this situation.

5. How does the organization's structure affect your decision in Question 4? How would the provisions of Sarbanes-Oxley Act affect your decision in Question 4? What role should the audit committee play in that decision?

6. Assume that Walter Hayward steps in at this point and tells Cupertino to record both transactions as revenue in 2007 without regard to his proposal in Question 3. If you were in Cupertino's position, what would be your next step? Why? What would you do if the CEO and president back Hayward? Why?

Name Index

Locators with n indicate notes.

Subject Index

Locators with n indicate notes.